Tonality and Design in Music Theory

Volume II

Tonality and Design in Music Theory

Earl Henry

Webster University, St. Louis

Michael Rogers

University of Oklahoma, Norman

PEARSON
_____
Prentice
Hall

Upper Saddle River
New Jersey 07458

Library of Congress Cataloging-in-Publication Data

Henry, Earl.
   Tonality and design in music theory / Earl Henry, Michael Rogers.
      p. cm.
   Includes index.
   ISBN 0-13-081120-3
   1. Music theory—Textbooks. I. Rogers, Michael R. II. Title.

   MT6.H526 2004
   781.2—dc22

                           2004052228

Editor-in-Chief: Sarah Touborg
Senior Acquisitions Editor: Christopher Johnson
Editorial Assistant: Evette Dickerson
Marketing Manager: Sheryl Adams
Marketing Assistant: Cherron Gardner
Managing Editor: Joanne Riker
Production Editor: Randy Pettit
Manufacturing Buyer: Benjamin D. Smith
Cover Design: Kiwi Design
Full-Service Project Management and Composition: Preparé
Printer/Binder: Courier Companies, Inc.
Cover Printer: Lehigh

Credits and acknowledgments borrowed from other sources and reproduced, with permission, in this textbook appear on appropriate page within text or on page 581.

Pearson Education LTD.
Pearson Education Australia PTY, Limited
Pearson Education Singapore, Pte. Ltd
Pearson Education North Asia Ltd
Pearson Education, Canada, Ltd
Pearson Educación de Mexico, S.A. de C.V.
Pearson Education–Japan
Pearson Education Malaysia, Pte. Ltd

10   9   8   7   6   5   4   3   2   1
ISBN 0-13-081120-3

Contents

Preface

Music Theory is the study of how and why music works. This suggests that understanding the subject consists of something more than data bits, definitions, or a body of prescribed knowledge. While this set of textbooks offers plenty of instruction about names, labels, and an appropriate vocabulary for effective communication among musicians, we have designed the series to offer a good deal more. Without being dangerously speculative, we have tried to propose, where possible, the *reasons* which lie behind principles and procedures of aesthetically stimulating musical constructions—that is, an explanation for just how the rules came about and how they have influenced changing musical styles.

We have also approached theoretical study from the listener's perspective, so that our discussions and analyses refer not only to the printed notation of scores, but also to the reactions of educated audiences to the individual sounds and larger patterns of music. By alluding frequently to the aesthetic involvement of music and the psychological manipulation of master composers, for example, we have endeavored to enrich cognitive and perceptual experiences; these are simultaneously the byproducts of informed listening and the foundation of performing, composing, and teaching music.

Presented in proper manner and spirit, these books can enable theory teachers to not only foster intellectual development and aural growth for their students, but also to advance beyond that stage into the ambitious realms of changing opinions and attitudes, reworking beliefs and habits, judging sides of a controversy, and refining a set of values. Students may come to develop a sense of wonder about the mysteries and forces of music itself. In other words, training in music theory can support learning how to think and learning how to respond—the twin sides of a true musical education.

We draw from the well-established tradition of Comprehensive Musicianship in choosing and organizing topics for these books. Lessons and assignments are presented not only in basic tonal harmony, but also in fundamentals, concepts of melody, counterpoint, form, analysis, composition, writing essays, and various aspects of contemporary music—all within a stylistic and historical context. Although our emphasis is on Western musical art, text material is amplified by the music of both men and women, differing styles, various cultures, and examples drawn from popular and ethnic sources. Distinctive features as well as commonalities and universals are identified in comparing works.

The methodology of *Tonality and Design in Music Theory* is intentionally eclectic. We present a wide variety of analytic techniques, including both traditional approaches (harmony and form, for example) and also a generous representation of linear analysis. We introduced the latter topic without any formal or restrictive adherence to Schenkerian principles because we feel that these topics are a worthy subject for advanced study in their own right, but only after a beginning groundwork has been established. Our book will not, for example, teach students to draw elaborate graphs. Instead, it will enable them to not only appreciate the long-range attractions and links that pitches have for one another, but also to understand and create graphic representations of these relationships in a variety of ways. Single-line melodic study is covered along with selective representations of structural reductions (as simplified notation) in both harmonic and contrapuntal settings in order to clarify the skeleton and scaffolding of music. These reductions permit distinctions to be made between events that give meaning and those that take meaning.

One of the most challenging aspects of writing the actual words, sentences, and paragraphs for an introductory theory course is to establish an appropriate tone, style, and level of readability for students of varying backgrounds—one that is forceful and clear for the learner while being engaging and thought-provoking for the facilitator. In short, we have written a book that we hope is simple and direct, but at the same time, properly sophisticated and nuanced so that while concepts are not diluted, there is no underestimation or dishonoring of the profusion of music itself. We have devoted special care and attention to the problem of writing a text for readers who are coming to a topic for the first time, and can only hope that a satisfying and challenging balance has been achieved so that the books will have appeal as well for the teacher.

ACKNOWLEDGMENTS

We are indebted to numerous individuals who provided valuable assistance in the preparation of this book. Kendall Stallings, Glen Bauer, Robert Chamberlin, Gay Spears, and Karen Trinkle used the book in class testing and provided many invaluable suggestions and corrections. Carole Gaspar and Kathryn Stieler assisted with text translations. In addition, we thank the students at Webster University who used various transformations of these materials over several years. The involvement of students in pointing out typographical errors, unwieldy exercise problems, and ambiguous explanations has helped us produce a more useful book. The books are *for* students, after all, and we have profited greatly from their input on virtually every page. Finally, we would like to thank our Prentice Hall production editor, Randy Pettit, for his careful supervision of the manuscript as it progressed from stacks of loose pages, through various rounds of proof, and on to a finished book. We appreciate Randy's encouragement and helpful advice throughout the production process.

Earl Henry
Michael Rogers

USING THE TEXT

To Students

Tonality and Design in Music Theory is the final manuscript version of a two-volume textbook to be published by Prentice Hall with a January, 2005, copyright date. We hope that you will enjoy using this book and will find it helpful in your studies. Please note how the text has been organized to facilitate study and comprehension.

Organization

Each chapter centers on a full and detailed discussion of one major aspect of traditional Western music. These prose discussions are then divided into two, three, or four smaller parts that likewise present self-contained topics. There are over thirty of these smaller divisions in each volume, so that while the chapters cover a broad aspect of Western musical art, chapter divisions progress in "bite-sized" pieces. Each chapter division ends with a *Review and Application* consisting of important terms, class and individual exercise problems, and music for analysis. Be sure that you understand each of the terms and its relationship to the central topic. The exercises can be completed either in class or at home, as directed by your instructor. *Chapter Projects* conclude each broad area of study. These projects include analysis, composition, essay, and a wide range of other endeavors that will help you apply the knowledge you have gained to a wider range of interests and studies.

Following each *Review and Application*, chapter divisions contain *Self-Tests*. These quizzes are short, and center on objective questions about the material concerned. You should take each self-test at home in a *timed* situation. The time limits in the text are only suggestions; you may want to allow yourself more time, but note carefully how much of the self-test you have covered in the prescribed time. Remember that in many aspects of music theory, *speed* in analysis and construction is as important as a knowledge of procedure. The answers to self tests can be found on the website for both volumes (www.prehall.com/henry). Where questions are objective, the given answers can be scored correct or incorrect; in other situations, however, you will find an answer given, but with the indication that other correct answers are possible. When in doubt, check your answers with your instructor. Score each self test as directed on the basis of 100 points and note your progress.

Workbook/Anthology.   The two Workbook/Anthologies that accompany the texts are optional at the discretion of institutions and individual instructors. These volumes contain a wide range of problems, drill exercises, composition activities, and music for analysis. As you progress through the text, you will note references to specific pages in the Workbook/Anthology that correspond to the text material. Your instructor will assign some or all of these materials as supplementary studies. Each chapter of the Workbook/Anthology contains one or more complete works of movements for study and analysis.

CD 1, TRACK 04
Robert Schumann, "Träumerei"
(Dreams) from *Scenes from Childhood*
Simple Beat Division

CD 1, TRACK 6-1 MIXED VALUES (2 PARTS)
Ludwig van Beethoven, Quartet, Op. 18
Rhythmic Variety

Compact Disc Recordings.   Each volume corresponds to two compact discs that contain recorded examples of text material. Another CD corresponds to each volume of the workbook/anthology. These recordings will assist you in your study when a keyboard is not avaible. As shown in the next example, a logo lets you know when a text or workbook passage is recorded.

TRACK 6-2 MIXED VALUES
Robert Schumann, Trio, Op. 110
Rhythmic Economy

If the caption indicates that the example is in multiple parts ("2 parts," "3 Parts," and so on), you will need to pause the CD at the end of the first passage, and then resume the same track when you are ready to listen to the next example.

(pause CD)

While a few of the recorded examples are synthesized, most are live acoustic performances by both student and professional musicians.

Website.   From the Internet, you can connect easily to Prentice Hall's website for this book at www.prenhall.com/henry. On this site (available 2005), you will find additional study suggestions and materials that correlate with every chapter of *Tonality and Design.* As you work through the problems on the website, the correct answers and supplementary commentary are available at any time you choose. In addition, a student-centered forum will permit you to discuss related topics and swap ideas with other students, with professional musicians, and with the authors.

Form and Technique

Henry Purcell, "Thy Hand Belinda" and Dido's Lament
from *Dido and Aeneas*

Chapter 1
Variation Forms

Chapter 2
Canon and Fugue

As early as 1580, *The Camerata*, an influential group of Italian composers, poets, and intellectuals, was unified by a common disdain for contemporary imitative polyphony. In madrigals and other late Renaissance vocal works, the text was often rendered unintelligible amid converging lines and programmatic effects. Composers Jacopo Peri (1561–1633) and Giulio Caccini (1545–1618), the poet Ottavio Rinuccini (1562–1621), and others, discussed these issues in Florence at the estate of Count Giovanni Bardi (1534–1612). In concept, their vision of music, which they called MONODY, was "classical." Simple melodies, embellished with striking dissonances for dramatic effect, enhanced the text in the manner of an ancient Greek drama. In texture, monody is not contrapuntal, but an entirely new texture of melody and accompaniment. In 1600, Peri and Caccini collaborated with Rinuccini to produce the first opera, *Euridice*. The subject matter, Greek mythology, was rooted in the past; the new system of tonal organization, however, launched a three-hundred-year era of Western musical unity.

Reacting to the imitative counterpoint of the Renaissance, the members of the Camerata were fully aware that they had conceived not merely a new style, but a new musical *system*. Caccini, for example, published a collection of solo songs in 1602 under the title *Le nuove musiche* (*The New Music*). In the early seventeenth century, the new music of Peri, Caccini, and Claudio Monteverdi (1567–1643) was referred to as the "Second Practice." As we would expect in any era of significant

1

change, those who had a vested interest in the "First Practice" (the contrapuntal style of Palestrina) assailed composers like Monteverdi who dared to meddle with "sacred traditions." But despite the disapproval of establishment figures like Giovanni Artusi (1540–1613), by about 1680, there was no question that the "Second Practice" had become the *preferred* practice for Western composers.

The period between the first opera and the death of J. S. Bach (1600–1750) is known to us today as the BAROQUE ERA. The term "Baroque," from the Portuguese *baurreuco* (an irregularly shaped pearl), was applied to Italian art and architecture before its association with music. Innovations during the Baroque era are virtually too numerous to mention. The seventeenth century saw a rise in instrumental music, as the older family of viols was supplanted by the more flexible violin, viola, cello, and bass—instruments that remain the backbone of the orchestra today. Public concerts, music publication, and entrepreneurship in the arts were all brought to fruition in the Baroque, and alongside societal changes wrought by an emerging middle class, all of these factors affected the way music was written and performed.

Perhaps the most important new *genre* of the Baroque was opera. Opera fused music with acting, poetry, lavish set construction, and costume design. Originally an entertainment for the nobility, by the end of the seventeenth century, opera production was big business all over Europe, as rival houses competed for the grandest singers and the most celebrated composers. If French was the preferred language for international politics, Italian reigned in music. Words that we still use today like "finale," "solo," and "da capo" first came into the Western musical vocabulary four hundred years ago, when Italian opera was performed from London to Moscow.

In today's celebrity-centered popular culture, we may have difficulty imagining a time—four centuries past—when the notion of a performer or composer as "star" first emerged in the West. Celebrated opera singers like the castrato Farinelli (Carlo Broschi, 1705–1782) were perhaps as wealthy and powerful in their own day as some rock stars have been in our time. As a result, most Baroque composers wrote one or more operas. Some of these works, like those of Nicola Porpora (1686–1768) and Johann Hasse (1699–1783), were popular for a time, but are virtually unknown today. While other operas, like *Xerxes* by Handel (1685–1759), have moments of undeniable beauty and are occasionally revived, only a handful of Baroque operas are still revered today as representing music in its highest order. *Dido and Aeneas*, composed by Henry Purcell, is one such work.

Henry Purcell (1659–1695), the greatest of English composers, studied music from an early age, and rose eventually to serve as royal organist to both James II and William III. In addition to pieces for harpsichord and organ, Purcell composed sacred and secular vocal music as well as incidental works to accompany stage plays. In 1689, he composed his only opera on a theme from Virgil's *Aeneid*. In the story, the Princess Dido has fled her homeland following the murder of her husband. She has founded the city of Carthage in North Africa where Aeneas, leader of the Trojans, is later shipwrecked. Dido and Aeneas fall in love; yet, when faced with a choice between his love for Dido and his duty to Troy, Aeneas chooses the latter. Heartbroken, Dido commits suicide in the famous "Lament," shown in the next example.

In the next excerpt from *Dido and Aeneas*, we see numerous elements both of opera and of the Baroque style in general. The selection begins with "Thy Hand, Belinda," a brief *recitative* (a passage of speech-song accompanied by keyboard and bass). This recitative is rhythmically free, with the text set syllabically in order to facilitate dramatic action within a minimal span of time. The *aria* (song) that follows is scored for full orchestra, reflects on action in the previous recitative, and, in the case of "When I Am Laid in Earth," is carefully organized both in tonality and form. "When I Am Laid in Earth" is a *Passacaglia*—a work that unfolds over a repeated bass pattern that occurs eleven times.

In Chapter 1 of the present unit, we will discuss variations like the passacaglia seen in Purcell's "When I Am Laid in Earth" and also types of later variation forms, such as the "Theme and variations." The topic in Chapter 2 is *fugue*—another crucial *genre* of the Baroque inventory.

CD 1, TRACK 02
Henry Purcell, "When I Am Laid in Earth" from *Dido and Aeneas*

RECITATIVE

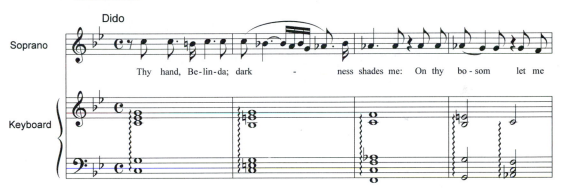

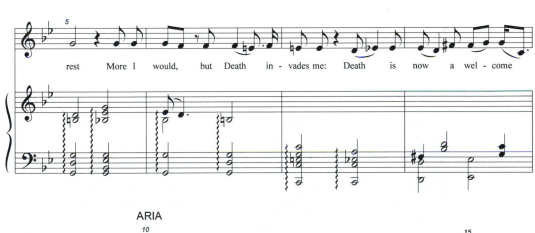

ARIA

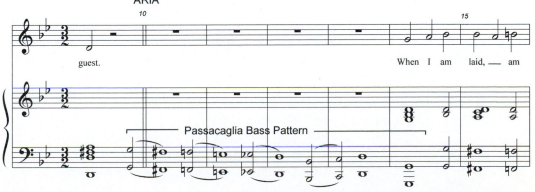

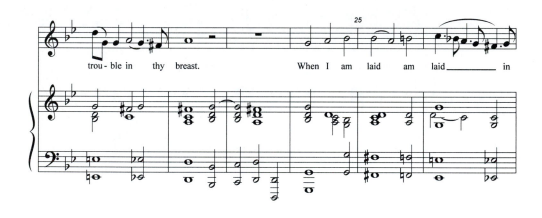

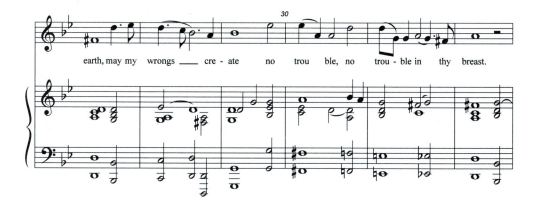

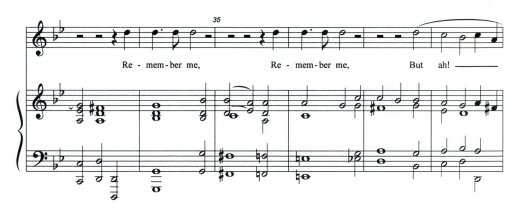

Re - mem - ber me,   Re - mem - ber me,   But ah! ———

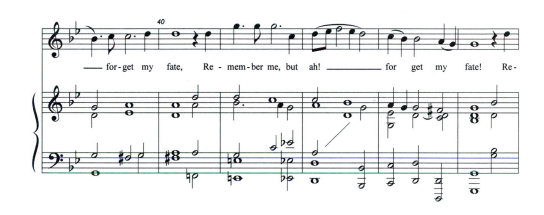

——— for-get my fate,   Re - mem-ber me, but ah! ——— for get my fate!   Re -

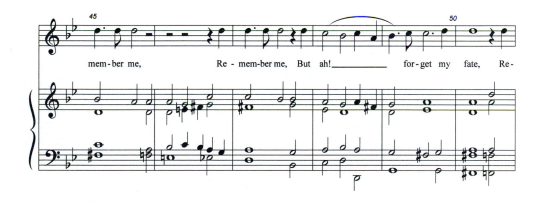

mem-ber me,   Re - mem-ber me,   But ah!——— for-get my fate,   Re -

mem - ber me, but   ah! _____ for - get my   fate!

CHAPTER 1

Variation Forms

Baroque music is often based on the characteristic rhythms of seventeenth-century court dances. About the same time that composers of the Camerata were debating a new approach to the art of music itself, for example, the *allemande* from Germany, the French *courante,* the Spanish *sarabande,* and the lively *gigue* from England were all the rage throughout Europe. In addition to providing court entertainment and a means of interaction between young men and women of noble birth, many of these same dances were enjoyed in concert performances as suites of instrumental pieces (for keyboard or orchestra).

Western musicians have long looked to forms from earlier eras—including dances—for artistic stimulus. Dance forms of the Baroque era continue to be composed even today. Maurice Ravel (1875–1937), for example, honored seventeenth-century French composer François Couperin with his *Le Tombeau de Couperin.* Likewise, Camille Saint-Saëns (1835–1921), Ralph Vaughan Williams (1872–1958), and Clement Delibes (1836–1891) explored modern adaptations of dances like the pavane. Another sixteenth-century court dance, the *gavotte,* provided inspiration for Igor Stravinsky (1882–1972) and Serge Prokofiev (1891–1953), among others.

Perhaps the most important reason that modern composers have chosen forms of the past, however, is that they embody principles of balance and momentum that appeal to Western sensibilities. While the style, harmonic approach, and metric plans of modern compositions may differ significantly from earlier models, many common-practice forms and techniques themselves have proven remarkably durable.

In Chapter 1, we will examine several different types of variation forms that continue to attract composers today. In addition, we will survey *realization*—the art of interpreting a figured bass to create keyboard accompaniments in the Baroque style.

Variation Forms

As a technique, variation is apparent in virtually all eras of Western music (from chant to the present day). One type of variation form, termed *continuous*, developed during the late Renaissance and is associated with multiple repetitions of a brief bass line. A second *genre* of variations, classified as *sectional*, originated in the Baroque era, but reached full development in the late eighteenth and nineteenth centuries. We will discuss these and other types of variation forms in this chapter.

CONTINUOUS VARIATIONS

In the seventeenth and eighteenth centuries, most variation forms were based on a single phrase of music that recurred dozens of times. These brief and numerous segments, termed CONTINUOUS VARIATIONS, flow from one to another without significant pause. Continuous variations embody the Baroque flair for spontaneity and improvisation. Over a repeated bass or harmonic pattern (or both), composers from Purcell to Bach wove complex works from a single, generative phrase. While some continuous variations were improvised, most were notated in full.

The Ground Bass (*Basso Ostinato*)

Many continuous variations are composed upon a repeated bass melody called a GROUND BASS. The term OSTINATO BASS (*basso ostinato* in Italian) is also applied to the recurring segment of a set of continuous variations. Based on Renaissance dance forms, some of these bass patterns are nothing more than descending tetrachords.

Other ground ostinato basses were associated with specific dances such as the *romanesca* and the *folia* ("fool's dance").

Romanesca

Folia

More common in the Baroque era is the newly composed ground bass. In his *Passacaglia for Organ* (a form to be discussed presently), Dietrich Buxtehude (1637–1707) employs twenty-eight statements of a four-measure ground bass. The phrase is heard in the keys of D minor, F Major, and A minor.

Dietrich Buxtehude, Passacaglia
Ground Bass

François Couperin (1668–1733) used the ground bass below to unify his *Passacaille.*

François Couperin, *Passacaille*

Although changes of key are common, composers sometimes treat a ground bass strictly, with the pattern seldom broken except to effect a major sectional division. In the next example, follow the four-measure ground bass that Henry Purcell composed to organize his aria "Ah! Ah! Ah! My Anna" (from *Dido and Aeneas*). The first five (of sixteen) statements are shown. Notice in the next example that the vocalist's phrases do not coincide with those of the bass. The eighth and ninth statements of the pattern (not shown) are in the dominant key.

 CD 1, TRACK 03
Henry Purcell, "My Anna," from *Dido and Aeneas*

Just as often, composers treat the bass ostinato pattern more freely. Study, for example the opening binary movement ("Aria") of Bach's *Goldberg Variations*. The bass seen in measures 1–8 organizes each of the thirty variations.

CD 1, TRACK 04-01 CANON (2 PARTS)
J. S. Bach, Goldberg Variations
Aria

Variation 12 is for three voices. Compare the bass line here with the less elaborate dotted-half notes of the aria. In addition to rhythmic alterations, the pitch content of the bass in Variation 12 is different as well. Nonetheless, the outlines of the original ostinato are obvious.

CD 1, TRACK 04-2 CANON
J. S. Bach, Goldberg Variations
Variation 12

As we have seen through the Purcell and Bach compositions, the use of a ground bass may range from a definitive structural device to a more general principle of organization. Accordingly, in the Baroque era, composers generally followed one of the two approaches to organize continuous variation forms. The first, associated with the *passacaglia*, is identified today as a set of variations over a repeated bass melody; the second, more often termed *chaconne*, is understood today as a repeated harmonic formula. We emphasize the modern distinction between the terms because composers of the Baroque era employed them in titles almost interchangeably.

Passacaglia

A PASSACAGLIA is the most important ostinato bass form of the Baroque era. While the bass pattern in a passacaglia may not be repeated exactly at every occurrence, it is rarely entirely absent or even obscure. The Purcell aria from *Dido and Aeneas* ("Ah! Ah! Ah! My Anna") given in part on page 9 is a passacaglia. Note the exact repetition of the ostinato bass in the five segments shown. Likewise, from the same opera, the aria "When I Am Laid in Earth" that opens this unit (page 3) is also a passacaglia. Heard eleven times in the complete movement, the ostinato bass is chromatic, descends an octave, and culminates in a strong cadence.

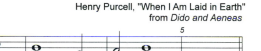

Henry Purcell, "When I Am Laid in Earth"
from *Dido and Aeneas*

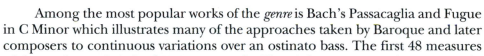

Among the most popular works of the *genre* is Bach's Passacaglia and Fugue in C Minor which illustrates many of the approaches taken by Baroque and later composers to continuous variations over an ostinato bass. The first 48 measures of the work are given in the next example. The eight-measure ostinato comprises a single phrase. In addition, notice that Bach increases momentum through an eighth-rest/sixteenth-note figure (measure 40) that is applied to the bass as well as to the upper voices.

 CD 1, TRACK 05
J. S. Bach, Passacaglia and Fugue in C Minor
Opening Ostinato Segments

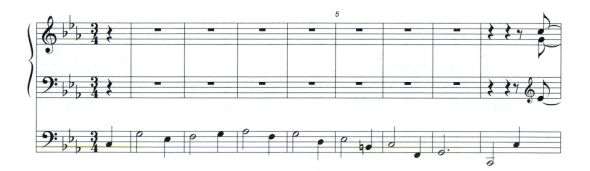

Later in the passacaglia, Bach transfers the ostinato figure to the soprano register. The change of texture is an additional means of emphasizing the sectional structure while increasing interest in the work as a whole.

CD 1, TRACK 06
J. S. Bach, Passacaglia and Fugue in C Minor
Ostinato in Soprano

While the form is itself a distinct *genre*, composers since the nineteenth century have sometimes included a passacaglia as one movement of a symphony or other major work. Johannes Brahms (1833–1897) used a passacaglia as the final movement of his Symphony No. 4 in E Minor; albeit in a significantly different style, the American William Schuman (1910–1992) began his third symphony with a similar set of continuous variations. Notice the preponderance of perfect fourths and fifths in Schuman's passacaglia melody.

Johannes Brahms, Symphony No. 4 in E Minor
Fourth Movement

William Schuman, Symphony No. 3
Part I

While the passacaglia is the most common form of continuous variations, another approach, the *chaconne*, was also popular during the Baroque era.

Chaconne

In the eighteenth century, the terms "passacaglia" and "chaconne" did not have the clear and separable meanings that they do today. In addition to a ground bass, for example, some Baroque works entitled "passacaglia" have an "obstinate" harmony as well; likewise, a work labeled "chaconne" may feature a reiterated bass that accompanies some or all of the harmonic segments. As we define the term today, a CHACONNE is a set of variations based on a recurring harmonic pattern.

André Campra (1660–1744) was a successful French composer who is credited with the creation of a new form of opera, more suited to French tastes than Italian *opera seria*. These *opera-ballets* combined ballet with musical scenes (called *entrées*) and were immensely popular with the Parisian public. Accordingly, Campra exerted substantial influence on later generations of French composers including Jean-Philippe Rameau (1683–1764). The work below opens an instrumental chaconne from Campra's opera-ballet, *Les Fêtes Vénitiennes* (Venetian Festivals). Only the first third of the work is given here, but notice the flexibility with which each repeated four-measure segment is treated. Unlike the approach that we now term "passacaglia," Campra's bass pattern does not recur exactly, but in varied form. In addition, the melody is constantly renewed with each repeated phrase. Still, we maintain our recognition of the basic structure through the descending octaves that signal the cadential point of each phrase.

CD 1, TRACK 07
André Campra, Chaconne

Measures 30–31 of Campra's chaconne exhibit a HEMIOLA CADENCE—an interesting Baroque mannerism in which the meter shifts at the cadence from triple to duple (without an actual change in the time signature). We might also look at this passage as a technique termed HYPERMEASURE: A new pattern, spanning more than one notated measure, emerges on a different level (the half note here).

George Frideric Handel (1685–1759) composed many chaconnes for keyboard. Notice that the eight-measure phrase of his Chaconne in G Major begins with the same bass line that Bach embellished and used in the *Goldberg Variations* (page 10). This bass is present in many, but not all of the fifty-two variations of Handel's chaconne. The harmonic progression, however, is consistent throughout. Note that while each variation ends with a strong cadence, the next begins without pause. The generative phrase and the first nine variations (less than one-quarter of the complete chaconne) are given in the next example.

CD 1, TRACK 08
George Frideric Handel, Chaconne in G Major

In a passacaglia, the ostinato bass "grounds" the work, but interest is usually centered in the upper voices. A chaconne, on the other hand, typically features shifts of interest among the voices as the variations unfold. In any chaconne, we might expect several different "stock" variation types. Review the referenced passage from Handel's Chaconne in G Major for a musical example of each type.

- *Solfeggio*   This type imitates vocal exercises (*solfeggio*) featuring various scales and triads in equal rhythmic values. (See Variations 2, 3, 5, and 7).

- *Dance-Type*   Dances were so popular during the Baroque era that the characteristic rhythms invariably crept into multimovement works of almost every type. The *sarabande* rhythm (♩ ♩. ♪ | ♩) is especially common in triple meter. (See Variation 4. Variations 5 and 9 have similar short–long motives.)

- *Counterpoint*   Chaconnes and passacaglias are inherently homophonic in texture. However, composers may cast one or more variations in strict, nonimitative counterpoint. (Variation 7 is an excellent example.)

- *Style Brisé*   The lute was still a popular instrument during the Baroque era and the style of broken arpeggios (*style brisé*) is common in works for keyboard. Composers typically notate each voice, employing numerous rests, to delineate separate lines. (See Variations 1 and 2 for an example of *style brisé.*)

- *Descant*   In early polyphony, a second voice was often improvised as a new melody above the *cantus firmus.* This technique, called *descant*, was also applied to chaconnes in the Renaissance. Even in the Baroque era, some variations feature a new, florid melody in the highest voice as a counterpoint to the bass (these latter variations are written out in full and not improvised). (Descant-type melodies can be seen in Variations 3, 5, and 6.)

- *Chorale*   To contrast with more active variations, a chaconne or passacaglia may include a passage set in chorale (or FAMILIAR) style. All voices maintain the same (or about the same) rhythms. (See Variations 4 and 8.)

Analyzing Continuous Variations

Even the most seasoned and knowledgeable performers carefully analyze works to ensure stylistic accuracy and faithfulness to the composer's intentions. In the analysis of continuous variations, begin by determining the relationship between *fixed* and *variable* elements. A FIXED ELEMENT is one that is maintained from the original ground, passacaglia, or chaconne phrase. Elements that are VARIABLE change from one variation to another. Composers typically vary only one or two elements at a time, leaving the others fixed to maintain the connection with the original segment. The following are common areas for variation:

- melody
- texture
- key
- rhythm
- register
- mode
- style

Meter and harmony are less commonly modified in continuous variations. Especially in the passacaglia, the meter is dictated by the ostinato bass pattern; in the chaconne, harmonic security is a cornerstone of the form.

Charting Variations.   Consider approaching the analysis of variation forms through a survey of fixed and variable elements. While the sample analysis given for the first nine variations of Handel's Chaconne in G Major (pages 17–18) has a table format, the same information might be jotted in the margins of the score as an aid to performance. Obviously, each variation is different; the table documents only the most significant changes. Because key is a fixed element in all of the Handel variations, that category is omitted from the table.

ANALYTICAL NOTES: HANDEL CHACONNE

Measures	Variation	Fixed	Variable	Comments
1-8	-	Chaconne Phrase		Homophonic texture
9-16	No. 1	Harmony, Bass	Melody, Rhythm, Texture	Style Brisé
17-24	No. 2	Texture, Harmony, Bass	Melody, Rhythm	Solfeggio style
25-32	No. 3	Harmony, Rhythmic flow	Texture, Descant Melody	Bass heard as variation of previous soprano
33-40	No. 4	Harmony, Bass	Texture, Rhythm, Melody	Sarabande rhythm; chorale style
41-48	No. 5	Harmony, Bass	Texture, Rhythm, Melody rhythm continues in soprano	Original bass line returns; Sarabande
49-56	No. 6	Harmony, Bass	Rhythm	Increase in rhythmic values; New descant melody
57-64	No. 7	Harmony, Bass	Texture	Two-voice counterpoint in solfeggio style
65-72	No. 8	Harmony, Bass	Texture, Rhythm, Melody	Descant melody
73-80	No. 9	Harmony	Bass, Texture, Melody	Thickened, two-voice structure; Original bass missing

As we can see from the analytical notes, the original harmony is inflexible. Likewise, the bass line is constant except in Variations 3 and 9 (please remember that there are fifty-two variations in the complete work). Texture is one of the most commonly varied elements, ranging from the chorale setting of Variation 4, *style brisé* in Variations 1 and 2, counterpoint in Variation 7, and a slowing of momentum in Variation 8.

Finally, in addition to a study of how individual variations differ from one another, an important aspect of analysis in variations concerns how a large-scale sense of form is projected. This may be through the pattern of subgroupings; by the overall flow of continuity and contrasts; in increases and decreases of tension and stability; and through the gradual or sudden accumulation of excitement. In short, a comparison of one variation with another is but the accumulation of data for an understanding of the work as a whole.

Dynamic and Expression Marks.   Most composers before 1750 did not often include dynamic and other detailed markings of expression in their scores. In later times, music editors have added these, but in Baroque music, any marks of nuance on a published score were probably not provided by the composer.[1] Consider this fact when you perform a Baroque work. Plan dynamic contrasts carefully. Baroque composers often favored TERRACED DYNAMICS which might be illustrated by an increase in intensity from *pp* to *ff*, but progressing one phrase at a time (and not gradually over several phrases).

Terraced Dynamics

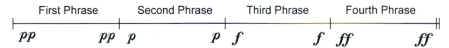

We have now discussed the most common forms of continuous variation forms in the Baroque era: the passacaglia (ground bass) and the chaconne. As we can see from the text examples, a passacaglia may have elements of the chaconne—a repeated harmonic scheme for some or all of the variations (see Bach's Passacaglia and Fugue in C Minor). Likewise, a chaconne may often be viewed also as a passacaglia if the bass pattern remains fixed for many segments (as in the Handel example). More important than formulating precise definitions is an appreciation of the ways in which Baroque composers used principles of variation to unify a longer work while maintaining a high degree of spontaneity.

 WORKBOOK/ANTHOLOGY II
I. Ground Bass, Passacaglia, and Chaconne, page 1

REVIEW AND APPLICATION 1–1

Continuous Variations

Essential Terms

basso ostinato	familiar	hypermeasure	solfeggio
chaconne	fixed element	monody	terraced dynamics
continuous variations	ground bass	ostinato bass	variable element
descant	hemiola cadence	passacaglia	

[1]Many modern editors enclose added dynamic and expression marks in brackets: [*ff*], [*cantabile*], [<], and so on.

1. A chaconne melody and five variations follow for analysis. Use the table provided to discuss fixed and variable elements of each variation. Consider the analysis on page 20 as a model.

CD 1, TRACK 09

George Frideric Handel, Chaconne in G Major

G. F. Handel, Chaconne in G Major

Measures	Variation	Fixed Elements	Variable Elements	Comments
1-8	Theme			
9-16	No. 1			
17-24	No. 2			
25-32	No. 3			
33-40	No. 4			
41-48	No. 5			

SELF-TEST 1–1

Time Limit: 5 Minutes

1. Choose a term from the list that applies to the given statement. Write the appropriate letter in the blank. *Scoring: Subtract 7 points for each error.*

   A. Passacaglia

   B. Descant

   C. Chaconne

   D. Continuous variations

   E. Fixed element

   F. Variable element

   G. Ground bass

   _____ a. An aspect of the original phrase or segment that remains unchanged in one or more variations

   _____ b. A work in which a harmonic pattern is maintained or varied in each of several variations

   _____ c. A group of variations that flows from one to another without a major break or pause

   _____ d. An aspect of the original phrase or segment that changes in one or more variation

   _____ e. A melody (originally improvised) that is heard in counterpoint with the bass or another melodic line

   _____ f. A type of variation form in which a bass line is repeated for many or all segments

   _____ g. An equivalent term for "basso ostinato"

2. Some of the following statements are true; others, false. Write "T" or "F" in the blank as appropriate. *Scoring: Subtract 8 points for each error.*

   _____ a. "Passacaglia" and "chaconne" are different terms for the same form.

   _____ b. Ostinato bass was popular in the Baroque era.

   _____ c. German composers such as J. S. Bach did not compose variation forms.

_____ d. In a hemiola cadence, the metric accents change from triple to duple at the cadence.

_____ e. George Frideric Handel composed *The Goldberg Variations.*

_____ f. If an element in continuous variations is fixed, it is varied in every section of the work.

3. Identify the composer of the opera *Dido and Aeneas. Scoring: Subtract 3 points for an incorrect answer.*

_____
answer

Total Possible: 100   Your Score _____

SECTIONAL VARIATIONS

While Baroque composers excelled at unifying a composition through dozens of brief variations, forms like the passacaglia and chaconne fell out of style by the time of Mozart and Haydn (ca. 1780). In the Classical era, a new type of variation form emerged—primarily from the Baroque dance suite. In addition to the principal suite movements (allemande, courante, sarabande, and so on), composers wrote variations to be performed immediately following the given dance. A courante, for example, might be followed by two *doubles* (variations) that accentuated the characteristic rhythms of that dance. Because dance movements were usually binary forms (as opposed to the phrase-length models of the passacaglia and chaconne), both the original dance and the doubles were treated as separate and complete movements. The result is a series of sections (usually three to ten), each of which is at least a double period in length. These SECTIONAL VARIATIONS are usually performed with a pause between each division.

Theme and Variations

The most important *genre* of sectional variations presents a complete binary movement (or another small form) as a theme; other divisions of the work are likewise complete, and often transverse a range of affective moods (march, waltz, expressive aria, and so on). Classical and Romantic composers termed such works THEME AND VARIATIONS. Unlike the ostinato bass of the baroque (limited to a melodic contour and characteristic rhythms), the theme of a set of sectional variations includes many different parameters: melody, harmony, rhythm, form, texture, and so on. Because there are relatively fewer sections in a classic theme and variations, the composer has more time to develop each different setting.

Where the individual segments of a continuous variation form may be identified on the score, the separate sections of a theme and variations are often included on a printed program. Especially in nineteenth-century music, each section may have a fanciful or programmatic title. In other works, the tempo marking may be included. The inclusion of sections on a program accentuates both their position in the work as a whole and their completeness individually.

Many composers of the Baroque era wrote music for their students (and for publication, of course), but the late eighteenth and nineteenth centuries saw a marked increase in amateur performance. A burgeoning middle class was eager to appreciate the joys and frustrations of music study and had the means to purchase virtually unlimited quantities of printed music. As a result, most composers found it lucrative to write music with popular tastes in mind. The theme and variations was among the most popular of these forms. Composers would begin with a folk melody, an aria from a popular opera, or the melody from a major symphonic work, and then compose a series of variations that were within the capabilities of average performers.

Variation Types.   Just as we would expect a passacaglia to include at least one section in sarabande rhythm and a chaconne to contain contrapuntal segments, composers of Classical- and Romantic-era forms approached variation according to the stylistic conventions of the time. While many composers remained true to some of the most popular Baroque methods of variation (texture, melodic embellishment, and so on), several new ones emerged in the works of Mozart and Beethoven, among others.

Change of Meter. One or more variation typically features a change of meter. While metric changes were impractical for the short segments of a passacaglia or chaconne, a binary variation afforded the composer plenty of time to explore the effect of the theme cast in a duple, rather than a triple meter, or with a compound, rather than a simple division (for example).

Change of Mode. When the original melody is major, one variation may be in the parallel minor. Likewise, a variation in minor is often provided for themes that are in the major mode. These modal variations are often labeled "Major" or "Minor" on the score.[2]

Rhythmic Effects. Classical and Romantic composers expanded the range of rhythmic effects. Syncopation, two-against-three, hemiola, borrowed division, and an ascending arpeggio effect (the stereotypical "rocket" motto) are among common variants in one or more sections of a theme and variation form.

Finale. Due to the greater length of many theme and variation forms, some composers wrote lengthy final sections (often labeled "Finale") to bring the work to an energetic close. A finale may abandon the form of the original theme and include a coda and even a cadenza-like passage.[3]

---

[2]Remember that throughout the seventeenth and eighteenth centuries (and even into the nineteenth), Italian was the language of music. Accordingly, the words "Maggiore" and "Minore" often appear, regardless of the composer's nationality.

[3]In an orchestral concerto, the cadenza is a passage for the solo instrument alone. Cadenzas typically feature a juxtaposition of lyric melody with virtuoso passage work.

Beethoven, Variations on "God Save the King"

Beethoven (1770–1827) wrote his variations on "God Save the King" in 1807. We know the tune as *America*, but in the nineteenth century, it was associated with the British monarchy (as Haydn's *God Save the Emperor Franz*—discussed in Volume I—was a song of respect in Austria). In many ways, Beethoven's variations comprise a catalog of the ways composers manipulated familiar themes in works of modest difficulty. The seven variations include changes of mode, meter, texture, rhythmic and melodic embellishment, syncopation, and a fiery finale. The melody itself is a six-measure repeated phrase followed by a phrase group of eight measures.

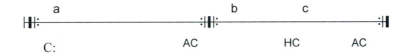

The theme is set in a simple folk style, but the careful soprano–bass counterpoint—especially over the bar line—is worthy of careful study.

Ludwig van Beethoven, Variations on
"God Save the King"

Variation I effects increased momentum with thickened texture and varying numbers of voices. Chromatic embellishment is common, as is syncopation. The harmony, meter, and cadential structure remain fixed.

Variation I

A major change of texture occurs in Variation II, along with a highly ornamented version of the melody. Form, harmony, and meter remain fixed.

Variation II

An Alberti bass accompaniment is an added feature in Variation III. The melody is fragmented and articulated rhythmically. Form and harmony are fixed elements.

Variation III

The fourth variation is basically chordal (contrasting with the two-part setting in the previous movement) and expands on the ascending arpeggio from the third variation. We see more use of the lower piano register in Variation IV than in previous movements.

Variation IV

   After the chordal flourish of Variation IV, the two-part structure, borrowed division, and minor mode of the fifth variation supply a welcome change. The harmony includes a number of seventh chords and a Neapolitan sixth (to be discussed in Chapter 4).

A change of meter with an emphasis on dotted rhythms characterizes the sixth variation. The final Variation, VII, begins without pause (termed *attaca*).

Variation VI

The finale of Beethoven's Variations on "God Save the King" begins in quadruple meter, but later changes back to the familiar $\frac{3}{4}$ and, for the first time in the work, form is a variable element. An extended coda begins in measure 140. Characteristic of Beethoven, a dramatic Adagio precedes the close of the work, with an embellishment of the melody in sixteenth-note triplets (against sixteenth notes in the accompaniment), that provides a drive toward the final cadence.

Variation VII

Few would suggest that Beethoven's variations on "God Save the King" rank with the composer's greatest works. Still, as a model of how a simple tune can serve as the basis of a more lengthy and complex composition, the piece provides an interesting compendium. We have variations of texture, mode, meter, form, register, and mood. The melody undergoes constant embellishment and metamorphosis; rhythm, fragmentation, borrowed division, the trumpet-like quality of the fourth variation, and the playfulness of the finale are all imaginative variants of the melody. All the while, the tune is recognizable, yet always fresh and invigorated.

Variations—both continuous and sectional—continue to attract composers today. Some of the most memorable works in the second half of the twentieth century are *Piano Variations* by Aaron Copland (1900–1990), *Five Pieces for Orchestra* by Arnold Schoenberg (1874–1951), and *Young Person's Guide to the Orchestra* (a set of variations on a theme of Henry Purcell) by Benjamin Britten (1913–1976).

> WORKBOOK/ANTHOLOGY II
> II. Sectional Variations, page 11

REVIEW AND APPLICATION 1–2

Sectional Variations

Essential Terms

sectional variations   theme and variations

1. Indicate whether the following statements pertain to continuous variations, sectional variations, or both, by writing the appropriate letter in the blank.

    A. Continuous variations

    B. Sectional variations

    C. Both

_____ a. May include the embellishment of a melody

_____ b. Most popular with composers before about 1750

_____ c. May include a variation in the major (or minor) mode

_____ d. Variations tend to be phrase-length

_____ e. May center on a *basso ostinato*

_____ f. Characterized by the theme and variations form

_____ g. Changes of texture frequent

_____ h. May include 20 or more variations

_____ i. May center on a fixed harmonic plan

_____ j. Often features changes of meter

2. Study the familiar melody below, then write three variations for solo flute. In the first variation, preserve the basic outlines of the melody, but add chromatic and diatonic nonchord tones as embellishments. Retain the basic melody in the second variation, but change the meter from $\frac{4}{4}$ to $\frac{3}{4}$ (retaining the eight-measure length of the melody). For the third variation, use the parallel minor mode with occasional chromatic embellishments.

Civil War-era Song, "The Cruel War"

Theme

a. Variation I (Embellishment)

b. Variation II (Change of Meter)

c. Variation III (Change of Mode)

SELF-TEST 1–2

Time Limit: 5 Minutes

1. Check the best answer for each question from the list (one answer correct).
   Scoring: Subtract 7 points for an error.

   a. Sectional variations

   _____ (1) are usually more brief than continuous variations.

   _____ (2) are more typical of the Baroque era.

   _____ (3) usually include an ostinato bass.

   _____ (4) are usually based on a periodic theme.

   b. Which of the following is usually *not* varied in a series of sectional variations?

   _____ (1) Harmony and melody

   _____ (2) Texture and rhythm

   _____ (3) Mode and meter

   _____ (4) Any or all of the above may be varied elements

   c. If variations are sectional,

   _____ (1) each begins and ends in the same key.

   _____ (2) each variation usually has a definitive ending.

   _____ (3) the theme is a passacaglia or chaconne.

   _____ (4) the meter is different in each variation.

   d. Sectional variations

   _____ (1) were popular in the Classical era.

   _____ (2) were popular in the Baroque era.

   _____ (3) evolved from the passacaglia.

   _____ (4) are based on a fixed harmonic pattern.

   e. A *double is*

   _____ (1) a dance performed after each section of sectional variations.

   _____ (2) a variation of a dance played immediately following the dance itself.

   _____ (3) the third movement of a theme and variations.

   _____ (4) the variation of any one section of a theme and variations.

2. Write the term or phrase that fits the given definition. These questions cover both continuous and sectional variations. *Scoring: Subtract 9 points for each incorrect or incomplete term.*

    a. _____ A series of continuous variations based on a harmonic pattern

    b. _____ The most popular type of variation form in the Classical era

    c. _____ The country in which opera originated

    d. _____ A common type of cadence in Renaissance and Baroque eras in which agogic accents effect a change of meter

    e. _____ The composer of the *Goldberg Variations*

3. List five aspects of a work that might be variable elements in a theme and variations. *Scoring: Subtract 4 points for each incorrect or omitted answer*

    a. _____

    b. _____

    c. _____

    d. _____

    e. _____

Total Possible: 100   Your Score _____

FIGURED BASS

As we discussed in the introduction to Unit 1, the composers who conceived the "new music" in the early seventeenth century were determined to break with the Renaissance ideal of interweaving melodic lines. Monody features a simple, ornamented melody with a strong bass and chordal accompaniment. So subordinate were the inner voices that composers often did not even notate them in full but, rather, indicated the intervals sounding above the bass with numerals.

The system of shorthand notation, associated almost exclusively with the Baroque era, is called FIGURED BASS. In the next example, study the facsimile of an instrumental work in a mid-Baroque style by Arcangelo Corelli (1653–1713). Notice that numerals and other symbols appear above the bass line. By 1680, FIGURED-BASS SYMBOLS were uniformly placed *below* the bass, where we are more accustomed to seeing them today. The work shown is a sonata for solo violin as it was published in 1700 from copper plates. The middle line is the violin melody; the upper one, an ornamented version. The bass is the lowest line; the numerals instruct the keyboard performer about the disposition of the inner voices.

Figured Bass Realization

In the days of Monteverdi, Corelli, and Bach (representing early, mid-, and late-Baroque styles, respectively), a keyboard performer was expected to read a score that contained only soprano and bass lines and complete the inner voices based on the instructions provided by the figured bass symbols. This process, important for many musicians today, is called REALIZATION. Skilled specialists in Baroque music (then and now) use voice-leading procedures that are virtually identical to those discussed in Volume I of this text: Parallel perfect fifths and octaves are avoided; leaps are minimal; doubling follows traditional practice; and contrary motion is emphasized.

The Continuo.   Central to the performance of Baroque music are a keyboard instrument (usually a harpsichord; often an organ in sacred works) and a stringed bass instrument such as a cello, lute, guitar, or any number of less common choices. Together, these two instruments comprise the CONTINUO (or *basso continuo*) which is the backbone of a Baroque ensemble. As a stabilizing—but not necessarily leading—force in performance, the continuo holds a position similar to the rhythm section in contemporary jazz. Whether the ensemble is large or small, the Baroque continuo is omnipresent. A performance of the solo violin sonata in the last passage (a chamber work) requires three performers: a violinist who plays the upper line in treble clef, a cellist who performs the bass line as written, and a harpsichordist who doubles the bass and fills in the inner voices according to the figured bass.[4] In a major orchestral work, such as Handel's *Messiah* or Bach's *Mass in B Minor*, an entire string section as well as brass and woodwinds play alongside the continuo.

Chamber Music [5]	Orchestral Music
Solo Violin	Flutes, Oboes, Bassoons Trumpets, French Horns (other instruments) Violins, Violas, Cellos, Basses
Continuo (Keyboard and Bass)	**Continuo** (Keyboard and Bass)

So much was written during the Baroque era about the art of realization that we have very clear guidelines for characteristic rhythms and textures in keyboard accompaniments. Realization of a figured bass in keyboard style is an important skill for pianists today. In addition, however, figured bass problems in a four-part vocal style have been a traditional facet of studies in music theory.

THE FIGURED-BASS SYSTEM

In limiting our study of figured bass to the chorale style, we may bypass the more complex issues associated with keyboard performance. From several chapters in Volume I, you already know many of the basic figured bass symbols, because the arabic numerals have been retained in contemporary harmonic analysis of triads and chords in tonal music.

	The *absence* of a numeral or other symbol specifies a diatonic triad in root position.
6	The numeral 6 or the numerals $^6_3$ denote a triad in first inversion.
$^6_4$	The numerals $^6_4$ stipulate a diatonic triad in second inversion.
♭ ♮ ♯	An accidental alone affects the third above the bass.

Notice that in the following examples, the spacing and doubling procedures are those that you learned earlier. Remember, however, that the figured

---

[4]The second treble-clef line is not a second instrument, but an ornamented version of the melody to be played when the melody is repeated.

[5]While many other types of chamber music were common in the Baroque era, the *Trio Sonata*, combining two solo violins and continuo (a total of four instruments) was among the most popular.

bass symbols specify a group of inner-voice pitches; the octave placement of those pitches is left to the discretion of the performer. Each of the following chords is a correct interpretation of the figured bass.

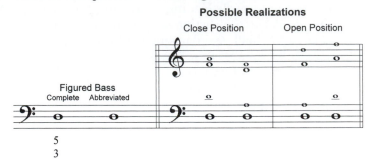

The numeral 6 alone or the numerals $^6_3$ stipulate a chord in first inversion. Conventional doubling in first-inversion chords is assumed. Because this particular chord is diminished, however, we would double the third (bass).

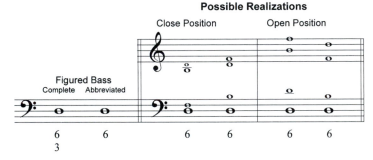

The figures $^6_4$ specify a triad or chord in second inversion. Almost invariably, the bass is doubled in a four-part setting.

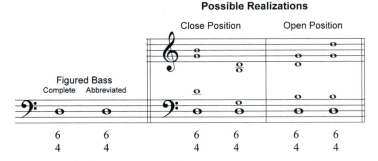

Accidentals alone always refer to the third above the bass.

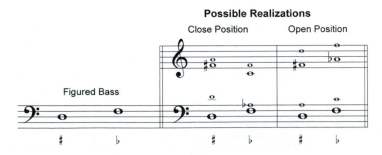

Seventh Chords. The arabic numerals we use to represent root-position and inverted seventh chords also come from figured bass. If third inversion is specified ($^6_4$), we know that the seventh is in the bass. Otherwise, or unless the soprano is given, the voice that contains the chordal seventh is not specified. Regardless of the voicing, however, the seventh itself resolves down by step as we have discussed in earlier chapters. Remember that pitches represented by figured-bass numerals are diatonic unless accompanied by an accidental or other symbol. In the next example, the numerals in parentheses are often omitted.

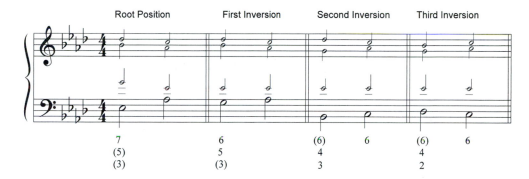

Composers may specify alternate doublings through figured-bass numerals. In the first progression below, a doubled root (and omitted fifth) is indicated for a seventh chord in root position; in the second, the figures specify a doubled third for the D-minor triad.

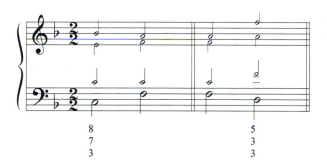

Accidentals. Because figured-bass numerals alone refer to diatonic pitches above the bass, Baroque composers employed a number of different notations to indicate chromatic pitches. In addition to accidental symbols (which are self-explanatory), a slash through the numeral or a plus sign before or after it indicates a diatonic pitch that is raised a half step. Be aware that the different figured-bass symbols employed by Baroque composers is virtually infinite; the examples below are but some of the more common.

6	6̸	6+	+6	♯6	♭6	♮6
Diatonic Sixth	Raised Sixth	Raised Sixth	Raised Sixth	Sharp Sixth	Flat Sixth	Natural Sixth

Various accidental symbols are shown in the next example.

Linear Motion.   In addition to an outline of the harmony, figured-bass symbols may indicate linear motion above the bass as well. While figured bass was employed almost exclusively in Baroque instrumental music, notice how we might stipulate inner-voice motion for Bach's harmonization of a Nikolaus Selnecker chorale melody, *Nun Lasst uns gehn und treten* ("Now Let Us Come Before Him"). The first two phrases of the chorale as Bach harmonized them are followed by a figured-bass version with Selnecker's melody and Bach's bass. Note how the inner-voice movement is specified by the figures.

 CD 1, TRACK 10-1 REALIZATION (2 PARTS)
J. S. Bach, "Now Let Us Come Before Him"
Melody by Nikolaus Selnecker (ca. 1600)

Figured Bass Version

Due to the many possibilities for inner-voice spacing, a realization of the figures in the last example would not necessarily duplicate Bach's harmonization—even with given soprano and bass. Any faithful realization, however, would adhere to Bach's harmony (beginning in G major and concluding with a cadence in D major).

Realization in Four-Part Vocal Style

Realizing a figured bass within the limitations of the four-part vocal style is an excellent means of understanding the system itself. This approach also allows us to avoid the complexities of instrumental realization, which are better treated in a separate course. In a vocal realization, we can employ a given melody (closer to the actual Baroque practice) or create a melody from within the harmony specified by the figures. In either case, the first task is a roman-numeral analysis of the given bass.

Analysis.   In recent years, authors of theory texts have less frequently employed altered numerals (♯6, *6̸*, +4, and so on) to specify the occurrence of chromatic pitches. Most now agree that in analysis, the chromatic alterations are obvious and need not be included in arabic-numeral labels.

Analysis of the figured bass prior to realization is important in identifying suspensions, six-four sonorities, seventh chords, and other traditional materials that require special treatment. The numerals 9–8, for example, might represent either an appoggiatura or a 9–8 suspension. Analysis will make this distinction clear (if the dissonant pitch is a member of the preceding chord, the figure is probably a suspension). Likewise, the figures $\frac{6}{4}$ denote a second-inversion triad with its distinctive doubling considerations.

Finally, combining figured-bass symbols with roman numerals visually clarifies key implications and enables us to capitalize on melodic and harmonic tendencies in performance.

Realization With Soprano Given

When a soprano melody is supplied along with a figured bass, we need only apply principles of voice leading and musical common sense to produce the composer's intended harmony. Remember that all inner-voice movement is denoted by the figured bass.

Study the figured bass with soprano in the next example. The first phrase is in G minor with a tonicization of C minor in the second phrase.

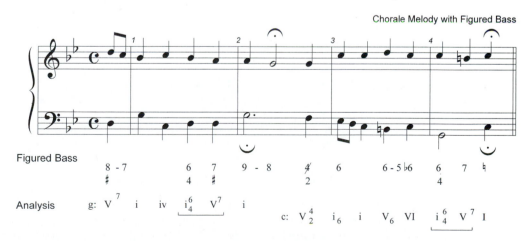

Chorale Melody with Figured Bass

We can make several observations about the bass and the process of realization.

- Chordal sevenths appear throughout.
- The seventh specified in measure 2 is already supplied.
- Cadential six-fours appear in measures 1 and 4 (we must make sure that these resolve characteristically through stepwise motion).
- The 9–8 suspension designated for measure 2 is already present in the soprano.
- The 6–5 in measure 3 is a passing figure that we must include in the alto or tenor.

CD 1, TRACK 10-2 REALIZATION
Four-Part Realization

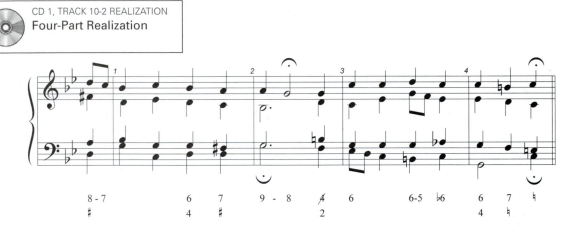

The realization above is but one of many possible, but in this version, the chorale conforms to the figured bass while voice-leading errors are avoided.

Realization Without Given Soprano

In Volume I, we studied the process of constructing a bass to complement a given soprano. Realizing a figured bass in vocal style without a given soprano is a similar process, since the melody must make an effective counterpoint with the given bass. But while we began our melody harmonization by devising a harmonic plan, with a figured bass, the harmony is designated through the numerals and symbols.

Begin a vocal realization as before—with a scrutiny of the figured bass and the specified harmony.

Figured Bass

An effective melody will move generally in contrary motion with the bass. In addition, however, while well-placed leaps may add interest and momentum, the melody should be easily singable and basically conjunct. Compose the melody first, then add the inner voices. The realization in the next example is an acceptable interpretation of the figured bass, but the melody lacks direction. This sort of melodic line often results from composing all three upper voices simultaneously.

Realization with Ineffective Soprano

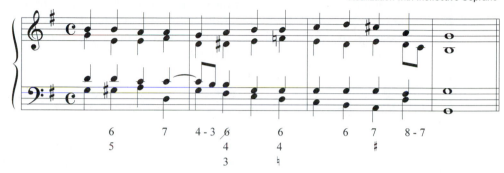

In the next example, the soprano is improved through an ascending line that complements the bass. While inner voices are often relatively less interesting in four-part chorales, the alto and tenor of the second version are improved as well.

Realization with Improved Soprano

Although authoritative editions of important Baroque works are widely available, many instructors include a modicum of studies in figured bass realization in the theory curriculum, both to foster an appreciation of the skills involved and to reinforce concepts of harmony and voice leading. Figured-bass realization for keyboard performance is a topic for advanced study. Composers in the early, middle, and late Baroque approached the art quite differently. Moreover, even in the same era, composers and performers in different parts of Europe employed diverse symbols and methods. After all, the Baroque was a

WORKBOOK/ANTHOLOGY II
III. Figured Bass, page 15

time of improvisation, and much of the skill of realization was in knowing how to support the soloist or ensemble performers while generally following the composer's instructions at the same time.

REVIEW AND APPLICATION 1–3 ────────────────────

Figured Bass

Essential Terms

basso continuo   continuo   figured bass   realization

1. Realize the given figured basses in four parts using traditional SATB format and conventional doublings. Add any necessary accidentals. Remember that an absence of figures indicates a root-position chord. Use the blank to provide an appropriate analytical symbol in the specified key.

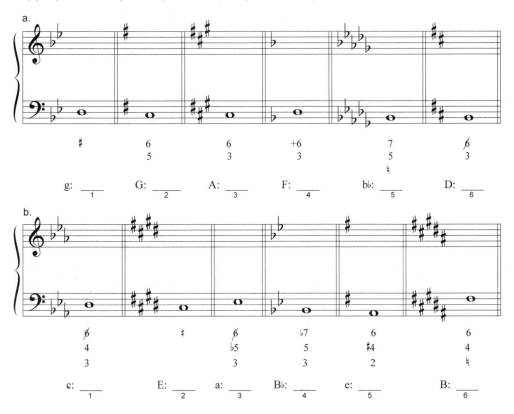

2. Realize the given phrases in four-part vocal style. Adhere closely to the figured-bass instructions. Add any necessary accidentals and provide analytical symbols in the keys specified.

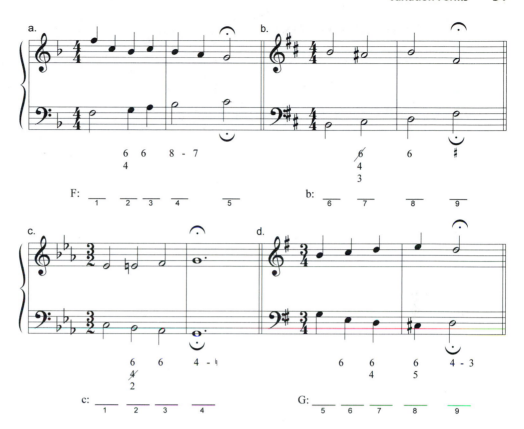

3. Realize these figured basses. Begin by writing a soprano that forms effective counterpoint with the bass. Next, add inner voices. You may need to add accidentals for some chords. Use the blanks to provide a harmonic analysis.

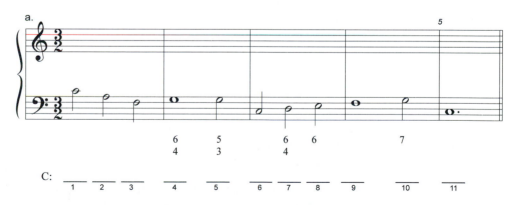

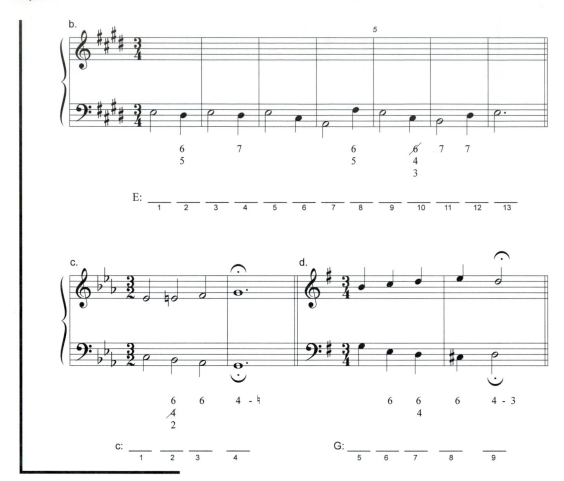

SELF-TEST 1–3

Time Limit: 5 Minutes

1. Indicate whether the following statements are true (enter "T" in the blank) or false (write "F"). *Scoring: Subtract 6 points for each error.*

   _____   a. Figured bass is characteristic of the nineteenth century.

   _____   b. At one time, figured-bass symbols were written above the bass.

   _____   c. There are three performers in a Baroque solo violin sonata.

   _____   d. An accidental symbol alone always refers to the third above the bass.

   _____   e. A first-inversion triad may be represented by the figures 6, $\frac{6}{3}$, or $\frac{6}{4}$, depending on the circumstances.

   _____   f. The symbols +6, 6+, ♯6, and $\not{6}$ are synonymous.

   _____   g. Figured-bass symbols may be employed both for harmonic and melodic motion.

2. Realize the given figured bass. Include necessary accidentals and adhere to conventions of four-part vocal scoring. Provide roman- and arabic-numeral analysis in the blanks (be sure to specify the key). *Scoring: Subtract 3 points for an incorrect key signature; 5 points for an incorrect roman-numeral symbol; and 6 points for each misspelled chord.*

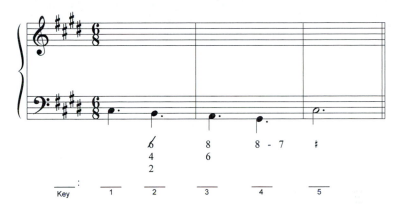

Total Possible: 100   Your Score _____

PROJECTS

Analysis

Prepare an analytical paper (or notes for a class presentation as directed) that centers on the Purcell aria in the text or Haydn's quartet movement that appears in the workbook/anthology.

Text

Henry Purcell, "When I Am Laid in Earth" from *Dido and Aeneas,* text pages 3–6. This passacaglia is discussed briefly in the introduction to Unit 1 (page 2). Undertake an analysis of this work as a series of continuous variations. First, comment on the structure of the bass ostinato (measures 9–14), then isolate later occurrences of the pattern. How is each ostinato statement made different from another? Is the harmony that accompanies the pattern (measure 14 and following) varied? Study the vocal melody and comment on how these phrases do or do not coincide with the ostinato. Discuss ways in which the ostinato bass and the melody combine to form a unified composition.

Workbook/Anthology II

Joseph Haydn, Quartet Op. 76, No. 3 (II), workbook pages 19–25. The second movement of Haydn's quartet is a theme with four variations. First, make a thorough study of the theme itself. Prepare a time line that shows melodic material, cadences, and measure numbers. Identify the melody form of the theme. In addition, note texture in the theme as well as the use of dissonance and secondary function.

Comment separately on each of the four variations, and identify fixed and variable elements. You will notice that a different instrument (and register) is featured in each variation. Center your comments on the accompanying material identifying texture, melodic embellishment, chromaticism, and other aspects as appropriate. Finally, explain how the five movements together make a satisfactory musical whole. How are movements contrasted in terms of texture, meter, key, and so on?

Composition

Variations on "Twinkle, Twinkle, Little Star". Mozart is among composers who wrote a set of variations on the French folk song "Ah! Vous dirai-je, Maman," which we know as "Twinkle, Twinkle, Little Star." Here is how Mozart stated the theme as a duet:

W. A Mozart, Theme, "Ah! Vous dirai-je, Maman"

Plan and compose a set of four sectional variations on this simple tune. The work can be for piano or (as directed by your instructor) for two instruments (flute and bassoon or violin and cello are among the logical combinations). Use your own creative instincts in planning fixed and variable elements, but consider using Beethoven's Variations on "God Save the King" as a guide. The examples that follow (with flute and bassoon in mind) represent just a few of the many possible approaches to variation. Only the first four measures are given; you may continue these in the same style or compose entirely new variations of your own. When you submit the assignment, recopy the theme as given, then notate your four variations complete with appropriate dynamic and phrasing indications.

CD 1, TRACK 11
Sample Variations

Variation I

Variation II

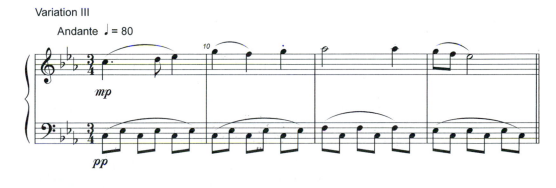

Variation III

Variation IV

For Further Study

"The Blues": A Twentieth-Century Chaconne. Complete a paper or prepare a class presentation (as directed) that centers on twentieth-century blues as a modern chaconne form. In addition to discussing typical blues harmonic patterns and approaches to improvisation, briefly trace the origin of the blues in Black American culture including the "field holler," blues in the rural south, urban Chicago blues styles, "rhythm and blues," and later movements. Identify major blues performers in each era ("Howlin' Wolf," for example) and assemble a list of recordings that will amplify your presentation.

CHAPTER 2

Canon and Fugue

By the end of the seventeenth century, most composers had embraced the new homophonic texture, but imitative counterpoint was far from abandoned. Contrapuntal passages in homophonic works afforded a means of managing the ebb and flow of tension while providing textural variety. In addition, Medieval and Renaissance forms that were based entirely on imitative counterpoint continued to attract composers in the Baroque—especially as instrumental music attained a new prominence.

In college and university music study, courses in counterpoint are usually offered in both sixteenth- and eighteenth-century styles. Renaissance vocal polyphony (MODAL COUNTERPOINT) is idealized in the works of Giovanni da Palestrina (1525–1594). J. S. Bach is considered the greatest master of TONAL COUNTERPOINT, which developed largely through compositions for organ and harpsichord. While tonal counterpoint is our focus in this chapter (and fugue in particular), we will first study more simple imitative *genre*, such as the round and the canon. In one way or another, these forms have been popular since the Middle Ages.

The Round

Most of us have sung a ROUND—a simple melody composed so that overlapping entries create a polyphonic composition. Rounds like *Row, Row, Row Your Boat* are characterized by staggered beginning and ending points. The first voice to enter is also the first to finish; the last voice to enter completes the composition alone. In the line below, the numbers above the score indicate that the second voice enters when the first has reached the third measure; the third voice enters when the first voice begins measure 5.

Viewed as a three-voice polyphonic composition in full score, *Row, Row, Row Your Boat* consists entirely of tonic harmony that is embellished with passing and neighboring tones.

In addition to *Row, Row, Row Your Boat*, most Americans will be familiar with other rounds (*Three Blind Mice, Hi, Ho, Nobody Home*) that are popular in school and camp settings because a simple melody generates a rich-sounding tertian polyphony.

Rounds in Western music date from before the Middle Ages. Perhaps the most famous canon of these (called a ROTA in Medieval terminology) is the fourteenth century *Sumer Is Icumen In,* a song in celebration of the changing seasons.

"Sumer Is Icumen In" (*ca.* 1300)

Summer is a-coming in, loudly sing cuc-koo,
Soweth seed and bloweth mead, and springeth woods anew.
Ewe now bleateth after lamb, low'th after calf the cow,
Bullock starteth, buck now verteth, merry sing cuc-koo,
Well singest thou cuc-koo, nor cease thou never now.

"Sumer" has a text in Old English (including nonsense syllables) that is marginally comprehensible to us today. We should also note that the secular round is both in the Ionian mode (major) and strictly metric. Most sacred works in the fourteenth century were less regular metrically and more often cast in one of the Church Modes. An additional feature of "Sumer" is the drone or *ostinato* accompaniment.

While multivoice polyphonic compositions were common by the time that "Sumer" was composed in the early fourteenth century, ostinato, an older technique for thickening texture, is an important part of the work. As we discussed in Chapter 1 of this volume, OSTINATO is a repeated melodic and rhythmic fragment that continues throughout a section or entire composition. In *Sumer is Icumen In*, there are two different four-measure ostinatos that complement the canonic voices.

Ostinatos with "Sumer Is Icumen In"

Including the ostinatos, the simple round becomes an interesting and forceful composition. The first ten measures are given in full score in the next example.

"Sumer Is Icumen In"

Canon

While a round concludes with a staggered ending (as in *Row, Row, Row Your Boat*), a *canon* is a more sophisticated form. A CANON is a work in strict imitation for two or more voices: One voice assumes the role of leader; the other voice or voices follow at a specific interval of pitch and time (entering a perfect fifth higher and eight beats later, for example). Canons usually include a final passage that permits all voices to reach a cadence simultaneously.

Other Possibilities for Canonic Imitation.   In the previous example, the leading and following voices (the *dux* and the *comes* in Renaissance terminology) begin with the same pitch; this is called "canon at the unison." If the canon were at the octave, the second voice would enter an octave above or below the first. Especially in the Baroque era, canon at intervals other than the octave and unison is common. If canon is at the fifth, for example, the following voice enters a fifth higher or a fourth lower than the leading voice; if canon is at the second, the following voice imitates the first a second higher (or a seventh lower), and so on.

In 1742, J. S. Bach composed a series of thirty variations on an original "aria" for his harpsichord pupil, Johann Gottlieb Goldberg. We know these movements as *The Goldberg Variations*. Each of the thirty variations is organized around the original bass line and, as Ralph Kirkpatrick has said, the work as a whole may be viewed as "an enormous passacaglia."[1] Like the aria upon which they are based, each variation is binary in form. Every third variation is a canon at successively wider intervals:

No. 3	Canon at the unison		No. 18	Canon at the sixth
No. 6	Canon at the second		No. 21	Canon at the seventh
No. 9	Canon at the third		No. 24	Canon at the octave
No. 12	Canon at the fourth		No. 27	Canon at the ninth
No. 15	Canon at the fifth			

Variation 3 is a two-voice canon at the unison in G major (shown below in part). The bass is independent, but complementary. The three-stave notation (not Bach's original) helps us to follow both voices of the canon as they cross frequently. Emphasizing the canonic structure of each line is crucial in performance.

> CD 1, TRACK 12-1 VARIATIONS (2 PARTS)
> **J. S. Bach, Goldberg Variations (No. 3)**
> **Canon at the Unison**

J. S. Bach, Goldberg Variations
No. 3, Canon at the Unison

---

[1] Ralph Kirkpatrick (1911–1984) was widely acknowledged in his lifetime both as a scholar and as a performer of music for the harpsichord. His catalog of Domenico Scarlatti's works is definitive.

TRACK 12-2 VARIATIONS
J. S. Bach, Goldberg Variations (No. 18)
Canon at the Sixth

Variation 18, a canon at the sixth (with independent bass), is less figural and more easily followed on traditional grand-staff notation.

Given complete in the next passage, Variation 27 is a canon at the ninth. There is no accompanying bass.

CD 1, TRACK 13

**J. S. Bach, Goldberg Variations (No. 27)
Canon at the Ninth**

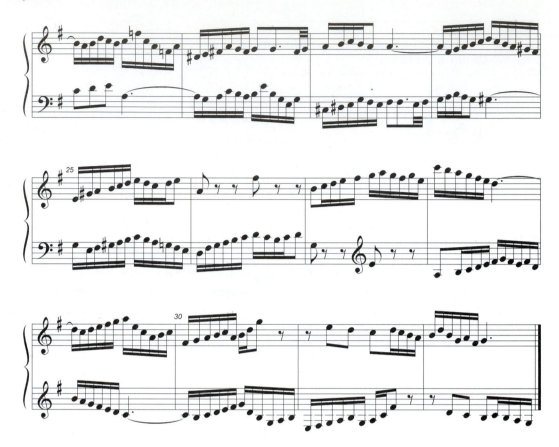

WORKBOOK/ANTHOLOGY II
I. Rounds and Canons, page 27

DEVELOPMENT OF THE FUGUE

While strict canon continued to be popular throughout the Renaissance, the *genre* that we know as *fugue* awaited two other developments in its evolution. The first of these, imitative counterpoint, is associated with the Renaissance master Josquin Desprez (1450–1521); the second, the monothematic *ricercar*, provided the mature fugue with its essential style and design.

Imitative Counterpoint (Points of Imitation)

In the late fifteenth and early sixteenth centuries, Josquin and others developed imitative counterpoint as a somewhat less rigid compositional approach than canon. After about 1500, sections of longer works were organized through the imitation of motives; these POINTS OF IMITATION permitted the composer to effect sectional contrast while maintaining textural continuity. Josquin's approach to imitative counterpoint is seen in *Faulte d'argent* (*Lack of*

Money), a five-voice *chanson* (song). The first two (of five) points of imitation are shown:

The third and fourth points (not shown) are based on contrasting motives, while the fifth point (not shown) returns to the opening material to round out the work.

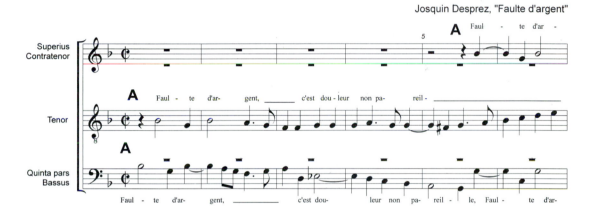

As the chanson continues, notice a third motive (B[1]) that is heard along with statements of point B, and further calls attention to each entry. The idea of independent melodic material that complements imitative counterpoint is an important part of traditional fugal structure.

Lack of money is an evil without equal.

Notice that in measure 7 of the chanson (page 65), the entry of point A in the contratenor (alto) duplicates the original intervals, but a perfect fifth higher. Likewise, the occurrence of point B in measure 17 is at a different pitch level than the original. In addition, observe that point B has two distinct motives heard in different voices (labeled B and B^1). The descending stepwise motive is heard in augmented rhythmic values in the tenor (measures 20–21) and the bassus (measures 21–22). Finally, be aware that the opening two or three pitches are sufficient to convey the idea of a point entry even if differences occur later in the line.

Canzona and Ricercar

While the Renaissance was an era of supreme achievement in vocal polyphony, composers were increasingly attracted by purely instrumental works as well. The nobility were still the major consumers of new music, and few courts lacked a complement of stringed and wind instruments, organs, and one or more *clavichords* or *harpsichords.*[2] Like his contemporary, Josquin Desprez, Heinrich Isaac (1450–1517) was Flemish, and composed masses and motets that continue to be performed today.[3] Unlike Desprez, however, Isaac is remembered for his *canzonas* and other music for keyboard.

Canzona. In the first chapter, we discussed how the terms we use today to identify certain forms and procedures were not as clear-cut in previous eras. As we define the term today, a CANZONA is a Renaissance instrumental work that employs imitative counterpoint in some or all of several different sections. Many canzonas start with a long–short–short (dactylic) rhythm. Isaac's canzona begins and ends in transposed Dorian (note the absence of E♭). Four different motives are treated in the fourty-two-measure work. The first two of these (measures 1–18) are shown in the next example. Note the extended use of sequence in measures 7–18.

CD 1, TRACK 14
Heinrich Isaac, Canzona

The first section of Isaac's canzona (measures 1–6) is a point of imitation for three voices; the third entry, in the alto, is transposed at the fifth and

---

[2]The CLAVICHORD is a small keyboard instrument (usually rectangular in shape) with a soft, intimate tone quality. When a key on the clavichord is depressed, a mechanism strikes the string (meaning that the performer may control volume through differences in touch). A HARP-SICHORD has the familiar curved appearance of the modern piano, but depressing a key results in a note's being *plucked*. Accordingly, the performer has no control over the volume of sound produced. While the harpsichord was the dominant keyboard instrument before about 1750, it was gradually replaced by the more versatile piano (*pianoforte*), which was invented around 1725.
[3]Flanders once comprised parts of modern Belgium, France, and The Netherlands.

concludes with an authentic cadence on D. While the first section is contrapuntal, measures 7–14 comprise descending diatonic sequences in soprano, tenor, and bass (the tenor is consistent in pitch and rhythm, but not sequential). The second section of the work ends with a ii$^6_5$–V–i cadence formula, although, as is common in early Renaissance works, the ("imperfect") third is omitted from the final tonic chord.

In many ways, the Renaissance canzona, with its sectional structure and emphasis on two or more principal motives, can be seen as the predecessor of the Baroque sonata. The monothematic ricercar, on the other hand (discussed in the next section), led to another important Baroque *genre*—the fugue.

Ricercar.   While a canzona might be characterized as a "lively" instrumental work, another form, the RICERCAR, is typified by solemn and generally slow-moving imitative lines.[4] Marco Antonio Cavazzoni (ca. 1490–1560) was a Bolognese composer who is closely associated with the development of the imitative ricercar as a keyboard form. Cavazzoni's works in this vein are typically brief and noble. The example below, shown in its entirety, is in three voices. The work begins and ends in Dorian mode (Mode I in Medieval and Renaissance terminology). Notice also that the cadences in Cavazzoni's ricercar lack the *musica ficta* (the absence of a C♯ here) that was typical in the early sixteenth century. The result is a work that sounds—even to us today—vaguely "old-fashioned." Note the picardy third in the final cadence.

CD 1, TRACK 15
M. A. Cavazzoni, Ricercar

---

[4]Italian in origin, the form in the singular is spelled both "ricercar" and "ricercare" in primary sources. The spelling in plural references is uniformly "ricercare." In the singular, we will employ "ricercar" in this text.

Cavazzoni's ricercar is in three voices throughout. The opening soprano motive is duplicated at the octave in the bass (measure 2). When the tenor enters in measure 4, however, the motive is imitated at the fifth, as we encountered in both Josquin's chanson and Isaac's canzona. In the next example, the three voices are aligned metrically for illustrative purposes. In the score on page 68, notice that the third entry actually begins on the second half of measure 4.

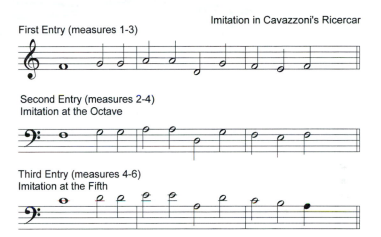

The tonic–dominant relationship, crucial to seventeenth-century tonal harmony, is anticipated in many imitative works in the fifteenth and sixteenth centuries. The relationships seen in Cavazzoni's ricercare facilitated the evolution of a more important *genre*: the *fugue*. In the next section, we will discuss

WORKBOOK/ANTHOLOGY II
II. Imitative Counterpoint, page 31

fugue and its component elements. For now, review canon and early imitative counterpoint through Review and Application 2–1.

REVIEW AND APPLICATION 2–1

Canon and Ricercar

Essential Terms

canon	ostinato	round
canzona	point of imitation	tonal counterpoint
modal counterpoint	ricercar	

1. Identify the intervals of imitation in the examples below (third, fifth, sixth, and so on). Write the answer in the blanks below. Consider only the first few notes of imitative lines.

a.

Interval of Imitation_____

b.

Io   mi   ri - vol - go in die - tro.

Io   mi   ri - vol - go in die - tro.

I look back at every step.

Interval of Imitation _____

c.

Fire and light - ning from heav'n   fall,   fire and light - ning from heav'n - fall.

Fire   and light - ning from heav'n   fall,   fire and light - ning from heav'n fall.

Interval of Imitation_____

2. Consider the fragments below to be motives for canonic imitation. As specified, transpose the motive to begin above or below the given notes. Begin on the diatonic pitch specified and duplicate the original rhythmic values. Add accidentals as necessary.

SELF-TEST 2–1

Time Limit: 5 Minutes

1. Choose a term from the list that matches each description. *Scoring: Subtract 8 points for each error.*

   A. ricercar   D. rota

   B. canon   E. round

   C. canzona   F. point of imitation

   _____ a.   A sectional imitative work that is typically lively in nature

   _____ b.   A composition based on the literal or transposed imitation of a single motive and with a written ending so that all voices end at the same time

_____ c.   A Renaissance technique through which sections in a composition are organized through the imitation of a motive

_____ d.   A Medieval and Renaissance term for round

_____ e.   A sectional imitative composition that is generally solemn and slow moving

_____ f.   A work based on the imitation of a single melody (usually at the unison), but without a composed ending (voices end at different times)

2. Write "T" in the blank if the statement is true, write "F" if false. *Scoring: Subtract 7 points for an incorrect answer.*

_____ a.   Two or more voices are required for canon.

_____ b.   Tonal counterpoint was written in the Renaissance by composers such as Palestrina.

_____ c.   *Sumer Is Icumen In* is an English tune with a Latin text.

_____ d.   Several points of imitation may occur in one contrapuntal work.

_____ e.   Canons at various intervals occur in Bach's *Goldberg Variations.*

_____ f.   Canzona and Ricercar were late Renaissance/early Baroque forms.

_____ g.   In canon at the fifth two voices move in strict canonic imitation five beats apart.

3. Name the Renaissance composer who is generally credited with the development of imitative counterpoint. *Scoring: Subtract 3 points for an incorrect name.*

_____
Composer

Total Possible: 100   Your Score _____

FUGUE

FUGUE is an imitative *genre* that has attracted composers since the seventeenth century. We may regard fugue (from the Latin *fuga* or "flight") as both a technique of composition and as a form. Yet because each fugue has its own unique structure, the definition of a formal design is elusive. Moreover, composers have written complete fugal sections and inserted them into longer works. The *techniques* that define fugue (statement, imitation, restatement, and so on) do not preclude their employment as contrapuntal sections within a homophonic work.

On the other hand, a fugue is itself a complete musical work, with several interval divisions that convey varying levels of tension and stasis. Rather than dwelling on a more specific definition, we might acknowledge that fugue can be *both* a form and a technique. In a longer composition, the technique of fugue permits textural contrast and increases tension. As a short contrapuntal composition, fugue is a dynamic and challenging musical form.

Some approaches to music that were popular in the Baroque era reappear in twentieth-century jazz: the use of improvisation, for example, and the presence of a continuo (or rhythm section of a jazz ensemble). In terms of tension and release, a fugue unfolds in a continuous development of a central idea, as jazz does. And while we might diagram a binary form as statement–tension–release (first diagram below), fugues and jazz improvisations *spiral* from beginning to end (represented by the second graphic). In both, we have the impression that the performer might have gone on indefinitely, but chose a point of cadence almost arbitrarily, when the time "seemed right."

Melody Forms   **Fugue/Jazz**

The Subject

Whether technique or form, fugue is based on the statement and imitation of a brief, but memorable melodic fragment called a SUBJECT. As discussed below, a fugue subject differs significantly from a melody and from a motive.

Subjects and Melodies.   Melodies often dictate the structure of musical form, as we discussed in Chapters 9 and 12 of Volume I. A phrase, for example, may grow into a period, a double period, or even a binary or ternary form. By contrast, a fugue subject does not define, but rather facilitates the continuous evolution of melodic material throughout the work. German composers and scholars used the term *fortspinnung* (which we might translate loosely as "spinning forth") to describe the burgeoning of a complete composition from a melodic fragment.

In addition, melodies, associated principally with homophonic works, are usually complete within themselves, at least nominally symmetrical, and balanced with points of strong and weak cadence. A fugue subject, on the other hand, is inherently spontaneous: One entry (usually only a few notes in length) "spins" into another and another. These entries, combined with contrasting material, form a complete and balanced musical whole.

Subjects and Motives.   A subject also differs from a motive as we use the latter term in discussing periodic melody. Motives are building blocks that launch full melodic statements such as phrases and periods. A fugue subject may comprise two or more discernable motives. The subject generates the melodic content of a fugue, not only through statements of the subject, but also by imitation, sequence, rhythmic augmentation, melodic inversion, and other manipulations of one or more motives.

The Well-Tempered Clavier.   J. S. Bach is considered by many to be the greatest master of the fugue. In Bach's day, composers and performers were expected to improvise fugues—often on subjects supplied by others. Yet Bach also composed and notated many fugues, including the two volumes of *The Well-Tempered Clavier*—series of twenty-four preludes and fugues in all major and minor keys.[5] We can better understand the special nature of a fugue subject by examining the first ten subjects from the *WTC* (Volume I).

---

[5]Bach wrote two series of twenty-four preludes and fugues. We know them as *Well-Tempered Clavier*, Volume I (1722) and Volume II (1740), respectively.

CD 1, TRACK 17
J. S. Bach, *Well-Tempered Clavier I*
Ten Fugue Subjects

No. 1 in C Major

No. 2 in C Minor

No. 3 in C♯ Major

No. 4 in C♯ Minor

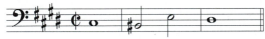

No. 5 in D Major

No. 6 in D Minor

No. 7 in E♭ Major

No. 8 in D♯ Minor

No. 9 in E Major

No. 10 in E Minor

Characteristics of Fugue Subjects

Within the ten fugue subjects in the last example, we can see important similarities and consistencies in rhythm, pitch content, and general character. At the same time, however, differences among them are striking. As we have discussed, each fugue subject is unique. Still, we can formulate basic models of rhythm, melodic character, and tonality.

Rhythm and Meter.   Duple and quadruple meters are common (but not exclusive) in Bach's fugue subjects. The rhythms are distinctive, yet generally uncomplicated. Most subjects include only two or three different durational values, so that the listener may follow the development of important rhythmic motives throughout the fugue. All of the subjects in the preceding examples are either two or three measures in length. They vary from three to eleven beats.

Melodic Character.   As we know, a fugue subject is not intended to be a complete musical idea. While we may chart the course of a fugue on a time line, our spiraling graphic (page 73) is a more helpful illustration. Fugue begins with a monophonic statement of the subject, then increases gradually in intensity until the final cadence is reached. Spontaneity—not symmetry—is the essence of fugal procedure.

A typical fugue subject has a well-defined melodic contour and a balance between conjunct and disjunct motion. Most of the Bach fugues shown on pages 74–75 are an octave or less in range (No. 3 has the range of a tenth; No. 7, a ninth). Observe that the limited range of rhythmic values and the melodic style of Fugue No. 4 in C♯ are typical of a slow-moving or "ricercar-type" subject.

Tonal Identity.   The subject defines the tonality of a fugue. Within Bach's ten fugue subjects (pages 74–75), for example, the initial pitch is $\hat{1}$ in every case except Nos. 3 and 7 (in which the first pitch is $\hat{5}$). As we will discuss later in this chapter, the first pitch of a fugue subject is crucial in defining the next voice to enter—the *answer*. Notice also that the last pitch of a fugue subject is often the tonic pitch, although in the ten Bach examples shown previously, there is somewhat more variety. All fugue subjects except Nos. 4 and 6 end with $\hat{1}$ or $\hat{3}$; the subject of the Fugue in C♯ Minor (No. 4) ends on $\hat{2}$; $\hat{5}$ is the last note of the D Minor Fugue (No. 6).

Fugue Number	Key	First Pitch	Last Pitch	Fugue Number	Key	First Pitch	Last Pitch
1	C Major	$\hat{1}$	$\hat{3}$	6	D Minor	$\hat{1}$	$\hat{5}$
2	C Minor	$\hat{1}$	$\hat{3}$	7	E♭ Major	$\hat{5}$	$\hat{3}$
3	C♯ Major	$\hat{5}$	$\hat{1}$	8	D♯ Minor	$\hat{1}$	$\hat{1}$
4	C♯ Minor	$\hat{1}$	$\hat{2}$	9	E Major	$\hat{1}$	$\hat{3}$
5	D Major	$\hat{1}$	$\hat{3}$	10	E Minor	$\hat{1}$	B Minor: $\hat{3}$

Tonal implications in the fugue subject are often quite subtle. The dominant key, for example, is implied merely by beginning on or emphasizing $\hat{5}$; a full-fledged modulation is not necessary. Traditional fugue subjects usually follow one of three tonal plans:

1. The subject begins and ends in the tonic key (ending with $\hat{1}$ or $\hat{3}$).
2. The subject begins in the dominant (with $\hat{5}$ or $\hat{7}$) and moves to the tonic.
3. The subject begins in the tonic and moves to the dominant.

All three subject plans are seen in the first ten fugues from Volume I of Bach's *Well-Tempered Clavier*. The first approach (beginning and ending in the tonic key) is the most common overall and is evident in Nos. 1, 2, 4, 5, 6, 8, and 9. Fugues 3 and 7, on the other hand, start with $\hat{5}$ and are heard theoretically as beginning in the dominant. Finally, Fugue 10 begins in the tonic and modulates to the dominant.

Harmonic Implication in Subject		Fugue Number
Tonic	Tonic	1, 2, 4, 5, 6, 8, and 9
Dominant	Tonic	3 and 7
Tonic	Dominant	10

Tonal implications in the subject determine whether the second voice to enter—called the *answer*—is an exact or an adjusted transposition.

The Answer

Most simply, an ANSWER is a transposition of the subject to the dominant. The transposition may be exact (a *real* answer) or adjusted (a *tonal* answer). Both of these possibilities will be discussed presently in detail. In a traditional fugue, voices enter in succession with either the subject or the answer. In a three-voice fugue, for example, statements of the subject are separated by the answer. A four-voice fugue includes two subjects and two answers in alternation.

Three Voices

Four Voices

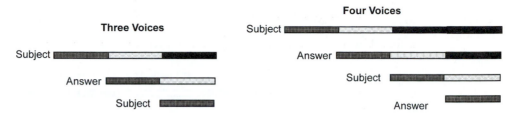

Most traditional fugues are in three or four voices; if a fifth voice appears, it will be a final subject entry.

Five Voices

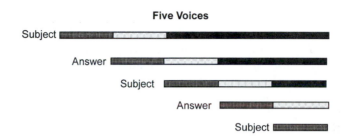

Real Answer.   If the answer is an exact intervallic duplication of the subject, it is termed a REAL ANSWER. When the answer occurs, the voice that stated the subject continues in free counterpoint against it. A typical real answer is

CD 1, TRACK 18-1 REAL ANSWERS (2 PARTS)
J. S. Bach, Fugue in C Major

seen in Bach's Fugue in C Major (WTC I). The subject (stated first in the alto) is in C major; the answer, in the soprano, is in G major.

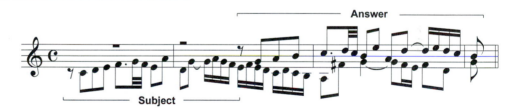

A similar real answer occurs in Fugue No. 6 in D Minor from the same collection. In this three-voice fugue, the two-measure subject in the soprano is answered exactly in the dominant (in the tenor voice). As we would expect, the soprano continues in counterpoint over the answer.

TRACK 18-2 REAL ANSWERS
J. S. Bach, Fugue in D Minor

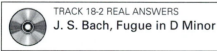

After the answer, a third voice enters with a restatement of the subject in the tonic key. Both the first and second voices then continue in free counterpoint. This process is repeated until each voice has entered.

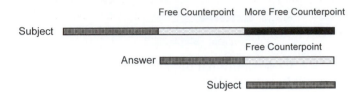

Many fugue subjects end and venture into free counterpoint when the answer enters. But while this guideline may be helpful, there are many exceptions. The end of a subject may overlap with the beginning of the answer, for example, and in later versions, a subject's length may not always coincide with the original statement. Subject–answer pairs may be separated by one or more measures of linking material (as discussed on page 88). Likewise, a transitional passage of free counterpoint may appear after the last voice has completed the subject or answer.

The Fugue in E Major (No. 9 in the *second* book of the *Well-Tempered Clavier*) is in four voices. The ricercar-type subject begins and ends in the tonic key; accordingly, the answer is *real*—an exact transposition to the dominant. The first nine measures, shown in the next example, include subject or answer entries in each voice, beginning with the bass. A cadential extension (measures 7–9) permits a definitive close in the dominant key.

CD 1, TRACK 19 REAL ANSWER
J. S. Bach, Fugue in E Major (*WTC* II)

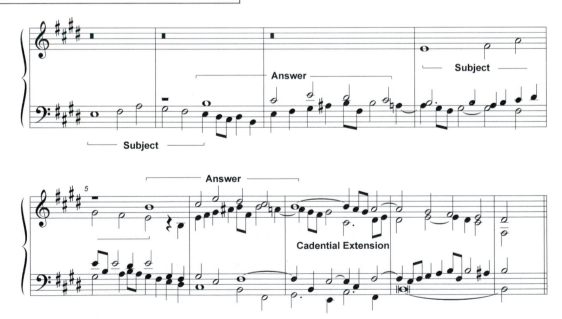

Tonal Answer.   To appreciate the distinction between real and tonal answers, we must try to view key change from an eighteenth-century perspective. Beethoven's distant key relationships, the chromaticism of Chopin, the tonal ambiguity of Wagner and Debussy—these were all future developments in Bach's day. To Baroque audiences, even a modulation to the dominant was a "big deal" and composers treated it accordingly. Especially within the first few measures of a fugue, distant modulation—to the dominant of the dominant, for example—had the potential to actually jolt listeners.

When a subject begins and ends in the tonic (see the E Major Fugue in the last example), the answer is usually *real*.

If the subject itself begins with a strong feeling of the dominant, however, a real answer would imply the *dominant of the dominant* (V/V). To avoid a distant key, Baroque composers retained a feeling of the tonic key within the first few pitches of the answer. Such an *adjusted* answer is termed TONAL. Bach's Fugue in C♯ Major from *WTC* I has such a subject-and-answer arrangement. Beginning with 5 in C♯, we hear the subject as moving from the dominant to the tonic.

A real answer would require a transposition of the subject to G♯ Major; the first pitch, therefore, would be heard as V/V (the dominant of the dominant) in the tonic key.

Like his contemporaries, Bach begins the answer in the C♯ Major Fugue with the tonic pitch, before introducing the remaining pitches transposed to the dominant. Compare the answer in Bach's fugue (below) with a real answer as shown in the last example.

As you study the guidelines that follow, remember that the purpose of a tonal answer is to smooth the transition to a new key. While this fluency had more logic for Baroque composers and audiences than it has today, the practice is often retained in contemporary fugues and fugal sections.

Subjects Beginning with 5̂.   As seen in Bach's C♯ Major Fugue, if a subject opens with 5̂, composers usually avoid the V/V implication in the answer by beginning, not on the fifth scale degree of the dominant key, but on the tonic pitch. Subsequent pitches in the answer typically duplicate the subject a perfect fifth higher (or perfect fourth lower, of course).

CD 1, TRACK 20-1 TONAL ANSWERS (2 PARTS)
J. S. Bach, Fugue No. 16 in G Minor
(*WTC* I)

Few "rules" are applicable to the analysis and composition of fugues. In general, however, if a fugue subject begins with 5̂, the answer begins with the tonic pitch. The Fugue in G Minor (*WTC* I) further supports these observations. While we hear the first pitch of the subject as 5̂ in G minor, the first pitch of the tonal answer is 1̂ in G minor, flowing from that point on to the dominant.

TRACK 20-2 TONAL ANSWERS
J. S. Bach, Fugue in G Minor (*WTC* I)

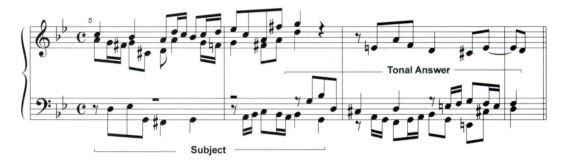

Keep in mind that the term "answer" refers to the second entry in a *pair* of statements (subject/answer). The third and fourth entries in Bach's G Minor Fugue, for example, follow this same pattern.

Subjects with Prominent Fifth or Fourth.   Another factor, the perfect fifth or fourth, is so important in defining key that its mere presence in a subject may require special handling in the answer. Simply put, a perfect fifth at or near the beginning of a fugue subject will be answered by a perfect fourth. Bach's Fugue in E♭ Major (*WTC* II), with one of the composer's longer subjects, opens with a perfect fifth (E♭–B♭). Despite a clear tonic emphasis throughout the subject, Bach used the traditional perfect fourth in the tonal answer.

J. S. Bach, Fugue No. 7 in E♭ Major (*WTC* II)

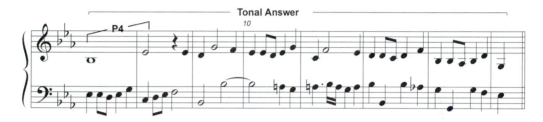

Composers often follow the same procedure when a subject includes an important perfect fourth (not typically the opening interval). In his Fugue No. 2 in C Minor (*WTC* I), Bach answers the descending perfect fourth on the second beat (C–G) with a perfect fifth (G–C). The tonic emphasis lingers with the $\hat{5}$–$\hat{1}$ descending fifth.

J. S. Bach, Fugue No. 2 in C Minor (*WTC* I)

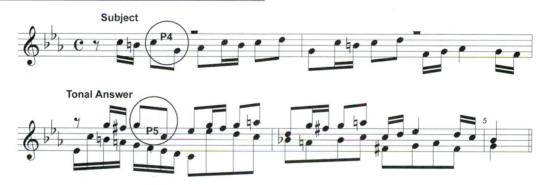

The choice of a real versus a tonal answer is rooted as much in the creative process as it is in convention. Bach's Fugue in E Minor (*WTC* II), for example, is exceptional in several respects. First, the work involves only two voices (more typical of a canon). In addition, although the subject modulates conclusively to the dominant, Bach employs a real answer.

CD 1, TRACK 22
J. S. Bach, Fugue No. 10 in E Minor
(*WTC* II)

While we can enumerate specific subject characteristics that usually take a tonal answer, the question is really one of historical interest and perspective. Real and tonal answers alike exist to provide a graceful and refined connection between two opposing keys. But where a true modulation does not quite occur, tonal implications have already been accommodated by the way the subject was composed in the first place.

WORKBOOK/ANTHOLOGY II
III. Fugue Subjects and Answers, page 33

REVIEW AND APPLICATION 2–2

Real and Tonal Answers

Essential Terms

answer	real answer	tonal answer
fugue	subject	*Well-Tempered Clavier*

1. Indicate whether the answers to the given fugue subjects are real or tonal. In addition, be prepared to discuss factors in each subject that led to the choice of an answer type.

2. Study the fugue subjects that follow. Based on the characteristics of the subject, speculate on whether the composer chose a real or a tonal answer and check the appropriate blank below the example. Be prepared to cite reasons for your opinion.

a. J. C. Bach, *Fugue for Organ*

Real _____ Tonal _____

b. Dietrich Buxtehude, *Toccata for Organ*

Real _____ Tonal _____

c. Joseph Haydn, Quartet, Op. 20, No. 5
Fourth Movement

Real _____ Tonal _____

d. J. S. Bach, Fugue No. 5 in D Major
Well-Tempered Clavier I

Real _____ Tonal _____

e. J. S. Bach, Fugue No. 14 in F♯ Minor
Well-Tempered Clavier I

Real _____ Tonal _____

SELF-TEST 2–2

Time Limit: 5 Minutes

1. Place a check mark by the best answer for each of the following questions.
Scoring: Subtract 10 points for each error.

a. A fugue is

_____ (1) a form

_____ (2) neither a form nor a technique

_____ (3) both a form and a technique

_____ (4) a technique

b. A fugue subject

____ (1) concludes with a definitive cadence

____ (2) is a memorable musical fragment

____ (3) may be described as a melody

____ (4) is a musical form

c. An answer is a transposition of the subject to

____ (1) a distant key

____ (2) the subdominant

____ (3) the dominant of the dominant

____ (4) the dominant

d. If the answer is an exact transposition of the subject,

____ (1) it is real

____ (2) it is incomplete

____ (3) it is tonal

____ (4) it is modal

e. Which of the following characteristics *does not* necessitate a tonal answer?

____ (1) subject begins in the tonic and modulates to the dominant

____ (2) subject begins in the tonic and ends in the tonic

____ (3) subject begins with $\hat{5}$ or $\hat{7}$

____ (4) subject includes a prominent perfect fifth

f. Which of the following *is not* true of the *Well-Tempered Clavier?*

____ (1) the composer is J. S. Bach

____ (2) the collection touts Twelve-Tone Equal Temperament

____ (3) the collection was written in the eighteenth century

____ (4) the collection is also known as *Goldberg Variations*

g. The principal reason for using a tonal answer is

____ (1) to avoid the dominant key

____ (2) to reinforce the tonic key

____ (3) to smooth the transition to the dominant

____ (4) to reinforce the dominant of the dominant

2. Determine whether each of the fugue subjects in the next example would require a real or a tonal answer. In the blank frame, provide the probable first two pitches of the answer. In addition (in a few words), indicate the reason that the answer would be real or tonal (as appropriate). *Scoring: Subtract 8 points for an incorrect answer pitch; subtract 7 points for an incorrect rationale.*

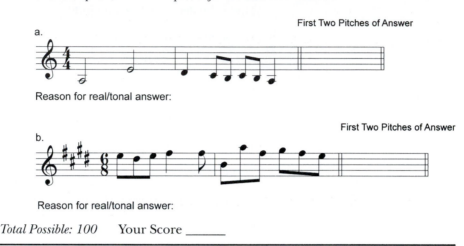

Reason for real/tonal answer:

Reason for real/tonal answer:

Total Possible: 100   Your Score _____

The Countersubject

In some fugues, the answer and all (or most) subsequent statements of the subject are accompanied by a complementary melodic idea called a COUNTERSUBJECT. Not all fugues have countersubjects, but if material heard with the initial answer recurs with the next (and most subsequent) statements of the subject, this identification is appropriate. Note well that we cannot identify a countersubject until after *both* the subject and the answer have been heard.

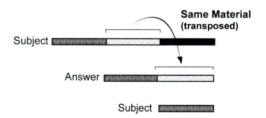

From the first volume of the *Well-Tempered Clavier*, Bach's three-voice Fugue in C Minor (discussed earlier and shown complete in the next examples) includes descending sixteenth notes and a dramatic ascending minor tenth, heard in the alto (measure 3) as free counterpoint to the answer. At its first occurrence, this material might or *might not* be a countersubject; we have no way of knowing. Following a brief linking passage (measures 5–6), the subject enters in the bass. Again, the descending sixteenth notes and the ascending tenth (soprano, measure 7) are heard along with the subject. Because this is an exact transposition of the alto counterpoint in measure 3, we can identify the material as a countersubject.

CD 1, TRACK 24
J. S. Bach, Fugue No. 2 in C Minor (*WTC* I)
Countersubject

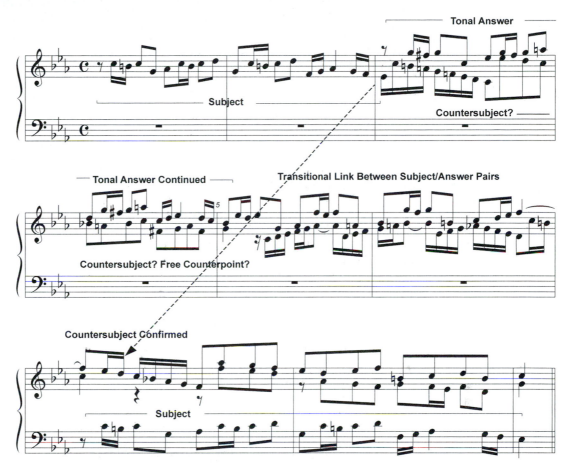

Slight differences among occurrences of a countersubject are not uncommon, although in Bach's C Minor Fugue, the soprano (measures 7–8) is an exact transposition of the alto in measures 3–4. Throughout the fugue, a subject (or answer) entry is accompanied by the countersubject. Note, however, that in some fugues, the appearance of a countersubject is not as regular. Verify a countersubject in the first part of a fugue as follows:

1. Study the counterpoint heard along with the answer (*not* the answer itself).

2. At the next entry of the subject, determine whether this material recurs (most probably at another pitch level). If so, the material may be understood as a countersubject; if not, the fugue has *no* countersubject.

SECTIONAL DIVISIONS OF A FUGUE

As we have discussed, fugue is as much a technique of composition as it is a form. Accordingly, we can make only the most general observations about internal structure. Almost every formal fugue (as opposed to a fugal *section* in a symphony or chamber work, for example) has three sectional divisions. These are usually more or less proportional (although the final section may be abbreviated).

- The *statement section* in which each voice enters with the subject or the answer
- A *middle section* where subject entries are less formal, and where contrasting material may appear
- A *final section* that brings the work to a close back in the tonic

The Statement Section

The STATEMENT SECTION of a fugue presents the subject or the answer once in each voice.[6] We have already discussed the statement section in our examination of the subject, answer, and countersubject. In addition to these crucial components, a LINK may occur between subject/answer pairs.[7] In addition, a transition that both facilitates modulation and heightens the approaching importance of the middle section may occur after the last subject or answer entry. Be aware, however, that the momentum of a fugue rarely slackens. The end of the statement section and the beginning of the middle section are often elided.

Time-line analysis is helpful in understanding fugal design. The diagram that follows identifies the major events in the statement section of Bach's Fugue No. 2 in C Minor (*WTC* I) printed in sections beginning on page 87.

STATEMENT SECTION   Bach, Fugue in C Minor

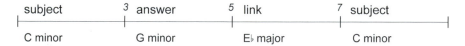

subject	3 answer	5 link	7 subject
C minor	G minor	E♭ major	C minor

Counter-Statement.   In some fugues, the final movement of Bach's Brandenburg Concerto in D Major, No. 5, for example, a complete second pair or group of subject-answer entries occurs immediately following the statement section. A brief transition may connect the statement and the counter-statement, but the key remains the tonic.

Double Fugue.   If the second statement presents a different subject than the first, the form is characterized as a DOUBLE FUGUE.

---

[6]In many sources, the statement section is identified as the "exposition." We have avoided the latter term, however, because of its closer association with sonata form (Chapter 5).

[7]The "link," of course, is also a transition. The use of the former term for typically brief passages that separate subject/answer pairs, however, is helpful in understanding fugal structure. Use the term "transition" for music that has a broader role.

The Middle Section

After each voice has been presented in the statement section, most fugues proceed to an alternation of subject entries with passages of free counterpoint called *episodes*. The MIDDLE SECTION provides contrast to the predictability of tonality in the statement section and develops motives from the subject. Please note that the middle section may begin with *either* an episode or a subject entry, but it will often be in a key other than tonic (allowing us to differentiate the beginning of the middle section from a counter-statement).

Subject Entries.   The term SUBJECT ENTRY denotes a statement of the subject *after* the initial series of subject/answer pairs (heard in the statement section). Subject entries occur at various tonal levels and may or may not be followed by "an answer" (that is, a transposition a perfect fifth higher). While we would expect the subject or answer to appear in each voice in a statement section, a subject entry may occur in only one or two voices in the middle section.

Episodes.   An EPISODE is a passage in which no complete statement of the subject occurs. Episodes usually begin in one key and end in another, their primary purpose being to link subject entries. The melodic material of an episode is related to the subject or countersubject and most frequently is developed sequentially.

In Bach's Fugue in C Minor, the middle section begins in measure 9 with an episode that opens in the tonic, and leads to a subject entry in E♭ major (measure 11). The descending scales of the first episode now ascend in the second (measures 13–14) and lead to a subject entry in G minor (measure 15). Finally, a third episode, built of subject fragments, returns the listener to C minor and the final statement (measures 17–20).

CD 1, TRACK 25
J. S. Bach, Fugue No. 2 in C Minor (*WTC* I)
Middle Section

MIDDLE SECTION

Shown in the time-line analysis that follows, the middle section of Bach's Fugue in C Minor (*WTC* I) is centered more on the subject and more clearly on the tonic key than is the case in many other fugues.

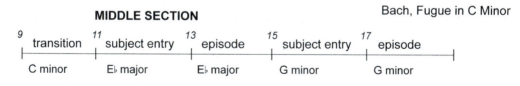

In addition to developmental techniques employed by Bach in the C Minor Fugue, others, such as augmentation or diminution, mirror inversion, and false entry, are common as well.

Augmentation and Diminution. In addition to a melodic manipulation of the subject (transposition, sequence, fragmentation, and so on), composers may state the subject in augmented or (less commonly) in diminished rhythmic values. Bach's four-voice Fugue in C Minor (*WTC* II) offers an excellent example of rhythmic augmentation. The fugue opens with a one-measure subject that is followed by a tonal answer.

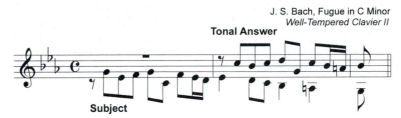

In the middle section, Bach overlaps a subject entry in the original rhythmic values (soprano voice) with a statement in the tenor of the same pitches in augmentation (with rhythmic values doubled).

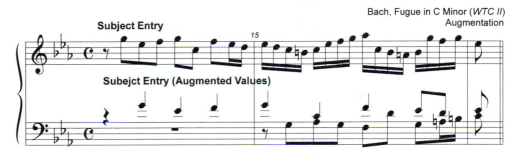

Inversion. Presenting intervals of the subject in the opposite direction—called INVERSION (or MIRROR INVERSION)—is a common technique in the middle and final sections of a fugue. In the last example, notice that the bass enters in measure 15 with an inverted version of the subject. The intervals are *nonliteral* (that is, not duplicated exactly), but because the rhythms are identical with those of the subject, we make the connection easily.

False Entry. Composers sometimes begin the subject with its memorable first few notes, then allow it to fall off into free counterpoint as a FALSE ENTRY.

 CD 1, TRACK 26-1 FALSE ENTRY (2 PARTS)
J. S. Bach, Fugue No. 6 in D Minor (*WTC* I)
Subject

In Bach's three-voice Fugue No. 6 in D Minor (*WTC* I), the subject is characterized by an ascending scalar pattern followed by a sixteenth-note turn on the tonic pitch.

At the conclusion of the middle section in the D Minor Fugue, Bach offers a subject entry in F major (measure 33), but concludes it quickly (omitting the sixteenth notes). In the next measure, a true subject entry begins in the bass (measure 34). As is common in middle sections, subject entries may be altered (as is the case here). Another false entry occurs in the soprano in measure 35 and begins a transition that leads to the final section in measure 39 (not shown).

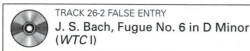

TRACK 26-2 FALSE ENTRY
J. S. Bach, Fugue No. 6 in D Minor (*WTC* I)

The Final Section

The concluding or FINAL SECTION of a fugue may be the most difficult to discern in analysis. As we have discussed, the middle section commences after all voices have entered. The beginning of the final section, however, may be more subtle. The final section is often marked by a subject entry in the tonic key, by a strong cadence in another key, or by a pedal point. In addition, composers also often employ *stretto* (discussed on page 94) to delineate the last section of a fugue.

A subject entry in the tonic key announces the beginning of the final section of Bach's C Minor Fugue (measure 20). After a lengthy sequential episode based on subject fragmentation, a final subject statement occurs in conjunction with a tonic pedal (measure 29–31). The picardy third in the final cadence is typical in eighteenth-century keyboard music.

CD 1, TRACK 27
J. S. Bach, Fugue No. 2 in C Minor (*WTC* I)
Final Section

FINAL SECTION

If there is a "typical" fugue, Bach's Fugue in C Minor (*WTC* I) may constitute a model in several respects. First, the three voices enter in typical fashion:
subject–answer–subject. A brief, two-measure link connects the subject/answer
pair (soprano and alto) with the second statement of the subject (bass). The
middle section begins with an episode, followed by statements of the subject (in
contrasting keys) and alternating with additional episodes. The three main

sections of the fugue are more or less equal in length and are crafted to introduce the tonic key, move away from it, and then return in the final section. On a time line, we may diagram the most important events of the complete fugue (including the final section) as shown below.

Bach, Fugue in C Minor

STATEMENT				MIDDLE				FINAL			
subject	³answer	⁷subject	⁹transition	¹¹subject entry	¹³episode	¹⁵subject entry	¹⁷episode	²⁰subject entry	²²episode	²⁶subject entry	²⁹subject entry
c	g	c	c	E♭	E♭	g	g	c	c	c	c
Tonic/Dominant				Related Keys				Tonic			

While Bach's C Minor Fugue is typical in many respects, fugues frequently employ another technique called *stretto*.

Stretto

When the subject is introduced in the statement section, its length is defined by the entry of the answer. We expect the answer to occur after a certain number of beats or measures, as defined by the first pair of voices. If subject entries are dovetailed (that is, if they occur at more closely spaced intervals of time), however, tension is increased significantly. STRETTO (It. "tightening") is such an overlapping of subject entries. In a stretto passage, a subject entry begins, but before it has finished (as defined by its length in the statement section), another voice enters with the subject. Stretto may occur in either the middle or the final section (it is rare in the statement section).[8]

CD 1, TRACK 28-1 STRETTO (2 PARTS)
J. S. Bach, Fugue No. 11 in F Major
(*WTC* I)

Bach's Fugue No. 11 in F major is for three voices. In the statement section, we hear the four-measure subject, its tonal answer, and a second occurrence of the subject. Notice that the sixteenth notes heard in the tenor in measures 5–6 recur in measures 10–11 (soprano) as a countersubject.

---

[8]See page 91 of this chapter for an example of stretto that includes augmented rhythmic values in one voice.

Answer continued

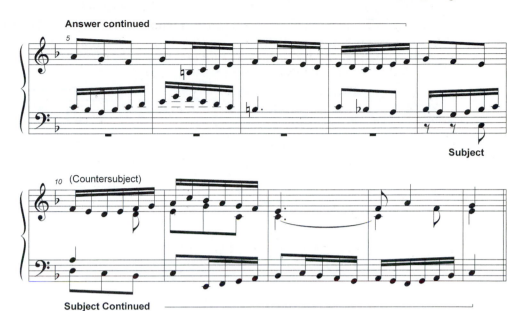

Subject

(Countersubject)

Subject Continued

TRACK 28-2 STRETTO
J. S. Bach, Fugue No. 11 in F Major
(*WTC* I)

In the middle section of the fugue, subject entries are spaced not four measures apart, but in stretto, at the distance of two measures and then one measure.

Subject

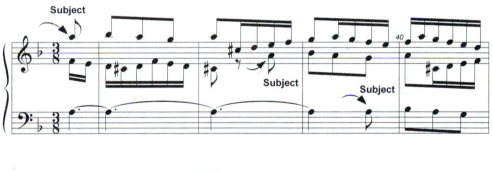

Subject

Subject

Another example of stretto occurs in the middle section of the D Major Fugue from the second volume of Bach's *Well-Tempered Clavier.* The subject is two measures in length.

J. S. Bach, Fugue No. 5 in D Major
Well-Tempered Clavier II

CD 1, TRACK 29
J. S. Bach, Fugue in D Minor (*WTC* II)
Stretto

Beginning in measure 21, subject entries occur one measure apart. In measure 27, entries are overlapped by one beat.

In this chapter, we have surveyed the most essential elements of fugue through many of the works in Bach's two volumes of the *Well-Tempered Clavier.* An exhaustive study would include many additional topics, such as a double fugue (one with two different subjects), invertible counterpoint (written so that intervals, when inverted, continue to be consonant), and the various approaches to fugue taken by composers of the Classical, Romantic, and Contemporary eras.

WORKBOOK/ANTHOLOGY II
IV. Fugal Structure, page 37
V. Composition, page 41

REVIEW AND APPLICATION 2–3

Traditional Fugue

Essential Terms

augmentation	episode	middle section
countersubject	final section	statement section
diminution	false entry	stretto
double-statement	inversion	subject entry

1. Bach's Fugue No. 16 in G Minor (*WTC* I) is given complete, below. Analyze the fugue; then locate the first example of each of the following. Provide measure numbers, and specify beat location when a more precise location is required. Note that the elements are *not* listed in order as they occur in the fugue. Locate the *first* occurrence of the following:

Event	Measure/Beat	Event	Measure/Beat
Episode	_____ 1	Answer	_____ 5
Subject	_____ 2	Middle Section	_____ 6
Countersubject	_____ 3	Final Section	_____ 7
Stretto	_____ 4		

2. Construct a time-line analysis of the G minor fugue that shows the three major divisions (opening, middle, and final sections) as well as other important events such as episodes, subject entries, stretto, and so on. Rely on your answers to question 1 above for the information. Include measure numbers and the key indications at important points in the work. Use the time line for Bach's C Minor Fugue (page 94) as a model.

[Not Recorded]

J. S. Bach, Fugue No. 16 in G Minor
Well-Tempered Clavier I

SELF-TEST 2–3

Time Limit: 5 Minutes

1. This problem includes material from the entire chapter. For each description, provide the most specific and appropriate term. *Scoring: Subtract 8 points for an incorrect term.*

   _____   a. a passage of free counterpoint that separates subject entries in the middle section

   _____   b. a passage in which subject entries are overlapped

   _____   c. A subject entry that is stated in part, but lapses into free counterpoint before its completion

   _____   d. A second statement section that follows immediately after the first

   _____   e. accompanying material that appears with a subject or answer throughout the fugue

2. In the following lists, check *all* that are true. *Scoring: Subtract 2 points for each error.*

   a. A fugal answer

   ____ (1) is a transposition of the subject to the dominant.

   ____ (2) may be real or tonal.

   ____ (3) always begins with the tonic pitch.

   ____ (4) may be accompanied by a counter-exposition.

   ____ (5) is always paired with a subject statement.

b. In structure, a fugue

____ (1) is usually in three parts.

____ (2) typically has two subjects.

____ (3) moves from tonic to related keys and back to tonic.

____ (4) is comprised mainly of episodes.

____ (5) is often in binary form.

c. Stretto

____ (1) does not occur in some fugues.

____ (2) is a lessening of tension before the final statement.

____ (3) means "flight."

____ (4) may appear in the middle or final sections.

____ (5) consists of diminished rhythmic values.

d. Tonal counterpoint

____ (1) is idealized in the music of Palestrina.

____ (2) was popular in the late Renaissance.

____ (3) is found in Bach's *Well-Tempered Clavier.*

____ (4) may be free or imitative.

____ (5) fell into disfavor with composers after about 1700.

3. Study the fugue subject; then check "real" or "tonal" to designate the type of answer that would likely follow. In addition, provide the most likely first two pitches of the answer based on your analysis. *Scoring: Subtract 10 points for an incorrect answer to either part.*

First Two Pitches of Answer

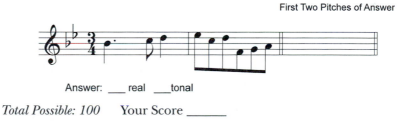

Answer: ___ real ___ tonal

Total Possible: 100   Your Score _____

PROJECTS

Analysis

Compile notes for an analytical paper or a class presentation as directed by your instructor. The following movements are available in the text or Volume II of the Workbook/Anthology.

Text

J. S. Bach, Fugue in G Minor (Well-Tempered Clavier, Volume I), text pages 97–100. This brief fugue has a straight-forward structure and also includes many of the elements discussed in Chapter 2. Prepare an analysis of this work. Begin by locating a recording and listening to the fugue several times. Next, identify the three major divisions of the fugue (statement, middle, and final sections). Prepare a time line that traces these major divisions along with the most important tonal areas and measure numbers. In addition, comment on the following as appropriate:

a. the tonal implications of the subject

b. the answer and its characteristics

c. the countersubject (if any)

d. transitional links (if any)

e. the episodes: their character, key, and melodie material

f. appearance of stretto (if any)

Workbook/Anthology II

Johann Caspar Ferdinand Fischer, Fugue from *Ariadne Musica*, workbook page 43.
J. S. Bach, Fugue in E♭ Major (*Well-Tempered Clavier* Volume I), workbook pages 44–46).
    In addition to the suggestions for analysis to be found in the workbook, refer to areas listed above for analysis of the G Minor fugue.

Composition

Canon at the Unison.   Compose a brief canon at the unison that can be sung or played by three to four voices. Begin by composing a subject of two to four measures that features a relatively slow harmonic rhythm.

Introduce the second voice with the canon subject as the first voice continues in free counterpoint. Maintain the derived harmonic plan for the second voices as well.

A third voice enters with the canon subject; the second voice is assigned the free counterpoint just heard in the first voice, and an additional segment of counterpoint is composed for the first voice as it continues.

A fourth voice begins the canon subject as first, second, and third voices continue the layering process. Avoid the temptation to increase the embellishment of the leading voice with each new contrapuntal segment.

When you have finished the canon in score format, recopy it on a single staff. Voices will enter as indicated and in octaves as necessary.

For Further Study

Prelude and Fugue Cycles. Bach was not the only composer to write a set of preludes and fugues. Prepare a class presentation or a brief formal paper in which you explore the prelude and fugue cycles of three composers:

Johann Caspar Ferdinand Fischer (1662–1746)

Dimitri Shostakovich (1906–1975)

Paul Hindemith (1895–1963)

Provide a biographical sketch of each composer and briefly discuss the structure of their individual prelude/fugue cycles (the number of works, relative length and complexity, and the range of keys included). Two of the composers are from the twentieth century; Fischer lived and worked before J. S. Bach. Select one prelude and fugue from each composer's cycle, listen to a recording, and document your reactions.

UNIT *2*

Chromaticism

Schubert, *Moment Musical*, Op. 94, No. 2

Chapter 3
Borrowed and Augmented-Sixth Chords

Chapter 4
**Neapolitan, Diminished-Seventh, and
Enharmonic Chords**

CHROMATICISM is simply the state of being chromatic. If we accept the term "chromatic" to designate pitches outside a given key, then chromaticism has existed for most of Western musical history. In Medieval music, for example, accidentals (*musica ficta*) were employed to avoid the tritone, for purposes of transposition, and simply to provide the right pitch at the right time. As music became more harmonically conceived, accidentals were a favored means of effecting finality at cadential points. In the fourteenth and fifteenth centuries, the concept of contrasting pitch centers in different sections of the same work added to the list of chromatic possibilities. By the end of the Renaissance, chromatic alterations were extremely common in some *genre*—the madrigal among them. In fact, chromatic alterations to characteristic intervals in the Medieval Church Modes eventually blurred their differences and helped usher in the era of major–minor modality.

Part of the attraction to chromaticism in the early 1800s was driven by technical improvements in the piano. Invented in the early eighteenth century by an Italian, Bartolommeo Christorfi (1655–1730), the *gravicembalo col piano e forte* (as the instruments were first termed) presented impressive advantages over the harpsichord; by 1825, a number of lingering technical problems had been overcome. A one-piece cast iron frame, for example, could withstand the tension of thicker strings, and the use of cross-stringing (a novel arrangement that spread out the mid-register and upper strings under those of the bass register) allowed performers to achieve greater virtuosity and range of tone color. These and other innovations in piano construction and technique launched a new era of keyboard music and encouraged composers to test the limits of chromatic relationships.

In Unit 2, we will survey several harmonic sources of chromaticism in the common-practice era. We have divided the materials into two chapters, largely for pedagogical efficiency. Accordingly, you are encouraged to view the material in Chapters 3 and 4 as one body of harmonic study. Some of these materials, such as *borrowed chords*, came about through an interchange of pitches between major and parallel minor keys. Other sonorities, such as *augmented sixths* and the *Neapolitan*, are not really chords at all, but the result of linear motion in individual voices. By the middle of the seventeenth century, composers had not only come to appreciate the color of the *diminished-seventh chord*, but had learned to use its instability to reinforce tonality.

A CHARACTER PIECE is a brief work for solo piano, or piano and one solo instrument. The *genre* is particularly associated with music of the nineteenth century. Translated, the titles of these sectional works may be programmatic (*Twilight, Rustle of Spring*), expressive of a particular mood (*Nocturne, A Dream of Love*), or simply *Prelude, Scherzo,* or *Caprice.* Most significant composers of the nineteenth century wrote character pieces. In addition to being performance choices in concerts and recitals by professionals, these works were often within the grasp of amateur pianists.

Compared to a keyboard sonata, a character piece is shorter and generally less weighty in spirit. Innovative composers such as Frédéric Chopin (1810–1849), Robert Schumann (1810–1856), and Johannes Brahms used the character piece as a vehicle to experiment with unique harmonic effects. As we will discuss in Chapters 3 and 4, a liberal view of mode in these works helped dilute the major–minor system as it had been established by Corelli, Bach, and others in the seventeenth and early eighteenth centuries.

Franz Peter Schubert was born in Vienna in 1797. Early on, he exhibited talent as a performer and composer, studying for a time with Mozart's contemporary and rival, Antonio Salieri (1750–1825). Schubert taught music at his father's school, but before the age of 17, he had found time to compose piano works, string quartets, choral music, symphonies, and an opera. Schubert is known primarily for his many *lieder* (over six hundred of them) as well as for several song cycles. While our contemporary reverence for Schubert is understandably centered on his contributions to vocal literature, much of his symphonic and keyboard music has likewise withstood the test of time.

Written in 1828 (the year of his death at age 31), Schubert's *Moment Musical* (Op. 94) is a series of six character pieces, typical of the *genre* in many ways. The second of these movements (No. 2 in A♭ Major) is a favorite of both performers and audiences. The work is harmonically innovative, yet its sectional structure imparts a security of both key and theme.

[Not Recorded]

Franz Schubert, *Moment Musical*
Op. 94, No. 2

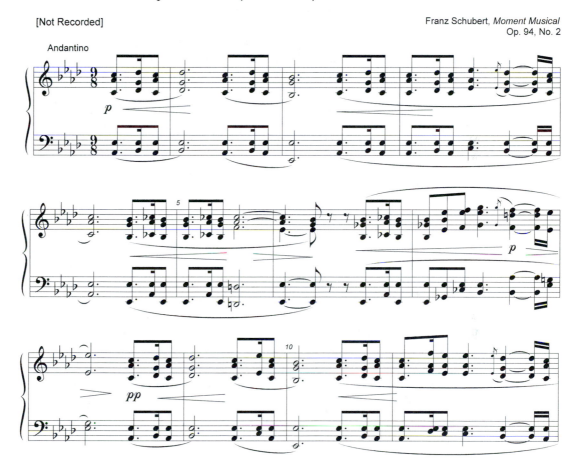

CHAPTER 3

Borrowed and Augmented-Sixth Chords

A number of chromatic chords began entering the common-practice vocabulary as early as 1700. Eventually, these sonorities offered traditional composers a resource of almost unlimited flexibility. While composers in the Classical era usually pursued diatonic key relationships in their works, harmonic chromaticism added interest to any key. In the early nineteenth century, Beethoven, Chopin, and Brahms employed some of these same chromatic chords as pivots to effect rapid modulations to distant keys, and by the end of the nineteenth century, Richard Wagner, Claude Debussy, and others had found even more uses for color chords that diminished the importance of harmonic function itself.

In the present chapter, we will cover two major categories of chromatic chords: (1) those that include "borrowings" from the parallel major or minor, and (2) a group of chords that contains an augmented sixth above the bass. A third category of chromatic chord, the Neapolitan, will be surveyed in Chapter 4, along with a study of how various chords are employed in chromatic and enharmonic modulation.

BORROWED CHORDS

The choice between major and minor is a cornerstone of common-practice music. As we discussed in Volume I, diatonic triads in major are predictable in quality. The tonic, subdominant, and dominant are *always* major; supertonic, mediant, and submediant triads are minor; and the leading-tone triad is diminished. This stability in triad quality is one of several factors that make us feel the effect of tonality. In minor, composers usually made choices that rendered the dominant and leading-tone triads the same as in major. In addition, notice in the next example that the root and fifth of the tonic and subdominant triads are identical in major and minor.

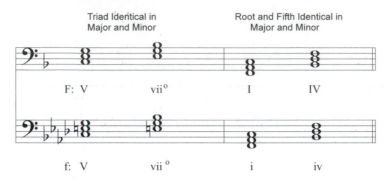

Especially in the Classical and Romantic eras, composers sometimes emphasized the duality of major and parallel minor by employing a *minor* tonic or a *minor* subdominant to add color in a major key. Such relationships are termed BORROWED CHORDS.

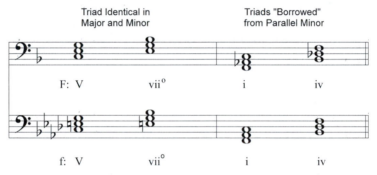

Joseph Haydn (1732–1809), for example, uses a borrowed minor tonic chord in the final movement of his Sonatina in C Major. Without tonal disorientation, the minor triad is simply substituted for the diatonic major one (boxed in the next example). In analysis, roman numerals are altered to show the sounding quality of the specified chord (I = major; i = minor).

CD 1, TRACK 30
Joseph Haydn, Sonatina in C Major
(III)

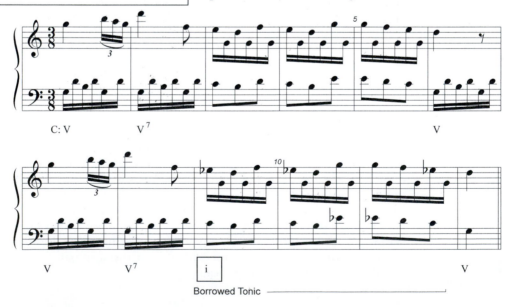

A borrowed (minor) subdominant colors the final measures of Beethoven's Sonata in C Major, Op. 53 (the first movement). Notice that the roman-numeral symbol iv_6 (as opposed to IV_6) specifies a minor triad built upon $\hat{4}$. Again, no tonal disorientation occurs, because the root and fifth of the major and minor subdominant are identical.

CD 1, TRACK 31

Ludwig van Beethoven, Sonata in C Major Op. 53 (I)

In a passage from Schubert's *Moment Musical,* we might explain the appearance of C♭ (measures 4–5) as a chromatic upper neighbor or as a borrowed tonic chord (as shown in the following analysis). As long as the examination remains consistent, either approach is acceptable to designate a turn toward the parallel minor. Compare the static melodic motion of the bass in measures 1–4 (analyzed here as nonchord tones) with the strong perfect fourths in measures 4–5 that suggest a harmonic basis.

CD 1, TRACK 32
Franz Schubert, *Moment Musical*

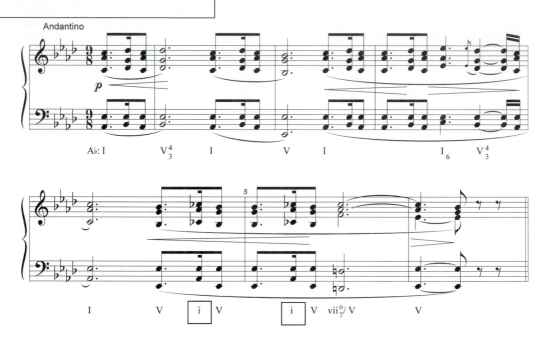

Borrowed Mediant and Submediant.

In addition to the borrowed tonic and subdominant (chords that have the same roots in major and minor), traditional composers were also fond of the other parallel relationships. BORROWED MEDIANTS (the mediant and also the submediant) have significant harmonic energy because they include two chromatic pitches.[1] Although function is not affected by modal borrowing, in analysis we emphasize the altered root of borrowed mediant and submediant triads with a flat or natural sign attached to the roman-numeral symbol.

CD 1, TRACK 33
Johannes Brahms, Symphony No. 3
in F Major (II)

Johannes Brahms ends his Symphony No. 3 in F Major with borrowed subdominant and submediant chords. The final cadence is plagal, but the minor mode affords additional color.

---

[1]We should emphasize an important difference between borrowed mediants, just discussed (triads diatonic in the parallel major or minor), and *chromatic mediants*—mediant and submediant triads that are altered in *mode* and *are not* diatonic in the parallel key. See page 160 for a fuller discussion of chromatic mediants.

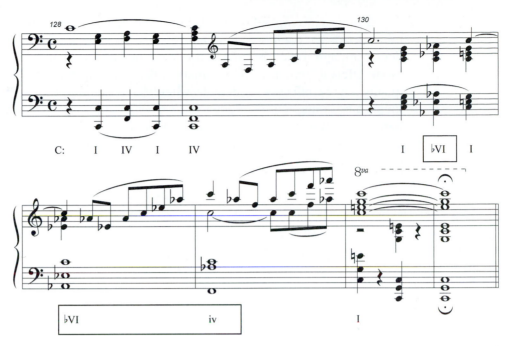

Works such as Brahms's Symphony No. 3 show us how, in about three hundred years, Western music came full circle: from the modal ambiguity of the Renaissance to a period of major/minor tonality (in the eighteenth and early nineteenth centuries), and returning in the late nineteenth century to a freer use of mode and key.

Borrowed Chords in Minor

In Volume I, we discussed the PICARDY THIRD— an example of a chord borrowed from parallel major for use in a minor key. This particular borrowing, however, also had a unique purpose in the seventeenth and early eighteenth centuries. In Renaissance systems of tuning keyboard instruments (Mean-Tone Temperament), the major triad was more perfectly in tune than the minor; it is not surprising, therefore, that composers chose a more stable sonority for the final chord in a work or section.

A common use of the picardy third occurs at the end of Bach's G Minor Fugue (*WTC* I). Notice that the analytical symbols do not take into account every harmonic fluctuation or bass position. Such an approach is often entirely appropriate in studying music for performance purposes.

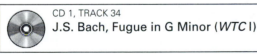

CD 1, TRACK 34

J.S. Bach, Fugue in G Minor (*WTC* I)

Composers employ borrowed chords less often in minor. This is because when minor triads are made major, we tend to hear them as dominants. Except at a cadence, a major tonic triad in a minor key is heard as V/iv. In addition, the minor mode offers its own array of chromatic inflections with ↑6̂/↓6̂ and ↑7̂/↓7̂. Triad quality may be affected incidentally where ↑6̂ is employed through linear movement, but we might also consider the *harmonic* employment of a major subdominant to be "borrowed." The first part of the next example offers a passage with linear employment of ↑6̂ in D minor. In the second progression, the B♮ is clearly a chord tone and *lacks* the ascending melodic motion that we associate with ↑6̂.

 CD 1, TRACK 35-1 ALTERATIONS IN MINOR (2 PARTS)
Progression with Raised 6̂

 TRACK 35-2 ALTERATIONS IN MINOR
Progression with Borrowed Subdominant

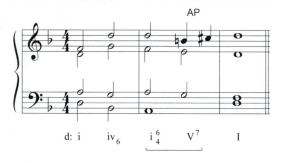

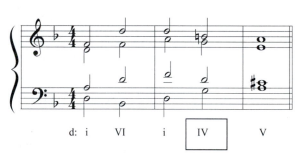

Henry Purcell harmonized the descending passacaglia bass of "Dido's Lament" with a major subdominant that is tonicized for additional emphasis. The passage below is in G minor; the pitch E♮ (measure 7) is a chord tone with

 CD 1, TRACK 36
Henry Purcell, *Dido and Aeneas*

the E♭ passing on to D in measure 8. We would not consider the E♮ to be ↑6̂ in this case since it does not ascend.

Voice Leading in Altered Chords.   The resolution of an altered pitch usually follows the direction of the alteration: Flats tend to descend; sharps, ascend.

In vocal works, composers generally adhere to three additional guidelines for scoring altered chords:

1. *Prepare altered tones by step.*

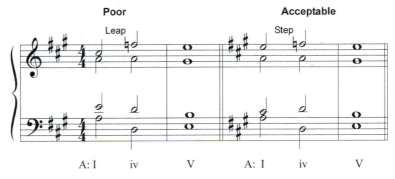

2. *Avoid cross relationships.*

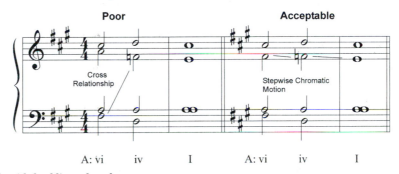

3. *Avoid doubling altered tones.*

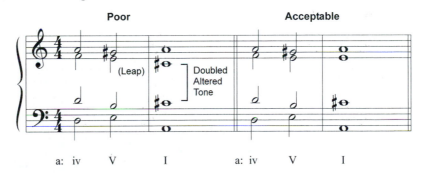

In Bach's harmonization of the melody "*Ach, Gott und Herr*" ("O God and Lord"), most of the chromatic motion occurs in the bass voice. The chorale begins in B♭ major, but within the space of only four measures, D minor, G minor, and E♭ minor (the borrowed subdominant relationship) are tonicized. Despite all of the chromaticism, however, the lines are relatively easy to sing, due to the careful treatment of altered pitches. The arpeggiated tonic six-four in measure 9 is noteworthy.

B♭:   V$^6_5$ IV$^6_5$ V$^6_5$ VI$_6$ vii$^{o}_7$/vi vi   V$^6_5$/ii ii   V$^6_5$ i   i$_6$ i$^6_4$ I
                    iii   iv

Borrowed chords provided a useful resource for composers throughout the eighteenth and nineteeth centuries. Substituting a minor subdominant, for example, or a major tonic requires no tonal reorientation, because the chord roots are identical. Likewise, a borrowed submediant in major is readily accepted, because mode—and not the tonal center—is affected. In the next section, we will discuss several ways in which traditional composers used diminished seventh chords to add color to tonal works.

Diminished Sevenths as Color Chords

The diminished-seventh chord, with its strong tendencies, was a mainstay of the harmonic vocabulary throughout most of the common-practice era. J. S. Bach was especially fond of enlivening tonicizations with the diminished seventh. Harmonizing Nikolaus Hermann's melody, *"Hinunter is der Sonnenschien"* ("The Happy Sunshine Now is Gone"), for example, Bach employs a fully diminished seventh to tonicize the supertonic area in F major.

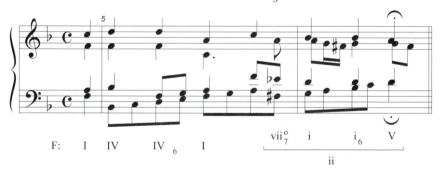

F: I   IV   IV$_6$ I   vii$^{o}_7$ i   i$_6$ V
                                              ii

In four parts, diminished sevenths are often resolved according to natural tendencies of the two tritones (augmented fourths expanding; diminished fifths contracting). This approach results in a doubled third in the chord of resolution. Just as often, however, resolution involves parallel fourths in contrary motion with the bass (as seen in "The Happy Sunshine Now Is Gone," in the last example).

Classical and Romantic composers employed the diminished seventh liberally—especially in transitional and developmental sections. A series of two or three consecutive diminished sevenths creates an especially strong expectation of resolution. In the first movement of his String Quartet, Op. 18, Ludwig van Beethoven crafts a passage of colorful, but inherently tonal harmony through a series of diminished sevenths. Measures 147–150 employ eleven of the twelve pitches of the chromatic scale, yet when the resolution to B♭ occurs (measure 151), our tonal conditioning permits us to "sort out" the series of diminished sevenths retroactively, as related by descending fifth: in effect, a distinctive vi–ii–V–i progression.

CD 1, TRACK 39
Ludwig van Beethoven, Quartet No. 18 in F Major (I)

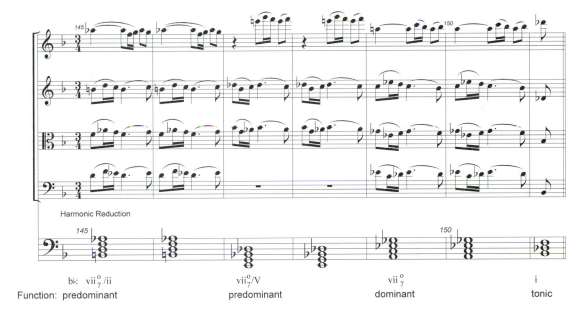

Harmonic Reduction

b♭: vii°₇/ii   vii°₇/V   vii°₇   i

Function: predominant   predominant   dominant   tonic

While we can analyze the descending-fifth root relationships in the Beethoven quartet passage as entirely functional, later composers employed the diminished seventh to obscure tonality and create music that was intentionally *nonfunctional*.

Finally, review a passage from Schubert's *Moment Musical* that opens Unit 2. In addition to a borrowed tonic (measure 80), note the diminished seventh chord that tonicizes the subdominant (measures 80–81). These two color chords not only offer harmonic variety, but they reinforce the A♭ major tonality as well.

CD 1, TRACK 40
Franz Schubert, *Moment Musical*

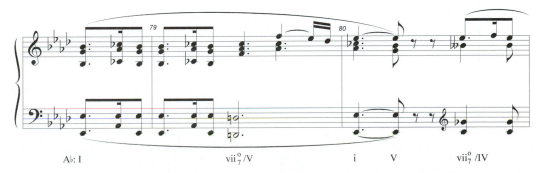

A♭: I   vii°₇/V   i   V   vii°₇/IV

IV   V$^4_2$/IV   IV$_6$ V^7 I

Chromatic alterations affect triads and chords in all three functional categories: predominant, dominant, and tonic. When function remains clear, chromaticism draws our attention toward harmonic goals even more effectively than diatonic pitches do. In the hands of mid- and late nineteenth-century composers, however, borrowed chords and diminished sevenths, among other materials, provided a springboard for harmonic experimentation that culminated in a new system of music.

 WORKBOOK/ANTHOLOGY II
II. Diminished-Seventh Chords, page 49

REVIEW AND APPLICATION 3–1

Borrowed and Diminished-Seventh Chords

Essential Terms

borrowed chord	borrowed mediant	character piece
chromaticism	picardy third	

1. Some of the chords in the next examples are diatonic; others reflect customary alterations resulting from ↑$\hat{6}$ and ↑$\hat{7}$; and still other chords are borrowed sonorities or diminished sevenths. In the key specified, provide an appropriate roman numeral symbol (include arabic numerals and other symbols as necessary). If a chord has two possible interpretations, choose an analysis that best reflects the materials in this chapter.

a.

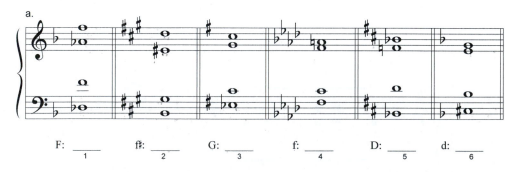

F: _____   f♯: _____   G: _____   f: _____   D: _____   d: _____
    1   2   3   4   5   6

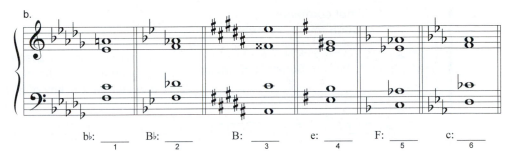

bb: ____ (1) Bb: ____ (2) B: ____ (3) e: ____ (4) F: ____ (5) c: ____ (6)

2. Chromatic color chords are specified in the following frames. Begin by choosing chords that might logically precede and follow the one given. Provide a roman-numeral symbol in the two blanks. Next, in traditional four-part style, write the three-chord progression. Avoid cross relationships and adhere to other guidelines of effective vocal writing.

a.

Ab: ____ i ____ (1 2 3)   D: ____ bVI ____ (4 5 6)   d: ____ vii°₆/iv ____ (7 8 9)   C: ____ bIII ____ (10 11 12)

b.

E: ____ iv ____ (1 2 3)   G: ____ vii°₆/IV ____ (4 5 6)   bb: ____ IV ____ (7 8 9)   Bb: ____ bVI ____ (10 11 12)

CD 1, TRACK 41-1 REVIEW AND APPLICATION 3-1 (3 PARTS)
Robert Schumann, *Ich Grolle Nicht* from *Dichterliebe*

3. Provide roman-numeral analyses for the passages given.

a.

Ich grol - le nicht,   und wenn das Herz   auch bricht,

C: ____ (1) ____ (2) ____ (3) ____ (4) ____ (5) ____ (6)

I'll not complain,
though my heart break.

W. A. Mozart, Sonata in E♭ Major

Analyze the next passage in detail—with arabic numerals and other symbols. Remain within the key of B♭ major.

The next excerpt could be analyzed in several different ways. In this exercise, remain in the key of E♭ major, employing borrowed explanations and secondary function. You need not specify the chord bass position with arabic numerals.

Franz Schubert, "Du Bist die Ruh"

You are rest, mild peace;
You are desire, and stillness.

SELF-TEST 3-1

Time Limit: 8 Minutes

1. Some of the statements that follow are true; others, false. Write "T" or "F" in the blank as appropriate. *Scoring: Subtract 5 for each error.*

    _____ a.   The piano was invented in Italy around 1625.

    _____ b.   Used in a major key, borrowed submediant and subdominant chords have two accidentals.

    _____ c.   The picardy third is an example of a chord from major that is used in the parallel minor.

    _____ d.   In vocal writing, cross relationships should be avoided in scoring borrowed and other altered chords.

    _____ e.   Used in a major key, a diminished seventh constitutes a category of borrowed chord.

    _____ f.   Chromatic chords entered the common-practice vocabulary as early as 1700.

    _____ g.   The character piece is a Romantic-era *genre* that is a short work for string ensemble.

2. Construct the following chords in four parts. *Scoring: Subtract 8 points for an incorrect spelling.*

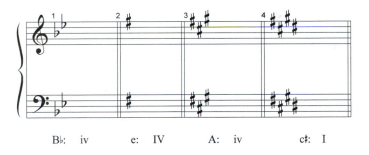

3. Study the chords in the next example. Some are borrowed; others are diatonic in the key specified. Provide a roman-numeral analysis of each chord. *Scoring: Subtract 11 points for each incorrect analysis.*

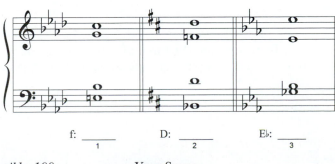

Total Possible: 100   Your Score _____

AUGMENTED SIXTH CHORDS

A second category of chromatic harmony, popular throughout the common-practice era, has a linear origin. Familiar to us from their use at points of harmonic strength, *augmented-sixth* chords result from converging melodic lines, and have in common an altered sixth above the bass.

The first and fifth scale degrees ($\hat{1}$ and $\hat{5}$) are pivotal points in a tonal composition. Melodies tend to gravitate toward one of these goals, with soprano and bass voices often converging in contrary motion. The harmony sketched in the next passage, for example, is common in Baroque music. Beginning with the tonic, soprano and bass move in contrary motion through logical progressions that culminate in a half cadence.

TRACK 42-1 EVOLUTION OF THE AUGMENTED SIXTH (3 PARTS)
Linear Motion

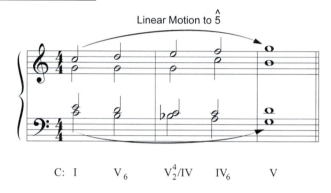

Linear Motion to $\hat{5}$

C: I   V$_6$ V$^4_2$/IV   IV$_6$ V

TRACK 42-2 EVOLUTION OF THE AUGMENTED SIXTH
Progression In Minor

In minor keys, the progression is virtually identical, and the cadence may be Phrygian.

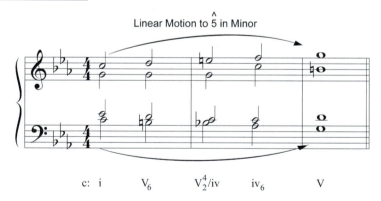

Linear Motion to $\hat{5}$ in Minor

c: i   V$_6$ V$^4_2$/iv   iv$_6$ V

To accentuate the force of convergence on $\hat{5}$, composers sometimes created a raised $\hat{4}$ as a passing tone to effect half-step motion to $\hat{5}$ in both soprano

TRACK 42-3 EVOLUTION OF THE AUGMENTED SIXTH

Half-step Motion

and bass. For purposes of smoother voice leading, the dominant was often preceded by tonic six-four as shown in the next example.

Half-Step Motion to $\hat{5}$

c: i   V$_6$ V$_2^4$/iv   iv$_6$ i$_4^6$ V

The raised-fourth scale degree, creating an augmented sixth with the bass, became a cliché during the Baroque era, and the pitch was soon absorbed as a consonant member of a group of sonorities termed AUGMENTED-SIXTH CHORDS. Almost invariably, the augmented sixth between the bass and an upper voice expands to an octave in contrary motion. Both of the resolutions in the next example are common.

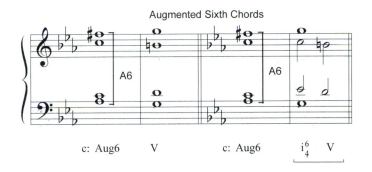

Augmented Sixth Chords

c: Aug6   V   c: Aug6   i$_4^6$ V

The progression in the previous example occurs in the theme from a series of thirty-two variations by Beethoven. The arrows above the soprano line trace the ascending linear movement toward $\hat{5}$; descending stepwise motion is present in the bass as well. While we might analyze the chords in measures 6–7 as subdominant, they do not *function* that way. The role of the F-major chord, and also of the sixteenth notes in measure 7, are better understood as the embellishment of a cadential six-four/dominant.

An augmented-sixth chord is distinctive in that, theoretically, it has no root: Soprano (or another upper voice) and bass expand to an octave, and converge upon $\hat{5}$. But while we may discount a harmonic origin for the augmented sixth, the chord is predominant in function, with a resolution to the dominant or to tonic six-four. In fact, the altered pitches in augmented-sixth chords increase the urgency for resolution.

Linear Motion in Augmented-Sixth Framework

Various possibilities exist for the inner voices of an augmented sixth chord, but traditional composers relied basically on three different structures. While the origins of the names are obscure (and most certainly have little to do with nationalistic preferences), we know these chords as the *Italian, German,* and *French* augmented sixths, respectively.

Italian Augmented Sixth.   In addition to the augmented sixth, that expands in contrary motion to $\hat{5}$, the ITALIAN AUGMENTED-SIXTH CHORD includes a major third above the bass. The resolution is to dominant or tonic six-four. Analytical designations for augmented sixth chords are not standard. In this text, we will employ the symbol It^{+6} for the "Italian" version.

Italian Augmented Sixth Chords

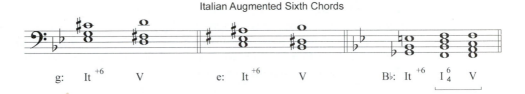

Despite the melodic origin, we may conveniently view the Italian augmented sixth as a first-inversion subdominant in minor, with the sixth above the bass raised a half step. In major keys, the Italian augmented sixth occurs as a *borrowed subdominant*, with similarly altered sixth above the bass. In major or minor, the third above the bass is doubled in a four-part setting.[2] Notice that in the third example, the augmented sixth and its resolution occur in an inner voice.

(Exceptional Resolution)

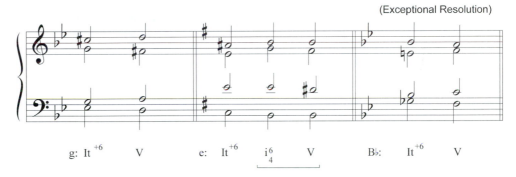

The development section of Haydn's Sonata in G Major begins in the parallel minor (with an emphasis on the mediant area within this key). An Italian augmented sixth occurs in measure 117 and resolves to the dominant.

CD 1, TRACK 44
Joseph Haydn, Sonata in G Major

After about 1750, augmented sixths were so common and so unmistakable in function that the chord, together with its resolution, suggests a key center even if the expected tonic is absent. As we see from the next example (from the third movement of Beethoven's Sonata in C Major, Op. 13), composers may make introductions sound "introductory" by avoiding a clear tonality. Chords may not resolve

---

[2]Western composers have been consistent in their avoidance of doubling either pitch of an interval with strong tendencies. In the It^{+6}, the tonic pitch is usually doubled because it is not included in the augmented-sixth interval itself. This is the same approach that traditional composers employ with respect to the tritone and other unsteady intervals.

immediately in introductions, and we would not be surprised to find modal dominants, diminished sevenths, augmented sixths, and other color chords. We could
analyze the passage from Beethoven's "Waldstein" in a number of different ways,
but because an F-major tonality is not established until measure 9 (not shown), we
should not suggest that any area is tonicized. In measure 1, the Italian augmented

CD 1, TRACK 45
Ludwig van Beethoven, Sonata in C
Major, Op. 53 (III)

sixth and its resolution establish A minor without
the tonic chord itself. Beethoven employs another
Italian augmented sixth chord in measure 5.

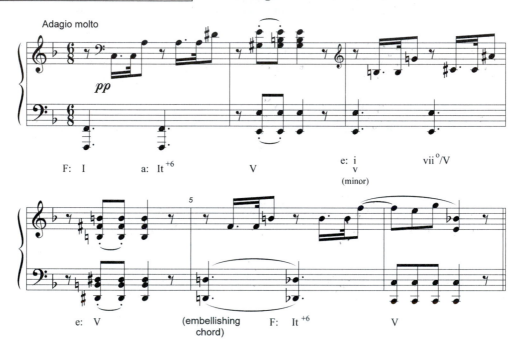

Constructing Italian Augmented-Sixth Chords.   Theoretically, we may construct augmented-sixth chords in either of two ways. The first method more
clearly follows the way composers actually used the chord in literature, and the
system has the advantage of a uniform strategy in major and minor. The second
approach, through an altered subdominant triad in minor, however, is simpler
for some students. Consider learning both methods. Employ one of them to
construct the chord; the second, to check your spelling. The same two methods
may be employed to construct other varieties of augmented-sixth chords to be
discussed later in this chapter.

Construction through Linear Motion.   Follow the steps below to create an
Italian augmented sixth through its characteristic linear motion.

1. Begin by determining $\hat{5}$ in the specified key. Write (or visualize) this pitch in
   soprano and bass.

2. Precede $\hat{5}$ in the soprano by a diatonic half step below; approach $\hat{5}$ in the bass
   by a diatonic half step above.

3. The third pitch (and the one characteristically doubled) is a major third
   above the bass and in all cases, will be the tonic pitch.

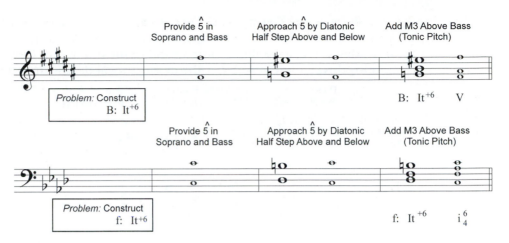

Construction From Subdominant in Minor.   A second method of constructing an Italian augmented sixth begins with a subdominant triad in minor (a borrowed chord if the key is major).

1. In the key specified, construct a minor subdominant triad in first inversion (*Remember:* This is a borrowed chord in major keys).

2. Raise the sixth above the bass.

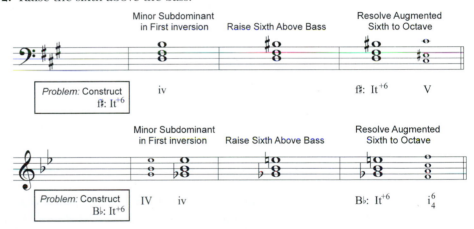

The Italian augmented-sixth chord, consisting of only the characteristic altered interval plus the tonic pitch, is the simplest of the three types that were employed by common-practice composers. Moreover, in other versions of the chord the "Italian" sonority is always present.

WORKBOOK/ANTHOLOGY I
III. Italian Augmented-Sixth Chords, page 51

German Augmented Sixth.   Many of the characteristics associated with the Italian augmented sixth apply equally to other forms of the chord. The GERMAN AUGMENTED-SIXTH CHORD includes all three pitches of the Italian version *plus* a perfect fifth above the bass. The symbol Gr^{+6} identifies the German augmented sixth in this text.

Italian and German Augmented Sixth Chords

Because the German augmented sixth includes a perfect fifth above the bass, the resolution is most often to tonic six-four in order to avoid parallel fifths that result from direct progression to the dominant. Composers typically employ this resolution whether the music is vocal or instrumental.

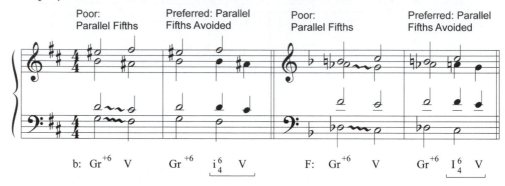

We can find augmented-sixth chords in the music of virtually every composer after 1800. In an introduction to one of his *lieder*, Franz Schubert uses a German augmented sixth and its characteristic resolution to tonic six-four. Note the simultaneous nonchord tones in measures 1 and 3. In measure 3, the bass F and the treble D are suspensions (4–3 and 9–8, respectively); the B♮ is a retardation.

CD 1, TRACK 46-1 AUGMENTED SIXTH IN ROMANTIC LITERATURE (2 PARTS)
Franz Schubert, "At the Grave of Anselmo"

The richness of nineteenth-century harmonic spirit is also apparent in Robert Schumann's "Waltz" from a collection entitled *Albumblätter* (*Album Leaves*). The work begins in the key of A minor with a German augmented sixth. Although obscured through metric placement, the augmented sixth itself resolves characteristically to an octave in the following tonic six-four.

TRACK 46-2 AUGMENTED SIXTH IN ROMANTIC LITERATURE
Robert Schumann, "Waltz" from *Albumblätter*

Mary Carr Moore (1873–1957) was an American composer and conductor who wrote chamber and choral music as well as grand opera. Her Sonata for

Violin and Piano, Op. 81, No. 6, begins with a broad, dramatic gesture that includes a German augmented sixth.

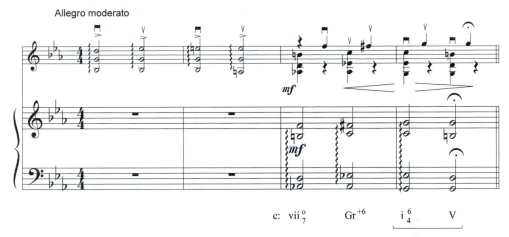

In the last passage, the violin plays *triple stops* in which the bow is drawn over three different strings simultaneously. In addition, the symbol ⊓ (down bow) instructs the performer to draw the bow downward from the "frog" to the tip; for an up bow (∨), the violinist begins with the tip of the bow on the string (or strings) and pushes the bow upward toward the frog.

Constructing German Augmented-Sixth Chords. Regardless of your favorite method of augmented-sixth-chord construction, the German type requires only that one pitch be added to the basic "Italian" sonority.

1. Construct an Italian augmented-sixth chord using either of the methods discussed on pages 130–131.

2. Add a perfect fifth above the bass.

The Enharmonic German Augmented Sixth. Especially in major keys, composers occasionally used the Gr^{+6}–V progression in an enharmonic spelling. Instead of notating a perfect fifth above the bass, the same pitch is spelled as a doubly augmented fourth. While the respelling may have lessened traditional concerns about parallel fifths, the sound, of course, is the same.

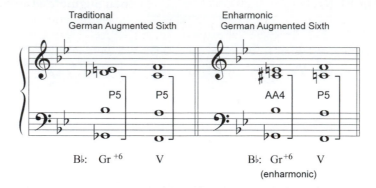

Even when the German augmented sixth resolved to tonic six-four in major, composers still occasionally utilized the enharmonic notation. In Robert Schumann's *lied "Am Leuchtenden Sommermorgen"* (On A Shining Summer Morning), the chord spelling was chosen to clarify voice leading

CD 1, TRACK 48
Robert Schumann, "On A Bright Shining Morning" from *Dichterliebe*

On a bright summer morning,
I walk around the garden.

French Augmented-Sixth Chord. The last of the three augmented sixth-chord types is known as "French." The FRENCH AUGMENTED-SIXTH CHORD contains the three pitches of the Italian chord *plus* an augmented fourth above the bass (this is always $\hat{2}$). The resolution of the French sixth (Fr^{+6}) is to dominant or tonic six-four. Voice-leading conventions are equivalent to those of other augmented sixth chords.

Compare the three augmented-sixth-chord types in the keys of C major and E♭ minor.

Composers have used the French sixth less frequently than the other augmented-sixth chords. Fanny Mendelssohn Hensel (1805–1847) was the sister of Felix Mendelssohn and an accomplished composer in her own right. Her piano work, *Abschied von Rom* (*Departure from Rome*), includes a French augmented-sixth chord and a characteristic resolution to tonic six-four. The augmented sixth itself occurs between bass and alto in this passage.

CD 1, TRACK 49
Fanny Hensel, *Departure from Rome*

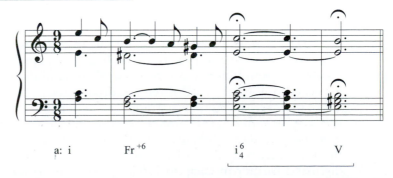

Hugo Wolf (1860–1903) was an Austrian composer of *lieder* in the generation after Brahms. Wolf's works are often only quasi-tonal (see Chapter 7) and he made consistent use of color chords—often without their traditional resolutions. The song *Das Verlassene Mägdlein* (*The Forsaken Maiden*) exhibits a French sixth in measures 11–12. Worth noting is the careful selection of pitches for voice and piano that are fused into a single expressive whole; neither part is complete without the other. Finally, observe the atypical resolution of the Fr^{+6} (measures 11–12) in the accompaniment. Especially in keyboard music, late Romantic composers allowed themselves considerable latitude to forsake voice-leading conventions when musical considerations dictated.

CD 1, TRACK 50

Hugo Wolf, "The Forsaken Maiden"

Dawn, when the roosters crow,
Even with the morning stars,
Must I then tend the herd,
Build up the fires.

The "Tristan" Chord.   By the middle of the nineteenth century, augmented sixth and other color chords, as well as a new approach to the resolution of dissonance, combined to produce a weakening of the tonal principles that had governed music for nearly three hundred years. Among innovative composers who employed traditional harmonic materials in new ways was the German, Richard Wagner (1813–1883), whose music dramas (operas) such as *Tannhäuser* (1845), *Lohengrin* (1850), and *Tristan und Isolde* (1865) remain in the repertory today. This last work was pivotal in many respects, and will be discussed further in Chapter 7. The prelude to *Tristan* begins with a series of three phrases—each comprises two motives (identified in the opera with "sorrow" and "longing," respectively). The first harmonic sonority in the prelude has been discussed so often that it is known as the "Tristan chord."

"Tristan" Chord

Some authorities view the **"TRISTAN CHORD"** as a French augmented sixth, obscured by a lengthy appoggiatura (as analyzed in the next example). Others have described the chord as a half-diminished seventh. In fact, the "Tristan chord" fits neatly into neither category; it is an entirely new predominant sonority and one that recurs throughout the opera. In an otherwise ambiguous tonality, these chords and their resolutions anchor phrases in the keys of A minor and C major, respectively, without the appearance of either tonic. In the third phrase, in which Wagner suggests E major, the altered French sixth is replaced by yet another predominant outside the common-practice vocabulary. For music that is clearly less functional, our system of roman-numeral analysis is correspondingly limited. We have analyzed this new sonority as an altered submediant, but other interpretations are possible, depending on which tones are judged to be nonchordal.

CD 1, TRACK 51
Richard Wagner, *Tristan und Isolde*

Augmented-sixth chords in the common-practice era run the gamut from the traditional (represented by the Beethoven theme on page 128) to the revolutionary (as in the Wagner passage just cited). As music changed in the late nineteenth century, augmented sixths were viewed by some composers as clichés of a past era, and their use in twentieth-century tonal works was minimal. Yet, for composers from Purcell to Wolf, augmented-sixth chords afforded an effective means of enlivening a central tonality through chromatic alteration.

WORKBOOK/ANTHOLOGY II
IV. German and French Augmented Sixth Chords, page 53

REVIEW AND APPLICATION 3–2

Augmented Sixth Chords

Essential Terms

augmented-sixth chord   German augmented sixth   Tristan chord
French augmented sixth   Italian augmented sixth

1. For each octave given, provide the augmented sixth that would precede it in an augmented-sixth/dominant progression. Write only the augmented-sixth interval. The first frame has been completed as a model.

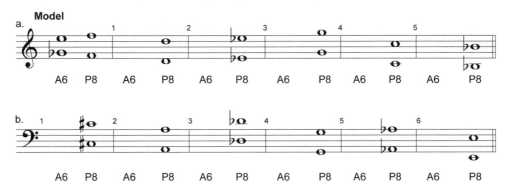

2. Note the given major or minor key. Next, write the dominant pitch in an octave in the right-hand area of the frame (you need not use accidentals, since the key signature is provided). Approach this octave with an augmented sixth as you did in Exercise 1. Please note that you will need to add one *or more* accidentals to form the augmented sixth. Finally, create an Italian augmented-sixth sonority by adding a pitch that lies a major third above the bass. The first frame is completed as a model.

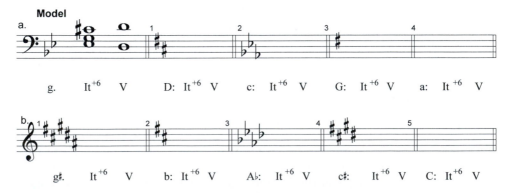

3. Use the second method described in the text (page 131) to create augmented-sixth chords from minor subdominant triads. Begin by providing iv₆ in the first frame. Please note that this is a *borrowed chord* in major keys; provide any necessary accidental. Repeat this chord in the second frame, but raise the upper pitch to form an augmented sixth above the bass. In the third frame, show the octave resolution of the augmented sixth to the dominant or tonic six-four (write only the octave itself and not a full chord).

a.

f♯:　iv₆　　It⁺⁶　　V　　　B♭: iv₆　　It⁺⁶　　V　　　e: iv₆　　It⁺⁶　　V　　　A♭: iv₆　　It⁺⁶　　V

b.

G: iv₆　　It⁺⁶　　V　　　E♭: iv₆　　It⁺⁶　　V　　　b: iv₆　　It⁺⁶　　V　　　e♭: iv₆　　It⁺⁶　　V

4. In the exercises below, begin by writing an Italian augmented sixth, then provide one additional pitch to create a German or French sonority as specified.

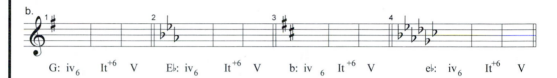

a.

A:　It⁺⁶　Gr⁺⁶　　　d:　It⁺⁶　Fr⁺⁶　　　G:　It⁺⁶　Fr⁺⁶　　　G♭:　It⁺⁶　Gr⁺⁶

b.

f:　It⁺⁶　Gr⁺⁶　　　E:　It⁺⁶　Fr⁺⁶　　　g:　It⁺⁶　Fr⁺⁶　　　D:　It⁺⁶　Gr⁺⁶

5. Construct and resolve the specified augmented-sixth chords in four parts. Employ conventional doublings and spacings. Provide all necessary accidentals.

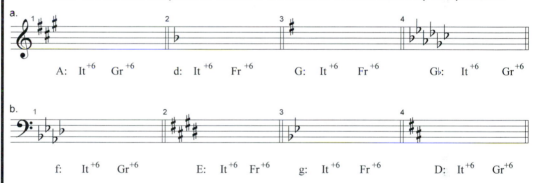

a.

c: Gr⁺⁶　i⁶₄　　　G: Fr⁺⁶ V　　　b♭: It⁺⁶　i⁶₄　　　E: Gr⁺⁶　I⁶₄

b.

F: Gr⁺⁶ I⁶₄　　　g♯: Fr⁺⁶ V　　　B♭: It⁺⁶ I⁶₄　　　f♯: Gr⁺⁶ i⁶₄

SELF-TEST 3–2

Time Limit: 8 Minutes

1. Each chord in the next example is an augmented sixth. Indicate the type as Italian, German, or French (It^{+6}, Gr^{+6}, or Fr^{+6}). *Scoring: Subtract 5 points for each incorrect response.*

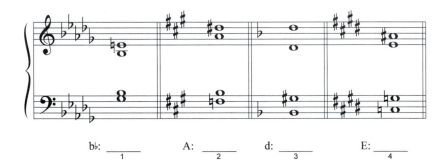

bb: _____   A: _____   d: _____   E: _____
    1   2   3   4

2. Answer the following questions about borrowed and augmented-sixth chords. Enter the appropriate word or phrase in the space below the question. *Scoring: Subtract 4 points for each error.*

   A. The Gr^{+6} usually resolves to tonic six-four to avoid:

   B. In all categories of augmented-sixth chords, the augmented-sixth interval resolves as follows:

   C. When scoring a borrowed chord in four parts, how is any altered pitch (or pitches) ideally approached?

   D. Provide a working definition of "chromaticism."

   E. In four-part vocal writing, which pitch is traditionally doubled in an Italian augmented sixth?

3. Write and resolve the following progressions. Furnish any necessary accidentals. *Scoring: Subtract 10 points for an incorrect chord (a total of 40); subtract another 10 points for any improper voice leading between chords (a total of 20).*

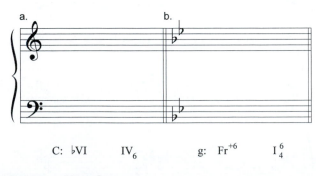

C: bVI   IV$_6$ g: Fr^{+6} I$^6_4$

Total Possible: 100   Your Score _____

PROJECTS

Analysis

Prepare notes that will serve either as the basis of an analytical paper or a class presentation. Summarize and document your understanding of one or more of the compositions listed below. The following areas are appropriate:

    a. A brief biographical sketch of Schubert or Schumann and a few words to set the particular work in context in his overall output. Remember that this type of information often requires identification of the source.

    b. An analysis of form (possibly including a time-line diagram). Your comments on form might also show how other areas (items c-e on this list) affect formal development.

    c. The key scheme and tonal variety (tonicization, modulation, and the establishment of a central tonality).

    d. Harmonic vocabulary. Consider making a reduction of selected passages to clarify the chromatic harmony.

    e. A discussion texture and variety.

Text

Franz Schubert, "Dona nobis pacem" from Mass in E♭ Major, text page 143.

Workbook/Anthology II

Robert Schumann, "The Poet Peaks" from *Scenes from Childhood*, workbook pages 58–59.
Franz Schubert, "Restless Love" Op. 5, No. 1, workbook pages 59-63.
See the workbook instructions for additional suggestions on analyzing this work.

Composition

Chorale for Brass Quartet. Compose a chorale for two B♭ trumpets, horn in F, and trombone. The chorale should make use of numerous chords studied in Chapter 3 (borrowed chords, dimished sevenths, augmented sixths, and so on). Begin by composing the chorale at concert pitch in a four-voice vocal style. The completed work will be for brass instruments, however, and your instructor may suggest that you use a freer approach to voice leading. Begin with a chord progression for each phrase such as the one that follows:

Next, plot out block chords based on your roman numerals.

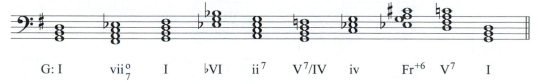

G: I   vii°₇   I   ♭VI   ii⁷   V⁷/IV   iv   Fr⁺⁶ V⁷   I

With an interesting and workable progression chosen, select a meter and compose a melody line (first trumpet) that is chromatic. Remember that you may add traditional nonchord tones (diatonic or chromatic) as you see fit.

As you would with a four-part vocal chorale, write the bass, then fill in alto and tenor. The result is a concert-pitch score for the brass ensemble. Avoid parallel perfect unisons, fifths, and octaves, but you may find it convenient to approach doubling and spacing in a more relaxed manner.

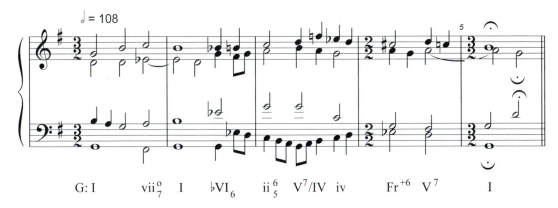

G: I   vii$^{o}_{7}$ I   ♭VI$_6$ ii$^{6}_{5}$ V^7/IV   iv   Fr^{+6} V^7 I

Complete a full score with parts transposed as necessary (refer to Appendix B for ranges and intervals of transposition). Continue this chorale for another two or three phrases or begin anew with your own melody and harmonization.

CD 1, TRACK 52
Chromatic
Chorale

Chromatic Chorale

Trumpet I

Trumpet II

Horn in F

Trombone

G: I   vii$^{o}_{7}$ I   ♭VI   ii^7 V^7/IV   iv   Fr^{+6} V^7 I

For Further Study

Harpischord to Piano. While the harpisichord was the predominant keyboard instrument of the Baroque era, the piano (pianoforte) gained favor steadily after about 1750. In the nineteenth century, technical improvements in piano construction permitted a dynamic and expressive range that significantly influenced the romantic style. In notes for your own edification, for a class presentation, or as the basis of a formal paper, investigate some of the following areas:

    a. Summarize the essential difference between the harpsichord and piano.

    b. Discuss the pianoforte of Mozart's era. What were the limitations of the instrument in comparison to later versions?

    c. What is piano "action?" Name and comment on two different actions employed in the eighteenth century.

    d. Summarize on technical achievements in the nineteenth century. Name and discuss briefly two or three major instrument builders of the Romantic era.

    e. Differentiate among different types of keyboard instruments. What is a "grand" piano, for example? a spinet? an upright?

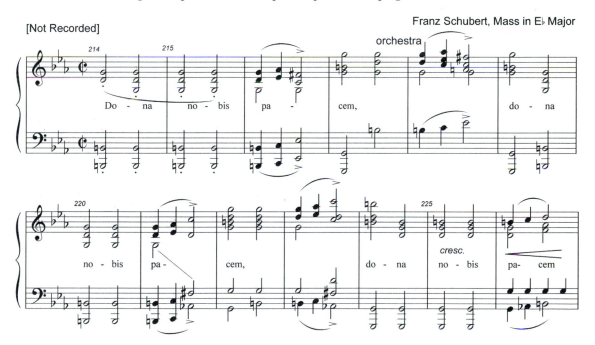

Franz Schubert, Mass in E♭ Major

CHAPTER *4*

Neapolitan and Other Chromatic Resources

While the eighteenth century saw the piano emerge as musically superior to the harpsichord, the nineteenth century was a time of dramatic changes in the construction of orchestral instruments. As we discussed in Volume I, trumpets and horns were fitted with valve mechanism by 1815; about a decade later, Theobald Böhm (1794–1881) invented a system of keys and rings for woodwind instruments that permitted greater flexibility and improved intonation. Most woodwind and brass instruments are still constructed with these same principles today. As soon as it was technically feasible to write virtually any pitch for any instrument, composers were quick to exploit new chromatic and enharmonic possibilities.

We discussed borrowed and augmented sixth chords in Chapter 3. Now our study of chromatic harmony continues with two new topics. First, the *Neapolitan sixth* is a colorful predominant sonority that was first associated with a group of eighteenth-century Italian opera composers working in Naples.[1] Second, by about 1775, composers throughout Western Europe began to dramatize distant modulations that had become popular through Twelve-Tone Equal Temperament. Enharmonic interpretations (E–G♯–B = F♭–A♭–C♭) had long been possible theoretically, but in the late Classical and Romantic eras, applications of these relationships became feasible as well. In Chapter 4, we will study how composers used listeners' functional conditioning to establish two different tonal settings for a single chord— one immediate; the other, retroactive.

The Neapolitan

In the Baroque era, composers often looked to melodic and harmonic formulas as a means of structuring the various parameters of a composition. The ground bass, for example, presented a great deal of flexibility within the security of a recurring

---

[1]Principal among these composers are Alessandro Scarlatti (1660–1725) and Giovanni Battista Pergolesi (1710–1736).

formula: Tonal progressions governed harmonic movement, and melodic patterns (especially those between bass and soprano) provided additional tonal direction.

CD 1, TRACK 53-1 ORIGIN OF THE NEAPOLITAN SIXTH (2 PARTS)
Basic Progression

Like augmented sixths, the Neapolitan chord grew from the linear embellishment of a familiar diatonic progression in minor.

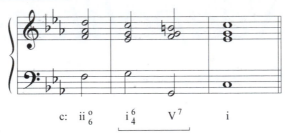

c: ii$^{\,o}_{6}$ i$^{6}_{4}$ V^7 i

As they did with augmented sixth chords, composers first added passing chromatic motion toward $\hat{1}$ in the tonic six-four; later, as shown in the second frame of the next example, this pitch was incorporated into

TRACK 53-2 ORIGIN OF NEAPOLITAN SIXTH
Passing Tone/False Consonance

the chord as a FALSE CONSONANCE—a consonant pitch that is made to sound dissonant by its surroundings.

False Consonance

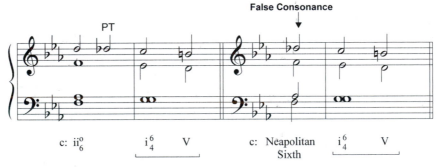

c: ii$^{o}_{6}$ i$^{6}_{4}$ V   c: Neapolitan   i$^{6}_{4}$ V
                                                            Sixth

Like augmented-sixth sonorities, the NEAPOLITAN SIXTH (specified N$_6$ in this text) is a predominant chord that appears as a vertical arrangement of three pitches:

- The fourth scale degree serves as the bass (other possibilities will be discussed presently).

- A minor third and a minor sixth occur over the bass.

G: N$_6$ g: N$_6$

In minor keys, the minor sixth above the bass is an accidental. In major, *both* the minor third and the minor sixth lie outside the key signature. We should note that while the Neapolitan sixth has no theoretical root (being formed through linear motion), the pitches are those of a first-inversion major triad on $\downarrow\hat{2}$. In the next example, compare Neapolitan sixths in the keys of D major and minor, B major and minor, and A♭ major and minor. In each case, the bass is doubled.

As we will discuss fully later in this section, the Neapolitan sixth resolves most characteristically to tonic six-four; less often to the dominant.

Neapolitan Sixth Chords in Major and Minor

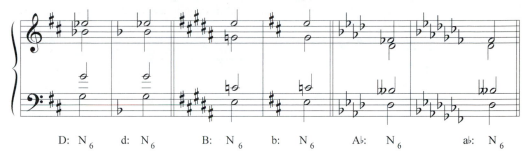

Throughout the eighteenth and nineteenth centuries, the Neapolitan sixth was a favored sonority. Josephine Lang (1815–1880), for example, was celebrated in her day for songs that included interesting harmonies as well as well-crafted and musical phrases. In the work below, notice several different color chords: diminished sevenths, borrowed chords, and, in measures 66–67, a Neapolitan sixth that resolves to tonic six-four. Observe that $\text{vii}^\circ_7/\text{V}$ follows I^6_4 and precedes the resolution to dominant (measures 67–68). In this case, the dominant is strengthened both through the Neapolitan and through the secondary diminished seventh. Such colorful embellishments of dominant harmony were common in the mid- and late nineteenth century.

 CD 1, TRACK 54
Josephine Lang, "I Gave You Back to Your Fate"

Täu - schung trifft,   ein   et was   das wir nicht ver - schmer   - zen,

(I)   V^7 ♭VI   N$_6$ i$^6_4$ vii$^{\circ}_7$/V   V

It is a wondrous feeling that forever cripples the heart,
When we experience our first disappointment—
A feeling that we never get over.

Frédéric Chopin wrote a series of twenty-four preludes—one in each major
and minor key. Prelude No. 20 in C Minor (given complete in the following
example) offers a range of tonicizations and chromatic chords that includes a
root-position Neapolitan (resolving to the dominant) and a French augmented
sixth (measures 6 and 10). In measure 5, we initially hear the third beat as vii$^{\circ}_7$ in C
minor. The appearance of an F♯, however, leads us to a tonicization of G minor.

Chopin's brief prelude is cast in an A B B form. The first four measures
(A) include a harmonic sequence (C minor and A♭ major) and end with a half
cadence in the original key. The repeated second (B) part is dominated by a
chromatic bass and includes more ambiguous
harmonic function. Still, the root-position N–V^7–i
cadence formula provides a strong ending in C
minor.

CD 1, TRACK 55
Frédéric Chopin, Prelude, Op. 28,
No. 20

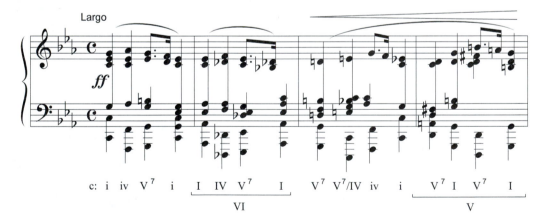

Largo

_ff_

c: i iv V^7 i   I IV V^7 I   V^7 V^7/IV iv i   V^7 I V^7 I

VI   V

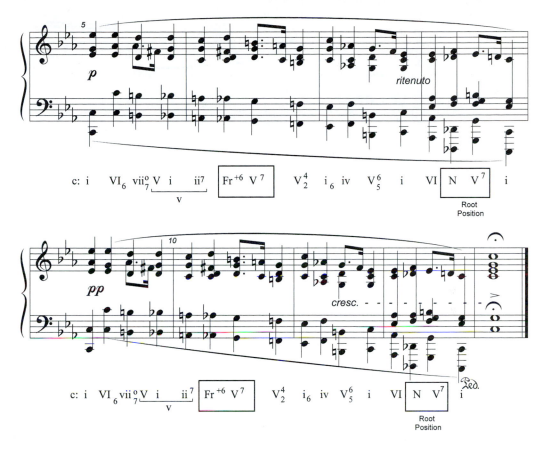

In "The Miller and the Brook" from the song cycle *Die Schöne Müllerin* (*The Beautiful Miller Woman*), Franz Schubert resolves a Neapolitan sixth to the dominant. Notice the diminished third between A♭ and F♯ in the piano accompaniment (measures 8–9). Whether the music is vocal or instrumental, composers approached voice leading from universal guidelines.

CD 1, TRACK 56
Franz Schubert, "The Beautiful Miller Woman"
from *The Miller and the Brook*

(g:) i   N 6   V   i

When a faithful heart of love dies,
Then the lilies wither in every garden.

Constructing Neapolitan-Sixth Chords.   Despite the linear origin of the Neapolitan sixth, you may find it most convenient to notate the chord as a major triad built upon the lowered second scale degree (adding accidentals as necessary). The Neapolitan appears most often in first inversion, although root position and second inversion are viable exceptions.

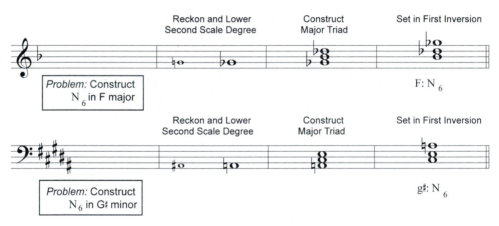

The Neapolitan Sixth in Four-Part Style.   The Neapolitan chord is common both in vocal and instrumental music of the late eighteenth and nineteenth centuries. In four-part vocal style, the linear movement $\hat{3}-\downarrow\hat{2}-\hat{1}$ is common in the soprano. When the chord resolves to dominant, however, $\uparrow\hat{7}$ may appear between $\downarrow\hat{2}$ and $\hat{1}$. This diminished third is characteristic of the N_6–V progression.

CD 1, TRACK 57
Resolution of the Neapolitan Sixth

Resolution to Tonic Six-Four   Resolution to Dominant

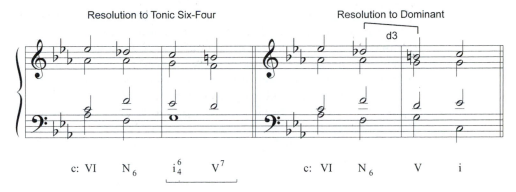

$$\text{c: VI} \quad \text{N}_6 \quad \text{i}^6_4 \quad \text{V}^7 \qquad\qquad \text{c: VI} \quad \text{N}_6 \quad \text{V} \quad \text{i}$$

Tonicization of the Neapolitan Area.   Because the Neapolitan sixth is spelled like a major triad, it has the potential to sound like a stable tonic.[2] While the tonicization of the Neapolitan area is not especially common, Chopin and other nineteenth-century composers did exploit this remote relationship. We recognize a tonicization of the Neapolitan area only after the fact: The relationship with the tonic key is clear when the Neapolitan itself resolves to tonic six-four or dominant.

Tonicization of Neapolitan Area

$$\text{a: i} \quad \text{V} \quad \text{i} \quad \text{iv} \quad \text{V}^7/\text{N} \quad \text{N} \quad \text{V} \quad \text{i}$$

The harmony sketched in the last example is from Chopin's *Mazurka*, Op. 7, No. 2. The first major section of the work ends with a tonicization of the Neapolitan area in A minor. The resolution to dominant is a strikingly effective reinforcement of the primary tonality.

$$\text{a:} \quad \text{V}^4_3/\text{iv} \quad \text{iv} \qquad\qquad \text{VI} \quad \text{i} \quad \text{V}^7$$

$$\text{(a:)} \quad \text{iv}_6 \quad \text{VI} \qquad \text{V}^7/\text{N} \quad \text{N} \qquad\qquad \text{V}^7 \qquad\qquad \text{i}$$

---

[2]The Neapolitan sixth can also be heard as a dominant as discussed on page 167.

Including the Neapolitan, traditional composers had a wide range of predominant chords at their disposal. The common element in these chords is the convergence of either $\hat{4}$ or $\hat{6}$ (or both) upon the dominant. As shown in the next example, one or both of these pitches may be altered, but always in a direction to draw *nearer* to $\hat{5}$. The chords in the next example are only some of those with predominant function and they are shown resolving variously to the dominant and tonic six-four. In general, chords and resolutions are equivalent in major and minor. Note that we have included the "Tristan Chord" and labeled it "Tr^{+6}". While far from standard, such identifications convey the origin and function of the chord.

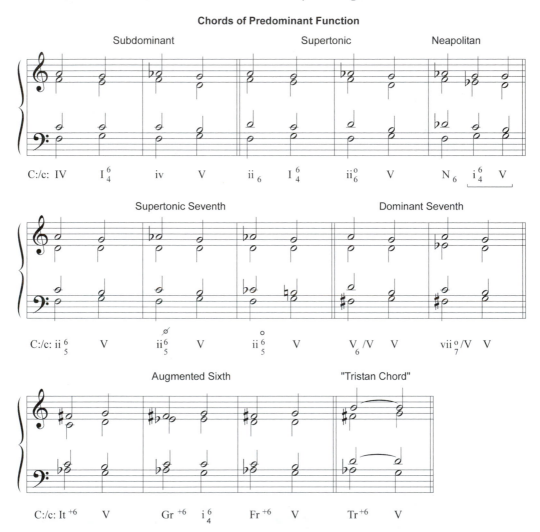

Chords of Predominant Function

The last example shows a few ways in which nineteenth-century composers stretched predominant function to include a remarkable degree of color. Frequently employed at a cadence, augmented sixths, borrowed seventh chords, and the Neapolitan, among others, create an almost electric quality of excitement that alerts the listener to an important event. When Chopin and others tonicized the Neapolitan area, they not only enriched the traditional vocabulary, but, as we will discuss in the next section, they also laid the groundwork for enharmonic interpretations that permitted rapid and distant modulation.

I. WORKBOOK/ANTHOLOGY II
Neapolitan Sixth, page 65

REVIEW AND APPLICATION 4–1 ─────────────

Neapolitan Sixth

Essential Terms

false consonance   Neapolitan sixth

1. In four-part vocal style, provide an appropriate chord of preparation; then construct and resolve the other two chords specified. Add accidentals as necessary. In addition to the Neapolitan, you will find augmented sixths and other predominants.

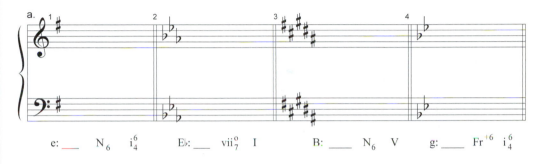

e: ___ N₆ i⁶₄   E♭: ___ vii°₇ I   B: ___ N₆ V   g: ___ Fr⁺⁶ i⁶₄

c♯: ___ N₆ V   a♯: ___ N₆ i⁶₄   F: ___ ii⁶₅ V   b: ___ Gr⁺⁶ i⁶₄

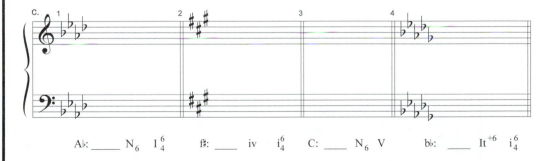

A♭: ___ N₆ I⁶₄   f♯: ___ iv i⁶₄   C: ___ N₆ V   b♭: ___ It⁺⁶ i⁶₄

2. The chord given is a Neapolitan sixth or otherwise has predominant function in a major key *and* its parallel minor. Determine the key; then provide a key signature (major or minor as you choose) that creates a predominant setting for the given chord. Note that when you add the key signature, one or more of the given accidentals may be redundant. Finally, be aware that the notation (spelling) of chords indicates the key of function. Do not interpret pitches enharmonically.

Model

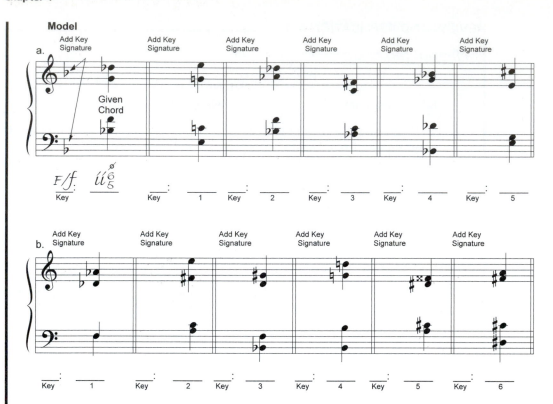

CD 1, TRACK 59-1 REVIEW AND APPLICATION 4-1 (3 PARTS)
Ludwig van Beethoven, Sonata in C♯ Minor, Op. 27, No. 2 (I)

3. Provide roman-numeral analyses of the following passages.

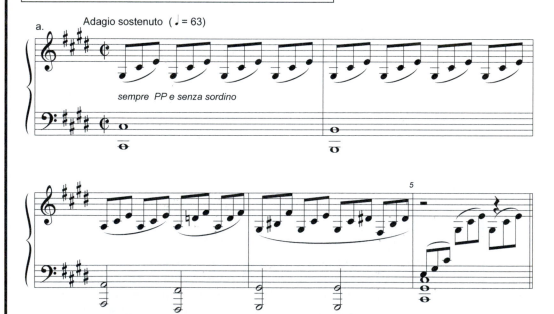

TRACK 59-2 REVIEW AND APPLICATION 4-1
Franz Schubert, Sonata in E♭ Major (III)

TRACK 59-3 REVIEW AND APPLICATION 4-1
George Frideric Handel, Chaconne

SELF-TEST 4-1

Time Limit: 5 Minutes

1. Place a check mark in the blank beside the correct response to each statement about the Neapolitan chord. *Scoring: Subtract 5 points for each incorrect answer.*

   a. An early Baroque composer associated with the use of the Neapolitan chord is

      ___ (1) Domenico Scarlatti

      ___ (2) Alessandro Scarlatti

      ___ (3) J. S. Bach

      ___ (4) C. P. E. Bach

   b. The Neapolitan chord evolved

      ___ (1) through linear motion

      ___ (2) as a dominant substitute

      ___ (3) through an embellished V–i progression

      ___ (4) through an embellished iv–V progression

   c. In a resolution to dominant, a feature of the Neapolitan sixth is the melodic interval of

      ___ (1) an augmented second

      ___ (2) a diminished fifth

      ___ (3) an augmented fourth

      ___ (4) a diminished third

   d. In function, the Neapolitan chord is

      ___ (1) tonic

      ___ (2) predominant

      ___ (3) dominant

      ___ (4) ambiguous

   e. In scoring the Neapolitan sixth in four-part vocal style, composers most often double the

      ___ (1) soprano

      ___ (2) bass

      ___ (3) altered tone

      ___ (4) fifth

2. Write and resolve the following progression in four parts. Supply a chord that would likely precede the Neapolitan. Add any necessary accidentals and adhere to conventional voice-leading guidelines. *Scoring: Subtract 12 points for an incorrect chord. Consider each chord entirely correct or entirely incorrect.*

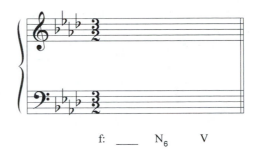

f: _____ N₆ V

3. Provide roman numerals (and symbols for bass position) where blanks appear. *Scoring: Subtract 6 points for an incorrect roman-numeral symbol. Subtract only 3 points if the arabic-numeral designation is incorrect.*

CD 1, TRACK 60

Ludwig van Beethoven, Sonata No. 23 in F Minor, Op. 57 (I)

4. Provide the term that describes a consonant pitch that is made to sound dissonant by its surroundings. *Scoring: Subtract 3 points for a wrong answer.*

Total Possible: 100   Your Score _____

CHROMATIC AND ENHARMONIC MODULATION

With only a few exceptions (the "Tristan chord," for example), the chromatic chords we have discussed in Unit 2 were employed by composers from the beginning of the eighteenth century throughout the common-practice period. Distant modulation, however, was extremely limited before the acceptance of Twelve-Tone Equal Temperament. Late-Baroque and even Classical-era composers limited their modulations to closely related keys, only occasionally ranging further afield in development sections. In the nineteenth century, however, when essentially all keyboard and wind instruments were equipped to play equally well in any key, distant modulation became an increasingly enticing choice.

Modulation by Borrowed Common Chord

In Volume I, we discussed modulation by common chord—a process in which one chord is heard as diatonic in two different keys. While the range of possible common-chord modulation is limited, composers as early as 1800 employed a *borrowed* chord as an harmonic pivot to reach distant keys. The tonalities of A major and C major, for example, are distant, and no common chord exists between them.

A Major-C Major: No Common Chords

A: I   ii   iii   IV   V   vi   vii°

C: vi   vii°   I   ii   iii   IV   V

With a change in mode, any of several additional triads might serve as a pivot chord in a modulation from A major to C major.

A Major-C Major: Borrowed Common Chords

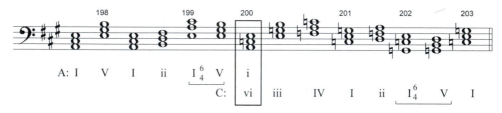

A: i   ii   ♮III   iv   V   ♮VI   vii°

C: vi   vii°   I   ii   iii   IV   V

If the tonic in A major is made minor in quality, the tonality remains stable, but we now have a viable pivot chord for the modulation to C major.

Modulation Through Borrowed Common Chord

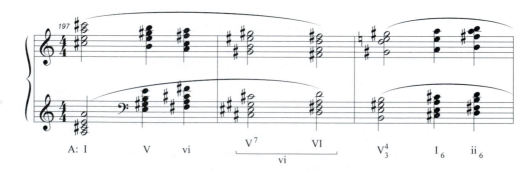

A: I   V   I   ii   I$^6_4$ V   i

C: vi   iii   IV   I   ii   I$^6_4$ V   I

The progression sketched in the last example occurs in the first movement of Beethoven's Sonata in C Major, Op. 53.

A: I   V   vi   V^7 VI   V$^4_3$ I$_6$ ii$_6$
                    vi

A: I^6_4 V i

C: vi iii IV I ii I^6_4 V^7 I

A similar change of mode in the tonic chord occurs in Schubert's *Sehnsucht* (*Longing*). Beginning in G major, the passage shown in the next example modulates to the distant key of E♭ major through a change of mode in the tonic chord that is then reinterpreted as a mediant in the new key: G: i = E♭: iii.

CD 1, TRACK 62
Franz Schubert, "Longing"

G: ii_6 I^6_4 V i

E♭: iii V^6_5 I ii^6_5

(E♭:) I^6_4 V IV V^7 I ii^6_5 I^6_4 V^7 I

[Chasing] winter away.
The earth is clad in velvet,
And the blossoms form red fruit.

Chromatic Mediants As Pivot Chords.   A CHROMATIC MEDIANT is not "borrowed," but is a mediant or submediant that is altered in mode so as to function as a pivot chord in a distant modulation. In C major, for example, the major mediant (III) and submediant (VI) may serve as predominants in a modulation to B major or minor (as well as C♭ major) and E major, respectively.[3] If the modulation is from C major to B major, the chromatic mediant provides a smooth connection between keys.

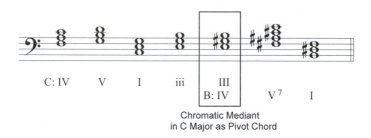

Chromatic Mediant
in C Major as Pivot Chord

After about 1800, examples of modulation through borrowed and chromatic pivot chord abounded in Western music, as composers exploited the striking, yet tonally secure relationships between major and parallel minor. Modulation through borrowed pivot chord utilizes a change of mode; as we will discuss in the next section, other techniques of chromatic key change exploit enharmonic relationships.

Enharmonic Modulation

In Bach's day, triads like B major and C♭ major were recognized as equivalent (especially in view of the new system of Twelve-Tone Equal Temperament), but faithfulness to the system of diatonic harmony generally prevented the employment of such relationships. Baroque and even Classical composers viewed tonality as the essence of a successful musical work. While two triads might be enharmonically equivalent, they belonged to two completely different tonal systems. By the beginning of the nineteenth century, however, chromaticism, modal borrowing, and altered predominants were sufficiently ingrained that enharmonic relationships—and in particular enharmonic modulation—became a common way for composers to assert their originality. Distant modulations, which had always been possible through enharmonic relationships, were exploited by Chopin, Brahms, and others, as composers searched for new means of musical expression.

Enharmonic Pivot Chord.   In a modulation through enharmonic pivot chord, a diatonic triad or chord in one key is also heard as a member of another diatonic collection. In A major, for example, the dominant triad (E–G♯–B) is enharmonically equivalent to the subdominant in C♭ major (F♭–A♭–C♭). Likewise, the subdominant triad in D♭ major sounds the same as the dominant triad in B major.

---

[3] If these chords have dominant function they are simply secondary dominants.

Although the range of potential enharmonic relationships is not without limit, and while the pivot chord must be functionally viable in both old and new keys, Romantic-era composers effectively used these materials to facilitate distant modulations. In *Moment Musical*, Schubert connects the distant keys of D♭ major and F♯ minor through an enharmonic common chord: The tonic triad in D♭ major is enharmonic with the dominant triad in F♯ minor. Schubert concludes the first section of the work in D♭ major; when the following section be-

CD 1, TRACK 63
Franz Schubert, *Moment Musical*

gins with an F♯ minor triad, we hear the tonic triad in D♭ major retroactively as the dominant in the new key.

Chopin employs an enharmonic pivot chord in his Prelude, Op. 25, No. 3. In the passage shown, the key is F# minor (despite the key signature). The dominant chord in F# minor (C#–E#–G#) is reinterpreted as a borrowed submediant in F major (Db–F–Ab). The union of two keys through an enharmonic *borrowed* chord (bVI in F major) is a logical extension of the same principle seen in Schubert's *Moment Musical*.

CD 1, TRACK 64
Frédéric Chopin, Prelude, Op. 25, No. 3

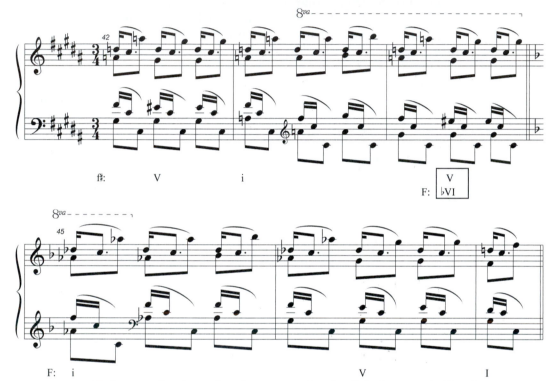

Enharmonic pivot chords, as seen in the Schubert and Chopin excerpts, provided composers with the opportunity to expand the harmonic palette within the limits of tonal design. In the final section of this chapter, we will explore three familiar sonorities (diminished seventh, German augmented sixth, and Neapolitan sixth) that, when resolved enharmonically, facilitate still other distant key relationships.

WORKBOOK/ANTHOLOGY II
II. Borrowed and Enharmonic Pivot Chords, page 69

The Diminished-Seventh Chord as Enharmonic Pivot

With its two tritones, the diminished seventh is both one of the most volatile and one of the most useful chords in establishing tonality. Where Baroque and Classical composers resolved the diminished seventh directly to its immediate goal, in the nineteenth century, the ambiguous quality of the diminished seventh was applied to effect distant modulation. Consisting entirely of minor thirds, inversions of the diminished seventh are impossible to distinguish aurally. The chords below, for example, though notated differently, all have the same sound.

Varying Notations of A Single Diminished-Seventh Chord

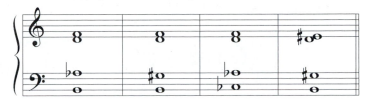

In traditional tonal harmony, each of the chords in the last example would serve to define a different tonic. The root of the chord is ↑$\hat{7}$ in the key in which it functions. The four chords in the last example, therefore, would function as dominants in the keys of C, A, E♭, and F♯, respectively.[4] As always in tonal music, function is defined through context: the gravitation of unstable (dissonant) pitches to their harmonic goals. With dominant function, each chord below is defined through regular resolution.

CD 1, TRACK 65
Enharmonic Resolutions

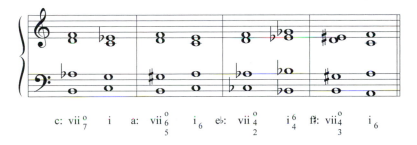

c: vii°$_7$ i   a: vii°$_6^5$ i$_6$ e♭: vii°$_4^2$ i$_4^6$ f♯: vii°$_4^3$ i$_6$

If C has already been established as tonic, we would assume that the first diminished seventh in the last example is primary, and we would anticipate a resolution to tonic (as shown in the first frame). If the resolution is not to C, but to an A-minor triad, however, we retroactively identify the diminished seventh as having dominant function in A minor. Melodic tendencies are redefined, with the pitch A♭ (↓$\hat{6}$ in C major) now being heard as ↑$\hat{7}$ in A minor.

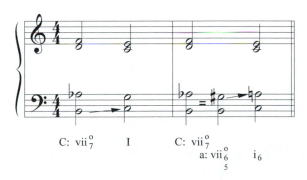

C: vii°$_7$ I   C: vii°$_7$
a: vii°$_6^5$ i$_6$

The keys of C major and A minor (last example) are closely related, and other methods of modulation exist. The process and the same diminished-seventh

---

[4]Examples here are given in the minor, but the enharmonic relationships in this section are appropriate for major and minor alike.

chord, however, facilitate modulation to the distant keys of E♭ major or minor and F♯ major or minor.

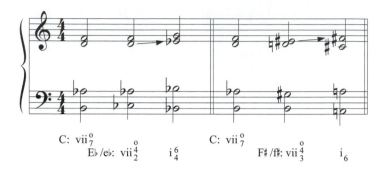

Beethoven's Sonata in C Minor, Op. 13 provides a helpful example of the enharmonic diminished seventh as used in traditional literature. In the next example, the key of G minor is established through a vii°₇–i progression. Beethoven repeats the diminished seventh, but effects an unexpected resolution to tonic six-four in E minor.

Beethoven, Sonata in C Minor
Enharmonic Modulation

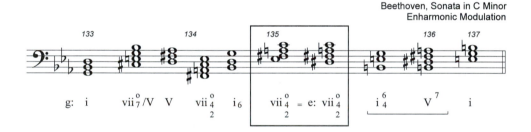

In the excerpt that follows, notice that Beethoven notates the diminished seventh according to its resolution. Not all composers provide this assistance to the performer; the listener, of course, is unconcerned about notation, expecting only an eventual functional outcome.

CD 1, TRACK 66
Beethoven, Sonata in C Minor, Op. 13 (I)

German Augmented Sixth as Enharmonic Pivot

Modulation through an enharmonic diminished-seventh relationship is effective because the chord itself is immediately recognized as dominant in function. The strong tendencies to resolve enable us to perceive retroactively any one of several possible tonics. Another chord, the German augmented sixth, provides a similar potential for enharmonic interpretation. Aurally, the German augmented sixth cannot be distinguished from a dominant-seventh chord in root position.

Dominant Seventh   German Augmented Sixth

We differentiate between the two chords through function and resolution. The dominant seventh is dominant in function and progresses to tonic (or a tonic substitute); the German augmented sixth, a predominant choice, resolves to the dominant (or to tonic six-four).

The spelling of chords in tonal music is dependent on the key system, but when chords of differing function are enharmonic equivalents, that function is conveyed through resolution and not notation. Using this phenomenon, we can modulate down a minor second by resolving a dominant seventh as if it were a German augmented sixth. Reversing the process, a reinterpretation of a German sixth as a dominant seventh permits a rapid and convincing modulation up a minor second. These modulations are summarized in the next table.

Chord	Reinterpreted As	Effects Modulation
Dominant Seventh	German Augmented Sixth	To the key a minor second lower
German Augmented Sixth	Dominant Seventh	To the key a minor second higher

If the tonic key is D major, we can modulate down to C♯ major (or minor) by resolving the dominant seventh (A–C♯–E–G) so that it sounds like a German augmented sixth (A–C♯–E–F𝄪.) Both resolutions were familiar to listeners in the common-practice period, and the alternate choice was readily accepted in retrospect.

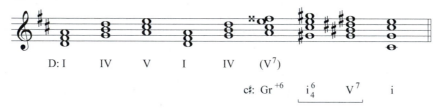

Reversing the process effects a modulation to a key a minor second higher. In C minor, for example, a German augmented sixth may be resolved as if it were a dominant seventh in D♭ major.

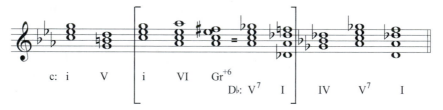

The bracketed portion of the last example appears in Chopin's Prelude in D Minor, Op. 28, No. 24. The key of C minor has been established in the measures preceding the passage shown. Likewise, the key of D♭ major is verified as the section continues. The link between keys, however, is the German augmented sixth that resolves as a dominant seventh in the new key.

CD 1, TRACK 67
Frédéric Chopin, Prelude, Op. 28, No. 24

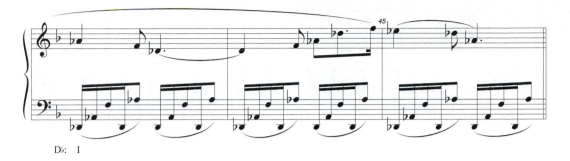

Db: I

Neapolitan Chord as Enharmonic Pivot

Despite its linear origin, the Neapolitan-sixth chord *sounds* like a major triad; like all major triads, it has potential dominant function. As we have discussed, the Neapolitan sixth was traditionally a predominant choice. If the chord is resolved as a major triad in first inversion with *dominant function*, however, the chord assumes a different role. The result of this reinterpretation is a modulation to the key a tritone higher or lower. In the harmony sketched below, the key of A major is established. The Neapolitan sixth resolves as a first-inversion dominant triad in Eb major and subsequent functional progressions in the new key validate our enharmonic reinterpretation.

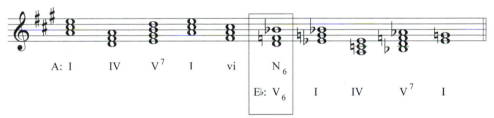

A: I   IV   V^7 I   vi   N$_6$

Eb: V$_6$ I   IV   V^7 I

As a first-inversion sonority, the reinterpreted Neapolitan sixth lacks some of the inherent dominant tension that we normally would exploit to establish a new key. Still, some composers carefully manipulated melodic and rhythmic parameters so that the key change is convincing. In his *Phantasiestücke* (*Fantasy Piece*), for example, Robert Schumann reinterprets a tonic triad in Db major as a Neapolitan sixth in C major. In the passage shown, Schumann employs a root-position Neapolitan. In the following measures, we hear C major not as a new tonal center, but as the dominant of F minor—a key closely related to Db major. Schumann could have employed a traditional common-chord modulation between the two keys, but chose the enharmonic route for its color and expressive potential.

CD 1, TRACK 68
Robert Schumann, *Phantasiestücke*,
Op. 12, No. 3

Db: V^7/vi   vi   vii$^{o}_7$/V   V^7/V   V^7

(D♭:) I

C: (N)   V⁷   I

                                              f: V   V⁷   i

By 1875, composers were no longer limited to the diatonic chords in any one major or minor key. Augmented-sixth, Neapolitan, and diminished seventh chords provided variety as they facilitated modulation to remote areas. The freedom composers allowed themselves to progress less in terms of function than color, gradually led to a questioning of the tonal system itself. Moreover, the musical public, once conditioned to the supremacy of a single tonal area and a narrow range of harmonic possibilities, supported composers in their use of innovative materials and techniques. Thus, as we will discuss fully in Chapter 7, Western music changed. Improvements in the construction of instruments, Twelve-Tone Equal Temperament, and the individual and collective quest for an expansion of the tonal system set the stage for its dissolution in the works of Debussy, Mussorgsky, and others.

III. WORKBOOK/ANTHOLOGY II
Enharmonic Modulation, page 71

REVIEW AND APPLICATION 4–2

Enharmonic Relationships

Essential Terms

chromatic mediant

1. Construct Neapolitan-sixth chords in the keys suggested. Supply all necessary accidentals.

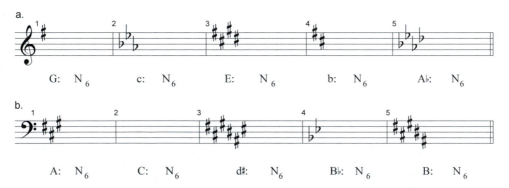

a.

G: N₆   c: N₆   E: N₆   b: N₆   A♭: N₆

b.

A: N₆   C: N₆   d♯: N₆   B♭: N₆   B: N₆

2. The following chords contain chromatic alterations. Use roman numerals and other appropriate symbols to identify each sonority in the key suggested. Consider dominant and leading-tone triads in minor, secondary dominants, diminished-seventh chords, augmented sixths, and Neapolitan sixths.

a.

A♭: ____   e: ____   E♭: ____   b: ____   F: ____   g♯: ____
    1   2   3   4   5   6

b.

D: ____   C♭: ____   G: ____   c: ____   b: ____   a: ____
    1   2   3   4   5   6

3. The following passage illustrates two different types of enharmonic modulation as discussed in this chapter. Provide a complete roman-numeral analysis, changing keys as necessary. The passage begins and ends in F major. Comment on the techniques of modulation to a distant key and back.

 CD 1, TRACK 69
Franz Schubert, Sonata in A Minor, Op. 164 (I)

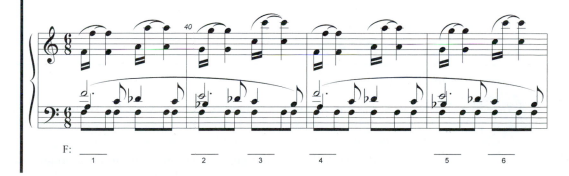

F: ____
  1   2   3   4   5   6

SELF-TEST 4–2

Time Limit: 15 Minutes

1. Some of the statements that follow are true; others, false. Write "T" or "F" in the blank as appropriate. *Scoring: Subtract 5 points for each incorrect answer. These statements concern material covered in the entire chapter.*

_____ a. Reinterpreting a German augmented sixth as a dominant seventh facilitates a modulation to a key a half step lower.

_____ b. Because minor triads consist of superimposed minor thirds, inversions cannot be discerned aurally.

_____ c. With a proper resolution, any one of the four pitches of a diminished seventh chord may be heard as the root.

_____ d. A Neapolitan sixth may be reinterpreted as a dominant triad in first inversion.

_____ e. Borrowed chords are not suitable as enharmonic pivot chords.

_____ f. In a Neapolitan sixth, $\downarrow\hat{2}$ is an example of a false consonance.

2. In four-part vocal style, write and resolve the progression specified. Add any necessary accidentals. Resolve the diminished seventh according to melodic tendencies in the new key. *Scoring: Consider each chord right or wrong; subtract 10 points for each error. Even if all chords are correctly notated, examine your finished work also for characteristic resolution of active pitches, resolution of the dominant seventh, correct doubling, appearance of any parallel octaves or fifths. Subtract 2 points for each minor error; 5 for each occurrence of parallel octaves or fifths.*

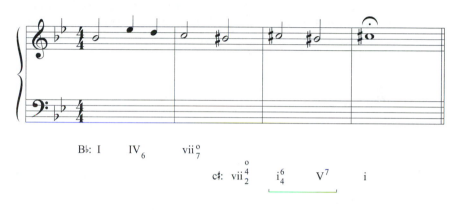

B♭: I   IV₆   vii°₇

c♯: vii°₄₂   i⁶₄   V⁷   i

Total Possible: 100   Your Score _____

PROJECTS

Analysis

Schubert, Chopin, and Brahms were three of the most important keyboard composers of the nineteenth century. Works for analysis appear both in the text and in the Workbook/Anthology. Follow the instructions and complete an analysis of one or more of these keyboard compositions. If directed to do so, compare and contrast two of the works as follows:

a. form

b. key scheme; tonicization and modulation

c. texture and accompaniment pattern

Text

Franz Schubert, Moment Musical Op. 94, No. 2, text pages 107–112.
   This composition is discussed briefly in the text, but many areas remain for your investigation.

Workbook/Anthology II

Frédéric Chopin, Waltz, Op. 9a, No. 14, workbook page 75.
Johannes Brahms, Rhapsody Op. 119, No. 4, workbook pages 76–77.
Otto Malling, Impromptu, Op. 30, No. 7, page 78.

Composition

Choral Arrangement: "Streets of Laredo." The folk song that many of us know as "Streets of Laredo" was first an Irish ballad, "A Handful of Laurel."[5] Make an arragement of this song for four-part chorus with piano accompaniment. Begin and end the first verse (given below) in G major. Compose a brief modulating transition for piano that employs one of the chromatic or enharmonic relationships discussed in Chapter 4, then state the second verse in a distant key. End the composition after the second verse (remaining in the distant key). Your instructor may ask you to provide a brief piano introduction or a concluding passage after the second verse.

Feel free to alter the harmony of "Streets of Laredo" to provide more harmonic color. Consider setting the first verse with diatonic harmony, for example, and with a chromatic chord selection for the second verse.

Irish-American Folk Song, "The Streets of Laredo"

Second Verse
"I see by your outfit that you are a cowboy,"
These words he did say as I boldly walked /by,
"Come sit down beside me and hear my sad story,"
"I'm shot in the breast and I know I must die."

The sample transition that follows could be used to connect the first and second verses. The chorus ends the verse with a cadence in G major. The piano interlude exploits a motive from the melody and modulates to B♭ major. The connection between keys is made through a borrowed submediant in G major; the following chord can be heard as diminished seventh in both keys.

---

[5]Composers in the eighteenth century often wrote new sets of words to familiar tunes. The national anthem, "The Star-Spangled Banner" is another example. We credit Francis Scott Key with our national song, but the melody was first a drinking song by John Stafford Smith entitled "To Anacreon in Heaven."

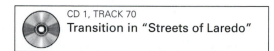

CD 1, TRACK 70
Transition in "Streets of Laredo"

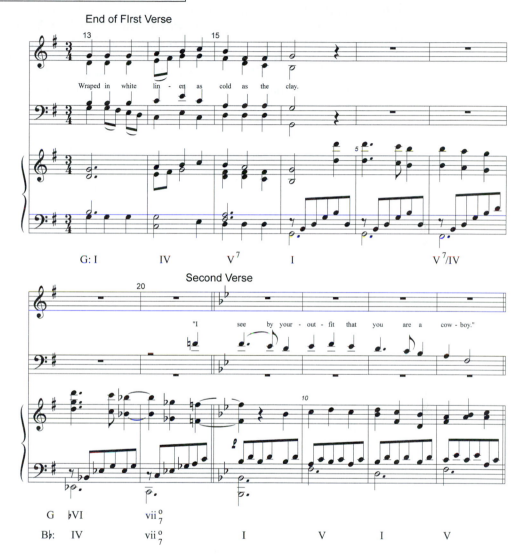

For Further Study

Women in Music: The Nineteenth Century. In addition to the celebrated male composers who dominated Western music in the days of Beethoven and Brahms, many talented women made and performed music in the nineteenth century. One of the most well known of these is Clara Wieck Schumann (1819–1896) who was an accomplished pianist and composer. Unfortunately, after her marriage to Robert, Clara rarely performed her own music, preferring to champion her husband's works. After Robert's death in 1858, Clara was left with the responsibilities of seven children, yet still managed to compose and perform. She wrote solo piano and chamber works as well as numerous *lieder.*

Clara Schumann wrote in a Romantic style and many of the chromatic materials discussed in Chapters 3 and 4 may be found in her works. As a project, choose one of her *lieder* or a brief piano composition as may be available in your library. Compile notes for a paper or presentation that includes a brief biographical sketch as well as your analysis of the work in question. Instead of submitting a formal paper, your instructor may ask that you turn in an outline of the material along with a brief listening list of Clara Schumann's works and your reaction to one or more of them.

Numerous other women composers might be included in a survey. While none of those listed below has equaled Clara Schumann's popularity, some of their works are readily available in scores and recordings.

Amy Cheney Beach (1867–1944)

Cécile Chaminade (1857–1944)

Rebecca Clarke (1886–1979)

Louise Farrenc (1804–1875)

Fanny Mendelssohn Hensel (1805–1847)

Josephin Lang (1815–1880)

Alma Mahler (1879–1964)

Maria Theresa von Paradis (1759–1824)

Nancy Reich (1819–1896)

Louise Reichardt (1779–1821)

Pauline Viardot-Garcia (1821–1910)

UNIT *3*

Grand Forms

Mozart, Serenade for Strings, K. 525 (*Eine Kleine Nachtmusik*)

Chapter 5
Sonata Form

Chapter 6
Rondo

A SONATA is an instrumental *genre* that unfolds in several distinct movements. In the Renaissance, the word "sonata" meant nothing more than a work intended for instrumental performance (as opposed to a "cantata"—one to be sung). By Bach's day, however, most composers wrote sonatas in three to six movements and in contrasting tempos, styles, and textures. The first movement of a Baroque sonata, sometimes preceded by a brief introduction, is typically fast and imitative. Other sonata movements, reflecting the genre's origin in the dance suite, may include a *Lento* or *Adagio* (sometimes imitating a vocal aria in its melodic embellishment), a fantasia, passacaglia or chaconne, and one or more dances (minuet, sarabande, allemande, gigue, and so on). Sonatas often begin with more formal and weighty material and then conclude with a movement that is light or even humorous in tone.

Many great sonatas were written by J. S. Bach, Antonio Vivaldi (1678–1741), Georg Telemann (1681–1767), and others, but the clearest image of "sonata" for most concert-goers today is the three-movement genre as composed by Haydn, Mozart, Beethoven, and their contemporaries. The first movements of these works usually retain the serious character of the Baroque sonata. Likewise, the second movement is most often slow and lyric; the third, energetic and rhythmic. In form, the second movement of a "typical" Classical-era sonata

175

may be binary, ternary, a theme and variations, or any one of numerous other designs. The last movement (often termed the *finale*) is frequently a rondo (to be discussed in Chapter 6). The first movement structure (the subject of Chapter 5), has the same designation as the genre itself: *sonata form*.

Alongside Romantic-era genre such as *lieder* and the character piece, nineteenth-century composers continued to write sonatas, string quartets, concertos, and symphonies. Invariably, one or more movements of these major works was cast in a traditional GRAND FORM (so-called in opposition to small forms such as binary and ternary). While Sonata form evolved from a baroque binary design, in the hands of composers like Mozart and Haydn, the structure became an important model for balancing the opposing forces of stability and momentum in a longer work. Nineteenth-century composers expanded sonata form in terms of length, the number of themes, and the importance of development, but they still remained faithful to the basic tonal precepts involved.

Sonata form is found in many genre besides sonatas, symphonies, and quartets. In the eighteenth century, a number of generally lighter compositions entitled "serenade," "cassation," and "divertimento," for example, were written originally for performance outdoors, and may include one or more sonata movements.

Wolfgang Amadeus Mozart was born in 1756 in Salzburg, Austria, where his father, Leopold (1719–1787), was a musician at the court of the Archbishop. Wolfgang's genius emerged at an early age as he learned harpsichord and violin, composed a minuet at five (K. 1), and a symphony at age eight. In promotion of his children (Nannerl, Wolfgang's older sister, was also a child prodigy), Leopold exhibited them throughout Europe, including tours to Vienna, Prague, London, Rome, Paris, and Munich. As a young man, Wolfgang was employed by the Archbishop, but for the remainder of his life sought unsuccessfully to find employment in a position that matched his prodigious talents. By the late 1780s, Mozart was celebrated throughout Europe for works in choral, instrumental, and chamber media. His comic operas literally redefined the genre, and the majority of his extant works continue to be performed today. Still, for reasons that are not entirely clear to scholars, he died virtually penniless in 1791.

One of Mozart's most popular works with today's general public is the Serenade for Strings, K. 525 subtitled *Eine Kleine Nachtmusik* (*A Little Night Music*). Composed in 1787, *Eine Kleine Nachtmusik* is scored for double string quartet plus bass (reading the same part as the cellos, but sounding an octave lower). The work is in four movements, with the first being a rather straightforward sonata form. Listen to the work now as an introduction to Unit 3. After you have completed basic studies of sonata form in this chapter, listen again to a recording of the first movement as you study the score that follows.

W. A. Mozart, Serenade for Strings, K. 525
First Movement

[Not Recorded]

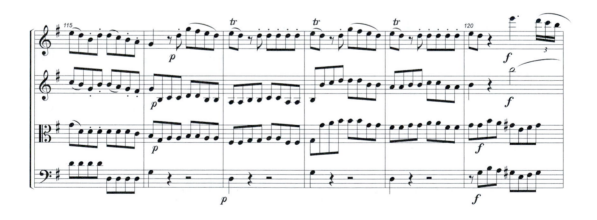

CHAPTER 5

Sonata Form

In its essential structure, sonata form is directly related to the rounded binary form that we discussed in Chapter 12 of Volume I. Some confusion may result, however, from the fact that the same word—sonata—is used to designate both a form and a *genre*. In the latter use of the term, SONATA is a group of movements for keyboard or for one solo instrument with keyboard accompaniment. As a *genre*, the sonata was phenomenally popular in the eighteenth and nineteenth centuries; most composers wrote several—even dozens.

SONATA FORM, based on the statement and contrast of themes and keys, is a formal scheme often found in the first movement of a sonata *genre*. Any movement (and all movements) of a sonata may be in sonata form, but this design is especially common in the first movement. Before about 1975, sonata form was often identified as "sonata–*allegro* form" to designate the most common tempo of the first movement. Today, we more frequently refer simply to "sonata form" in acknowledgment of movements that may be slow or moderate in tempo.

SONATA STRUCTURE

Audiences in Haydn's day were accomplished listeners. While untrained listeners today may be vaguely aware of modulation in a popular song or other simple work, the expectation of moving through a pre-set key sequence is unnecessary for appreciation. Eighteenth-century audiences, on the other hand, were still largely noble and privileged individuals who learned music at an early age and maintained a life-long patronage. As a consequence, the digression from an opening key to another tonality (reinforced by corresponding thematic material) created an actual state of tension. Audiences anticipated the return of the tonic key and the accompanying relaxation of that tension.

Tonal Dissonance.   We might describe this tension as a large-scale TONAL DISSONANCE that dominates a sonata. While the dissonance of a suspension or appoggiatura is resolved quickly in tonal music, the dissonance associated with the interplay of keys is more supple: We *enjoy* the tension, strive to understand it as we listen, and anticipate the ways in which a composer might approach eventual resolution. To our ears, the return of the tonic key is almost an anticlimax, because we are so accustomed to far greater dissonances. But in the eighteenth century, the notion of tonal polarity was still relatively new.

Sonata form is usually discussed as having three major divisions: *Exposition, Development,* and *Recapitulation.* The exposition launches the tonal dissonance by moving away from the tonic key. In the development, this tension (the dissonance) is heightened through a number of means that we will discuss in detail. Finally, in the recapitulation, the tonal dissonance is resolved through a return to the tonic key.

Exposition

The EXPOSITION of a sonata form introduces the two principal keys and themes around which the movement will center. In addition to the tonic key, a POLAR KEY provides contrast and creates tonal dissonance. A sonata exposition comprises four basic elements: the first theme, a transition to the polar key, the second theme, and a closing section.

The First and Second Themes.   The FIRST THEME is heard in the tonic key. Depending on the proportions of the movement, the first theme may be stated several times, and may have two or more different melodic ideas. EPISODES of figural material may appear between statements of the first theme. After we are familiar with the first theme and comfortable with the tonic key, the TRANSITION begins a movement away from the tonic and toward the polar key. This event begins the tonal dissonance that we will follow throughout the movement. The SECOND THEME accentuates the polar key.[1] Like the binary form from which it originated, a sonata movement may be *monothematic* if the first theme is reinterpreted in the polar key.

Time-Line Identification of Themes.   While a sonata movement revolves around two themes (identified as "first" and "second"), there may be two or more distinct melodies or episodes associated with the tonic key, the polar key, or both. These are THEME GROUPS, and while the materials might be quite different in character, their *function* is always clear: to accentuate either the tonic or the polar key.

Many scholars today use roman numerals (I or II) to specify the first and second themes, respectively. If there are two or more melodies or episodes associated with a given theme group, lowercase roman letters are used: Ia, Ib, IIa, IIb, and so on. Study the sample time line that follows. This hypothetical exposition has two distinct melodies in the first theme group; two in the second group; and a linking episode to the closing section.

---

[1] If the tonic key is major, the polar key is most likely to be the dominant. In minor keys, several possibilities exist, including the relative major and the dominant minor. Be aware that other terms are synonymous with the "polar key": "related key," "contrasting key," "secondary key," and the like.

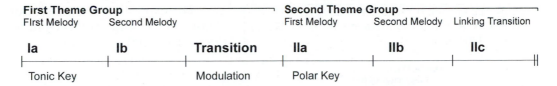

The Closing Section.   Following the second theme (and still in the polar key), the exposition of a sonata form ends with a CLOSING SECTION— material that is clearly secondary in importance to the first and second themes, but which celebrates the polar key. Again, one or more episodes may link members of the second theme group. In most sonatas, the closing section includes either or both of two elements: preparation for the *focal cadence* and a *codetta.*

Preparation for the Focal Cadence.   The strongest cadence in the polar key typically occurs just before the end of the exposition. This point is called the FOCAL CADENCE since it rivets attention upon the polar key and accentuates the tonal dissonance. The preparation is usually figural with scales, arpeggios, and melodic fragments. This passage work culminates in the focal cadence itself.

Codetta.   Following the focal cadence, we often hear an unassuming phrase or phrase group that serves to extend the polar key through the final cadence of the exposition. When such a passage occurs, it is termed a CODETTA (It. small coda).

Closing Section

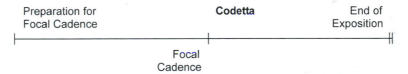

Observe that there are many exceptions to the format in the last illustration. Usually, the identification of a codetta is sufficient; it begins immediately after the focal cadence and continues to the end of the exposition. In summary, the most characteristic elements of the exposition are shown in the next diagram.

Exposition

Between 1777 and 1778, Mozart wrote eight piano sonatas while traveling in Paris and Mannheim (Germany). The first movement of his Sonata in F Major, K. 332 is from this group and is typical, in many respects, of sonata form in the mature Classical era. We will use this movement to illustrate the themes, keys, and other elements of sonata form that have been discussed previously in general terms. While only portions of the score are displayed with the discussion, the full score appears beginning on page 196.

CD 1, TRACK 71-1 FIRST THEME GROUP (2 PARTS)
W. A. Mozart, Sonata in F Major, K. 332 (I)
Theme Ia

The exposition of Mozart's Sonata in F Major opens with a three-phrase group (identified as Ia).

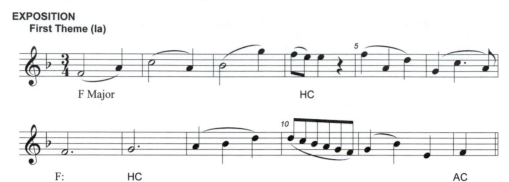

Next, Mozart continues the first theme group and the tonic key with material (Ib) that has a dance flavor and is underscored by the horn fifths in measures 13 and 17. Note that theme groups may be divided into two or more distinct phases. In Mozart's sonata, theme Ia is lyric; theme Ib is more rhythmic.

TRACK 71-2 FIRST THEME GROUP
Mozart, K. 332
Theme Ib

In measure 23, Mozart begins the transition through a dramatic excursion to D minor. Arpeggios, diminished-seventh chords, and descending scalar patterns culminate in C minor (beginning in measure 31). At this point, we have reached the polar key (C), but in the minor mode. In measures 35–40, the dominant of the polar key (G) is embellished through a German augmented sixth and a pedal (measures 37–40).

CD 1, TRACK 72
Mozart, K. 332
Transition to Second Theme

Dominant Caesura. One of several clichés often found in sonata form is a dramatic pause called a DOMINANT CAESURA, that appears immediately before the second theme. The last measure in the previous example is such a dominant caesura. The silent third beat (and the lack of melodic or rhythmic momentum for the entire measure) alerts the listener to an event of significance: the polar key. In Mozart's sonata, the dominant caesura leads directly to the second theme in C major. Where the first theme is legato in style and moves basically in quarter notes, the second theme (IIa) contrasts by beginning with a staccato group and including an ornamented line of eighth notes. In form, the second theme is a parallel double period.

CD 1, TRACK 73
W. A. Mozart, Sonata in F Major, K. 332 (I)
Second Theme Group (IIa)

Second Theme Group (IIa)

C Major

Mozart links the second theme with a more extensive closing section through an animated passage constructed from the motive

and combined with arpeggios that touch on the keys of C minor and E♭ major before returning to the polar key (C major). This material is episodic and not thematic; still, because it is associated with the polar key, we employ the designation IIb.

CD 1, TRACK 74
Mozart, K. 332
Second Theme Group (IIb)

Second Theme Group IIb (Episode)

C Minor   V   C Major: V   IV

Notice the metric accentuation in the last passage (marked by octaves in the bass and written dynamics). In measures 60–63, these accents reinforce the triple meter. Beginning in measure 64, however, Mozart employs hemiola that has the effect of pushing the music ahead more quickly without a change of tempo. The term *internal acceleration* is used by some to describe this effect.

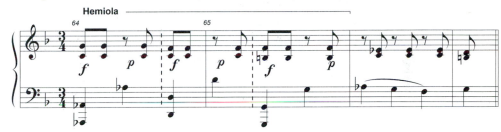

The Closing Section. While some closing sections are little more than flourishes to intensify the polar key, this part of K. 332 is a thematic preparation for the focal cadence.

CD 1, TRACK 75-1 SECOND THEME AND CODETTA (2 PARTS)
Mozart, K. 332
Theme IIc (Preparation for Focal Cadence)

Second Theme Group (IIc)
(Preparation for Focal Cadence)

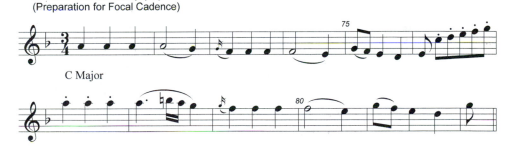

C Major

The focal cadence itself occurs in measures 85–86. A codetta (IId—based on material from the earlier episode (IIb)—ends the exposition.

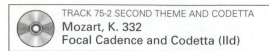

TRACK 75-2 SECOND THEME AND CODETTA
Mozart, K. 332
Focal Cadence and Codetta (IId)

Consider the time line of the entire exposition and observe the principal events and keys.

EXPOSITION

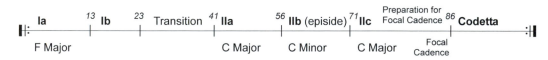

Development

In a rounded binary form, the related key has been established at the end of the first part, and the second part begins with a new theme (or a statement of the first theme in the related key). In a sonata movement, however, two themes have already been heard, and the second division begins with a section of increased tension and complexity called the DEVELOPMENT. Composers employ a wide range of techniques to manipulate melodic, rhythmic, and harmonic material from the first theme, the second theme, or both. In addition, because the exposition ends with the closing section, this material may also be prominent in the development.

Thematic Development.   Periodic themes are usually not heard in their entirety in a development section. More often, a melodic fragment from one of the themes occurs sequentially to touch on several new keys. To maintain textural tension, a longer development section may include a short fugue or other imitative passage. Less often, a development includes one or more entirely new themes.

Increased Tonal Tension.   The development continues the tension that began in the exposition. While the development opens in the polar key (in which the exposition ended), however, there are usually passages in a number of additional tonal areas. A shorter development section may state a theme (or material from it) in the relative major or minor, the subdominant, or another contrasting key. In movements of longer overall proportions, distant as well as closely-related keys may be heard. Yet, while virtually any key is possible in a development section, composers usually avoid the tonic in order to maintain the tonal tension.

Retransition.   The last element of the development section, termed a RETRANSITION, is a preparation for the return of the tonic key. Where the transition of the exposition is a movement *away* from the tonic, the retransition facilitates its return. In shorter works, the retransition may be nothing more than a dominant chord; in others, the return of the tonic is signaled by a lengthy dominant prolongation that may run for dozens of measures and effect a virtual halt in harmonic momentum.

A "model" sonata movement—from the beginning of the exposition to the end of the development—is shown on the time line below.

EXPOSITION			DEVELOPMENT	
First Theme	Second Theme	Closing Section	**Various Keys/Themes**	**Retransition**
Tonic Key	Polar Key		Polar Key Other Keys	Tonic Key: V

The development section of Mozart's K. 332 begins with a variation of material from the closing section (IIc). This material, however, is expanded melodically into a more lyric and absorbing melody of period length. The same theme is then repeated an octave lower to complete a sectional double period.

Mozart next returns to the rhythmic motive heard as an episode between the second theme and the closing section (IIb). The passage begins as it did originally—with triad outlines in the bass. Instead of moving toward E♭ as he

CD 1, TRACK 76-1 RETRANSITION (2 PARTS)
Mozart, K. 332
Excerpt I

did in the exposition, however, Mozart touches upon the keys of G minor and D minor, then ends with an emphasis on the dominant in the latter key (measures 123–126).

(Development)
Retransition to Recapitulation

RETRANSITION TRACK 76-2
Mozart, K. 332
Excerpt II

But while Mozart seems headed for a full modulation to D minor and more development, a shift in mode precedes a dominant seventh in C major and begins a retransition (measure 127).

(Development)
Retransition to Recapitulation, continued   **RECAPITULATION**

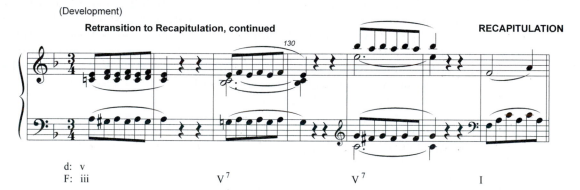

d: v
F: iii   V⁷   V⁷   I

A time line shows that material from the closing section opens and closes the development of Mozart's K. 332. More notable, perhaps, is the *absence* of both the first and second themes in the development. The keys employed are closely related with an emphasis on the dominant minor (C minor).

DEVELOPMENT

94 IIc   109 IIb   123 IIc   Retransition

C Major   C Minor   G Minor   D Minor   F: V⁷

Recapitulation

The role of the RECAPITULATION is to relax the tonal dissonance created in the exposition and continued throughout the development. In most sonata forms, we hear a restatement of the tonic key and some or all first-theme material. The transition appears as it did in the exposition, but instead of leading to the polar key, it blusters briefly, then returns to the tonic. The second theme is likewise stated in the tonic.

To add variety to the recapitulation, composers may add new accompaniment figures, create contrasting textures, vary transitional passages, change register, alter instrumentation in orchestral works, and otherwise endeavor to enliven material heard previously. While the second theme is associated with the polar key in the exposition, it reinforces the return of the tonic key in the recapitulation. Concluding the recapitulation, as well as the movement as a whole, is a return of the closing section—also in the tonic key. In longer movements, composers may use a *coda* (discussed on page 213) to provide a more definitive ending.

RECAPITULATION

The recapitulation of K. 332 offers few surprises. The first theme group returns in measure 133 exactly as it occurred in the exposition. Likewise, the transition recurs in measure 155, although this material is four measures longer than in the exposition. Mozart moves through D minor and C minor as before, but in preparation for the second theme in the *tonic key,* four added measures emphasize B♭ minor (measures 165–168); a modal shift (measures 171–176) enlivens both F major and the second theme (measure 177).

The remainder of the recapitulation is a transposition of exposition material to the tonic key. The episode (IIb) recurs (measures 192–206) including the hemiola, and the closing material is in F major as we would expect (measure 207).

On a time line, interest centers on the reinforcement of F major in the second theme and closing section.

RECAPITULATION

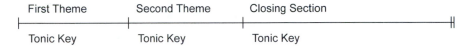

As a whole, the first movement of Mozart's Sonata in F Major is 229 measures long, with exposition, development, and recapitulation comprising sections of 93, 39, and 97 measures, respectively. The work is of average proportions for the late eighteenth century and follows the model of sonata form closely. The next time line shows the major events and the keys associated with them. Listen to a recording or a live performance while you follow the score.

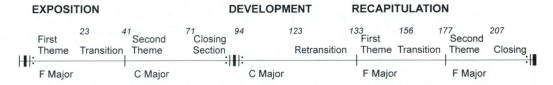

[Not Recorded]

EXPOSITION

First Theme Group (Ia)

F Major

First Theme Group (Ib)

F Major

Transition (Ic)

D Minor

C Minor

RECAPITULATION
First Theme Group (Ia)

F Major

First Theme Group (Ib)

F major

Transition (Ic)

D minor

Codetta (IId)

WORKBOOK/ANTHOLOGY II
Ia. Haydn, Sonata in C major, page 79
Ib. Mozart, Sonata in B♭ Major, K. 333, page 83

REVIEW AND APPLICATION 5–1

Sonata Form

Essential Terms

closing section	episode	polar key	sonata form
codetta	exposition	recapitulation	theme group
development	first theme	retransition	tonal dissonance
dominant caesura	focal cadence	second theme	transition

1. Match a term from the list with each of the statements given. Note that these questions include all terms covered in the chapter. Some terms may be used more than once; others, not at all.

A. tonic key   E. exposition

B. polar key   F. development

C. retransition   G. closing theme

D. transition   H. dominant caesura

_____ a. the key in which the exposition begins

_____ b. an emphasis on the dominant (or V/V) just before the second theme is heard

_____ c. a passage that connects the tonic and polar keys

_____ d. the key of the second theme in the recapitulation

_____ e. the key in which the second theme appears in the exposition

_____ f. a passage of figural material that first occurs at the end of the exposition and emphasizes the polar key

_____ g. a passage that prepares for the return of the tonic key just before the recapitulation

_____ h. the section of a sonata movement in which the tonic key is established

2. These matching questions concern the three major divisions of a sonata movement. Choose one *or more* answers from the list; then match it (them) with one of the descriptions given. Note that answers may be used more than once.

    A. exposition

    B. development

    C. recapitulation

_____ a. second theme in tonic key

_____ b. dominant caesura

_____ c. first occurrence of the tonic key

_____ d. second theme in polar key

_____ e. first occurrence of polar key

_____ f. second theme reinterpreted in the tonic key

_____ g. the transition connects tonic and polar keys

_____ h. appearance of the retransition

_____ i. the transition connects first and second themes in the same key

3. On the time line below, provide the key names at the appropriate points where blanks appear. The keys for this hypothetical sonata movement are D major and A major. Write the letter "D" or "A" in each blank.

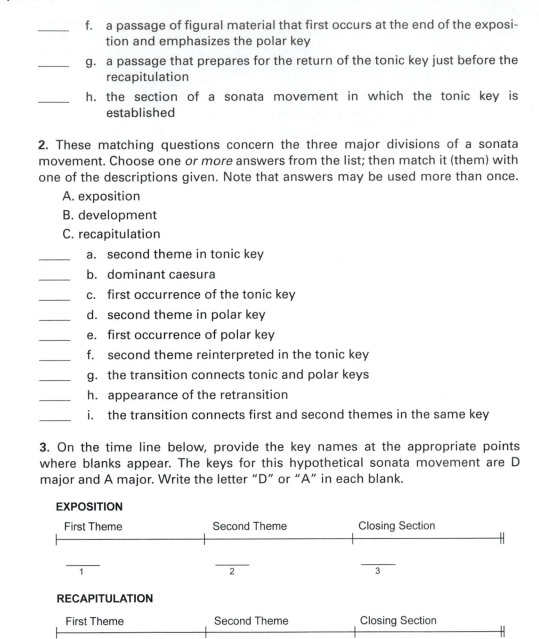

EXPOSITION

First Theme	Second Theme	Closing Section
1	2	3

RECAPITULATION

First Theme	Second Theme	Closing Section
4	5	6

SELF-TEST 5–1

Time Limit: 5 Minutes

    1. Place a check mark beside the best answer for each of the following statements. *Scoring: Subtract 7 points for each incorrect answer.*

a. A rhythmic and harmonic pause just before the second theme is called

   ___(1) dominant pedal

   ___(2) dominant caesura

   ___(3) dominant preparation

   ___(4) dominant seventh

b. The transition occurs

   ___(1) between the exposition and the development

   ___(2) between dominant caesura and second theme

   ___(3) between tonic and polar keys

   ___(4) between dominant pedal and recapitulation

c. A closing section

   ___(1) begins in the polar key and ends in the tonic

   ___(2) is usually less melodic than first or second themes

   ___(3) is usually heard at or near the end of the recapitulation

   ___(4) all of the above are true of the closing section

d. The retransition

   ___(1) begins in the polar key

   ___(2) is an extension of the exposition

   ___(3) provides a smooth link to the recapitulation

   ___(4) none of the above is true of the retransition

2. The time line below includes one crucial error. Locate and circle the error, and in your own words, explain the inaccuracy. *Scoring: Subtract 13 points for an incorrect identification of the error; subtract 13 for an incorrect or incomplete explanation (26 possible for this problem).*

EXPOSITION				DEVELOPMENT	RECAPITULATION		
First Theme	Transition	Second Theme	Closing Section	Retransition	First Theme	Second Theme	Closing Section
Tonic Key		Polar Key		Polar and Other Keys	Tonic Key	Polar Key	Tonic Key

Explanation:

3. Fill in the blank with a term, date, composer's name, or other information regarding sonata form. Please note that these questions concern Chapter 5 (pages 185–203) as well as the introductory material for Unit 3. *Scoring: Subtract 5 points for each error.*

_____   a. Baroque form from which sonata form evolved

_____   b. A modern term for the "tension" that was created in audiences of Mozart's day by tonal polarity

_____   c. Country of Mozart's birth

_____   d. A major composer who was contemporary with Mozart

_____   e. Typical number of movements in a sonata *genre*

4. Provide the names (in order) of the three major divisions of a sonata movement. *Scoring: Subtract 7 points for each incorrect identification.*

a. _____

b. _____

c. _____

Total Possible: 100   Your Score _____

SONATA FORM IN THE NINETEENTH CENTURY

Although the same tonal dissonance can be found in virtually every sonata movement, many nineteenth-century composers continued an expansion of the form. Mozart's K. 332 has an exposition of 93 measures (with its theme groups, transition, and codetta). As we will discuss in this section, Beethoven, Schubert, Brahms, and others composed longer sonata movements. The exposition of Beethoven's Sonata No. 8 in C Minor ("Pathetique"), for example, is 132 measures long. Late-nineteenth-century symphony composers routinely created sonata movements of 500 measures and more. In addition to repetition, transition, episodes, and theme groups, composers lengthened the basic sonata form with a slow introduction, extended development, and a coda.

Introduction

Slow introductions that precede the exposition are common, and have three functions. First, they establish a harmonic backdrop against which the tonic key will emerge eventually. Introductory material strengthens the first theme and the tonic key when they finally arrive. Second, introductions quote melodic fragments and distinctive rhythm patterns that will emerge in the exposition as a complete theme. Melodies in the introduction begin, but trail off before they are completed; key shifts, often every few measures, cause us to anticipate the stability of a tonic key and a memorable theme. Finally, an introduction establishes a mood that may be somber, witty, dramatic, whimsical, and so on. Introductions are usually *Grave* or *Lento*, and the exposition may begin with a faster tempo and a stable key center.

Peter Illyich Tchaikovsky (1840–1893) wrote six symphonies; the last three of these have been in the standard orchestral repertory for over a hundred years. Composed in 1893, Tchaikovsky's Symphony No. 6 in B Minor "Pathétique" begins with an introduction that is typical of late nineteenth-century sonata movements. In the full score that follows (page 207), note the brooding bassoon (*fagotti*) line in E minor (the subdominant of the tonic to follow). This material is complemented by low strings and woodwinds. We would not classify the bassoon solo as a "melody," but as a melodic fragment that foreshadows the vigorous first theme. In measure 15, the violas conclude the introduction with a descending stepwise line that leads to a dominant preparation in B minor. Note also the detailed performance instructions (dynamics, crescendos, and so on) that are typical of the late Romantic era.

INTRODUCTION

P. I. Tchaikovsky, Symphony No. 6 in B Minor
("Pathetique") First Movement

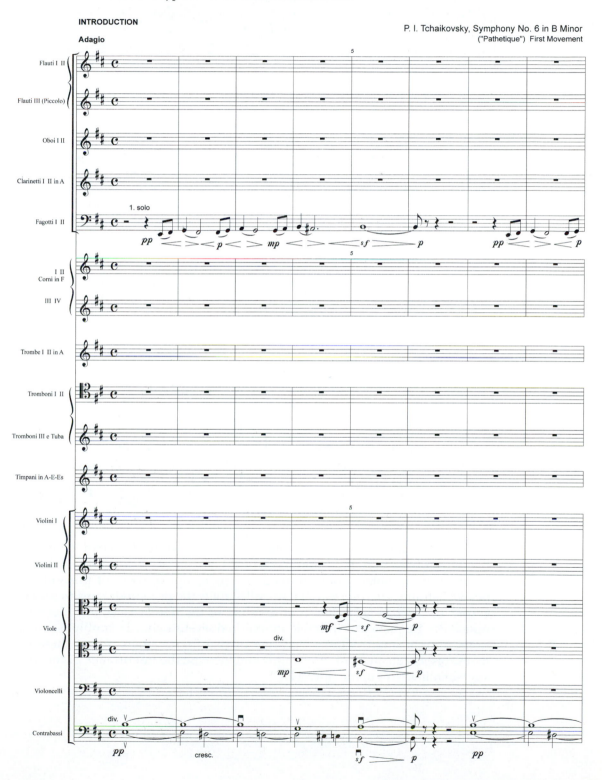

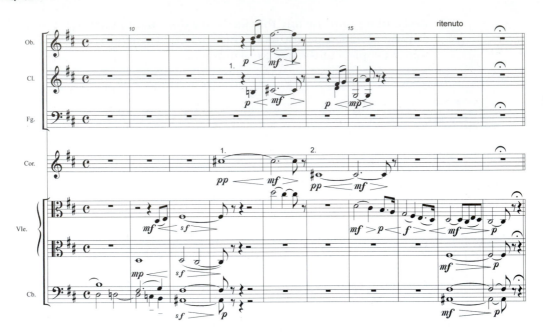

When the exposition of Tchaikovsky's symphony begins in measure 19, the key of B minor is quickly established. The first theme exhibits the momentum that the introductory material lacks.

Over a hundred years before Tchaikovsky wrote his sixth symphony, Beethoven began the first movement of his Sonata No. 8 in C Minor, Op. 13 (1789) with a similar slow introduction. The complete score of this work appears beginning on page 214, but we will amplify the present discussion with excerpts. In the passage below (the first half of the ten-measure introduction), notice the frequency of unstable diminished-seventh chords, multiple suspensions, and an improvisational passage of sixty-fourth notes. All of these elements project an effect of uncertainty and increase the importance of the tonic key when it arrives in measure 11.

CD 1, TRACK 77
Ludwig van Beethoven, Sonata No. 8 in C Minor, Op. 13 ("Pathetique") (I)
Introduction

Following the introduction, the first theme of Beethoven's Op. 13 is the "rocket" effect that is associated with Johann Stamitz (1717–1757) and other composers who served the court at Mannheim. The left-hand accompaniment pattern of broken octaves, more dramatic than Alberti arpeggios, is another late-Classical cliché that is sometimes termed "murky bass."

CD 1, TRACK 78
Beethoven, Op. 13
First Theme

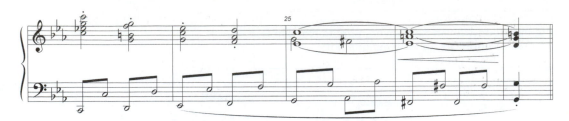

While composers like Mozart and Haydn generally wrote complete, periodic themes, Beethoven and some of his contemporaries more frequently used melodic fragments and interesting rhythmic and harmonic effects in their place. After a single presentation of the first theme, for example, Beethoven

CD 1, TRACK 79
Beethoven, Op. 13
First Theme, Part Ib

provides an additional theme fragment (Ib). We can identify this material as a member of the first-theme group through its clear C-minor tonality.

The transition (not shown) begins in measure 35 with Ia heard in G major, then A♭ major. A dominant caesura (measure 49–50) signals the approach of the polar key (see page 214 for complete score).

Key Relationships in Nineteenth-Century Sonata Movements

As we have discussed, in music from the early eighteenth century, the term polar almost invariably designates the dominant if the key is major, and the relative major or dominant minor if the tonic key is minor. The Mozart sonata discussed previously conforms to this model. With Beethoven and other nineteenth-century composers, however, the key associated with the digression may be distant. Especially common are third-related keys. If the tonic is C major, for example, the polar key might be E major, E♭ major, A major, or A♭ major—all keys that present interesting chromatic possibilities and challenging problems of continuity. Similar flexibility may occur if the movement is in minor. In this case, in addition to root relationships by third, the second theme may also be in a minor key. Moreover, composers sometimes chose one distant key for the exposition and a different one for the corresponding point in the recapitulation. In this latter case, however, there are often two statements of the second theme in the recapitulation—one in a distant key, another in the tonic. The key relationships in the following time line occur in Beethoven's Sonata in C Major, Op. 53 (Waldstein).

In Op. 13, Beethoven uses the transition (measures 35–50) to establish the dominant of the expected related key—E♭ major. When the theme arrives, however, it is in the minor mode, and the melody is broken between bass and soprano registers. The first four measures embellish the tonic triad (E♭ minor) and a second four-measure segment is devoted to the dominant seventh.

CD 1, TRACK 80
Beethoven, Op. 13
Second Theme (IIa)

Second Theme IIa

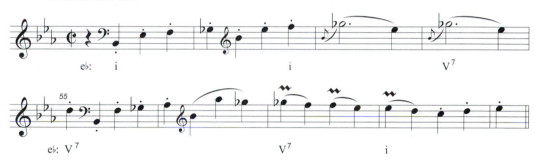

Now in E♭ major, a 12-measure transition begins in measure 89 and is repeated without change in measures 103–112. This dense passage, reminding us of Ia material, gives way in measure 113 to a brief closing section. The focal cadence occurs in measures 112–113. In addition to standard figural material as a codetta, Beethoven quotes the first theme a final time, ending the exposition with a dramatic series of octaves over the murky bass accompaniment. The exposition concludes on a dominant-seventh chord in C minor.

A time-line analysis of Beethoven's exposition is similar to the one on page 195 for Mozart's K. 332. We might note significant differences in key relationships, however, and the relative length of linking passages.

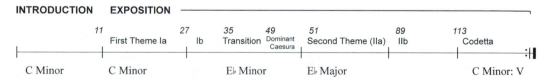

The development section begins in measure 135 with a brief return to the introductory material. From G minor, Beethoven reaches the distant key of E minor through an enharmonic reinterpretation of a diminished seventh.

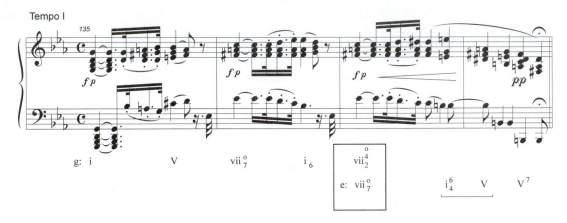

Considering the proportions of the movement as a whole, the development is relatively brief. Beethoven begins with the first theme in the distant key of E minor. He then states this material in F major (with liberal use of chromatic appoggiaturas) in measures 139–166, then shifts eventually to the minor mode within this tonality. By measure 169, not thirty measures into the development, Beethoven already begins the retransition with a pedal G that anchors chromatic figuration. In measure 186, a descending passage of eighth notes, built of a motive heard earlier (Ib), leads directly to the recapitulation in C minor.

DEVELOPMENT

Beethoven begins the recapitulation traditionally in C minor, but the first theme (Ia) is heard only once. Likewise, instead of the Ib material (with its half notes tied over the barline), the half notes belonging to the first theme, Part I, are extended to form a brief link to the second theme. A dominant pedal in measures 221–222 suggests that the second theme will be in C minor as we would expect. However, Beethoven begins the second theme in F minor (measure 223), although a second statement (measures 239–246) modulates to C minor. As in the exposition, the second theme dissolves into fragmentation, and the material heard earlier in the exposition (between the second theme and the closing section) occurs also in the recapitulation (measures 255–278). Finally, a closing section in C minor (measure 279–296) ends with octaves in the right hand, as it did in the exposition. For the close of the work, however, Beethoven composed a *coda*.

Coda

Beethoven is generally credited with enriching traditional key relationships, increasing the importance of the development, and maximizing the use of an ending formula called a CODA (from the Latin, *tail*). Beethoven's codas are not only longer than those of Haydn and Mozart, but they have a different purpose. Many composers before Beethoven, for example, employed codas as a means to effect a strong final cadence. Although the coda of Op. 13 is brief and relatively conservative, in some of Beethoven's sonata movements, the coda becomes a second development section that is a discrete and integral part of the sonata structure. Later composers like Tchaikovsky and Mahler expanded on Beethoven's innovations with even more formidable codas. The first movement of Tchaikovsky's Symphony No. 5 in E Minor, for example, is 565 measures in length; the coda that ends the movement is itself nearly 140 measures.

The coda of Beethoven's Sonata No. 8 in C Minor begins with a third statement of the *Grave* material. Each time we have heard the pounding diminished sevenths of the introduction, an important event has followed. The exposition provided theme and key security following the introductory *Grave;* likewise, the development has its own introduction of the same material. When we hear the dotted rhythms for a third and final time, the movement is virtually at an end.

RECAPITULATION

As you did with the Mozart sonata, follow the score and listen to Beethoven's Op. 13 in its entirety. As you listen, be conscious of the dramatic nature of Beethoven's work (often associated with a eighteenth-century German literary movement known as *Sturm und Drang* ("Storm and Stress"). Notice the motivic nature of Beethoven's themes and the ease with which they lead from one key to the next. You might also be conscious of the key relationships—not just the tonality of the second-theme statements—but also of ways in which C minor is maintained overall as a principal key. Finally, assess the effect of the introductory material as a harbinger of important structural events throughout the movement.

L. van Beethoven, Sonata No. 8 in C Minor, Op. 13
("Pathetique"). First movement

[Not Recorded]

EXPOSITION
First Theme

Transition II

Eb Major

Eb Major

C Minor

Closing Section

C Minor

WORKBOOK/ANTHOLOGY II
II. Sonata Form in the Nineteenth Century
Beethoven, Sonata in D Minor, page 93

REVIEW AND APPLICATION 5–2

Later Developments in Sonata Form

Essential Terms

coda   introduction

1. For each characteristic of sonata form listed, choose the best answer from the given list.

A. Introduction   C. Both Coda and Introduction

B. Coda   D. Neither Coda nor Introduction

_____ a. extends the overall length of the sonata movement.

_____ b. may be tonally insecure.

_____ c. can rise to the importance of a second development section.

_____ d. may be *grave* or *lento* in tempo.

_____ e. enabled composers after Mozart and Haydn to personalize basic sonata form.

_____ f. usually centers around a key other than the tonic.

_____ g. occurs just before the development section.

2. The time lines below represent hypothetical sections of a sonata movement. First, identify the section in which such an arrangement of keys and themes might occur, by choosing *one or more* appropriate letters. If the suggested passage would not normally occur in a sonata movement, choose "D. None." Next, speculate on whether the time line represents basic sonata form (Haydn and Mozart) or an expansion of the sonata principle as represented by the works of Beethoven and others. Be prepared to discuss the basis of your conclusions.

A. Exposition   C. Recapitulation

B. Development   D. None

a.
First Theme	Transition	Second Theme
G Major		D Major

Section _____

b.
Ia	Ib	Ic	Dominant Caesura
G Major	E Minor	G Major	D Major

Section _____

c.
Second Theme	Transition	Closing Section
G Major		C Major

Section _____

d.
First Theme	Transition	Second Theme
G Major		E♭ Major

Section _____

SELF-TEST 5–2

Time Limit: 5 Minutes

1. Choose the best answer for each of the following questions. *Scoring: Subtract 20 points for each incorrect response.*

a._____ Which of the following is *not* a characteristic of a coda in sonata movements?

(1) extends the movement as a whole

(2) enhances final cadence

(3) reaffirms the related key

(4) provides an additional opportunity for development

b._____ Which of the following occurs just before the initial entry of the second theme?

(1) dominant caesura

(2) dominant pedal

(3) secondary dominant

(4) dominant transition

c._____ Which of the following is *not* a characteristic of introductory sections?

(1) may be tonally unstable

(2) often allegro in tempo

(3) includes theme fragments

(4) may include chromatic harmonies and embellishments

d._____ When a sonata movement is in minor, the most common related key is

(1) the tonic minor

(2) the subdominant

(3) the parallel major

(4) the relative major

e._____ Which characteristics are typical of composers of sonata movements in Beethoven's era and later?

(1) an interest in precise notation of dynamics and special effects

(2) distant keys associated with the digression

(3) longer development sections

(4) all of the above

Total Possible: 100   Your Score _____

PROJECTS

Analysis

The formal analysis of a sonata form is daunting for some. On the one hand, we have the means and may want occasionally to study the smallest elements of a sonata movement such as motives, phrases, periods, and double periods. Most often, however, we identify only the outlines of the sonata form itself: themes and keys, major sectional divisions, and the degree to which a movement does or does not conform to our expectations. Several movements appear in the present chapter with various degrees of analysis provided. In addition, note the following movements that appear in the text or the workbook without analytical notes. As directed, provide an analysis of one or more of these works. Identify keys as well as major sonata component parts and be prepared to discuss areas such as motivic development, contrast, texture, and so on.

Text

W. A. Mozart, Serenade for Strings, K. 525 (I), text pages 177-182. Viewing the score, we might assume Mozart's K. 525 to be a traditional string quartet. The work is labeled "Serenade," however, because it was intended for outdoor performance. Accordingly, the score specifies a *double* string quartet with an added bass. Trace the form of this work and mark keys, themes, sectional divisions, and other aspects of sonata form. Comment on the development section: Which themes are heard? How long is the development section?

Workbook/Anthology II

Joseph Haydn, Sonata in C Major H. 10 (I), workbook pages 79–81.
W. A. Mozart, Sonata in B♭ Major, K. 333 (I), workbook pages 83–91.
Ludwig van Beethoven, Sonata in D Minor Op. 31, No 2 (I), workbook pages 93–103.

Composition

Sonata Exposition.   Compose the exposition of a sonata for piano that is designed for younger performers. Begin by choosing tonic and polar keys, then compose a simple theme in both keys or plan a monothematic work in which one theme serves both tonic and polar roles. An appropriate theme will be a double period in length and might be repeated with an alternate accompaniment pattern. This sample theme is a sectional double period that comprises of parallel and contrasting phrase groups.

Our sample second theme is in F major and is another sectional double period.

Before composing the linking transition, consider accompaniment figures that will be appropriate for the first and second themes. Alberti bass is usually a good choice; reiterated chord tones and a quasi-contrapuntal texture (as in the next three examples) are additional possibilities.

There are many approaches to composing the transition. Because harmonic momentum is so important, you might begin with a chord progression such as the one that follows.

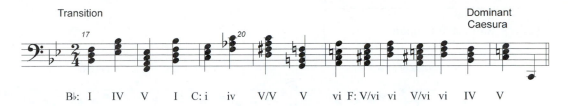

Transition   Dominant Caesura

B♭: I   IV   V   I   C: i   iv   V/V   V   vi   F: V/vi   vi   V/vi   vi   IV   V

Compose a simple melodic line for the transition that includes sequence and employs scalar figures. As we have discussed, many different accompanying patterns are appropriate.

Transition with Accompaniment

B♭: I   IV   V   I   C: i   iv   V/V   V

C: I   F: V/vi   vi   V/vi   vi   IV   V

Now, put the three pieces together for a sonata exposition through the statement of the second theme. Observe that only the last four measures of the first theme and first four measures of the second theme are shown.

CD 1, TRACK 82
Sample Transition

For Further Study

Domenico Scarlatti and the Evolution of Sonata Form. While we associate mature sonata form with Haydn and Mozart, the Baroque composer Domenico Scarlatti (1685–1757) was instrumental in the development of the form. In many of Scarlatti's works, for example, we can trace the emergence of polar keys and other elements that typify a later sonata form. Scarlatti was born in the same year as Bach and Handel, but is remembered today more as a transitional composer between the Baroque and Classical eras of Western music.

Write a paper or prepare notes for a presentation on Scarlatti and his importance. Include basic biographical information, a summary of his works, discussion of important positions held at various European capitals, and include an analysis of at least one sonata movement. Two complete Scarlatti sonatas are included in Volume I of the Workbook/Anthology: G Major, K 412, L. 182 and G major, K. 377, L. 388. A range of other sonatas should be available in your library. Specifically recommended for analysis are the sonatas in D Major, K. 96, L. 465 and B♭ Major, K. 544, L. 497.

CHAPTER 6

The Rondo

Considering the overwhelming distribution of pop-oriented electronic styles since the 1970s, some listeners have lamented the end of "classical" music as embodied in the works of Mozart, Brahms, and Debussy. From our perspective at the beginning of the twenty-first century, we may indeed forget that Western music has been in constant flux since its origin in the early Christian church. Most music composed in any given era has rather quickly disappeared as tastes changed, and as the passing of time separated great works from those that were mediocre. We have no reason to believe that the styles and media of "today" will be any more durable than those of yesterday.

One useful measure of universal value is adaptability. As we discussed in the previous chapter, sonata form was sufficiently flexible to interest composers not only in the Classical and Romantic eras, but into the twenty-first century as well. Another standard of durability is the relative length of time that an organizational principle has influenced musical composition. In this respect, sonata form is a relative newcomer in comparison to the *rondeau.*

The Baroque *Rondeau*

Baroque composers employed the term *RONDEAU* for sectional keyboard works in which a repeated phrase (the *rondeau*, also known as the REFRAIN) alternates with new material (the *COUPLET*). We use uppercase letters to represent both the refrain and the couplets. In the Baroque *rondeau*, both the *rondeau* theme and the intervening couplets are usually brief. The refrain occurs typically in the tonic key, while the couplets may be in the tonic or in related keys. *Rondeaux* (plural of *rondeau*) of different structures occur in seventeenth- and eighteenth-century keyboard literature. Those with five parts (three refrains and two couplets) and seven parts (four refrains and three couplets) are common.

Five-Part Rondeau

A	**B**	**A**	**C**	**A**
rondeau	couplet 1	rondeau	couplet 2	rondeau

Seven-Part Rondeau

A	**B**	**A**	**C**	**A**	**D**	**A**
rondeau	couplet 1	rondeau	couplet 2	rondeau	couplet 3	rondeau

François Couperin (1668–1733) was a French composer who is known today mainly for his works for the CLAVECIN, a small, rectangular keyboard instrument with an intimate tone quality. His *Soeur Monique* (*Sister Monique*) is a seven-part rondeau with an eight-measure refrain theme in F major. The first couplet (measure 10) is in C major.

CD 1, TRACK 83

François Couperin, *Soeur Monique*
Rondo Theme and First Couplet

After a return to the *rondeau* theme, the second couplet appears in D minor. Notice that both texture and melody are quite similar to the theme itself. Only the first four measures of the couplet are shown in the next example.

François Couperin, *Soeur Monique*
Second Couplet

SECOND COUPLET
(Measures 1-4)

D Minor

Couperin, *Soeur Monique*
Third Couplet

The third and final couplet brings an acceleration in momentum with sixteenth-note figuration in the bass and a faster moving melody. Again, only the first four measures of the couplet are shown.

THIRD COUPLET
(Measures 1-4)

F Major

A final statement of the *rondeau* theme concludes the work. Using letters to represent the various sections, the entire movement emerges as a seven-part form. Notice that the third couplet is in the tonic key and, along with *rondeau* statements that recur in the tonic as well, provides tonal security throughout the work.

A	B	A	C	A	D	A
Rondeau	First Couplet	Rondeau	Second Couplet	Rondeau	Third Couplet	Rondeau
F Major	C Major	F Major	D Minor	F Major	F Major	F Major

Baroque *rondeaux* are polyphonic works that alternate both a recurring melody and tonality with new material in one or more related keys. As discussed in the next section, however, the Classical-era rondo (with a more familiar spelling) is the form that composers often employed as the final movement in a sonata, symphony, concerto, or other major work. While the Baroque *rondeau* is interesting from a historical standpoint, the *rondo* begins in the eighteenth century with composers like Haydn and Mozart.

RONDO IN THE CLASSICAL ERA

Classical composers adapted the *rondeau* principle to the styles and tastes of eighteenth-century audiences. Four different rondo forms are common. The five- and seven-part rondos are similar to their Baroque counterparts. The *"classical" rondo* (page 244) employs a thematic structure similar to that of sonata form; the sonata-rondo, discussed on page 258, is yet another form that fuses the two principles.

In discussing and analyzing eighteenth- and nineteenth-century rondo forms, we use a special terminology. The refrain is better termed the RONDO THEME; the digressions to sections of new material are known as EPISODES. The rondo theme is virtually *always* in the tonic key, while the episodes occur in various contrasting keys. A FIVE-PART RONDO includes three statements of the rondo theme and two episodes; in the SEVEN-PART RONDO, we hear the rondo theme four times in alternation with three episodes. While the terminology is slightly different than we use in discussing Baroque *rondeau* movements, Classical rondos occur as similar sectional works with identical time-line structures.

Five-Part Rondo

A	B	A	C	A
Rondo Theme	First Episode	Rondo Theme	Second Episode	Rondo Theme

Seven-Part Rondo

A	B	A	C	A	D	A
Rondo Theme	First Episode	Rondo Theme	Second Episode	Rondo Theme	Third Episode	Rondo Theme

First, Second, and Third Rondos.   Rondo forms are often categorized as *first*, *second*, or *third*, respectively. The FIRST RONDO, with one episode, is equivalent to a simple ternary form (ABA). The five-part form is also known as SECOND RONDO (ABACA) and the THIRD RONDO is the seven-part form with three episodes (ABACADA). Although the use of the term "first rondo" is less common than "ternary," these designations have become alternate ways of referring to three-, five-, and seven-part rondos.

Five-Part (Second) and Seven-Part (Third) Rondos

Both five- and seven-part rondo forms are common in the Classical era. The rondo theme itself is usually periodic, with a well-defined melodic and rhythmic character. The mood is typically light and vivacious. Combined with rhythmic themes, sequence and repetition often make rondo melodies less serious in tone than sonata movements (although there are many exceptions). Likewise, the complete five- or seven-part rondo may be shorter than a sonata movement and, as discussed earlier, either form is common as the final movement in a sonata, symphony, concerto, or string quartet.

Key Relationships.   While the rondo theme itself is in the tonic key throughout, episodes may be in virtually any key. In sonata movements, structure revolves around the establishment of tonic and the digression to *one* polar key. A rondo is quite different in this respect. Our interest is still centered upon a central tonic key, but with multiple episodes, composers may choose two or three different CONTRASTING KEYS.[1] If the rondo theme is major, the first episode may be in the dominant; likewise, in minor, the relative major is a common related key. Subsequent episodes, however, are often in entirely new related keys. The subdominant is common, as is the relative or parallel major or minor. In addition, composers in the late eighteenth and nineteenth centuries employed third-related and other distant keys as well.

We will explore a basic five-part rondo using the third movement of Haydn's Sonata in D Major—an early work that includes the essential elements of the form without the complexities associated with later styles.

The rondo theme (**A**) of Haydn's Sonata in D Major unfolds with left and right hands joining in a hocket effect to articulate a single melodic line. The form of the theme is a sectional double period (two parallel periods). Notice that both

CD 1, TRACK 85

Joseph Haydn, Sonata in D Major (III)
Rondo Theme

periods are in D major. While only portions of the rondo are provided to amplify the present discussion, the full score appears on page 238 of this chapter.

RONDO THEME

D major

A sudden shift to the parallel minor launches the first episode (**B**). The texture changes, with right and left hands now in octaves. Again, the form is a sectional double period, but with the new material, the second of the periods begins F major (the relative major of the parallel minor key) and forms a third relation with the tonic. Haydn uses a four-measure transition in the second period to modulate from F major to D minor.

<hr>

[1]The term "polar key" is reserved for movements in sonata form because this relationship is so crucial to the form. In rondo and other forms, however, "contrasting key" denotes *all* possibilities other than tonic.

FIRST EPISODE

The rondo theme returns in measure 45 with the melody in the bass beneath figuration in the right hand—an embellished version of the initial presentation. Notice that with its recurring theme and key, rondo has the potential of serving as a type of variation form. In fact, at least one statement of the theme is actually a variation in most rondo movements. Only the first four measures of the second rondo statement are given below.

RETURN OF RONDO THEME

Haydn sets the second episode (**C**) in the dominant, which plays an important role in this rondo movement. Likewise, the use of a key signature (as opposed to accidentals) emphasizes the completeness of each section—a central characteristic of rondo form. The thematic material of Haydn's second episode is less regular in form than either the rondo theme or the first episode. Beginning in measure 61, the first part of **C** is a seven-measure (3 + 4) contrasting phrase group. This is followed by a sectional double period that is also asymmetrical (4 + 6; 3 + 4). The next example shows only the beginning of the second episode.

SECOND EPISODE

A Major

With the key back in D major, the final statement of the rondo theme appears in the bass. The right hand states an embellished version of the material that opened the work.

RETURN OF RONDO THEME

D major

Like many rondo movements, Haydn's work ends with a coda (measures 101–125). The first period of the original soprano/bass texture returns (this time in octaves), and is followed by a variation (repeated to end the movement).

A	**B**	**A**	**C**	**A**	
Rondo Theme ^{17}	First Episode ^{45}	Rondo Theme	^{61} Second Episode	^{85} Rondo Theme ^{101}	Coda
D Major	D Minor	D Major	A Major	D Major	

Although other composers wrote lengthier movements, Haydn's brief rondo has the essential components that define the form: a memorable rondo theme stated always in the tonic key, episodes of new material in contrasting keys, and a final coda that brings the work to a close. Likewise, observe that the rondo theme may return in an embellished or varied form in second and subsequent statements.

Listen to a recorded or live performance of Haydn's finale movement while following the score.

Finale
Allegro assai

A RONDO THEME

D major

B FIRST EPISODE

D Minor
(Modal Shift)

First Episode, Second Phrase Group

F Major

Transition to D Minor

Return of Initial Period

D Minor

A RONDO THEME

D Major

Rondo Theme, Second Period

C SECOND EPISODE

A Major

Second Episode,
Second Phrase Group

A RONDO THEME

D Major

Rondo Theme, Second Period

CODA   Rondo Theme

D Major

REVIEW AND APPLICATION 6–1

Rondo I

Essential Terms

clavecin	first rondo	rondo	second rondo
contrasting key	five-part rondo	*rondeau*	seven-part rondo
couplet	refrain	rondo theme	third rondo
episode			

1. Choose a letter from the list that reflects the best terminology for the characteristic given.

    A. Baroque *rondeau*

    B. Classical-era rondo

    C. None of these

_____   a. a sectional composition for piano

_____   b. modulates to the dominant at the end of the rondo theme

_____   c. may be found as the final movement of a sonata or symphony

_____   d. often performed on the clavecin

_____   e. includes one or more couplets

_____   f. includes one or more episodes

2. In discussing rondo forms, we often use the terms "first," "second," and "third." Choose one *or more* letters from the list to match with each given statement.

    A. First rondo

    B. Second rondo

    C. Third rondo

    D. All of the above

    E. None of the above

_____   a. includes three episodes

_____   b. composed for clavecin

_____   c. also known as simple binary form

_____   d. has three statements of the rondo theme

_____   e. has only one episode

_____   f. most common rondo form in the eighteenth century

_____   g. may include a coda

_____   h. key more important than theme in structural organization

3. Provide a time-line analysis for each of the forms suggested. Notice that the key for the first (**A**) part is stipulated in each case. Include uppercase letters to represent additional major sections. Finally, name likely keys for each episode and for each subsequent rondo theme statement.

a. First Rondo

A

B Major

b. Seven-Part Rondo

A

G Major

c. Second Rondo

A

B♭ Major

SELF-TEST 6–1

Time Limit: 5 Minutes

1. In each of the following groups, make a check mark by the correct statement. *Scoring: Subtract 20 points for each incorrect answer.*

   a. Which of the following statements best describes the key scheme of the eighteenth-century rondo?

   _____ (1) The rondo theme is always associated with the tonic key.

   _____ (2) Episodes are typically in related keys.

   _____ (3) Keys in a rondo form are more varied and flexible than in a sonata movement.

   _____ (4) All of these statements are true.

   b. Which of the following statements is *not* true of the rondo theme itself?

   _____ (1) The structure is usually a period or phrase group.

   _____ (2) The theme begins in the tonic and ends in a contrasting key.

   _____ (3) Subsequent statements may be variations.

   _____ (4) The rondo is always in the tonic key.

   c. The seven-part rondo

   _____ (1) is also known as a "second" rondo.

   _____ (2) includes four statements of the rondo theme.

   _____ (3) is not very common in the Classical era.

   _____ (4) has four different episodes.

2. Match one of the form sequences from the list with each description given.
Scoring: Subtract 8 points for each incorrect answer.

A. **A B A C A**   E. **A B C D A**

B. **A B C**   F. **A B A**

C. **A B C A D A**   G. **A B C A B C A**

D. **A B**   H. **A B A C A D A**

_____ a. First rondo

_____ b. Simple binary

_____ c. Seven-part rondo

_____ d. Simple ternary

_____ e. Second rondo

Total Possible: 100   Your Score _____

THE CLASSICAL RONDO

Five- and seven-part rondos were especially popular forms in the Classical era. One particular adaptation of the seven-part form, however, is known as a *classical* rondo because it embodies the late eighteenth-century preoccupation with thematic symmetry. A CLASSICAL RONDO is one that has the form **A B A C A B A**. The third episode is based upon the same melodic material as the first; the key may be the same or different.

Beethoven's Sonata in E Major, Op. 14, No. 1 concludes with a classical rondo. The rondo theme (**A**), shown in the next example, is a contrasting period and more motivic in structure than we would expect from a composer such

CD 1, TRACK 88
**Ludwig van Beethoven, Sonata in E Major, Op. 14, No. 1 (III)
Rondo Theme**

as Haydn or Mozart. The theme begins in the tonic key. Note on the score (pages 252–258) that the theme is presented in octaves with a triplet accompaniment.

After a partial repetition of the theme, a transition (measures 14–21) effects a modulation to the dominant. Note the imitative structure of the transi-

CD 1, TRACK 89-1 TRANSITION AND FIRST EPISODE (2 PARTS)
**Beethoven, Op. 14, No. 1
Transition**

tion; Beethoven provides continuity by using the most memorable motive from the rondo theme to advance toward the first episode.

Transition

The first episode (**B**) is an eight-measure repeated phrase (measures 22–30). While Beethoven wrote a seven-measure transition between the initial rondo statement and the first episode, the return to the rondo (and E major) is accomplished in a single measure. Refer to the full piano score on pages 252–258 to compare the left-hand triplets of the rondo theme with the sparse accompaniment of the first episode (merely a bass line for the harmonic progression ii_6–I_4^6–V–I in B major).

TRACK 89-2 TRANSITION AND FIRST EPISODE
Beethoven, Op. 14, No. 1
First Episode

FIRST EPISODE

B Major

The rondo theme returns in the last half of measure 30 (not shown in the example below). As the repetition of the first phrase begins, however, Beethoven shifts to the parallel minor and starts a transition to the second episode and the key of G major. Throughout the transition, the composer avoids the tonic, so that the beginning of the second episode and a firm establishment of G major coincide. Measures 41–46 of the transition occur over a dominant pedal and increase our expectation of the new key. Finally, observe that while an analysis of successive quarter notes in measures 38–41 makes harmonic sense (with the submediant substituted for the tonic), the harmony is incidental to the momentum of the bass line that begins with G_3 and descends stepwise all the way to D_2.

CD 1, TRACK 90
**Beethoven, Op. 14, No. 1
Return of Rondo Theme**

RONDO THEME

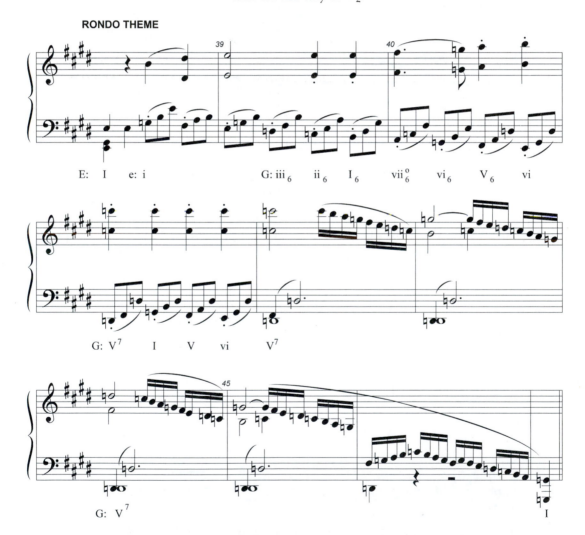

We would be hard pressed to call the second episode (**C**) a "theme." The arpeggiations in signature triplets ascend forcefully from G_2 (measure 47) to E_6 (measure 54). The real interest is in the bass where we hear a motive from the transitional passage.

Transition to First Episoide   Bass in Second Episode

Beethoven increases the tension in the second episode by initially stating only two of the six pitches (conveniently $\hat{5}$ and $\hat{1}$) rather than entire motive it-

CD 1, TRACK 91
Beethoven, Op. 14, No. 1
Second Episode

self. The passage opens in G major (measures 47–50), moves to A minor (51–54), and finally to B minor (measures 54–58.)

SECOND EPISODE

In measure 66 (see page 255), the second-episode material appears to re-peat in E minor, but a dominant pedal (measure 76) signals the return of the rondo theme. A chromatic scale spans four octaves, further emphasizing the pitch B and ending on $\hat{5}$ (measure 83).

Overall, the second episode has a decidedly developmental effect—although no full statement of the rondo theme occurs.[2] Study the full score of measures 47–80 as they appear on page 254. In a detailed analysis of this episode, we would want to note the most important keys, the appearance of the full transition motive, the repetition of material in E minor, and the dominant pedal. These elements are traced on a time line in the next example.

Second Episode

The third statement of the rondo theme (see page 256) presents the familiar octaves in the right hand combined with triplets in the left. The transition to the third episode, however (shown in the next example), is altered to permit a modulation to the subdominant (where in the first episode, the key is the dominant). As a contrasting area, the subdominant is slightly unusual but can be seen as a counterbalance to the dominant key in the first episode (the key a fifth above the tonic is balanced by the key a fifth below).

The third episode is a tonal reinterpretation of the first, and creates the symmetry characteristic of the "classical" rondo (analogous in some respects to the tonal reinterpretation in the recapitulation of a sonata form). Beethoven's choice of the subdominant, however, highlights the rondo's more flexible tonal structure. In a sonata movement, a recapitulation with the second theme in the subdominant key is extraordinary; in a rondo, with the stability of a recurring theme and tonic key, the subdominant is only another of many possible choices.

CD 1, TRACK 92
Beethoven, Op. 14, No. 1
Third Episode

THIRD EPISODE

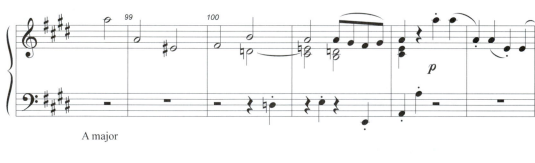

---

[2]When the second episode is a full-fledged development, with the statement of one or more themes, the form is termed a sonata-rondo (discussed on page 258).

The harmony in measures 103–108 of the previous example has more than one interpretation. First, we might view the passage as a shift to the parallel minor with the B♭ in measures 104–105 and numerous other pitches heard as nonchordal. A more sophisticated analysis, however, reveals a brief tonicization of F major prior to the return of the tonic key in measure 108. The passage begins in A major. With the D♮ and F♮ in measure 104, the harmony shifts to the parallel minor. Although the use and resolution are somewhat atypical, we may understand the B♭ major chord in measure 104 as a Neapolitan in A minor. At the same time, this chord is the subdominant in F major (which is established in measure 106). Beethoven slips back into E major through chromatic movement (F–F♯ in the bass and E–D♯ in the soprano).

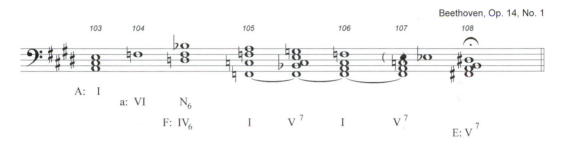

Beethoven, Op. 14, No. 1

As we discussed previously, passages with "complex harmonies," such as the one seen in measures 103–108, are usually not all that complex in works before the middle of the nineteenth century. At the same time, brief digressions to distant keys create a degree of instability that will be resolved when the tonic reappears. We might also note that while Beethoven created full transitions between the rondo theme and the first and second episodes, respectively, the modulation back to tonic in both cases is achieved through a cessation in momentum.

Beethoven concludes the movement with a final statement of the rondo theme (shown below in part). To increase tension and momentum, this last pronouncement centers on a rhythmic two- against-three figure. The eighth-note syncopation in the upper voice is paired with the familiar triplets in the left hand.

CD 1, TRACK 93-1 CONCLUSION (3 PARTS)
Beethoven, Op. 14, No. 1
Rondo Theme

RONDO THEME

While we recognize the rondo theme through the key and triplet accompaniment, Beethoven immediately digresses to stepwise lines in soprano and bass. Moving in contrary motion, the lines converge on a dramatic diminished

TRACK 93-2 CONCLUSION
Beethoven, Op. 14, No. 1
Transition

seventh (measures 117–119) and culminate with the familiar dominant-seventh fermata (measure 121).

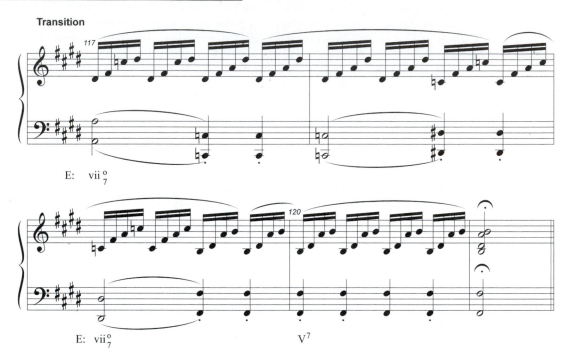

Throughout the final movement of Beethoven's Op. 14, No. 1, we have become accustomed to hearing a break in the tempo (with a dominant seventh or fifth scale degree) as the prelude to a major event. Accordingly, this last fermata heralds a coda beginning in the second half of measure 121. The composer further exploits the two-against-three rhythms before ending with the same transitional material that was heard in first, second, and third episodes. Thus, while the rondo theme announces the beginning of sections, the scalar material is heard at their conclusion.

TRACK 93-3 CONCLUSION
Beethoven, Op. 14, No. 1
Coda

CODA

The final movement of Beethoven's Sonata in E Major is a seven-part rondo with the characteristic we term "classical"—the first episode recurs as the third. All four instances of the rondo theme are in the tonic key. Digressions occur in B major (dominant), G major (a third relation to the tonic), and A major (subdominant). Earlier composers stated complete, periodic themes and linked them with transitions, but Beethoven centers many of his works on more minimal materials such as motives, subphrases, and phrases. These smaller units evolve during the composition to create both a higher degree of spontaneity and a developmental effect.

Study the time line below and then follow the score as you listen to a performance of the complete rondo movement.

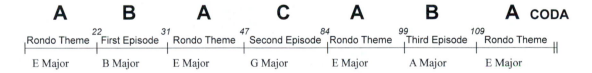

A	**B**	**A**	**C**	**A**	**B**	**A** CODA
	22	31	47	84	99	109
Rondo Theme	First Episode	Rondo Theme	Second Episode	Rondo Theme	Third Episode	Rondo Theme
E Major	B Major	E Major	G Major	E Major	A Major	E Major

[Not Recorded]

Ludwig van Beethoven, Sonata in E Major, Op. 14, No. 1
Third Movement

B major

A RONDO THEME

E: V^7 I

Transition to Second Episode

E minor (modal shift)

G: Dominant Pedal

Repetition of C material

E minor

E major: Dominant Pedal

A major

A **RONDO THEME** (Varied)

SONATA-RONDO

The popularity of sonata form affected many aspects of Western music. As we have seen in the classical rondo, the first episode returns as the third (often in a different key). In the late Classical era, some composers carried the integration a step farther, and provided a full development section as the second episode of the rondo movement. In this case, when the third episode is also heard as a "recapitulation" of the first, the form combines sections that we might describe as "exposition," "development," and "recapitulation." The hybrid form, diagramed below, is termed SONATA-RONDO.

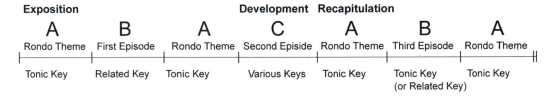

Exposition			Development	Recapitulation		
A	B	A	C	A	B	A
Rondo Theme	First Episode	Rondo Theme	Second Episide	Rondo Theme	Third Episode	Rondo Theme
Tonic Key	Related Key	Tonic Key	Various Keys	Tonic Key	Tonic Key (or Related Key)	Tonic Key

Sonata-rondo was popular during the late eighteenth and early nineteenth centuries, but declined after about 1840, as composers began to favor works that were generally shorter and less predictable. The form is common in the works of Mozart and Beethoven, however. The third movement of Mozart's Sonata in D Major, K. 576 is a sonata-rondo that offers an interesting introduction to the form. In addition to a development as the second episode, Mozart provides two themes for the first episode. The first of these is a restatement of the rondo theme in the dominant. As a general rule, the terms "monothematic" and "rondo" are mutually exclusive, but we will explore presently how the composer uses a dominant statement of the rondo theme to temporarily mislead the listener about the form. In addition to the excerpts cited in the following discussion of Mozart's K. 576 (third movement), the full score begins on page 264.

The rondo theme that Mozart composed for K. 576 is a parallel double pe-

CD 1, TRACK 94
W. A. Mozart, Sonata in D Major, K. 576 (III)
Rondo Theme

riod that centers on a prominent chromatic passing tone. The final phrase of the theme borrows from the triplet accompaniment, outlining diatonic triads.

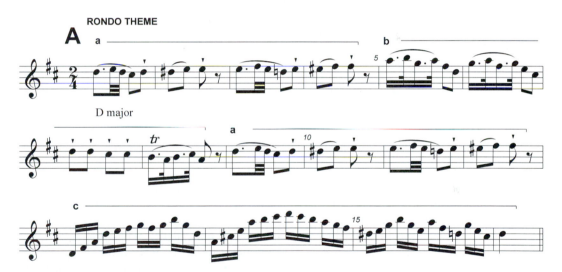

After a brief transitional passage (that later assumes the role of a closing section), a dominant caesura signals the next event—a statement of the rondo theme in the dominant. Despite our label "B, First Episode" (measures 22–29), the listener is unaware at this point in the work that the form is a rondo. The sequence of keys and themes suggests a monothematic sonata form.

CD 1, TRANSITION AND FIRST EPISODE, PART I
(2 PARTS) TRACK 95-1
Mozart, K. 576
Transition to First Episode (Part I)

Transition to First Episode

Dominant Caesura

B FIRST EPISODE

(Rondo Theme in Dominant)

A major

Following a passage in which the right and left hands alternate with the first measures of the rondo theme (not shown), Mozart begins a vivacious transition that includes triplets, syncopation, and another cadence in A major (measures 40–50). A new theme now appears in the dominant and is heard as the second member of the contrasting-key group (remember, as listeners, we would still assume that the movement is a sonata form). The new theme is unpretentious, but in its generally descending direction, provides contrast to the rondo theme. An embellished version of the first phrase follows to complete the period.

TRACK 95-2 TRANSITION AND FIRST EPISODE
Mozart, K. 576
First Episode, Part II

FIRST EPISODE, IIa

A major

For the first 64 measures of the K. 576 finale, the form is ambiguous. With the return of the rondo theme and the tonic key in measure 65, however, uncertainty is dispelled: The work is a rondo. Retroactively, we hear the statement of the theme in the dominant as the beginning of the first episode and not as the beginning of the second-theme group in a sonata form. The return of the rondo unfolds exactly as it did in the opening segment. The transitional material, first heard in measure 17, now leads to the second episode. Accentuating the form as a sonata-rondo, this section offers not a new theme (as would be the case with a conventional seven-part rondo), but the development of the rondo theme. On a time line (page 263), we use the designation **C** because the development functions as a second episode.

A modal shift to D minor (measure 84) initiates the development. Just as in typical sonata movements of Classical composers, the development section in this sonata-rondo (measures 84–116) hinges on motives from the main theme and its triplet accompaniment. The manipulation of these materials includes imitation as well as tonicizations of various keys, including D minor, F major, G minor, and others. Two brief passages from the development are shown in the next examples. In

CD 1, TRACK 96-1 EXCERPTS FROM DEVELOPMENT (2 PARTS)
Mozart, K. 576
Transition to Development

the first passage below (measures 84–88), notice the similarity to the second episode of Beethoven's Op. 14, No. 1. Arpeggios in the right hand are punctuated with strong dominant-tonic statements in the left.

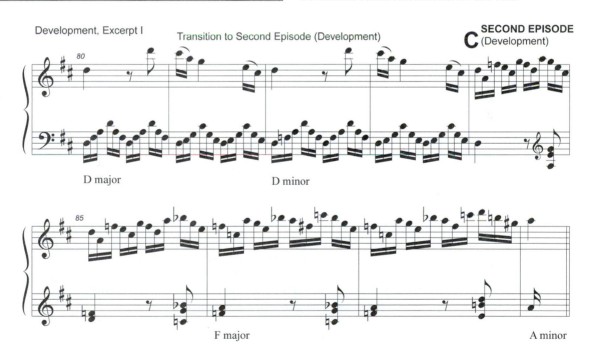

A second passage from the development (measures 103–116) shows Mozart's use of imitation to create a dense and volatile texture.

TRACK 96-2 EXCERPTS FROM DEVELOPMENT
Mozart, K. 576
Transition Back to Rondo Theme

The beginning of the rondo theme returns in measure 117 (a "recapitulation" in sonata parlance), although right and left hands continue to "trade" the motive between them. This material (measures 117–141) is largely a transposition of the first episode (measures 26–50) to the tonic. Now, the importance of the contrasting first-episode material (measures 51–58) is apparent (measure 142) as the third episode, and in the tonic key.

CD 1, TRACK 97
Mozart, K. 576
Third Episode

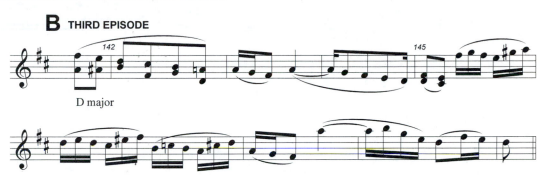

B THIRD EPISODE

D major

The movement concludes with a final statement of the rondo theme (measure 163) and a brief coda (measures 181–189). These are shown in full on pages 264–272.

In structure, Mozart's K. 576 finale is important, not only in accentuating the pervading influence of sonata form in the late eighteenth and nineteenth centuries, but in showing how ingenious composers pumped energy into well-known formal models. Consider how Mozart plays with the audience in this movement. While other forms are common, we naturally expect a rondo for the final movement. When the theme returns in the dominant, however, we reevaluate this perception and assume a monothematic sonata form. The recurrence of the theme in D major turns our expectations again toward rondo, however, and when the descending eighth-note melody (First Episode, Part II) appears as the third episode, we understand the composer's plan.

Study the time line below; then follow the score as you listen to a live or recorded performance of this interesting work.

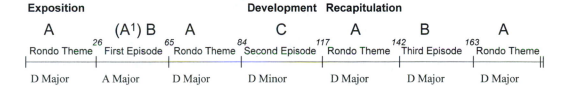

[Not Recorded]

Allegretto

W. A. Mozart, Sonata in D Major, K. 576
Third Movement

B **FIRST EPISODE, Part I**
(Rondo Theme in Dominant)

FIRST EPISODE, Part II

A major

Transition back to rondo theme

Dominant pedal

A   **RONDO THEME**

p

D major

(Closing Section)

D major

**C SECOND EPISODE
(DEVELOPMENT)**

D minor

F major

A RETURN OF RONDO THEME (RECAPITULATION)

D major

B THIRD EPISODE (First Episode, Part II)

D major

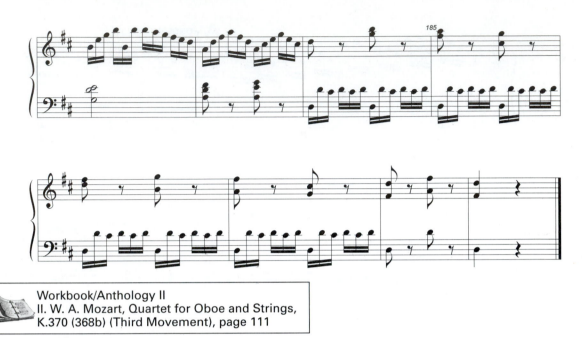

Workbook/Anthology II
II. W. A. Mozart, Quartet for Oboe and Strings,
K.370 (368b) (Third Movement), page 111

REVIEW AND APPLICATION 6–2

Variations of Rondo Form

Essential Terms

classical rondo   sonata-rondo

1. Provide an appropriate term for each of the following sectional works. In addition to rondo forms, consider others discussed in both volumes of the text (binary, sonata form, and so on). If the sketched form conforms to none of those studied (if, for example, the key scheme is atypical), then write "none" in the blank. Assume E♭ major as the tonic key in all cases.

_____ a.   **A**   **A¹**
                     E♭   B♭   B♭   E♭

_____ b.   **A**   **B**   **A**   **C**   **A**
                     E♭   B♭   E♭   c   E♭

_____ c.   **A**   **B**   **A**
                     E♭   B♭   B♭   E♭

_____ d.   **A**   **B**   **A**   **C**   **A**   **D**   **A**
                     E♭   B♭   E♭   c   E♭   A♭   E♭

_____ e.   **A**   **B**   **A**   **C**   **A**   **B**   **A**
                     E♭   B♭   E♭   c   E♭   E♭   E♭

2. For the characteristics listed, match one *or more* choices that apply.

A. seven-part rondo   D. expanded ternary

B. classical rondo   E. none of these

C. sonata-rondo

_____ a. Seven-part form

_____ b. Five-part form

_____ c. First part ends in the tonic key

_____ d. First part ends in a related key

_____ e. Includes a development section

_____ f. Third episode has the same material as the first episode

_____ g. Second episode is in the tonic key

_____ h. Includes only one episode

3. The time lines shown have discrete names. Provide the name of the form shown. Be aware that these diagrams include forms discussed in Volume I of this text as well as the first six chapters of Volume II. If a time line represents no form studied, write "none."

a.
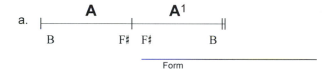

Form _____

b.

Form _____

c.

Form _____

d.

Form _____

e.

A   B   Development   A   B

c   E♭   E♭   c   c

Form _____

f.

Form _____

SELF-TEST 6–2

Time Limit: 5 Minutes

1. Make a check mark by the correct statement. *Scoring: Subtract 15 points for each incorrect answer.*

   a. In sonata-rondo form,

   _____ (1) the first episode begins in the tonic key.

   _____ (2) key choices are more flexible than in sonata form.

   _____ (3) there are four episodes.

   _____ (4) the third episode is a development.

   b. In a classical rondo,

   _____ (1) there are two different rondo themes.

   _____ (2) the first episode begins in the tonic key.

   _____ (3) the first and third episodes are the same in melodic material.

   _____ (4) the second episode is a reinterpretation of the first episode in the dominant key.

   c. The most essential difference between rondo and sonata forms concerns

   _____ (1) themes.

   _____ (2) keys.

   _____ (3) use of a dominant caesura.

   _____ (4) appearance of a coda.

   d. Which of the following is typical of rondo forms?

   _____ (1) sections are connected by a fermata and not transitional material.

   _____ (2) the parallel major/minor key is not a possibility for a contrasting key.

   _____ (3) there may be a coda.

   _____ (4) episodes occasionally appear in the tonic key.

2. In each of the following classical rondos diagramed, one element (and only one) is incorrect. This may be either a key designation or a letter representing musical material. Circle the incorrect or unlikely element *and* provide a correct response. In some cases, more than one correct answer is possible. The tonic key is B major. *Scoring: Subtract 10 points for each incorrect answer.*

		A	B	A	C	A	C	A
a.	Key:	B	F♯	B	E	B	B	B
b.		A	B	A	C	A	D	A
	Key:	B	F♯	B	E	F♯	B	B
c.		A	B	A	B	A	B	A
	Key:	B	B	B	e	B	F♯	B
d.		A	B	A	C	A	B	A
	Key:	B	F♯	B	g♯	B	F♯	F♯

Total Possible: 100   Your Score _____

PROJECTS

Analysis

Several rondo movements for analysis are available in the text and Workbook/Anthology. Be prepared to discuss aspects of assigned movements in some or all of the following areas:

a. Specify the overall form the work (seven-part rondo, sonata-rondo, classical rondo, and so on). Discuss key and theme relationships and prepare a time-line diagram.

b. Discuss how the composer handles transitions between major sections of the work. Are they similar in scope? different? What is the basis of melodic material in the transitions? Are there textural differences between transitions and themes/episodes?

c. What is the form of the rondo theme itself?

d. Comment on the melodic and rhytmic character of each episode. How are episodes contrasted with the rondo theme?

e. Is there a coda in the work? Does the work have unusual features otherwise?

f. Summarize the work in terms of harmonic vocabulary, the use of rhythmic or metric devices, melodic style, and proportion.

Text

W. A. Mozart, Serenade for Strings, K. 525 (III), text pages 278–284. The first movement of Mozart's double quartet K. 525 (*Eine Kleine Nachtmusik*) was used to begin Unit 3 of this volume (page 177). The final movement is offered here as a concluding project in the study of rondo form.

Workbook/Anthology II

Ludwig van Beethoven, Sonata in C Minor Op. 13 ("Pathetique") (II), workbook pages 105–109.

W. A. Mozart, Quartet for Oboe and Strings, K 370 (368b) (III), workbook pages 111–120.

Composition

Compose a classical rondo for unaccompanied B♭ clarinet or other instrument as specified by your instructor. Begin by writing a theme that is basically classical in style. Prepare a transposed score for the clarinet (sounding a major second lower). See Appendix B for the clarinet written range. This sample rondo theme is a sectional double period.

CD 1, TRACK 98-1 RONDO PROJECT (4 PARTS)
Rondo Theme

With a brief linking passage, you could simply repeat the theme. A longer transition, as shown in the next example, exploits the clarinet lower register and moves through the keys of G minor and D minor before arriving at the dominant in preparation for the first episode.

TRACK 98-2 RONDO PROJECT
Transition to First Episode

TRACK 98-3 RONDO PROJECT
First Episode

Because the rondo theme is rhythmic, we might compose a more lyric melody for the first episode.

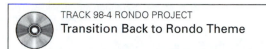

TRACK 98-4 RONDO PROJECT
Transition Back to Rondo Theme

After a lengthy transition from the rondo theme to first episode, the return to the rondo theme might be brief.

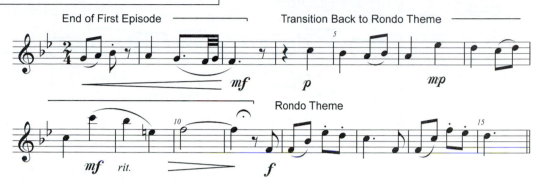

Consider Beethoven's motivic approach for a second episode. Clarinettists are accustomed to passage work, so let your performer shine. After the second episode (which might be brief), return to the rondo theme for a third time. Complete the movement by reinterpreting the first (lyric) episode in a new key (the subdominant, perhaps), state the rondo theme a final time, and end with a short coda.

For Further Study

The Concerto.   Depending upon the era, a *concerto* is a work for one instrument and orchestra (solo concerto) or a small ensemble and orchestra (called a *concerto grosso*). Investigate the development of concerto forms from the Baroque era to the nineteenth century. Divide your study into three parts. In the first part, gather information on solo and ensemble concertos in the Baroque era. Comment on the number of movements encountered and their characteristics. Mention *basso continuo* and its role in accompanying the solo instrument or instruments and the orchestra as well. Name several composers who wrote concertos in the Baroque era and prepare a listening list of two or three major works.

Devote the second part of your study to the solo concerto in the days of Haydn and Mozart. How many movements are usually found in the classical concerto? Which forms are most common for each? Who were major concerto composers? Which intruments were most popular in solo roles? What is a *cadenza* and how is this section contrasted with other sections of the concerto? Again, prepare a listening list with several representative works from the Classical era.

Finally, investigate *double-exposition sonata form* as is often encountered in the first movement of a classical-era concerto. Provide a diagram of this form and identify elements that are the same and those that are different from sonata form proper.

The first movement of Mozart's double quartet K. 525 (*Eine Kleine Nachmusik*) was used to begin Unit 3 of this volume (page 177). The final movement is given here. You might expect the form to be a rondo, but which type did Mozart employ? Provide a formal analysis, including time line as well as discussion of thematic content and key scheme.

W. A. Mozart, Serenade for Strings, K. 525
Fourth Movement

UNIT 4

Tonal Music in Transition

Debussy, "The Girl with the Flaxen Hair" from *Préludes I*

Chapter 7
Dissolution of the Common-Practice Style

Chapter 8
Impressionism

Chapter 9
National and Ethnic Resources

The term "Common-Practice Era" denotes Western music from about 1680 until the end of the nineteenth century. Like similar movements in art and literature, common-practice music originated from radical and controversial principles of organization in the early Baroque era. Later, these principles were held in universally high esteem as a classical era of tonal music evolved. However, as the traditional approach to harmony, melody, rhythm, and form began to be questioned after about 1830 (as young composers proposed their own radical and controversial ideas), the "classical" and the revolutionary existed side by side. The Frenchman Giacomo Meyerbeer (1791–1864) and Berlin composer Johann Hummel (1778–1837) are among those who continued to explore classical ideals in the decades after Beethoven; others, like Chopin and Wagner championed new, romantic expressions of music as a form of art. Yet all three periods—Baroque, Classical, and Romantic—are unified by a single musical system: *Functional Tonality*.

While music theorists and historians often center their studies on the emergence of a new musical system (meter in the fourteenth century; homophony in the seventeenth; serialism and other trends in the twentieth), the gradual dissolution of a time-tested approach to composing music is equally fascinating. In Chapter 7, we will discuss many of the harmonic and melodic

285

innovations that led to a gradual questioning of functional tonality as a central organizing principle. Composers like Chopin began experimenting with the resolution of dissonance, new key relationships, and innovative passages in which the tonality was intentionally obscured. Franz Liszt (1811–1886), Richard Wagner, and others, remained faithful to the notion of a tonal center, but developed their own special approaches to the relationships among diatonic triads.

In Chapter 8 of Unit 4, our studies center on both the musical style of Claude Debussy (1862–1918), known as Impressionism, and the many allied innovations that represent a major turning point in Western music. Debussy's music is tonal, but not often functional. Tertian chords are alternated with sonorities based on fourths; melodies may be major or minor, but just as often, they reflect patterns from the Renaissance as well as newly devised (synthetic) scales. Like the French painters who originated the Impressionist movement, color was important to Debussy. His use of traditional instruments to obtain unique shadings and special effects is another interesting facet of the Impressionist style.

While Debussy was employing quartal harmony and Medieval modal materials, other composers in the late nineteenth century independently adopted nonfunctional tonal styles that relied on melodies, rhythms, and harmonic resources from their native countries and regions. After all, the early twentieth century was a time of major discoveries in archeology; foreign travel was relatively safe; and international exhibitions inclined the listening public to look past their own cultures to sample a world of new and exotic sounds. The invention of the phonograph permitted the recording and transcription of folk music as it was performed in peasant villages throughout Europe. In Hungary, composers like Béla Bartók (1881–1945) and Zoltán Kodály (1882–1967) were inspired by such authentic folk materials and, as we will discuss in Chapter 9, this attraction is reflected in melodic patterns, rhythms, instrumental effects, and programmatic themes. At the same time, Gustav Holst (1874–1934) and Ralph Vaughan Williams (1872–1958) employed English folk melodies in their symphonies and choral works. In America, Charles Ives (1874–1954) developed a style that included not only traditional hymns, Civil War tunes, and popular melodies (sometimes simultaneously), but a wealth of novel and striking effects as well.

In Unit 4, we will focus not only on the end of the common-practice style, but on the quest for a new means of musical expression.

In 1877, **Achille-Claude Debussy** was a student at the Conservatory of Music in Paris. He clashed frequently with his harmony teacher, Emil Durand (himself a minor composer of traditional French opera). In his 1937 biography, *Debussy: Man and Artist*, Oscar Thompson relates how the young student enjoyed irritating his teacher by occupying the piano after lessons and improvising works that included exceptional harmonies and nontraditional melodies. More than once, Professor Durand slammed down the cover of the piano and exclaimed "You had better do your lessons!"[1] Thompson tells us that after class, Durand saved grading Debussy's papers for last.

---

[1] Oscar Thompson, *Debussy: Man and Artist* (Dodd, Mead & Co., 1937).

After Durand had examined and duly rated everyone else in the class, he applied himself to Achille-Claude's exercise book with the satisfaction of righteous indignation. Strokes of his pencil rained down, corrections fell like hail.

Today, Claude Debussy, the radical and impertinent student, is one of the most widely performed composers in the Western world; Emil Durand is remembered mainly as his teacher. Debussy is one of a handful of composers whose ideas were at once so powerful and so masterfully expressed that they literally changed the course of Western music.[2] Generations of later composers were influenced by his novel ideas about melody and harmony; more important, some of these men and women began with Debussy's innovative methods and established new and influential styles of their own.

Like Chopin, Debussy wrote a group of character pieces for piano called *Préludes.* The two books of *Préludes* are among Debussy's most significant compositions, since they represent a catalogue of Impressionist materials and techniques. Book I comprises twelve separate works and appeared in 1910; a second set of twelve (Book II) followed in 1913. "The Girl with the Flaxen Hair" is the eighth Prélude in *Book I.*

At first glance, "The Girl with the Flaxen Hair" (pages 288–289) appears to be little different from similar character pieces by Brahms and Chopin. As we will discuss fully in Chapter 8, however, many elements of the work are entirely outside the Romantic-era vocabulary. The opening melody, for example, is neither major nor minor, but *pentatonic.* Likewise, while a tonal center is typically present throughout the work, authentic cadences are rare (the first cadence, in measures 2–3, for example, is plagal). Chords are tertian, but their use generally eludes functional roles. Especially striking is the lengthy series of parallel seventh chords (measures 24–28) which constitutes a new organizational harmonic principle that we will discuss in detail. The work is ternary with an abbreviated final section. In Debussy's *Prélude,* however, the numerous transient points of color—none of them repeated exactly—are more characteristic than the ABA structure. In short, "The Girl with the Flaxen Hair" is far removed from the harmonic and melodic practices of Brahms or Chopin. In Unit 4, we will focus on how these changes came about, and assess their influence on generations of later composers.

[2]Many consider Claudio Monteverdi and Ludwig van Beethoven to have been similarly influential transitional composers from Renaissance to the Baroque era, and from the Classical to the Romantic eras, respectively.

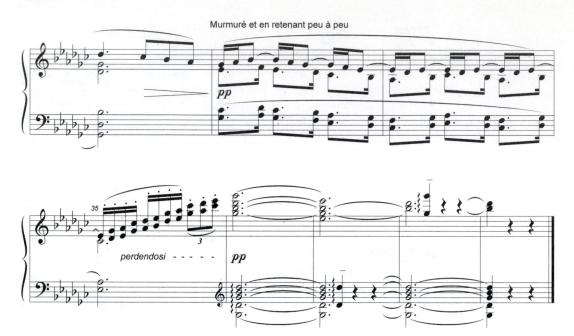

CHAPTER 7

Dissolution of the Common-Practice Style

Just as it took nearly a century for late Renaissance and early Baroque composers to fully grasp and utilize tonal principles as a means of organization, the gradual dissolution of the tonal system occurred over a similar period. We might surmise that the tonal system virtually began to dissipate from the moment it was perceived as being standard. Bach and other Baroque composers retained at least some vestiges of the old modal system in their works, but Haydn and Mozart represent tonality in its clearest sense. Not only did tonal principles define the relationships among themes, but composers of the Classical era used tonality to separate and clarify major sections of lengthy works. Even before 1850, however, innovative composers like Frédéric Chopin and Hector Berlioz (1803–1869) began to experiment within the tonal system. Later composers, Richard Wagner, Franz Liszt, and Claude Debussy among them, demonstrated to enthusiastic audiences that unambiguous tonality, was, in its "classical" sense, wholly unnecessary for a successful musical work.

We might prefer to take a chronological approach to documenting the gradual decay of tonality as a fundamental organizing principle, but we cannot. The process of change was on-going from at least the second quarter of the nineteenth century. Between about 1840 and 1890, innovative composers asserted their individuality through one *or more* of three primary means. First, they used melodic forces (ascending lines, descending lines, soprano and bass in contrary motion) to generate momentum toward a tonic. Others chose to alter and expand on models of the Classical and Romantic eras with chords and pitches that remained basically functional, but reveled in unique colors and exceptional resolutions. Finally, some composers wrote sections and complete compositions that were intentionally *nonfunctional* in comparison with common-practice ideals.

A RENAISSANCE OF MELODY

The nineteenth century was a time of expressive melody. *Lieder*, opera, and other vocal *genre* afforded composers an opportunity to create dramatic phrases that at times became the generating force for harmony. These same principles were often applied to instrumental media. In the keyboard work *Elegy* by the Norwegian composer Edvard Grieg (1843–1907), for example, the harmony is nothing more than a pedal in thirds (in the soprano). The melody in the left hand captivates our interest as it descends sequentially in two-measure segments from B_4 to $C\sharp_4$. A roman-numeral analysis of this passage is useless, since the phrase is melodically—not harmonically—conceived. We might note the root and quality of each chord formed incidentally by the pedal and melody together (some of them enharmonic), but there is no semblance of harmonic function. An alternate approach to *Elegy* is to trace the strong step progression that gives the melody its drive.

CD 2, TRACK 3
Edvard Grieg, *Elegy*
Melodic Generation

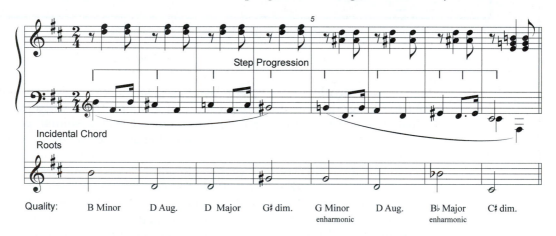

Nonchord Tones

For many traditional composers, nonchord tones were used primarily to decorate structural or secondary pitches. The dissonance added color just as an expected resolution reinforced tonality. In the passage below, from Haydn's Divertimento in C Major, traditional nonchord tones occur frequently. Note especially the half-note dissonances in measures 22 and 24 (7–6 suspension and an appoggiatura, respectively). These dissonances occur on strong beats, but with regular resolutions to chord tones.

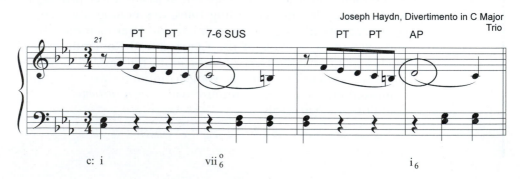

Even before 1850, composers like Chopin were making extensive use of nonchord tones to enliven functional tertian harmony and challenge audience expectations. In the Mazurka that follows, note the extensive use of decorative pitches in the melody, while the harmony is actually quite simple. In an analysis of this and similar works, arabic-numeral symbols to denote inversions are usually not necessary.

CD 2, TRACK 4
Frédéric Chopin, *Valse*, Op. 69, No. 2
Nonchord Tones

Throughout the last half of the nineteenth century, some composers chose to emphasize the dissonance of a nonchord tone rather than its resolution. The German, Hugo Wolf (1860–1903) adopted a style in which, although it retains basic harmonic function, dissonance is accentuated and tonality is sometimes briefly obscure. The song "Die du Gott gebarst" ("Thou Who Bore Our Savior") from the *Spanisches Liederbuch,* includes a series of passing tones that is reiterated in the right hand of the piano accompaniment. Notice the

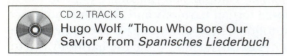

contrary motion between the ascending right-hand pitches and the descending thirds in the bass. Compare both of these lines to the vocal part which has a more static quality.

Thou who bore our Savior Jesus,
Did release us from chains and desolation,
Make me joyful.

In addition to the exceptional employment of nonchord tones, note Wolf's use of $\frac{6}{4}$ meter in the right hand against $\frac{2}{2}$ in the voice and the left hand. The effect in the right hand is the same as quarter-note triplets in $\frac{2}{2}$, but Wolf's use of *polymeter* (to be discussed in a later chapter) is another nontraditional aspect of the song.

Just as Renaissance composers combined melodic lines to generate tertian harmony, many nineteenth-century composers chose a similar path, creating semifunctional and even nonfunctional harmony. Rarely, however, did composers rely on only one technique outside the common-practice vocabulary. As we will discuss in the next section, various traditional approaches to composition—expanded or slightly altered—afforded new color, and diminished the influence of functional tonality.

WORKBOOK/ANTHOLOGY II
I. New Melodic Resources, page 121

ALTERATION OF TRADITIONAL MATERIALS

In addition to using tonality that is generated or obscured through the melody, nineteenth-century composers began with classical models (progressions, pitch centricity, and so on), but altered them so that the effect was completely new. We recognize Beethoven, for example, as an innovator who began his career with the classical models of Mozart and Haydn, but quickly thrust Western music on the path to a new era. We will discuss a number of these techniques and materials in the present section. Later, we will consider expanded tertian harmony and unique root relationships.

Absolute and Program Music

We might categorize music in the eighteenth century as "music for music's sake"; that is, ABSOLUTE MUSIC without programmatic or other literary connotations. Many nineteenth-century composers, on the other hand, wrote instrumental works that told stories—PROGRAM MUSIC. At age 27, for example, the Frenchman Hector Berlioz wrote a revolutionary five-movement symphony depicting a drug-induced fantasy, in which a single theme (which Berlioz called an *idee fixé*) occurs in various transformations. In the first movement, the *idee fixé* serves as the first theme in a sonata form and evokes serene remembrances of love.

Hector Berlioz, *Symphonie Fantastique*
First Movement

By the end of the forty-minute work, the *idee fixé* has been transformed to portray the former lover now murdered and become a witch. Not only do trills and grace notes transform Berlioz's love theme into a grotesque march, but the instrument we hear is a soprano clarinet in E♭—a shrill perfect fourth above the more familiar B♭ clarinet.

Fifth Movement, *Witches' Sabbath*

Where Classical composers manipulated motives more often in development sections, Beethoven, Berlioz, and others employed the motive as a new unifying device. Beethoven's Symphony No. 5, written two decades before Berlioz's *Symphonie Fantastique* (1830), is often cited as the first major work to unify several movements through a single motive. Such works, in which a few pitches generate a lengthy composition in multiple movements, are termed CYCLIC.

Orchestral Color

The nineteenth century witnessed numerous improvements in the construction of orchestral instruments: valves for brasses; keys and rings, for woodwinds; strengthened construction for violins, to accommodate tighter strings for bigger tone. In addition to the strings and pairs of winds that had made up Mozart's orchestra, new instruments were introduced to the ensemble in the nineteenth century, when the need for more color dictated. Harps, a range of keyboard instruments, English horns, tubas, an occasional saxophone, and a host of percussion instruments were all common in some nineteenth-century orchestras.

The orchestra of Mozart and Haydn was rarely more than forty members, but by 1850, larger concert halls and the drive for orchestral color resulted in ensembles of over one hundred players (as is common today). One of the most important aspects of nineteenth-century orchestration was the use of woodwind and brass instruments in *families*—groups of similar colors ranging from low to high registers. While Mozart was content with the traditional transverse flute, by Berlioz' day, the piccolo was a common addition to the flute section. In addition, nineteenth-century composers often wrote three different flute parts (first, second, and third). Even without the alto and bass flutes (which appeared later in the nineteenth century), the flute *timbre* regularly extended over three or more octaves.

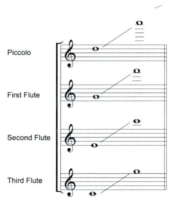

Likewise, a wide range of clarinets and double-reed instruments was available and in common use by the nineteenth century. In the passage on page 297, from *Death and Transfiguration* by the German Richard Strauss (1864–1949), note the expanded orchestration that includes three flutes, two oboes and English horn (an alto oboe), soprano and bass clarinets, bassoon and contrabassoon, four horns, three trumpets, three trombones, and tuba.

Distant Modulation

In Chapter 4, we surveyed some of the techniques that eighteenth- and nineteenth-century composers used to effect distant modulation (borrowed chords, the diminished seventh, and the German augmented sixth/dominant seventh-relationship). A number of composers in the nineteenth century found it unnecessary to connect two keys theoretically, but rather used the melodic line, chromatic movement, or unexpected enharmonic relationships to imply or establish a distant key.

In his *lied* "Am leuchtenden Sommermorgen" ("On a Bright Summer Morning") from the cycle *Dichterliebe,* Robert Schumann begins in B♭ major with a German augmented-sixth chord (notated enharmonically with a doubly-augmented fourth augmented fourth above the bass). The chords that follow are traditional, including the tonic six-four-to-dominant formula. In measures 8–9, however, an excursion to B major is unexpected and is effected through melodic motion in the vocal part. The three consecutive dominant seventh chords $(B^7–C^7–F^7)$ comprise another common nineteenth-century technique to be discussed later in this chapter.

CD 2, TRACK 6
Robert Schumann, "On A Bright Shining Morning"
Distant Modulation

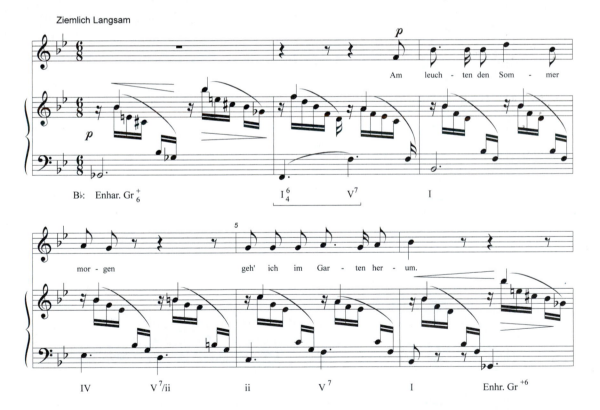

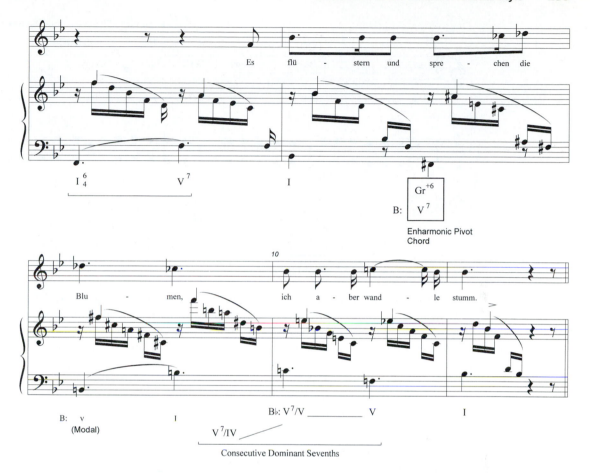

On a bright summer morning
I walk around the garden.
The flowers are whispering and speaking,
But I walk in silence.

Decreased Emphasis on the Dominant

You will remember that chromatic chords of predominant function (augment-ed sixth, Neapolitan, and so on) strengthen tonality by making the dominant (and its resolution to tonic) more important. In the mid- and late nineteenth century, however, many composers began to color the dominant itself by adding pitches, raising the fifth to create an augmented triad, and employing a modal dominant. Alteration of the dominant *decreases* tonal effect; this is one of many ways in which later nineteenth-century composers separated their music from that of Haydn, Mozart, and Beethoven.

Modal Dominants. Nineteenth-century composers rediscovered chords and progressions that had been popular in the Renaissance, but which were abandoned by Baroque- and Classical-era composers. Among these are the subtonic and the MODAL (MINOR) DOMINANT. In the Wolf *lied* cited earlier, notice the modal dominant in the second measure as the bass descends by step. The symbol "v" identifies E as the root, without implying harmonic function.

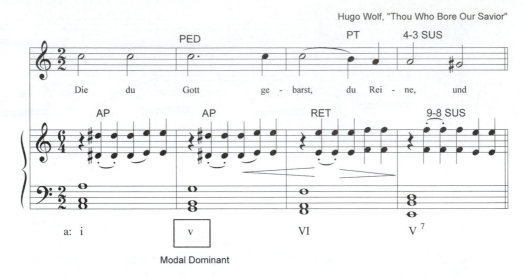

Hugo Wolf, "Thou Who Bore Our Savior"

The progression that opens Wolf's "Thou Who Bore Our Savior" (above) is typical of the later Romantic-era attitude toward harmonic function. In another sense, however, the modal dominant triad was a common formula that Baroque- and Classical-era composers used to harmonize a descending tetrachord ($\hat{8}$–$\hat{5}$) in the bass. Bach used the identical progression in his G minor Menuet (remember that a flat is missing from the key signature and written in as an accidental). In the analysis of functional music, however, we would tend to analyze the minor dominant as a passing chord and not as a minor dominant.

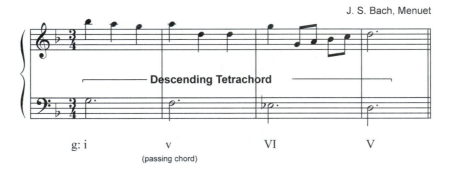

J. S. Bach, Menuet

Augmented Dominants. While augmented triads are very rare in the eighteenth and early nineteenth centuries, the augmented dominant triad became fashionable with some composers after about 1850. In effect, a V⁺–I progression permits a leading tone to both the root and the third of the tonic triad.

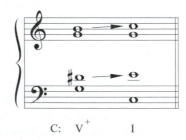

French composer Benjamin Godard (1849–1895) used a progression similar to the one in the last example in his *Florian's Song*. In addition to identification of the chord in measure 4 as an augmented dominant (seventh), we could also explain it as a passing chord. When tonality is only slightly obscure, there are usually two or more viable explanations using traditional roman-numeral symbols.

CD 2, TRACK 7-1 DECREASED DOMINANT EMPHASIS (2 PARTS)
Benjamin Goddard, "Florian's Song"
Augmented Dominant

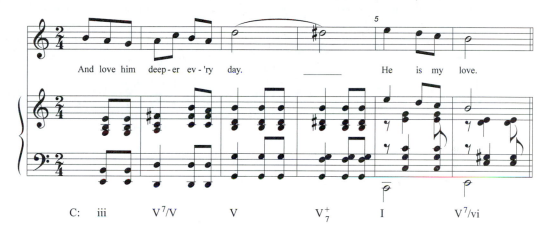

Voice Leading in Altered Chords. As we discussed in Chapters 3 and 4, guidelines for voice leading are more important in vocal music than in scoring for keyboard or instrumental ensemble. In the last example, observe that the accidental D♯ in the vocal line ascends to E as we would expect. Unusual resolutions, including leaps and other unanticipated twists and turns, are not uncommon, however. Likewise, guidelines for doubling are not as strictly observed in the later nineteenth century as they were in the time of Haydn and Mozart.

Modal and Exceptional Cadences. In addition to altered dominants, some nineteenth-century composers relied primarily on half, plagal, and exceptional cadences to avoid the tonal power of the descending-fifth root movement. The French composer Lili Boulanger (1893–1918) studied at the Paris Conservatory, and won the coveted *Prix de Rome*. Best known in her short life for choral works, Boulanger's song, "Au pied de mon lit" (*At the Foot of My Bed*) begins with the phrase below. The key of E minor is tentatively established in the melody (among structural pitches, and as the first sonority heard). Otherwise, most of the phrase, which moves by descending motion in the piano, sounds more in the key of A minor.

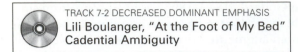

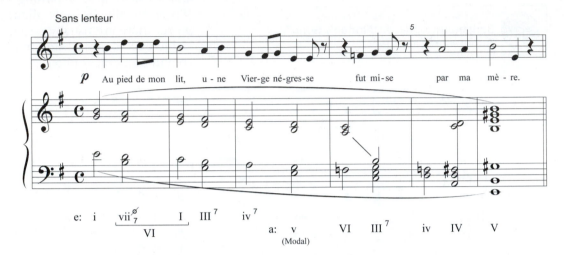

At the foot of my bed,
A black Virgin was placed by my mother.

Tonal Ambiguity

While composers like Mozart, Haydn, and Beethoven rarely obscured tonality in their works, intentional harmonic ambiguity, as seen in the Boulanger song, was common in Western music by 1850. The *lied Ekstase* (*Ecstasy*) by Alma Schindler Mahler (1879–1964, wife of the famous Austrian composer and conductor, Gustav Mahler), is similarly more ambiguous in key than we normally expect of Romantic-era music. In the passage shown, tonal tendencies in the melody are established in F major, but the extensive use of pedal and other nonchord tones in the accompaniment (as well as altered triads and unusual resolutions) makes this a nontraditional approach to tonal composition. Note that the phrase ends with an augmented triad as a point of cadence.

CD 2, TRACK 8
Alma Schindler Mahler, "Ecstasy"
Tonal Ambiguity

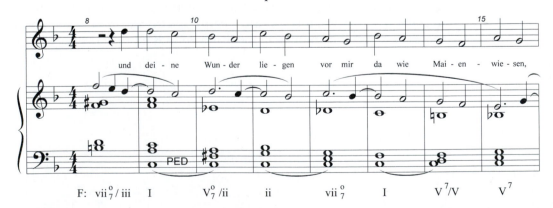

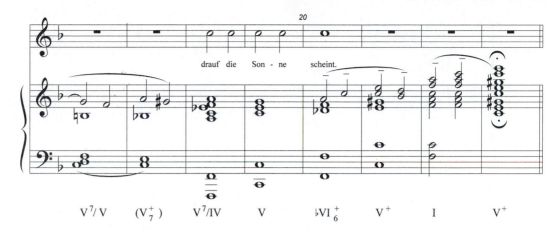

$$\text{V}^7/\text{V} \qquad (\text{V}^+_7) \qquad \text{V}^7/\text{IV} \qquad \text{V} \qquad \flat\text{VI}^+_6 \qquad \text{V}^+ \qquad \text{I} \qquad \text{V}^+$$

And your wonders lie before me
Like meadows in May on which the sun shines.

A number of nineteenth-century composers began with the traditional vocabulary of melodic and harmonic techniques, and expanded them through addition or alteration. Modal and augmented dominants, expanded orchestral color, and sudden and distant modulation were all used singly and in combination to create innovative works that are sometimes only vaguely tonal in the traditional sense. In the next section, we will consider a second group of materials and relationships that derive from traditional models.

WORKBOOK/ANTHOLOGY II
II. Altered Traditional Materials, page 125

REVIEW AND APPLICATION 7–1

New Uses of Traditional Materials

Essential Terms

absolute music	cyclic	program music
augmented dominant	modal dominant	

1. Several chords are given in the next example for resolution in four parts. First, identify the chord in the key indicated. Look for modal and augmented dominants, enharmonic notations of common-practice chords, and traditional triads and seventh chords as well. Use traditional voice-leading and doubling guidelines.

a.

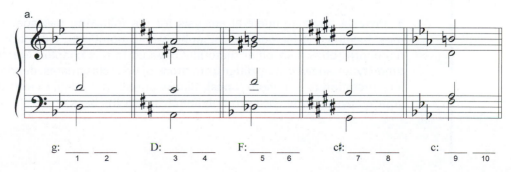

g: ___ ___   D: ___ ___   F: ___ ___   c#: ___ ___   c: ___ ___
   1   2   3   4   5   6   7   8   9   10

A: ___ ___   a: ___ ___   Gb: ___ ___   e: ___ ___   f: ___ ___
  1   2   3   4   5   6   7   8   9   10

2. Revise the passages below to include a variety of nonchord tones that resolve traditionally. Some nonchord tones may have delayed or metrically misplaced resolutions. Begin by providing a roman-numeral analysis of the existing passage. Retain the original harmony and four-part vocal format, but add one or more nonchord tones in each measure of the revision. Circle and identify all nonchord tones.

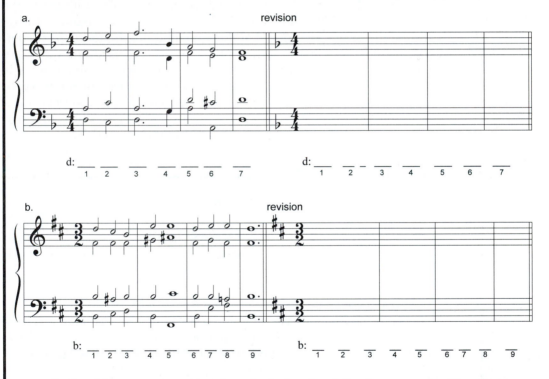

3. Provide a roman-numeral analysis for the following passage. The harmony may include modal dominants, enharmonic notations, exceptional cadences, nonchord tones, and other materials covered in this chapter. Identify nonchord tones (your analysis may differ from those of your classmates, depending on your interpretation of nonchord tones). Blanks are not provided, to afford flexibility in your analysis. Write each symbol directly under the bass of the chord.

CD 2, TRACK 09
Hugo Wolf, "Sleeping Child" Review and Application 7-1
Line 3-a

Blessed Virgin's heav'nly child!

SELF-TEST 7–1

Time Limit: 5 Minutes

1. Make a check mark by the correct statement in each of the following groups. *Scoring: Subtract 13 points for each incorrect answer.*

   a. An instrument that appeared in the symphony orchestra *before* the Romantic era is the

      _____ (1) saxophone.

      _____ (2) harp.

      _____ (3) viola.

      _____ (4) english horn.

   b. Music that tells a story is termed

      _____ (1) nationalism.

      _____ (2) nonfunctional.

      _____ (3) absolute.

      _____ (4) programmatic.

c. A *cyclic* composition features

_____ (1) two main themes.

_____ (2) single motive used throughout the first movement.

_____ (3) a single motive heard in two or more movements.

_____ (4) an extensive coda.

d. Typically, an orchestra in the days of Haydn and Mozart numbered about

_____ (1) 25.

_____ (2) 40.

_____ (3) 80.

_____ (4) 100.

2. Provide the chords specified. Use the four-part vocal format. *Scoring: Subtract 16 points for each error.*

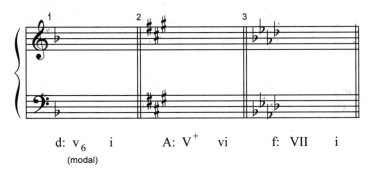

d: V_6 i   A: V^+ vi   f: VII   i
(modal)

Total Possible: 100   Your Score _____

EXPANDED TERTIAN RESOURCES

Earlier, we discussed a number of different common-practice techniques and philosophical viewpoints that were expanded or altered by later nineteenth-century composers. The next section centers on innovative uses of the traditional tonal system: Ninth chords (an extension of tertian harmony) and key and root relationships by chromatic third.

Ninth Chords

Tertian harmony evolved slowly, from converging melodic lines in the Renaissance to the functional tonality of the mature Baroque. In addition, composers in the late seventeenth century began to experiment with harmonic dissonances—the addition of a seventh above the root heard not as a nonchord tone, but as a full member of the chord. By the time Bach died in 1750, seventh chords were a common part of the traditional vocabulary. In the nineteenth century, composers extended the tertian principle yet further to include NINTH CHORDS—sonorities with thirds, fifths, sevenths, and ninths above the roots.

Triad   Seventh Chord   Ninth Chord

Like seventh chords, ninths occur in a variety of qualities. By far the most common of these is shown in the next example. The triad is major, the seventh is minor, and the ninth is major; this sonority is known as a DOMINANT NINTH CHORD.

Dominant Ninth Chords

B♭:   V⁹   F♯:   V⁹   A♭:   V⁹

Several additional qualities of ninth chords are available in major. While these chords may be useful in original composition today, only ii^9 and V^9 are common in traditional music. In fact, ninths on the tonic and the mediant are extremely rare. In jazz and popular styles, however, a host of colorful ninth chords—including the tonic—are prevalent.

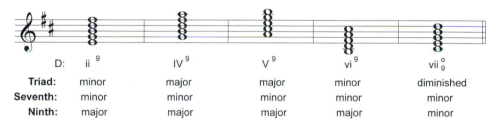

	D: ii⁹	IV⁹	V⁹	vi⁹	vii°⁹
Triad:	minor	major	major	minor	diminished
Seventh:	minor	minor	minor	minor	minor
Ninth:	major	major	major	major	minor

In minor, the use of ↑$\hat{6}$ and ↑$\hat{7}$ adds to the possibilities for ninth-chord quality.

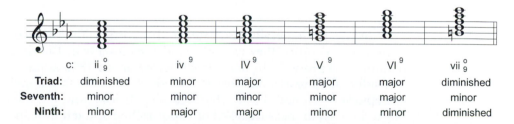

	c: ii°⁹	iv⁹	IV⁹	V⁹	VI⁹	vii°⁹
Triad:	diminished	minor	major	major	major	diminished
Seventh:	minor	minor	minor	minor	major	minor
Ninth:	minor	major	major	minor	minor	diminished

Resolution, Doubling, and Voice Leading.   In four voices (SATB), composers often omit the fifth of a ninth chord and resolve both the ninth and the seventh down by step. In more traditional works, the ninth may be prepared as a melodic dissonance figure (a suspension, a passing tone, or a neighboring tone). Both ninth chords in the following harmonic sketch are prepared as suspension figures; both resolve down by step. Remember that in all matters of voice leading, the observance of two principles solves most problems:

1. Avoid parallel fifths, octaves, and unisons.

2. Follow melodic tendencies in resolving active pitches.

Ninth Chords in Four-Part Writing

G: I   ii₆   V⁹   I   V⁷/IV   IV⁹   V⁷   I

Inversions.   Ninth chords usually appear in root position. Inversions are not entirely uncommon, however (especially first inversion). But because they are not part of the common-practice vocabulary, we do not often need the formality of indicating inversions with arabic numerals.

Especially when the harmonic rhythm is relatively slow, the ninth may move to another chord tone: the root, third, fifth, or seventh. In the case of a seventh, a traditional resolution follows. Characteristic doubling is seen in the last two examples; notice in the Schubert passage below that the third and fifth are present in the ninth chord (measure 4), but the seventh is omitted from the four-part texture until the third beat.

CD 2, NINTH CHORDS (2 PARTS) TRACK 10-1
Franz Schubert, Mass No. 6 in E♭ Major (*Kyrie*)

E♭: I   I₆   ii   V⁹   V⁷   I

While we generally associate ninth chords with the second half of the nineteenth century, they can be found occasionally in Classical and early Romantic works as well. In many cases before about 1850, a pitch that we might consider labeling as a member of a ninth *chord* is merely a nonchord tone with a stepwise resolution. In the Haydn passage below, however, the G♭ in measure 53 and the C♭ in measure 54—both approached and left by leap—are obviously chord tones a ninth above the bass. Notice that the resolution of the ninths is delayed, but characteristically down by step.

eb: vii $^{o}_{7}$/ii   V^9/V

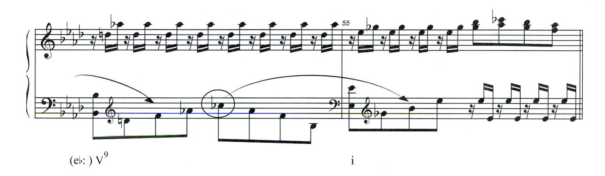

(eb:) V^9 i

As we have seen, while composers as early as 1800 used ninth chords occasionally, these harmonic dissonances became a more important part of the extended common-practice vocabulary in the later nineteenth century. In Chapter 8, we will discuss ninth chords as used by Claude Debussy and his contemporaries. Further extension of the tertian principle to include a completely new approach to ninth chords and other harmonic dissonances is one of several points introduced in Chapter 9.

Third Relation

Root movement by descending perfect fifth is central to common-practice harmony. As we discussed earlier, Baroque and Classical composers most often chose both root and key relationships by fifth. In the Romantic era, however, relationships based on the third became popular as well. In the first movement of his Sonata in C Major, Op. 53 ("Waldstein"), for example, Beethoven chooses E major for the second theme (instead of G major as Mozart would probably have done). Likewise, in the recapitulation, the second theme is in Ab major (and not C major as we would expect).[1] The relationship between C major and E major and between C major and Ab major is an example of chromatic THIRD RELATION—root relationships by third that involve a chromatic inflection between the two chords. While common-practice composers often employed

---

[1] See page 211 for a time-line diagram of this movement.

chords with third-related roots (as in the first example below), they generally lacked the chromatic color of third relation as employed by composers in the Romantic era.

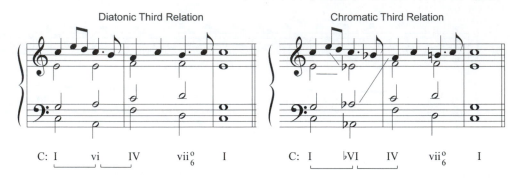

Composers of the late Romantic era generally conformed to three guidelines in the use of chromatic third relation:

1. Root movement is most often by *major* third.

2. Common tones are retained to link the two chords.

3. Two voices often move by half step.

Franz Liszt, a native of Hungary, was a late Romantic pianist and composer, who in one work or another, employed most of the techniques discussed in this chapter. In his *Wanderer's Nachtlied* (*Wanderer's Night Song*), the last three progressions (including the final cadence) are by chromatic third relation.

CD 2, TRACK 11-1 THIRD RELATION (2 PARTS)
Franz Liszt, "Wanderer's Night Song"

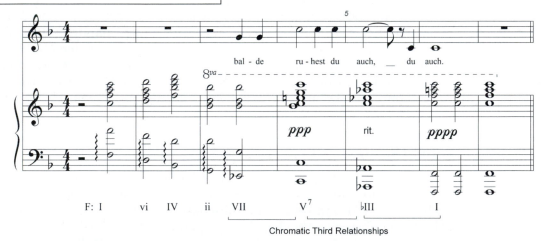

Soon thou, too, shall find rest, find rest.

In her *lied, Liebst du um Schönheit* (*If You Love Because of Beauty*), Clara Schumann colors an important cadence in D♭ major with a chromatic third relationship. Notice that in measure 9, the neighboring group in both hands of the accompaniment returns to the original dissonances before resolving in the next measure.

TRACK 11-2 THIRD RELATION
Clara Schumann, "If You Love Because of Beauty"

Chromatic Third Relation

If you love because of beauty, then do not love me!
Love the sun, it has golden hair!
If you love because of youth …

As the nineteenth century progressed, many composers increasingly sought new materials and techniques to separate their music from that of the older generation. Most of these innovations, like ninth chords and third relation, remained basically functional. In the next section, however, we will survey several compositional approaches that resulted in a total or temporary absence of tonal function.

> WORKBOOK/ANTHOLOGY I
> III. Ninth Chords, page 129

REVIEW AND APPLICATION 7–2

Ninth Chords and Third Relation

Essential Terms

dominant ninth chord   third relation   ninth chord

1. Choose an initial chord for the given progression that will permit preparation of the ninth as a suspension, a neighboring tone, or a passing-tone figure. Write and resolve the progressions in four parts. Use conventional doubling and spacing. Add accidentals as necessary.

2. Use roman numerals and other symbols to identify the chords below in the keys indicated. Two chords are given in each key, but they are not connected and are to be considered separately. The exercise includes not only ninths and third-related chords, but other materials studied in this and other chapters (augmented or modal dominant, augmented triad, any seventh chord, secondary dominants, borrowed chords, and the like). In some cases, there are two or more logical analyses.

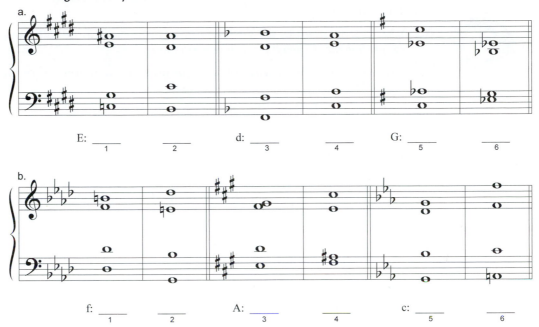

3. Complete this two-phrase period for piano with an inventive harmony that includes ninth chords, third relation, and a final cadence employing either an augmented or modal dominant (your choice). There are many possibilities, but take care to prepare and resolve ninth and seventh chords appropriately. Continue the accompaniment in the same texture.

SELF-TEST 7–2

Time Limit: 5 Minutes

1. Make a check mark by the correct statement in each of the following groups. *Scoring: Subtract 13 points for each incorrect answer.*

   a. Which of the following is not an appropriate preparation figure for a ninth chord?

   _____   (1) passing tone

   _____   (2) escape tone

   _____   (3) suspension

   _____   (4) neighboring tone

   b. In four parts, the voice most often omitted in a ninth chord is

   _____   (1) the root.

   _____   (2) the third.

   _____   (3) the fifth.

   _____   (4) the seventh.

   c. The most common type of ninth chord is

   _____   (1) major–minor–major.

   _____   (2) minor–diminished–minor.

   _____   (3) major–major–minor.

   _____   (4) minor–major–minor.

   d. Two chord roots are related by chromatic third when

   _____   (1) they are both in root position.

   _____   (2) they move by major third.

   _____   (3) they move by minor third.

   _____   (4) all pitches are altered.

2. Provide roman numerals and other symbols (including arabic numerals) as necessary to identify the following chords. Look for traditional diatonic sonorities as well as less traditional harmonies presented in the previous section. *Scoring: Subtract 12 points for each incorrect analysis*

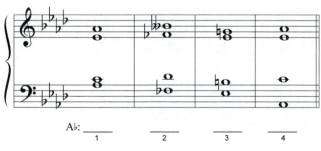

Total Possible: 100   Your Score _____

NONFUNCTIONAL HARMONY

We have previously discussed melodically generated harmony as well as innovative strategies for using traditional common-practice materials. A third approach that served to further dilute the tonal system concerns passages and complete movements that are *nonfunctional*. NONFUNCTIONAL HARMONY is organized with neither an orderly harmonic progression through the three functions nor a strict adherence to melodic tendencies. Romantic-era nonfunctional harmony is not atonal (lacking a tonal center); rather, composers like Liszt, Chopin, and Franck (1822–1890) established a feeling for key through individual and innovative means.

Augmented and Other Ambiguous Triads

Augmented triads are rare in the common-practice vocabulary, but by 1875, a number of composers were attracted to the ambiguity of superimposed major and minor thirds. While both diminished and augmented triads lack a perfect fifth, the former includes a tritone; when the tritone is resolved, the function of the diminished triad as a dominant is usually clear. However, no such clear functional implications exist in the augmented triad (comprising superimposed major thirds). In minor, the augmented mediant can be heard as having either weak tonic function or an unusual dominant tendency.

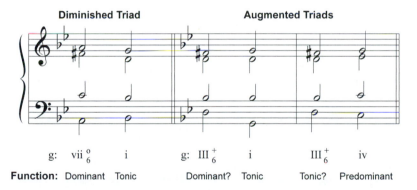

In the late nineteenth century, composers like Franz Liszt and the Russian Modest Mussorgsky (1839–1881), among others, anticipated Debussy in his view of the triad as an interesting and autonomous sonority in its own right and not merely one element in a series defined by its surroundings. Liszt's brief *Nuages gris* (*Grey Clouds*) is based almost entirely on augmented triads. The gentle alternation of B♭ to A in the bass suggests the listless motion of clouds. While *Grey Clouds* is nonfunctional, the opening motive (heard again beginning in measure 25) suggests G as a tonal center. The final cadence also creates a sense of tonal identity as the pitch F♯ moves to G in octaves over a dissonant (and unresolved) pedal.

[Not Recorded]

Franz Liszt, "Grey Clouds"

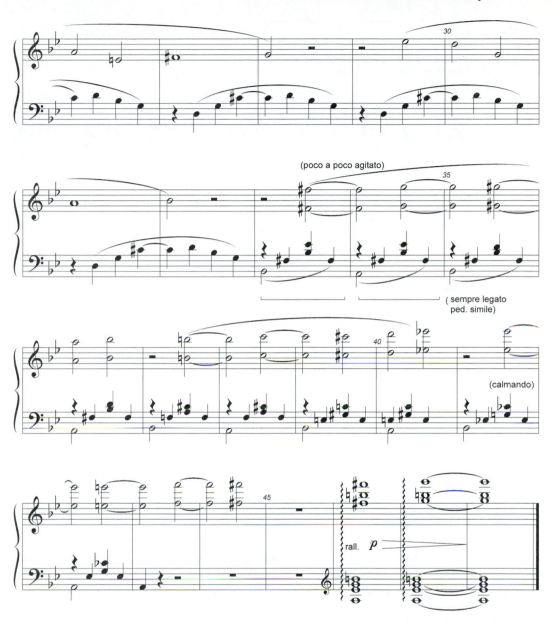

Another work by Liszt highlights a nonfunctional series comprising large-ly diminished-seventh chords. Roman numerals are of little value here (except to verify the lack of function); chords are better identified according to root and quality. Notice that the passage ends with a clear functional cadence, and after a long *cadenza* (a passage of an improvisational nature), the dominant seventh resolves in measure 5 to tonic (not shown).

Parenthetical Harmony

A series of nonfunctional chords that interrupts an otherwise tonal progression (as seen in the last example from Liszt's "Mazeppa") is often termed PARENTHETICAL HARMONY. We might think of such chords as a suspension of functional harmonic logic, just as a digression (in parentheses) interrupts the flow of ideas in a sentence. In the passage that follows by French organist and composer César Franck (1822–1890), notice that the harmony is quite ordinary The parenthetical harmonies create tension and heighten the expectation of resolution.

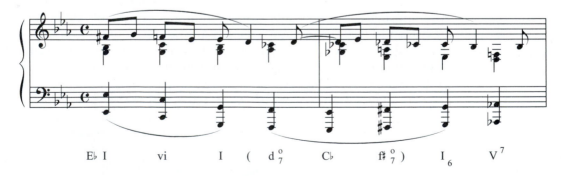

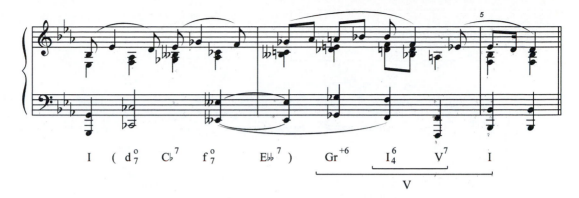

In addition to the two passages of parenthetical harmony in the Franck excerpt, the chromatic melody is rich with nonchord tones. Notice in the following reduction that, as with much music in the late nineteenth century, we must sometimes speculate about the root of a chord. Further, other interpretations of nonchord tones are possible. In this analysis, some nonchord tones appear in anticipation of their actual function (these are shown in parentheses).

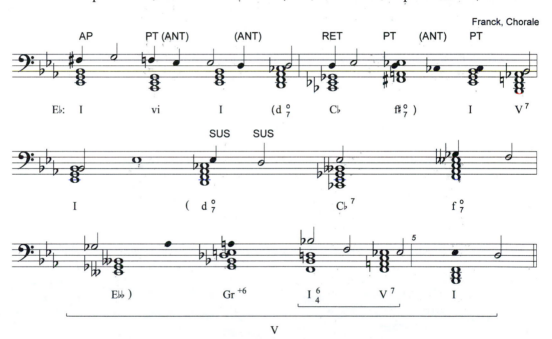

In the last 19 measures of his *Etude*, Op. 10, No. 1, Chopin employs two nonfunctional passages of parenthetical harmony (measures 63–64 and 70–74). The first parenthetical passage is a series of dominant sevenths; the second, a succession of diminished-seventh chords. That Chopin exploited two chords with strong tendencies is no accident; if a dominant or diminished seventh is left unresolved, tonality is obscured. When these and other unstable chords appear in a series, the composer retains the option to resolve the last of them conventionally.

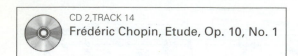

CD 2, TRACK 14
Frédéric Chopin, Etude, Op. 10, No. 1

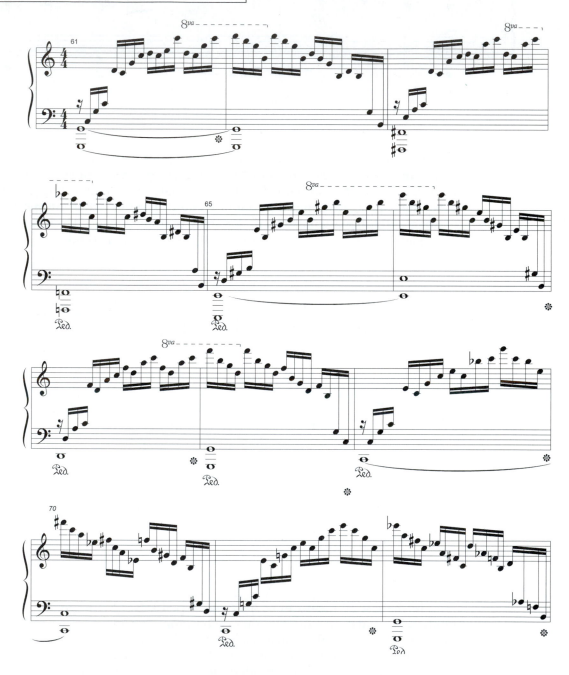

Tonal Pillars. Strong functional progressions often anchor passages of parenthetical harmony. These TONAL PILLARS (boxed in the reduction of Chopin's Etude, Op. 10, below) give a sense of direction to the harmony, even if it is otherwise largely nonfunctional. Note the tentative establishment of A minor through a secondary Fr^{+6}–V progression.

Chopin, *Etude*, Op. 10, No. 1

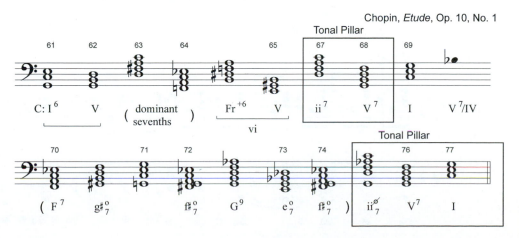

Chordal Mutation

CHORDAL MUTATION is a kaleidoscope of parenthetical harmony in which chords change one or two pitches at a time (usually by whole or half step), and with one or more common tones retained into the next harmony. Two consecutive chords may be quite distant from one another, but the common tone or tones permit the listener to perceive a closer organization. As seen in the next example, passages of chordal mutation typically include one or more tonal pillars.

CD 2, TRACK 15
Chordal Mutation

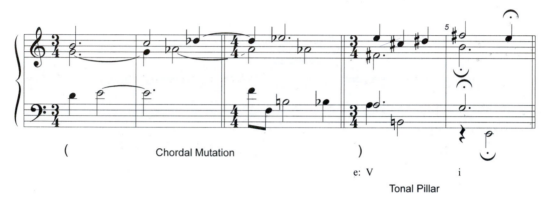

Chordal mutation and a number of other techniques appear in Chopin's Prelude in E major, Op. 28, No. 9. Our analysis of this work will serve as a model for use in approaching similar music. In only twelve measures, Chopin fuses the symmetry of traditional common-practice form and structure with significant theoretical principles that continue to govern tonal and quasi-tonal music today.

CD 2, TRACK 16
Frédéric Chopin, Prelude, Op. 28, No. 9

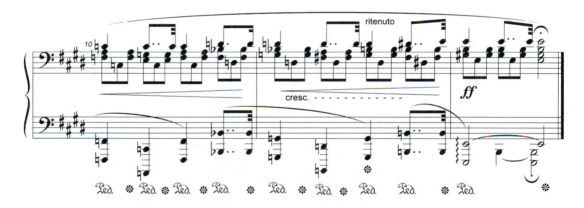

The analysis of a work like Chopin's Prelude might begin with a harmonic reduction that omits nonchord tones, rhythmic embellishments, and repeated tones. The block-chord format on page 324 has the soprano of the original score transposed up into the treble clef to facilitate understanding and performance at the keyboard.

Chopin, Prelude Op. 28, No. 9
Basic Chord Structure

Functional and Voice-Leading Logic.   The reduction reveals the presence of two different kinds of tonal logic in the E major prelude. First, FUNCTION-AL LOGIC, as we have discussed previously, both provides momentum and creates areas of stability. Movement through predominant, dominant, and tonic functions occurs three times early on in the Chopin Prelude. The third of these progressions includes a tonic proper (rather than a tonic substitute). At several points, the predominant function is omitted (see measures 7–8, 8–9, 10, and 11–12); dominant and tonic alone define the key.

VOICE-LEADING LOGIC governs nonfunctional passages and maintains continuity, while providing unexpected twists and turns in the harmony. The same principles are often present in distant changes of key. Chordal mutation, as seen in this and other works, rests on voice-leading logic: Common-chord connections smooth out links that might otherwise produce incongruous jolts because of distant (nonfunctional) root relationships. Chromatic mediants (usually major triads; root movement by third; stepwise motion in two voices; common-tone hold-over in the other) are the most frequent examples of this maneuver in Chopin's work.

The overall large-scale tonal plan of E–A♭ (G♯)–E produces the same chromatic-mediant relationship in key areas that also exists logically among many of the chords. Considering only roman-numeral analysis, the final cadence appears to be premature—the terminal V–I seemingly coming out of nowhere. The gradually rising soprano line stretched out now over 13 beats, however, helps to supply the necessary preparation for ultimate closure as it slowly inches up the scale toward the magnetic pull of tonic. The persuasiveness of final arrival, which otherwise might have been deficient in purely harmonic terms, is furnished through a powerful and strategically paced linear ascent.

In Chopin's E major prelude, we see many of the topics covered in this chapter, including unconventional use of nonchord tones, third relation, tonal pillars, chordal mutation, and ninth chords. We might also remember that Chopin set the stage for the dissolution of the common-practice style as early as 1840. Later composers like Debussy built on Chopin's innovations to create a new musical vocabulary where tonality was maintained, but not always through conventional functional relationships.

WORKBOOK/ANTHOLOGY II
IV. Nonfunctional Harmony, page 133

REVIEW AND APPLICATION 7–3

Nonfunctional Harmony

Essential Terms

chordal mutation	nonfunctional harmony	tonal pillar
functional logic	parenthetical harmony	voice-leading logic

1. Be prepared to answer the following questions regarding *Pompons and Fans* by Nathaniel Dett. Your instructor may ask you to answer the questions in written form.

   a. The chords are not all the same, but one quality predominates. What is it?

   b. Identify a passage in which "voice-leading logic" drives the music.

   c. How would you describe the cadence in measures 8–9?

   d. The work centers on the pitch G. How is this accomplished, given the numerous accidentals?

2. Undertake an analysis of the Mazurka by Chopin given in part below (compile notes for class discussion, or undertake a more formal paper—as specified by your instructor). Provide a roman-numeral analysis, and identify as many materials and techniques as you can that have been discussed in this chapter (not limited to the current section). Identify the form of the melody. Are there examples of chordal mutation? other nonfunctional harmony? Finally, consult a music dictionary for a concise definition of "Mazurka." How are the Mazurkas of Dett and Chopin similar? different?

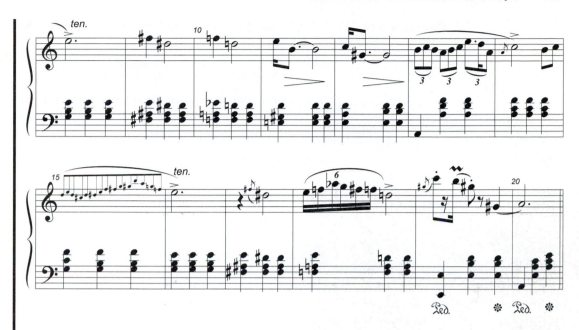

3. Prepare a chordal reduction of the Chopin Mazurka given in the last example. Include roman-numeral analysis and identification of significant nonchord tones. Model your reduction after the text example on page 324.

SELF-TEST 7–3

Time Limit: 5 Minutes

1. Match each statement with one *or more* of the techniques in the following list by writing the appropriate letter *or letters* in the blank. You may use some items more than once. *Scoring: Subtract 5 points for each incorrect (or incomplete) answer.*

A. Chordal Mutation

B. Tonal Pillar

C. Parenthetical Harmony

D. Functional Logic

E. Voice-Leading Logic

_____ a. Passages of nonfunctional harmony that often occur in conjunction with shifting tonality

_____ b. A series of unstable chords, such as dominant or diminished sevenths

_____ c. Usually involves movement by step in one or more voices with one or more common tones retained

_____ d. A strong tonal progression such as IV–V–I

_____ e. Nonfunctional harmony anchored by tonal pillars

_____ f. Governs a passage of chords that lacks traditional relationships

327

2. Provide a term that is applicable to each of the following definitions. *Scoring: Subtract 5 points for each incorrect term.*

_____ a. Two chords such as C major and E♭ major that include a chromatic cross relationship (inflection)

_____ b. A nonfunctional series of chords that interrupts an otherwise functional harmony

_____ c. A minor dominant chord

_____ d. A type of "logic" that helps organize nonfunctional harmony

_____ e. A triad built of superimposed major thirds

_____ f. A work that includes a single theme (or its transformation) in all or several movements

_____ g. Music that tells a story or relates the composer's view of events, places, or people

3. In four-part style, select a chord to precede the dominant ninth and write the appropriate roman numeral in the blank. Next, fill in the alto and tenor for all three chords. Be sure that the ninth is prepared and resolved. *Scoring: Subtract 6 points for an incorrect preparatory chord; subtract 6 points for an incorrect resolution of the ninth; deduct 3 points for each incorrect alto or soprano pitch.*

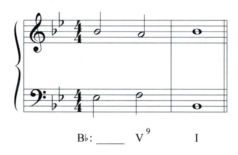

B♭: _____   V⁹   I

4. What was composer Franz Liszt's nationality? *Scoring: subtract 5 points for a wrong answer.*

_____
country

Total Possible: 100   Your Score _____

PROJECTS

Analysis

Deciding upon an approach to some areas of analysis in the works included in this chapter may be a challenge. Each work poses unique problems, and the dates of composition range from the early nineteenth century (Chopin) to twentieth-century jazz. Begin by determining how tonality is established, maintained, and (in many cases) obscured in both melody and harmony. Which techniques of late-nineteenth-century harmony are present? Are there tonal pillars? parenthetical chord series? Identify and be prepared to explain any rhythmic techniques present.

Text

John Coltrane, "Giant Steps," text page 331. While twentieth-century jazz composers employed improvisation to form a unique, American art form, with few exceptions, the harmonic vocabulary was solidly nineteenth century. Saxophonist John Coltrane (1926–1967) is considered by many to be one of those exceptions. He was one of the most original jazz composers in the period after world war II. In addition to performing with established jazz groups such as Thelonius Monk and Miles Davis, Coltrane led his own successful group, known for experimental compositions and extended. In many ways, Coltrane established jazz as an integral part of contemporary Western music in the 1960s. "Giant Steps" (1965) is a challenging improvisation vehicle that includes several of the harmonic techniques covered in Chapter 7.

Frédéric Chopin, Prelude in B Minor Op. 28, No. 6, text page 332. Chopin's series of preludes, Op. 28 is a directory of innovative melodic and harmonic techniques. Undertake a complete analysis of this brief work.

Workbook/Anthology II

Frederic Chopin, Prelude Op. 28, No. 4, workbook page 133.
Richard Wagner, Prelude to Tristan and Isolde, workbook pages 137-142.
Hugo Wolf, "Das verlassene Mägdlein," workbook pages 143-144.

Composition

Woodwind Trio. Compose a relatively slow-moving trio for flute, oboe, and bassoon (or other ensemble as directed) that employs chordal mutation, parenthetical harmony, and tonal pillars. Structure the work in three sections (either through-composed or ternary). The first section might be a chorale as shown in the next example. Chordal mutation, employed here, is most effective when entries are staggered (see also the text example on page 322). Make the first section of your chorale at least *twice* the length shown here.

CD 2, TRACK 18-1 PROJECTS (2 PARTS)
Trio with Chordal Mutation

The second section of the trio might contrast with the first through different rhythms and a varied harmonic approach. In the next example, the long second beat, the homophonic texture, and the use of parenthetical harmony (diminished seventh chords) all lend contrast with the chorale. Tonal pillars occur at the ends of both lines. Your second section should again be at least twice the length of the sample passage.

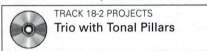

TRACK 18-2 PROJECTS
Trio with Tonal Pillars

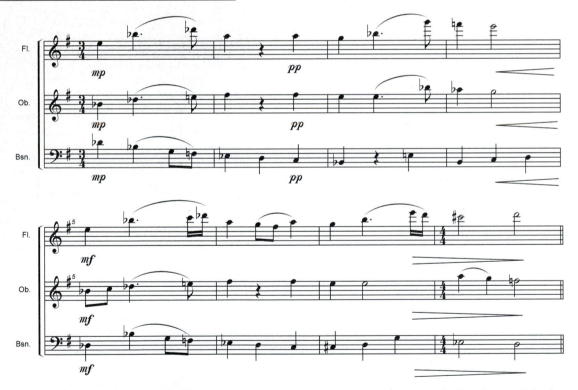

For the final section, return to a variation of the chorale (perhaps with the bassoon—rather than the flute—in the lead role) or compose a second contrasting section. Some instructors will ask students to complete the sample trio given here; in other cases, you should expect to begin anew with different ideas and harmonic approaches. In either case, the entire work should be about 50 measures in length; at a tempo of ♩ = 90, the trio will be 2-3 minutes long. Be sure that your score is accurate and detailed in terms of dynamic and phrase markings. If asked to do so, prepare a set of parts for performance.

For Further Study

Program Music.   While composers since the late sixteenth century have sought through their music to depict people, things, events, and places, we generally associate program music with the nineteenth century. One of the most important vehicles for program music was the tone poem (also called a symphonic poem). Write a formal paper or prepare notes for a class discussion that centers on program music in the nineteenth century and on the tone poem in particular.

Begin by differentiating between absolute and program music. Comment on the difference between subtitles ("Moonlight," "London," "Turkish," and so on) as sometimes are found attached to absolute musical works on the one hand, and music for which an extra-musical idea was the generating source on the other. Next, research the works of three major composers who wrote popular symphonic poems. Choose at least one of these, obtain essential biographical information about the composer, form a clear idea of the program or story, and listen to the work with the score. Document how the composer depicted events, places, things, and even emotions like love and hate through music.

These composers and works are only a few of those for which scores and recordings will be readily available in your library.

Paul Dukas (1865–1935), *The Sorcerer's Apprentice* (1897)

Franz Liszt, *Les Préludes* (1848)

Edward MacDowell (1860–1908), *Hamlet* (1884)

Felix Mendelssohn (1809–1847), *The Herbrides* (1832)

Richard Strauss, *Til Eulenspiegel's Merry Pranks* (1890)

Bedich Smetana (1824–1884), *The Moldau* (1879)

Peter Illyich Tchaikovsky (1840–1893), *Romeo and Juliet* (1870)

Frédéric Chopin, Prelude, Op. 28, No. 6

CHAPTER 8

Impressionism

The traditions of functional tonal harmony were firmly entrenched in the Western world by about 1875. While composers like Schubert, Schumann, and Chopin all died before 1860, their music continued to be popular with listeners and performers in Europe and the United States. Johannes Brahms (1833–1897), a model of German Romanticism, was known in 1875 as a composer of chamber music and *lieder*; he had yet to write the four great symphonies by which he is remembered by many today.

Arts in late nineteenth-century Europe were still partially under the influence of the Romantic movement that had begun in literature in the late eighteenth century. In the late nineteenth century, young painters who studied at the Conservatory of Fine Arts in Paris were required to demonstrate a mastery of traditional French styles before their works could be displayed at an official *salon* (exhibition). Paintings that veered too far from accepted subjects and techniques were shunned by the *salon* jury; as a result, artists could not easily display or sell their works. So many paintings were rejected from the official 1874 *salon*, in fact, that a number of young artists banded together and presented a rogue gallery: the *Salon of the Refused*.

THE "IMPRESSIONISTS"

Virtually unknown at the time, Claude Monet (1840–1926), Pierre Auguste Renoir (1841–1919), and Edgar Degas (1834–1917), among others, displayed their innovative canvases at the *Salon of the Refused*. Many of their paintings were titled simply "Impression." Art critics then universally attacked "The Impressionists," who used visible brush strokes, bright colors (unmixed with brown or black), and fuzzy images. Instead of scenes from Greek, Roman, and French history, the Impressionists painted dancers, haystacks, and children at play.

In the tight-knit community of late nineteenth-century French poets, painters, and composers, influences among the arts were inevitable. Even before 1874, we can see the roots of the Impressionist and Symbolist movements in the poetry of Stéphane Mallarmé (1842–1898) and Paul Verlaine (1844–1896), among others. Despite negative critical review of the *Salon of the Refused*, this movement spread, and eventually spawned new painting schools such as Neo-Impressionism and Symbolism.

Claude Debussy and His Influence

Claude-Achille Debussy was twelve years old in 1874, and a student at the Conservatory of Music in Paris, when the renegade "Impressionist" painters presented their *Salon of the Refused*. Rejecting basic traditions of form and technique, Debussy nevertheless won the coveted *Prix de Rome* from the Conservatory in 1884. As a young man, he traveled widely and was subject to the same influences that affected other composers in late nineteenth-century France: Japanese painting, the Indonesian gamelan ensemble, and a preoccupation with the exotic, supernatural, and illusionary. While Matisse and Van Gogh pursued Post-Impressionist painting styles that led eventually to new schools such as Picasso's Cubism, Debussy's musical practices were so powerful and inherently flexible, that he is generally credited with having established a bridge between the Romantic era and the twentieth century—almost single-handedly. Arnold Schoenberg and Igor Stravinsky, two towering figures in twentieth-century Western music, composed early works that might be described as "Neo-Impressionist," adapting Debussy's model to their own creative instinct.

Claude Debussy, who is universally known today as "an Impressionist," wrote to his publisher (*Durand et Cie.*) in 1908:

> I am trying to do something different—in a way, realities—what the imbeciles call "impressionism" a term which is as poorly used as possible, particularly by art critics.[1]

Despite his disdain for the term, Debussy was allied both personally and aesthetically with poets, painters, and others who shared the Impressionist ideal of nuance, ambiguity, and understatement. In this chapter, we will center our studies on Debussy's style and his use of melody, harmony, rhythm, and form. In addition, we will consider the music of several other composers who adopted enough of Debussy's style characteristics to be labeled "Impressionist."

MELODY

Many composers who today are considered models of Romanticism (Brahms, Schumann, and Schubert, for example) often wrote melodies that were either major or minor, relatively clear in tonality, lyric in style, and sometimes folk-like in their simplicity. Debussy's melodic style represents a substantial contrast. Modal ambiguity, unresolved dissonance, derived scales, and motivic variation

---

[1]Robert Schmitz, *The Piano Works of Claude Debussy*, Duell, Sloan, & Pearce, Inc., 1950 (Dover Books 1966).

are all characteristics of the Impressionist melodic style. In the following section, we will consider several scales—both old and new—that influenced Debussy and others in the late nineteenth century.

Modes and Exotic Scales

During the Renaissance, the use of accidentals (*musica ficta*) gradually transformed the four authentic Church Modes into just two patterns. By 1700, the use of scales other than major or minor was quite rare. In the late nineteenth century, however, several composers rediscovered the unique flavors of Dorian, Phrygian, Lydian, and Mixolydian modes.[2] The major modes (Lydian and Mixolydian) differ from the major scale by one accidental; Dorian and Phrygian, which are minor modes, are likewise removed by one accidental from the key signature for natural minor. Despite the common pitches among major or minor modes, the effects are striking.

We will alter a theme from Mozart's Symphony No. 41 in C Major (K. 551) to review the Church Modes. Mozart's scalar melody is major (Ionian); listen to the original version and to each following phrase that sets the melody in a different mode.

CD 2, TRACK 19-1 CHURCH MODES (2 PARTS)
Major Modes

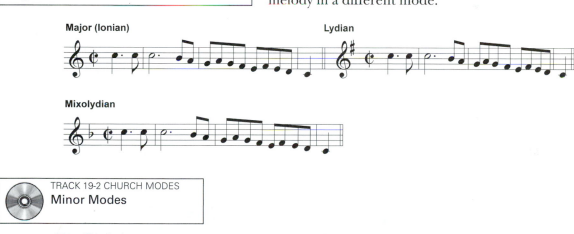

TRACK 19-2 CHURCH MODES
Minor Modes

---

[2]While Impressionist composers retained the names of the Medieval Church Modes, their use of these materials was far more flexible (in range and chromatic alteration, for example) than seen in the Middle Ages or Renaissance.

Debussy's two books of *Préludes* constitute a virtual catalog of Impressionist melodic techniques and materials. A memorable section of *La Cathédrale Engloutie* ("The Sunken Cathedral"), for example, is in Mixolydian mode. Shown in the next example, the melody revolves around the pitch C, but the appearance of B♭ creates Mixolydian. Observe that the phrase evolves from the opening three-pitch motive (1m) that is varied and extended throughout the 14 measures shown.

CD 2, TRACK 20-1 MODAL MELODIES (3 PARTS)
Claude Debussy, "Sunken Cathedral"

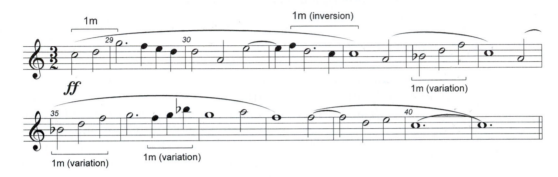

Maurice Ravel (1875–1937) was a French composer who, next to Debussy, is most closely associated with Impressionism. While the first movement of his Quartet (1903) is in sonata form, the second theme is in Phrygian mode on A. The pitch B♭ creates the lowered second scale degree that is characteristic of Phrygian.

TRACK 20-2 MODAL MELODIES
Maurice Ravel, Quartet (I)

Like Ravel, Debussy wrote one string quartet (1893). Also like Ravel, the first movement of the quartet includes a melody in Phrygian mode. The key signature and pitch center of the melody suggest G minor; the consistent use of A♭ as an accidental, however, creates Phrygian mode.

TRACK 20-3 MODAL MELODIES
Claude Debussy, Quartet (I)

In the generation after Debussy and Ravel, a number of Western composers were similarly attracted to modal scales and harmonies. Carlos Chávez (1899–1978), a Mexican composer, organist, and conductor, followed Chopin, Debussy, and others in writing a set of preludes for piano. The Prelude in C, shown in part in the next example, is in the Lydian mode. The opening measures center on C in both melody and accompaniment. But while the first phrase of the melody is in C major (with F♮ in measure 6), the accompaniment is C Lydian (with a consistent F♯). Notice that there is no pitch F in the melody until measure 6, allowing the listener to perceive the Lydian flavor of the accompaniment. Remember that while we may study one part of a polyphonic work alone, an understanding of any composition depends on the musical combination of all voices taken together.

TRACK 20-4 MODAL MELODIES
Carlos Chávez, Prelude

Composers in the late nineteenth century who espoused Nationalism (discussed further in Chapter 9) often wrote modal melodies because many of their native folk songs were modal. The English folk song *Scarborough Fair,* shown in the next example, uses the subtonic (F♮) that creates Aeolian mode on G. In measure 5, an E♮ (harmonized as a major subdominant) brings a Dorian inflection; the final cadence is melodic minor (employing both ↑6̂ and ↑7̂).

English Folk Song, "Scarborough Fair"

Scarborough Fair is not cast in any one mode, but shifts among Aeolian, Dorian, and melodic minor on G. This practice is typical of nineteenth-century modal use, as composers not only meander from one mode to another, but they also freely establish local key areas within an overall pitch reference. As an example, consider Debussy's *Des pas sur la neige* ("Footprints in the Snow") that begins in Aeolian mode on D, then shifts to Dorian mode on the same key center in measure 5.

CD 2, TRACK 21
Claude Debussy, "Footprints in the Snow" from *Préludes I*

Modal materials were common resources for Impressionist composers like Debussy and Ravel. As we will discuss in the next section, however, two modes or scales may also be combined to form a separate melodic resource known as a *synthetic scale*.

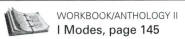

WORKBOOK/ANTHOLOGY II
I Modes, page 145

Synthetic Scales

Scales that do not conform to one of the traditional Renaissance or common-practice models are termed SYNTHETIC. One of Debussy's favorite major scales, for example, is a combination of the ↓$\hat{7}$ heard in Mixolydian plus the ↑$\hat{4}$ that characterizes Lydian.

The Lydian-Mixolydian synthetic scale dominates Debussy's 1905 orchestral work, *La Mer* (*The Sea*). Emphasis on the pitch A♭ and the cadences on D♭ lead us to hear the latter as the pitch center, yet the use of both G♮ and C♭ preclude any traditional scale.

CD 2, TRACK 22-1 SYNTHETIC SCALES (2 PARTS)
Claude Debussy, "From Dawn to Noon on the Sea" from *La Mer*

Several composers at the turn of the century adopted enough of the vocabulary to "sound like" Impressionists, yet a careful analysis of the music reveals many differences. The Lydian-Mixolydian synthetic scale that Debussy used in *La Mer* was attractive to other composers as well. The scale appears also in *Memories of My Childhood: Life in a Russian Village* (1924) by the American

TRACK 22-2 SYNTHETIC SCALES
Charles Martin Loeffler, *Memories of My Childhood*

Charles Martin Loeffler (1861–1935). While the first few measures establish Mixolydian on F, a Lydian inflection precedes the tonal cadence. The melody shown in the next example serves as the subject of a set of variations in Loeffler's tone poem.[3]

As we will discuss further in the next chapter, in addition to the Lydian-Mixolydian synthetic scale (cited in the previous Debussy and Loeffler examples), composers conceived many other scales with a variety of interval types and qualities. Some of these scales have more or fewer than seven discrete pitches. One of the most important new scales devised in the late nineteenth century—one particularly associated with Impressionism—has six pitches and only one interval type: the *whole-tone scale.*

The Whole-Tone Scale

A scale without half steps was unthinkable to common-practice composers; this, of course, is exactly why the WHOLE-TONE SCALE, a series of five consecutive whole steps, was so attractive to Debussy. Without melodic tendencies, it is impossible to tell whether a given pitch is at the beginning, the middle, or the end of the scale. The whole-tone scale was appealing to Debussy since its harmony generates augmented triads and because of its inherent non-Western flavor.

Enharmonic spellings of the whole-tone scale are acceptable (and preferable to double sharps or double flats). Each of the whole-tone scales in the next

[3]Loeffler was born in Alsace (France), but lived with his family for a time in Russia. He later immigrated to the United States and served both as violinist and assistant conductor of the Boston Symphony Orchestra.

example is a correct notation beginning on the pitch B♭; moreover, composers who employed the whole-tone scale did not always maintain any one notation for a section or complete work.

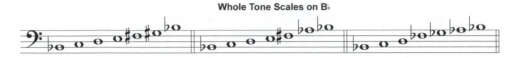

In the first book of piano *Préludes*, Debussy begins "Voiles" ("Veils") with a whole-tone scale harmonized in major thirds. Since traditional melodic tendencies are not present in the whole-tone scale, composers rely on other means to design a feeling for key. In "Veils," a B♭ pedal begins in measure 5 and provides an anchor throughout the work.

CD 2, TRACK 23

Claude Debussy, "Veils" from *Préludes* (Book I)

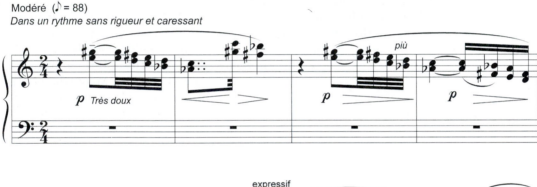

More often, composers used whole-tone *inflections* (with an emphasis on major thirds, major seconds, and the tritone) while the melody itself might deviate somewhat from pure whole tone. A melody from the first movement of Debussy's *La Mer*, for example, is basically whole-tone in A♭, but with a conspicuous half step (G♭–F).

CD 2, TRACK 24
Claude Debussy, "From Dawn to Noon on the Sea" from *La Mer*

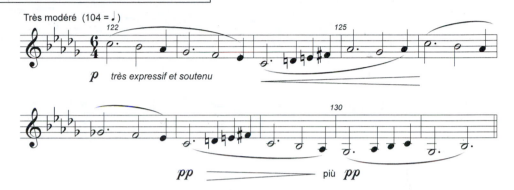

Because Debussy's whole-tone scale is so distinctive, listeners associated it with Impressionism. Accordingly, many other innovative composers of the same era used it tentatively or not at all in an effort to separate their styles from that of Debussy. In addition to the Church Modes, synthetic scales, and the whole-tone, several other new or rediscovered melodic resources were available.

Pentatonic Scale

The pentatonic scale is perhaps the oldest and most common of world scale forms. While it is especially associated with the East, the form of PENTATONIC SCALE seen most often in the West is a gapped series of whole steps and minor thirds. For purposes of construction, we might think of this scale as major without $\hat{4}$ and $\uparrow\hat{7}$.

Debussy's 1894 tone poem *Prélude à l'aprés-midi d'un faune* (*Prelude to the Afternoon of a Faun*) is probably his best-known work among the general public today. Loosely based on a poem by Stéphane Mallarmé, Debussy's *faun* embraces numerous Impressionist techniques, including a pentatonic melody that appears at the climax of the work.

CD 2, TRACK 25-1 PENTATONIC MELODIES (2 PARTS)
Claude Debussy, *Prelude to the Afternoon of a Faun*

Pentatonic melodies abound in hymns and folk literature. The traditional tune in the next passage is pentatonic. The words, with true "fire and brim-stone," were written in the late eighteenth century by the Englishman William Cowper (1731–1800).

Traditional American Melody, "Cleansing Fountain"
Words by William Cowper

Impressionist composers most often employed the pentatonic scale briefly for its familiar color, then veered in another melodic direction. In "General Lavine" from the second book of *Préludes*, when the preceding measures have been pentatonic in F, Debussy surprises the listener with an A♭ in measure 76.

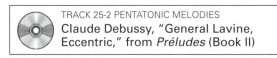

TRACK 25-2 PENTATONIC MELODIES
Claude Debussy, "General Lavine, Eccentric," from *Préludes* (Book II)

The Chromatic Scale

We could make a strong case that the chromatic scale had been a melodic resource for Western composers from about 1825. But while Chopin, Franck, and even Wagner employed chromaticism largely as an embellishment of functional harmony, Debussy and others reveled in the flavor of the chromatic scale itself. Just as the whole-tone scale constituted a resource without functional tendencies, Impressionists were untroubled by a series of consecutive half steps.

One of the most famous chromatic melodies is the one that opens Debussy's *Prelude to the Afternoon of a Faun*. Through repetition, we hear C♯ as a melodic focal point. The tritone between high and low pitches of the first two measures adds to the chromatic ambiguity.

Charles Tomlinson Griffes (1884–1920) chooses a chromatic scale that often exceeds an octave in *The White Peacock*. Consider the ascending chromatic motion in the right hand against the descending line in the left. In discussing music of the Impressionist era, contrary motion between lines is often termed *fanning*.

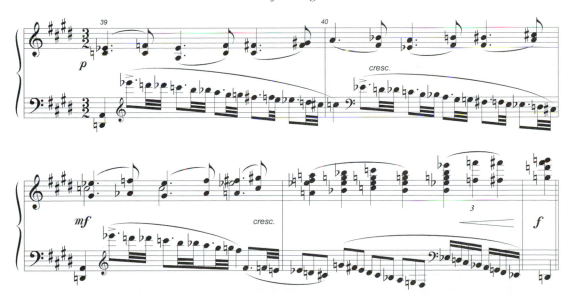

Debussy set the stage for numerous new movements in twentieth-century music. Among these is the mildly dissonant style adopted by several Russian composers, including Serge Prokofiev and Dimitri Shostakovich (1906–1975). Prokofiev wrote his *Vision Fugitive* in 1919—a year after Debussy's death. We will discuss Prokofiev and his style further in Chapter 9; for now, observe the descending chromatic motion in both right and left hands that dominates the phrase over a bass pedal.

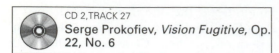

Prokofiev's chromaticism is different from that of Debussy, just as Chopin's innovations in the first half of the nineteenth century, and Wagner's after 1850, moved Western music forward. In melodic innovation, Debussy and some of his contemporaries remained committed to tonality, but they developed means other than harmonic function to foster organization. Many new schools in the twentieth century (Neo-Classicism, Expressionism, atonality, and Serialism, for example) owe at least some debt to the Impressionist aesthetic. In turn, as we will discuss in later chapters, new movements in the twentieth century themselves provided the impetus for the next generations of composers.

WORKBOOK/ANTHOLOGY II
II. Other Scales, page 147

REVIEW AND APPLICATION 8–1

Melody

Essential Terms

chromatic scale	impressionism	pentatonic scale
measured rhythm	synthetic scale	whole-tone scale

1. Identify the following ascending scales according to the initial pitch and scale type. Consider major and all forms of minor, the Church Modes, whole-tone, pentatonic, and synthetic. In the first examples, the pitches are listed in ascending or descending order; for subsequent exercises, determine the proper order based on the first pitch given (which, in all cases, you should consider the pitch reference).

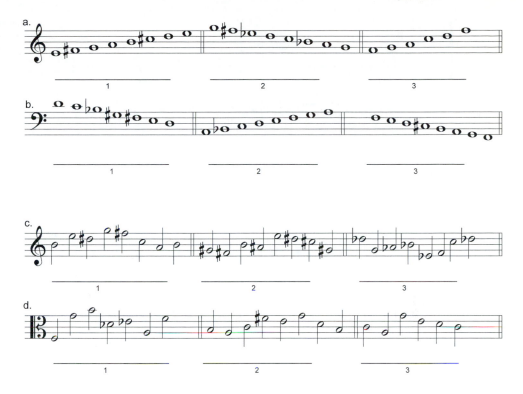

2. As in the previous exercises, identify the scale material of the following melodies. The pitch center is identified since, with melody alone, this may not be clear in all cases. Consider the same scale types suggested in Exercise 1.

Key Center: D   Scale Type: _____

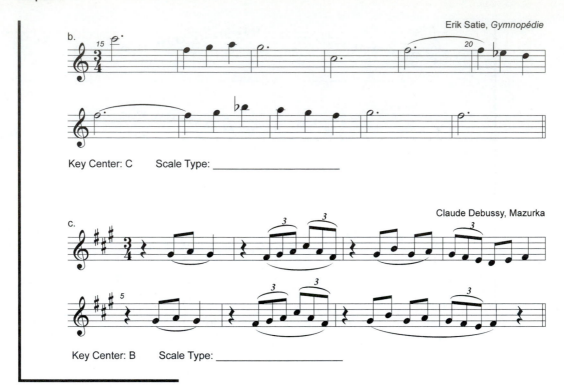

Erik Satie, *Gymnopédie*

Key Center: C   Scale Type: _____

Claude Debussy, Mazurka

Key Center: B   Scale Type: _____

SELF-TEST 8–1

Time Limit: 5 Minutes

1. Choose a scale type from the list that identifies each description. Use only one answer per blank (although in some cases, two or more answers are correct). Some answers may be used twice. *Scoring: Subtract 4 points for each incorrect response.*

   A. Whole Tone   F. Lydian
   B. Major   G. Pentatonic
   C. Dorian   H. Phrygian
   D. Mixolydian   I. Aeolian
   E. Synthetic

   _____ a. Minor scale with raised sixth degree

   _____ b. Natural minor scale

   _____ c. Minor with lowered second degree

   _____ d. Nontraditional scale

   _____ e. A gapped scale

   _____ f. Major scale with lowered seventh degree

   _____ g. Major scale with raised fourth degree

   _____ h. Ionian mode

_____ i. May be notated enharmonically

_____ j. Includes five discrete pitches

2. Write the following ascending scales on the tonics given. Include all necessary accidentals (as opposed to a key signature). *Scoring: Subtract 15 points for each error.*

                    Phrygian   Whole Tone   Mixolydian

3. Identify the scale material of the following melody. *Scoring: Subtract 25 points for an incorrect answer.*

Nathaniel Dett, *Legend of the Atoll*

Key Center: B   Scale Type:_____

Total Possible: 100   Your Score _____

HARMONIC ORGANIZATION

We cannot easily separate the melodic and harmonic practices of Impressionist composers. At times, melodies arise from an interesting series of chords that does not necessarily conform to functional guidelines. In other works, a modal, whole-tone, or alternate scale provides direction to the harmony. For Debussy and some of his contemporaries, embellishment and nuance may replace functional progressions; orchestral *timbre* may become a structural element. Likewise, the repetition and variation of motives may replace melodic tendencies. In this section, we will survey four of the most important Impressionist harmonic tools: extensive employment of pedal, cadences, *planing*, and *pandiatonicism*.

Pedal

Throughout the two volumes of this text, we have discussed pedal as a nonchord tone that sometimes supports, sometimes colors functional harmony. Bach, Haydn, Beethoven, and Schumann all employed pedal traditionally: a single pitch sustained through changing harmonies that is consonant at some points, dissonant at others. Impressionists, however, found a new strategy for the use of pedal. Not only does pedal often create the sensation of a pitch center (especially when the melody and harmony are ambiguous), but the pedal itself may be thickened with additional pitches and rhythmic figures. In "Golliwogg's Cakewalk" from

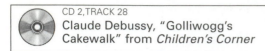

Claude Debussy, "Golliwogg's Cakewalk" from *Children's Corner*

Children's Corner (1908), for example, Debussy combines a pedal perfect fifth with a lively melody of ragtime rhythms.[4]

While Debussy's melody emphasizes B♭ and includes both C♭ and C♮, the E♭ pedal anchors the pitch focus. A sudden excursion to G♭ in measure 22 provides a burst of color; again, however, the pedal clarifies the chromatic mediant (♭III in E♭). The phrase ends with an authentic cadence in the dominant (measure 24–25).

---

[4]A cakewalk is an animated dance in duple meter, probably originated by slaves and their descendants in nineteenth-century America. Ragtime is a type of turn-of-the-century popular music (and a predecessor of jazz) that features syncopated (i.e., "ragged") rhythms. The American Scott Joplin (1868–1917) was a principal proponent of the style; in its manipulation of beat-subdivision accents, Debussy's "Golliwogg's Cakewalk" is typical of ragtime.

Impressionist composers utilized pedal both traditionally and in new ways as well. Charles Loeffler, in *Memories of My Childhood*, uses a layer of chords in superimposed fifths to accompany one of the variations on his Lydian-Mixolydian theme.

CD 2,TRACK 29-1 OSTINATO AND PEDAL (2 PARTS)
Charles Martin Loeffler, *Memories of My Childhood*
Ostinato

In measures 149–153 of the same work, Loeffler chooses a traditional pedal. The bass pitch, D_3, holds throughout the phrase while the theme appears in an inner voice and beneath a counterpoint in parallel fourths and fifths. Like other compositions of continuous variations, each of Loeffler's settings of the theme in *Memories of My Childhood* is unique.

TRACK 29-2 OSTINATO AND PEDAL
Charles Martin Loeffler, *Memories of My Childhood*
Pedal

Cadences

Cadence formulas in Western music date from their very origins in Gregorian chant. Medieval and Renaissance composers devised numerous stereotypical cadences that correspond roughly to half and authentic types in the Common-practice era. In the nineteenth century, composers were generally less preoccupied with strong tonal cadences (although works and important sections may still end with authentic cadences in the music of many composers).

In the Impressionist era, cadences remain a point of musical pause. When Debussy and his followers chose authentic cadences, however, it was frequently without that "set-up" (predominant) chord that we expect in Bach, Haydn, or Brahms. Without the predominant approach, an authentic cadence lacks the "push" that more clearly establishes tonal function in more conservative music. Cadences that have a half, authentic, or plagal *effect* are also common in the works of Debussy and his contemporaries. In "The Girl with the Flaxen Hair," the first cadence is a conventional plagal formula in G♭ major. The final cadence of the work is less traditional, but it also sounds plagal.

The cadences outlined in the last example are simple, but Debussy's use of melody and rhythm in the opening passage (next example) typifies the interest of Impressionist composers in individual intervals and chords. In addition, observe that the opening submediant seventh is unresolved, and the arpeggiations throughout the first four measures create a listless undulation.

CD 2, TRACK 30-1 CADENCES (2 PARTS)
Claude Debussy, "Girl with the Flaxen Hair"
from *Préludes* (Book I)
Opening Phrase

The final cadence (ii–I) in "The Girl with the Flaxen Hair" was also a common Renaissance ending formula. Notice that even without a dominant in close proximity, the plagal-like cadence both creates a pitch reference and lends an antique atmosphere to the work.

TRACK 30-2 CADENCES
Claude Debussy, "Girl with the Flaxen Hair" from *Préludes* (Book I)
Final Cadence

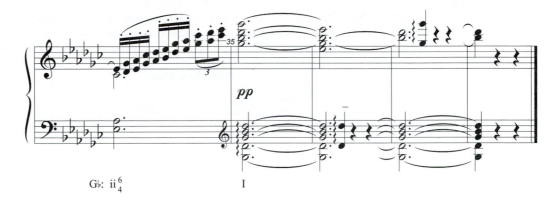

Gb: ii$^6_4$ I

Mediant as Dominant Substitute.   Nineteenth-century composers continued to employ authentic cadences, but often found new ways to color them. In
Volume I, we discussed the mediant triad as ambiguous, having two pitches in
common with both dominant and tonic triads. While Mozart and Beethoven
generally avoided the ambiguity of the mediant triad, Impressionist composers
exploited it. As shown in the next passage, from
Loeffler's *Memories of My Childhood*, the mediant
triad (including both $\hat{5}$ and $\uparrow\hat{7}$) makes a perfectly acceptable dominant substitute.

CD 2, TRACK 31
Charles Martin Loeffler, *Memories
of My Childhood*
Mediant as Dominant Substitute

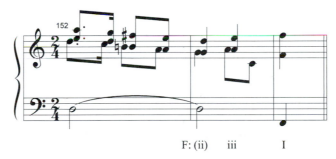

F: (ii)   iii   I

Observe the parallel fourths and fifths in the last two examples. While
common-practice composers avoided series of like perfect intervals, *parallelism*
is another facet of the Impressionist harmonic style.

Parallelism (Planing)

Common-practice harmony is based on chords that differ in quality and are ordered according to root-movement strength. As we have discussed, a series of triads with the same quality does *not* establish a key center. Traditional composers
used deviations in triad quality to orient the listener, just as half-step placement
identified the upper or lower tetrachord of a scale. In a major key, a major triad
might be heard as I, IV, or V, but *not* as ii, iii, vi, or vii°. In the late nineteenth century, Debussy was among the first to use chords in parallel motion—without regard
to root relationships. Because color was so important to Impressionist composers,
they often created *planes* of harmony that ascend or descend in chords of the same
quality or within a single scale system. The use of parallel harmony is termed
PLANING. Composers use three types of planing known as *chord-type*, *diatonic*, and
mixed, respectively.

Chord-Type Planing.   If we begin with a certain chord (a dominant ninth, for example) and shift that sonority up or down to successive chords of the same (or mostly the same) type and quality, the planing is known as CHORD-TYPE.

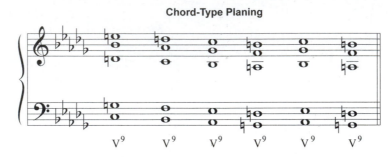

Chord-Type Planing

The chords in the last example are extracted from Debussy's "*La puerta del vino*" (Sp., "The Gate of Wine") from the second book of *Préludes*. While the soprano line in Debussy's passage is the same as the reduction, the chords in the original score are all in second inversion. Each chord is accentuated through an anticipatory flourish as the bass pedal establishes D♭ as a pitch reference. The arrow at the end of the first system indicates that chord-type planing continues into the next line.

 CD 2, TRACK 32-1 CHORD-TYPE PLANING (2 PARTS)
Claude Debussy, "The Gate of Wine"
from *Préludes* (Book I)

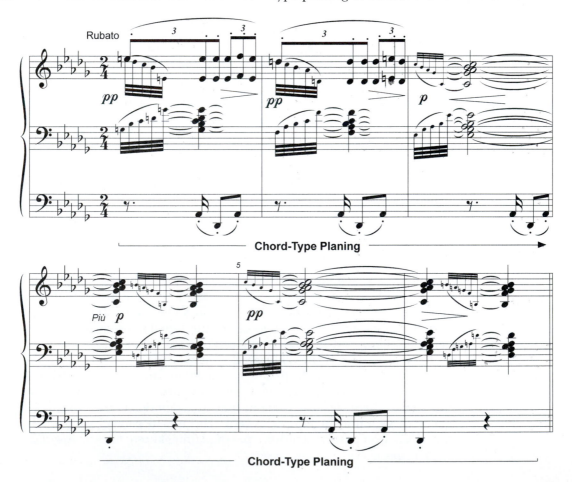

Chord-Type Planing

A *Tombeau* (*Fr.*, "tomb") is a suite written to commemorate the death of a friend or an important person. Another example of chord-type planing occurs in *Le Tombeau de Couperin* (1917) by Maurice Ravel.[5] The rigaudon is a court dance that was popular at the time of French Baroque composer François Couperin (1668–1733). The fourth of six movements in Ravel's *Le Tombeau de Couperin* is a rigaudon. Notice in the next example that the melody is not a single line, but a *plane* of root-position and first-inversion major triads.

TRACK 32-2 CHORD-TYPE PLANING
Maurice Ravel, Rigaudon from
Le Tombeau de Couperin

Diatonic Planing. The fifth movement of *Le Tombeau de Couperin* is a Menuet—a compound ternary (**A B A**) form. In Couperin's day, the second section of a minuet contrasted with the outer movements in key and texture. Following Baroque conventions, Ravel wrote this second section as a musette (with an ostinato pedal suggesting the drone of a bagpipe). The right hand at this same point employs DIATONIC PLANING—parallel motion in which all (or almost all) chords conform to a single scale system. In the Musette section of

CD 2, TRACK 33-1 DIATONIC PLANING (2 PARTS)
Maurice Ravel, Menuet from *Le Tombeau de Couperin*

Ravel's Menuet, the scale system is Dorian mode on G; the passage shown ends with a half cadence to a modal dominant.

---

[5]Ravel dedicated each of the six movements to a different friend who perished in World War I.

Debussy's "The Girl with the Flaxen Hair" includes several passages of diatonic planing. By definition, any type of planing is nonfunctional. In analysis, we might also identify the scale system when the planing is diatonic.

TRACK 33-2 DIATONIC PLANING
Claude Debussy, "Girl with the Flaxen Hair," from *Préludes* (Book I)

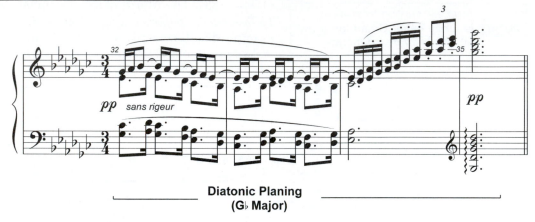

Diatonic Planing
(G♭ Major)

Mixed Planing.   Impressionist composers sometimes employed MIXED PLANING— parallel harmony *without* the predominance of any one chord type and *outside* any particular scale system. Identify mixed planing with some care. Just as a work in C major may contain accidentals while remaining within the tonic key, one or two exceptional chords within a given planed-chord type (a dominant seventh chord, for example, amid a series of minor sevenths) is not necessarily "mixed." Likewise, an occasional atypical chord may occur within the diatonic planing of a melody. Use the designation "mixed planing" when there is clearly neither a predominant chord type nor a discernable scale system.[6]

A characteristic passage of mixed planing occurs in Debussy's "The Gate of Wine" (a reference to a gate of the Alhambra palace in Grenada, Spain). The D♭ pedal clarifies the pitch focus, but the chords in the right hand are more problematic. Since the right-hand chords are mixed almost equally between major and minor, we would not refer to the planing as "chord-type." Likewise, the chords that descend chromatically in a step progression on the first beat of each measure are outside any one scale system. The parallel motion in the next passage may be correctly identified as mixed planing.

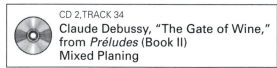

CD 2, TRACK 34
Claude Debussy, "The Gate of Wine," from *Préludes* (Book II)
Mixed Planing

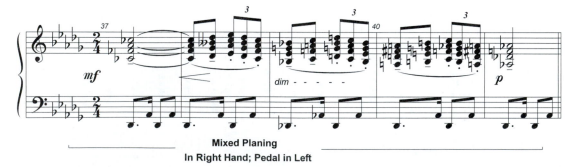

Mixed Planing
In Right Hand; Pedal in Left

[6]Remember that in addition to major and minor, diatonic planing may include a scale system that is modal, pentatonic, whole-tone, or synthetic.

Debussy and his contemporaries looked to techniques such as planing to organize nonfunctional harmony. Many Impressionist tools, however, are so distinctive that they were not often used by composers in the following generations. In the next section of this chapter, we will discuss other approaches such as *pandiatonicism* that proved somewhat more flexible in supporting early- and mid-twentieth-century styles.

Pandiatonicism

Like planing, *pandiatonicism* is an alternative harmonic approach. If a work is PANDIATONIC, structural and secondary pitches conform to a single "white-note" scale system or transposition (C major, B♭ minor, G Lydian, and so on). In other words, "pan" refers to every pitch of a scale or mode, with little or no sense of function; "diatonic" cites the seven scale degrees taken in any order. Passages that are pandiatonic are often linear in origin; like the masses and motets of the Renaissance, harmony results from converging melodic lines.

The first movement of Ravel's quartet begins with a pandiatonic passage within the F major scale. The harmony is nonfunctional, but focus is created through the gradual ascent in the viola and cello (in tenths), coupled with adherence to pitches in the F major scale. As the phrase continues, the lines descend and the scale system changes to minor (Aeolian) remaining on F.

CD 2, TRACK 35-1 PANDIATONICISM (2 PARTS)
Maurice Ravel, Quartet (I)

Pandiatonic in F Major

Pandiatonic in F Minor

Roman numerals are essentially valueless in the analysis of nonfunctional works. By definition, if a passage is constructed from planing or pandiatonicism, individual sonorities are less central to the harmonic effect.[7] Instead, consider an analytical approach that centers on identification through words and phrases:

1. Identification of the pitch that serves as a focal point
2. The scale system that colors the passage
3. Embellishment of pitches within the scale system
4. The relative length of each pandiatonic passage
5. Techniques by which points of pitch reference are maintained

In the final measures of "Jimbo's Lullaby" from *Children's Corner*, Debussy employs a pandiatonic passage that is anchored on the pitch B♭. As you study and listen to the excerpt shown in the next example, notice that we might analyze the music in B♭ major with traditional roman numerals. Closer inspection, however, reveals that melodic tendencies in B♭ major are often ignored. In fact, there is no pitch E♭ (4̂) anywhere until measure 78; ↑7̂ never resolves directly to 8̂ In addition, chords that we would need to explain as sevenths or other harmonic dissonances do not resolve traditionally. As shown in the next example, a more helpful analysis identifies pitch center, scale system, and the extensive use of pedal.

TRACK 35-2 PANDIATONICISM
Claude Debussy, "Jimbo's Lullaby" from *Children's Corner*

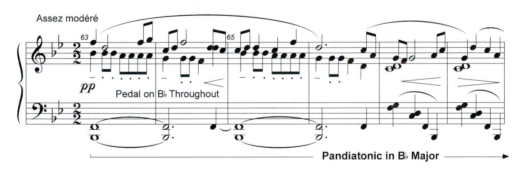

Assez modéré

pp

Pedal on B♭ Throughout

Pandiatonic in B♭ Major ⟶

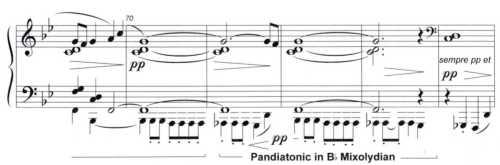

pp

sempre pp et
pp

pp

Pandiatonic in B♭ Mixolydian

---

[7]In Chapter 9, we will discuss a new way to analyze individual chords in nonfunctional passages.

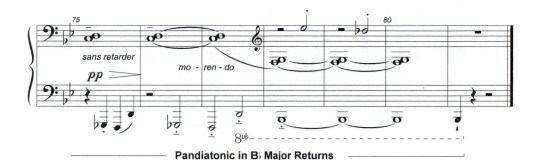

Pandiatonic in B♭ Major Returns

While diatonic planing is also pandiatonic, we usually prefer the former term, reserving the latter for passages in which no more specific explanation of harmonic organization is available.

In the hands of Impressionist composers, all four methods of harmonic organization discussed in this section are tonal (pedal, cadence, planing, and pandiatonicism). Yet, when it had been established that pitches within a diatonic scale system could be combined successfully without regard to melodic tendencies, other composers began to combine pitches of the *chromatic* scale to produce music that was *atonal*—without a pitch reference.

> WORKBOOK/ANTHOLOGY II
> III. Impressionist Harmonic Techniques, page 149

REVIEW AND APPLICATION 8–2

Harmonic Organization

Essential Terms

chord-type planing   mixed planing   planing
diatonic planing   pandiatonicism

1. Continue the first sonority in the treble clef to harmonize melodies with the type of planing specified. Use accidentals as necessary. Note that in some cases, many different solutions exist. Leave the lower staff blank for the time being.

a: **Diatonic Planing, G Dorian**

Leave lower staff
blank. See Exercise 2

b. **Chord-Type Planing**

Leave lower staff
blank. See Exercise 2

c. **Mixed Planing**

Leave lower staff
blank. See Exercise 2

2. Return to Exercise 1 and add a bass pedal as specified. Use the bass clef staff left blank earlier.

Line a. Create a rhythmic ostinato-pedal using the pitches G and D—singly or in combination. Be sure to establish G as the pitch reference.

Line b. Provide a bass pedal of repeated eighth notes that emphasizes the pitch D.

Line c. Use a more conventional pedal or longer note values. Establish C as the pitch center in measures 1–3; change to D as a reference in measures 4–6.

3. Provide an analysis of the passages given. Look for planing (possibly more than one type in a single example), use of pedal, and pandiatonicism. Locate and examine cadences; be prepared to discuss cadential type.

CD 2, TRACK 36-1 REVIEW AND APPLICATION 8-2 (2 PARTS)
Claude Debussy, Nocturne

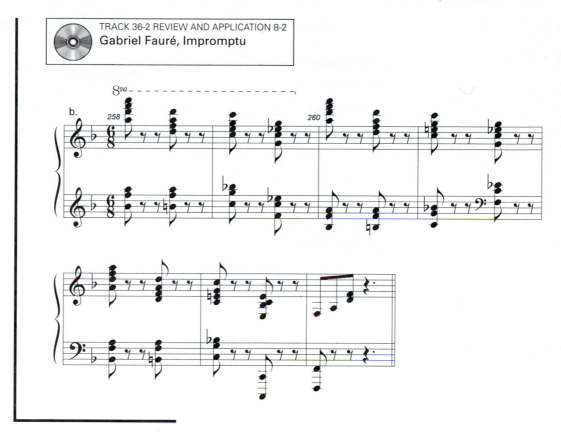

TRACK 36-2 REVIEW AND APPLICATION 8-2
Gabriel Fauré, Impromptu

SELF-TEST 8–2

Time Limit: 5 Minutes

1. Make a check beside the correct answer in each of the following groups. *Scoring: Subtract 9 points for each incorrect answer.*

a. Which of the following is *not* a common Impressionist harmonic technique?

_____ (1) Cubism

_____ (2) Parallelism

_____ (3) Pandiatonicism

_____ (4) Pedal

b. "Fanning" refers to

_____ (1) mixed planing

_____ (2) pandiatonicism

_____ (3) contrary motion

_____ (4) parallelism

c. Which of the following was an acceptable dominant substitute for Impressionist composers?

_____ (1) Subdominant

_____ (2) Supertonic

_____ (3) Mediant

_____ (4) Submediant

d. Planing that conforms to a particular scale system is termed

_____ (1) Mixed

_____ (2) Diatonic

_____ (3) Whole-tone

_____ (4) Chord-type

e. Pandiatonicism depends on adherence to

_____ (1) Functional tendencies

_____ (2) Plagal cadences

_____ (3) Parallel motion

_____ (4) A single scale system

2. Study the passage in the next example; then answer the questions posed.

Scoring: Subtract 11 points for each incorrect answer.

CD 2, TRACK 37

Claude Debussy, Sarabande from
Pour le Piano

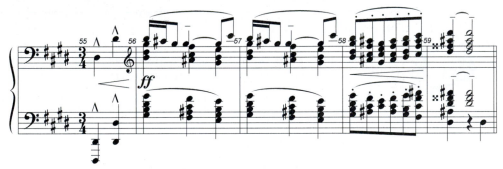

A. What is the pitch center of this passage?

_____

B. Which scale system is employed (mode or type)?

_____

C. What type of planing occurs in this passage?

_____

D. How would you describe the cadence in measures 58–59?

_____

E. Considering the contrapuntal motion between the highest soprano line and the lowest bass line in measure 58, what term is applicable?

_____

Total Possible: 100   Your Score _____

ANALYZING IMPRESSIONIST HARMONY

For passages that are organized around planing or pandiatonicism, an identification of pitch reference is often a sufficient analysis. In other cases, however, the identification of individual sonorities is necessary. Sometimes, as in the case of extended tertian and added-tone chords, we may use familiar letter-name symbols (EM, Em, E^7, and so on) or even roman numerals. When harmony is nonfunctional, the letter name sometimes identifies the bass (as opposed to stipulating a root).

Seventh, Ninth, and Added-Tone Chords

In passages that are functional, or at cadences and harmonic pillars, we may use roman numerals or letter designations to identify the root and quality of a chord. Seventh and ninth chords fall into this category. From our life-long tonal conditioning, chords like the dominant and diminished seventh imply a resolution to follow; when used in a series, such chords may be quickly heard as nonfunctional. We may identify chords in a series as "B^7, E♭^{7}," and so on. From the second book of *Préludes*, "*La terrasse des audiences du clair de lune*" ("The Terrace of Moonlight Audiences") appears quite complex, with three staves, cross-staff notation, and a multi-

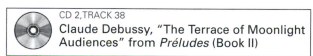

CD 2, TRACK 38

Claude Debussy, "The Terrace of Moonlight Audiences" from *Préludes* (Book II)

tude of accidentals. A closer look, however, reveals that after the first measure, all chords in the passage shown are dominant sevenths. Note also the pedal (C♯).

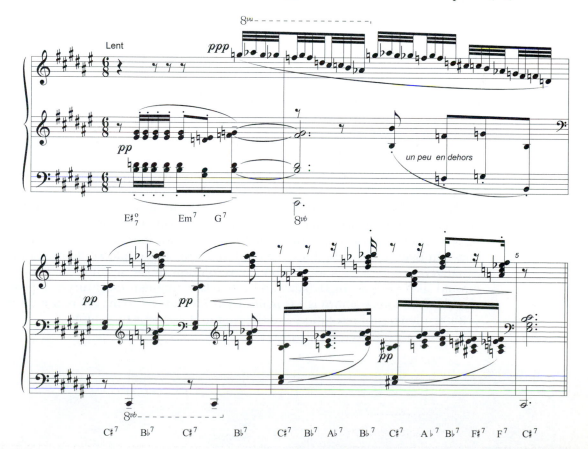

Ninth Chords. Debussy and other members of the Impressionist school employed ninth chords both individually and in nonfunctional series. Often, we can analyze these sonorities with letter names to identify the root. In "Canope" (a city in ancient Egypt), Debussy alternates dominant ninths on C and F. The letter-name identification of chords in this passage reveals quality and root relationships.

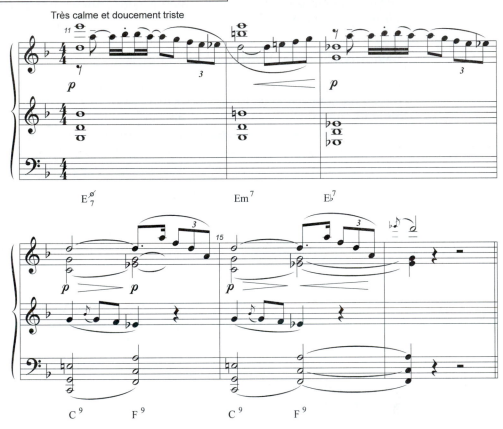

Added-Tone Chords. Impressionist composers often added pitches to tertian chords. The added dissonance is typically unresolved, so that the new ADDED-TONE CHORD becomes a new sonority in its own right. Debussy often dramatizes the added pitch by isolating it in terms of register or orchestral *timbre*. Pitches most frequently added are a second, fourth, or sixth above the bass. In Beethoven or Brahms, the triad in the next example would probably be analyzed as ii $\frac{6}{5}$ (with A as the root); a resolution of the seventh down by step would likely follow. In Debussy and other late-nineteenth-century composers, however, the same chord is a C major triad with added sixth. There are no specific tendencies of resolution and the root in this case is C—not A.

G: ii$^6_5$ C^{add6}

In the last example, notice that the added-tone chord is identified with the notation "add6" and not "+6." To avoid confusion, theorists use the references "add6," "add4," and so on, for added-tone chords. The plus sign is reserved for identification of augmented sixth chords (Fr^{+6}).

Erik Satie (1866–1925) was an eccentric French composer whose modal harmonies and simple, spacious rhythms were influential on Debussy and others. His three *Gymnopédie* (1888) are still popular today (the group Blood, Sweat, and Tears included an arrangement of a Satie *Gymnopédie* in their introductory 1970 album.) The passage shown in the next example has G as a pitch center. Frequent modal dominants and the modal cadence in measures 25–26

CD 2, TRACK 40
Erik Satie, *Gymnopedie*

contribute to a quaint atmosphere. Unresolved dissonances, including a seventh chord with added sixth (measure 20), create color in Satie's otherwise languid style.

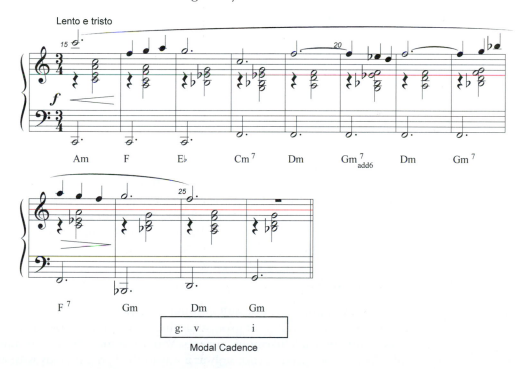

In another passage from Debussy's Sarabande, various added-tone chords are planed diatonically in F♯ minor.

CD 2, TRACK 41
Claude Debussy, Sarabande
Added-Tone Chords

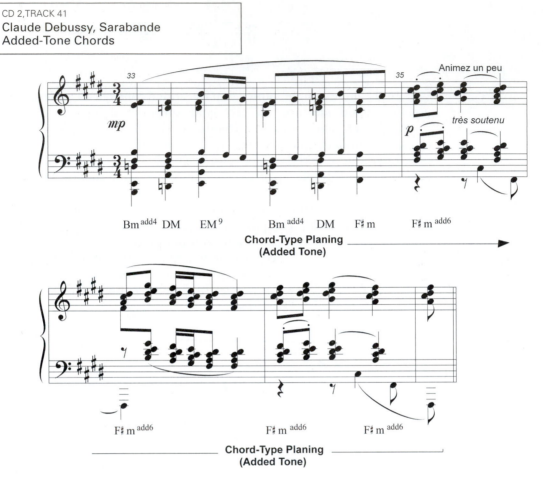

Determining the root of a chord in Impressionist music may be less important than identifying the pitch center and documenting the ways in which various sonorities lend support or contrast. The emphasis in the Sarabande passage shown is F♯; we can determine this from the strong root movement in measures 35–38 and the F♯$^{add\,6}$ that dominates the phrase.

Quartal Harmony

Impressionist composers not only pushed tertian harmony to its limits, but they were among several different groups of nineteenth-century pioneers who experimented with alternate harmonic systems. You will remember that tertian harmony evolved in the Renaissance not only as a way to thicken a melody with a consistent texture, but also because multiple voices permitted composers to assert a measure of creativity, even with music typically based on a chant melody. Yet harmonic systems other than tertian had always been theoretical possibilities. In the late nineteenth century, several different composers experimented with harmony based on superimposed fourths, known as QUARTAL HARMONY.

If we build a tertian triad upon G, the two upper pitches will be B and D. If the triad is quartal, however, the two upper pitches will be superimposed fourths—C and F.

Passages based on quartal chords lack the functional tendencies associated with traditional tertian harmony. Accordingly, numerous concepts such as chord quality, root, progression, key center, dissonance, and cadence must be viewed differently in a quartal system. Overall, however, quartal harmony in Impressionist music occurs most often as a moment of contrast with functional or nonfunctional tertian chords.

In Debussy's Sarabande from *Pour le piano*, the first major section concludes with a statement of the first theme in octaves and with a plagal cadence in C♯ minor (Aeolian). Following the cadence, Debussy begins a section in quartal harmony. The key center is still C♯, but the mode is Phrygian (measures 23–26). Harmonic sequence sets the same material in E Lydian (measures 31–32), but quartal chords soon give way to a return of tertian harmony and a cadence in E major.

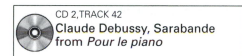

CD 2, TRACK 42

Claude Debussy, Sarabande
from *Pour le piano*

Analyzing Quartal Harmony. Quartal harmony is inherently nonfunctional; as with planing and pandiatonicism, traditional analytical methods are of little value. As we discussed earlier, determining the pitch reference is a first step toward understanding a quartal passage. In the Sarabande just cited, note that Debussy orients the listener first to C♯, then to E, by descending fifths in the bass and a dominance of the focal pitches in the soprano.

In analyzing specific quartal chords, find the QUARTAL-ROOT (the lowest pitch when stacked in successive fourths) and determine the number of fourths present above it. This process is virtually identical to reckoning the root and construction of a tertian sonority. To analyze a quartal chord, begin by eliminating any octave or enharmonic duplication; then arrange pitches in superimposed fourths. As with inverted triads, the bass and quartal-root may not be the same. In this event, arrange pitches in superimposed fourths exactly as you have done to find the root of an inverted triad or seventh chord (as with triads, only one arrangement in superimposed fourths is possible).

Original Chord	Octave and Enharmonic Duplications Omitted	Arrangement in Superimpoised Fourths

For an analytical symbol, count the number of pitch classes present in the "root-position" quartal chord, enter a numeral to specify the interval type ("4" for quartal), then identify the quartal-root.[8] We could identify the chord in the previous example as "4 × 4 on B♭."

ANALYSIS OF QUARTAL CHORDS

Number of Pitch Classes Present	**"X"**	Interval On Which Harmony is Based	**"on"**	Quartal Root

Examples:

4 x 4 on G	**3 x 4 on E♭**	**5 x 4 on F**
Four pitch classes	Three pitch classes	Five pitch classes
Quartal	Quartal	Quartal
G is Root	E♭ is Root	F is Root

While the fourths in chords *a* and *b* in the next example are all perfect, a diminished and an augmented fourth appear in chord *c*. Note also that in chords *a* and *c*, the bass and quartal-root are not the same. In the next chapter, we will discuss ways of accounting for differences in quality with quartal and quintal (fifths) harmony as well as the appearance of added tones and embellishments.

---

[8]This analytical method for secundal, quartal, and quintal harmonies is discussed further in Stephan Kostka, *Materials and Techniques of Twentieth-Century Music,* Second Edition, Prentice Hall, 1999.

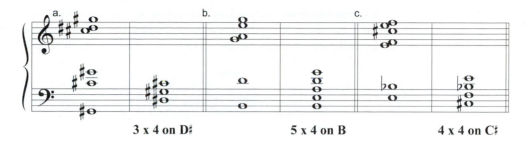

3 x 4 on D♯   5 x 4 on B   4 x 4 on C♯

Quartal harmony was pioneered in the late nineteenth century by Debussy and others—including those, like Charles Ives, who could hardly be termed Impressionists. At first, composers tapped an alternate harmony for color; later trend setters founded entirely new systems of harmony based on quartal, secundal, and quintal chords.

WORKBOOK/ANTHOLOGY II
IV. Analyzing Impressionist
Harmony, page 153

FORM, RHYTHM, AND OTHER PARAMETERS

Studies about Impressionist idioms tend to center on melody and harmony, since an understanding of these parameters necessitates new methods of analysis and a reorientation away from melodic tendencies and other functional principles. But in the parameters of form, rhythm, and orchestration, Impressionist composers broke new ground as well. Igor Stravinsky's use of motives, for example, can be traced directly to Debussy; the rhythmic complexities seen in some Impressionist works influenced later composers, including both Stravinsky and Arnold Schoenberg.

Impressionist Formal Design

The overall formal design of an Impressionist work may be binary, ternary, through-composed, or even sonata or rondo form. Most interest, however, lies in the development of phrases. MOTIVIC GENERATION, the manipulation of an incomplete melodic and rhythmic fragment, was not new with Debussy. Beethoven was among the first to fashion works from simple motives; the concept was enlarged through Hector Berlioz' *idee fixé*, and perfected in Richard Wagner's *leitmotif*. Debussy's formal design is often termed MOSAIC, since one or two motives, repeated, truncated, extended, and otherwise altered, flow from one to another throughout major sectional divisions.

"The Girl with the Flaxen Hair" (given complete on pages 288–290) is based on a single descending gesture heard unaccompanied in the first measure:

After repetition and truncation, the phrase ends with a variation ($1m^1$) that serves throughout the work to announce a cadence.

A second motive (derived as a rhythmically augmented inversion of 1m) occurs first in measure 5. Again, note the manipulation of the motive through three measures. The eighth/two-sixteenth figure in the extension reminds us of 1m.

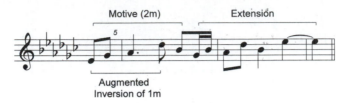

Following a repetition of measures 1–2 (not shown), the motive (1m) is manipulated into a five-measure phrase ending with the familiar descending tetrachord (1m¹). Measures 12–16 feature variations on motive 1m as well as ascending sixteenth notes in measure 15. The key is E♭, but the pitch reference moves gradually to G♭ by measure 24.

A new motive (3m) appears in measure 24, although it, too, is a variation in augmented values of the opening motive (1m). We might also view measures 27–28 as an expansion of the descending thirds heard in 1m.

The original motive (1m) returns an octave higher in measure 29. The key is now G♭ major. Notice that measures 31–33 constitute versions of 1m¹ (our cadential signal) in augmented rhythmic values.

After a brief return of material heard in measure 14, Debussy's "The Girl with the Flaxen Hair" ends with ascending parallel fourths and a cadence in G♭ major. Note the whole step plus minor third in the ascending line; this figure, as all material in the work, derives from the opening motive (1m).

Debussy based "The Girl with the Flaxen Hair" on a single motive. For convenience in analysis, we have identified three different motives, but the second and third are clearly derived from 1m.

We could make a detailed time-line analysis of "The Girl with the Flaxen Hair" based on the previous study of motives and their development. Unlike our earlier time lines of Classical- and Romantic-era forms, however, a prose description of the details may be more useful. In discussing an overall form for the brief work, we can rely on key scheme and melodic material, as well as tempo and phrase markings, to delineate sections. The work is an **A B A**[1] with a chromatic-mediant key relationship between the middle and the two outer parts.

Impressionist works often feature the kind of novel mosaic structure seen in "The Girl with the Flaxen Hair." On the other hand, we should not be surprised to find that compositions of almost any era and style fall into one of the small forms (binary and ternary).

Rhythm and Meter

Wholesale changes to the traditional system of Western meter were to occur in the generation after Debussy (with Stravinsky, Ives, Cowell (1897–1965), Bartók, and others). Impressionists were generally content with the same rhythmic and metric devices that existed in the music of Chopin and Brahms: mixed meter, syncopation, hemiola, two-against-three, unusual beat divisions, and the like. But while Brahms, for example, used hemiola frequently, Debussy and other forward-looking composers in the late nineteenth century were more prone to superimpose two or more exceptional rhythmic devices.

Layering. The process of combining two or more simple lines into a more complex whole is termed LAYERING. Found in the music of Africa, Indonesia, and other cultures, layering was not common in the West until the late nineteenth century.[9] Layering is most effective in ensemble music, where a line can be delineated by a different instrumental or vocal *timbre*, but Debussy's piano work *Hommage à Joseph Haydn* (1909) includes several examples of two- and three-voice layering. After a slow introductory section (measures 1–22, not shown), three distinct lines occur in $\frac{3}{8}$ meter. None of the lines actually supports the traditional strong-weak-weak accents; moreover, each line is offset from the other by one beat as it enters.

CD 2, TRACK 43
Claude Debussy, *Homage to Haydn*

The three separate lines in the last example are obvious with pitch notation. With rhythms only, however, the layered structure of this and more complex passages is even clearer.

Debussy, *Hommage à Joseph Haydn*

In many of Debussy's orchestral works, an even more elaborate layering occurs. The excerpt on page 375 from *Prelude to the Afternoon of a Faun* has four separate layers. The woodwinds and horns play the most intricate line: eighth-note triplets that are grouped in a hemiola pattern. This syncopation is supported by

---

[9]While Medieval organum is layered, our reference here is to a homophonic texture in which at least one voice is an accompaniment.

an uneven triplet in oboes and horns. The effect contradicts the notated triple meter and creates a series of nine quarter notes over each pair of measures.

Horns, Clarinets, Flutes, Oboes

Double basses and bassoons are assigned dotted half notes in the second layer.

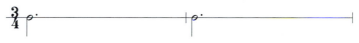

Bassoons and Double Basses

In the third layer, two harps play arpeggios that coincide with the triple meter.

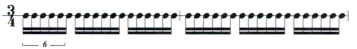

First and Second Harps

Finally, the pentatonic melody emerges in octaves in the violins, violas, and cellos. The massed sound of strings easily outweighs the more lightly scored harp, bass, and woodwind lines, but the background for the melody is rich with melodic and rhythmic effects. In this respect, "homophony" is a weak term for such an energetic texture.

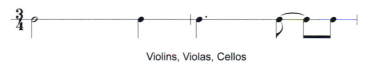

Violins, Violas, Cellos

Consider the four layers together. The complete orchestral score of this passage appears on page 375.

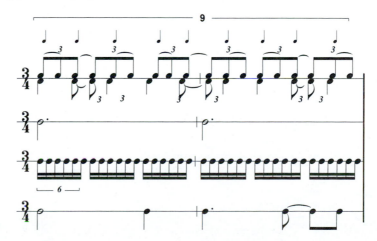

Polyrhythm. In another passage from *Hommage á Joseph Haydn,* Debussy creates a hemiola that is effectively $\frac{3}{16}$ in the right hand against $\frac{3}{8}$ in the left. When two meters occur simultaneously within a single meter signature, the effect is known as POLYRHYTHM; if two different meter signatures are employed simultaneously, the music is polymetric (discussed in Chapter 9).

CD 2, TRACK 44
Claude Debussy, *Homage to Haydn*
Polyrhythm

Debussy and other Impressionist composers considered the natural accents of a given meter only the most fragile guidelines for rhythmic construction. With no clear downbeat or strong/weak patterning, the resulting ambiguity is a perfect match to the Impressionist doctrine. Likewise, rhythms that obscure natural accents are more the rule than the exception and parallel the French language itself. As is apparent in the *Hommage á Joseph Haydn* and *Prelude to the Afternoon of a Faun* excerpts, Impressionists employed layered lines to generate a sparkling, but somewhat indistinct texture. In analysis, we should expect and point out various devices, but the real interest is in the interplay of individual lines.

Orchestration

By 1875, the Western symphony orchestra numbered over one hundred members. Strings (violins, violas, cellos, and basses) still dominated orchestral textures and comprised over half of the orchestra membership. The brass section, however, now included tuba and bass trombone; eight French horns were often employed (in contrast to two in Mozart's day). The woodwind section featured English horn and contrabassoon, as well as flutes and clarinets high and low. In addition to a host of percussion, one or more harps were often added to the orchestra, as was an occasional keyboard instrument or saxophone.

CD 2, TRACK 45
Claude Debussy, *Prelude to the Afternoon of a Faun*
Layering

Claude Debussy, *Prelude to the Afternoon of a Faun*

Hector Berlioz revolutionized orchestral scoring (orchestration) in the first half of the nineteenth century, with new instruments, increased technical demands, and an influential textbook on the subject. In the later nineteenth century, it was the Russian, Nikolay Rimsky-Korsakov (1844–1908), who taught and wrote about orchestration. For both Berlioz and Rimsky-Korsakov, strings constituted the backbone of the orchestra, with families of winds providing contrast. But while Debussy wrote for an orchestra of similar size, he employed the massed ensemble only rarely, preferring to select a chamber-sized group of distinctive colors for a few measures, then add or withdraw an instrument or two for the next phrase. Rather than scoring for the entire section of violins or cellos, for example, Debussy often scored a melody for one solo instrument.

In the passage from Debussy's *Prelude to the Afternoon of a Faun* on the previous page notice that the three supporting lines are actually two-measure ostinato patterns. Brahms or Tchaikovsky, on the other hand, preferred simpler accompanying textures that might include syncopated figures, repeated notes, or chords in longer values. Debussy's innovative use of simultaneous ostinato patterns creates an animation not possible with Romantic-era techniques. In this respect, Debussy again looms as the inspiration for later generations of composers.

Debussy's affinity for color led him to devise new orchestral combinations. In *La Mer*, for example, a sixteen-voice cello choir begins a major section in the first movement (shown in the next example). For Mozart and Haydn, cellos and basses usually played the same part in octaves; Beethoven and later composers occasionally specified *divisi* for a thicker texture. Requiring not six or eight, but *sixteen* cellos, however (let alone a four-part division), is illustrative of Debussy's genius.

CD 2, TRACK 46
Claude Debussy, *La Mer*

While Impressionism continued to be important well into the twentieth century, its primary function was to connect two eras. Just as Impressionist painters paved the way for Cubism and nonrepresentational art in the twentieth century, Impressionism began a trend away from harmonic function as a primary means of organization. Few composers in the first quarter of the twentieth century were not influenced by some aspect of Debussy's style: nonfunctional harmony, mosaic melodic construction, inventive accompaniment, or brilliant orchestration.

WORKBOOK/ANTHOLOGY II
V. Form, Rhythm, and Orchestration,
page 157

REVIEW AND APPLICATION 8–3

Summary of the Impressionist Style

Essential Terms

added-tone chord	mosaic	polyrhythm	quartal harmony
layering	motivic generation	quartal-root	

1. The passages in the next lines include quartal harmonies. Use the lowest staff to notate the chords with octaves and enharmonic duplications eliminated and with pitches stacked above the original bass note (an octave higher or lower for easier reading if necessary). In the blanks, provide analyses of the chords (as discussed on page 368).

2. Provide an appropriate analysis of each of the following passages (notes for class discussion or a formal presentation or paper as specified by your instructor). Consider some or all of the following parameters:

1. Scale system and pitch reference
2. Presence of planing (specific type) or pandiatonicism
3. Whole-tone, quartal, or other innovative harmony
4. Cadences
5. Importance of pedal
6. Rhythmic devices (polyrhythm, hemiola, and so on)

 CD 2, TRACK 47-1 REVIEW AND APPLICATION 8-3 (3 PARTS)
Claude Debussy, "Bruyères" from *Préludes*
(Book II)

a.

 TRACK 47-2 REVIEW AND APPLICATION 8-3
Claude Debussy, *Rêverie*

Andantino san lenteur

b.

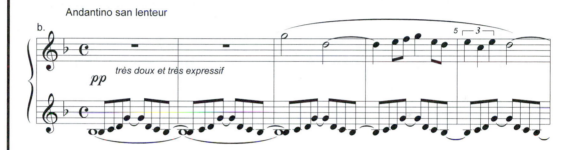

 TRACK 47-3 REVIEW AND APPLICATION 8-3
Claude Debussy, "The Sunken Cathedral,"
Préludes (Book I)

Sonore sans dureté

c.

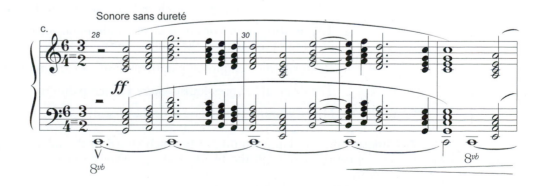

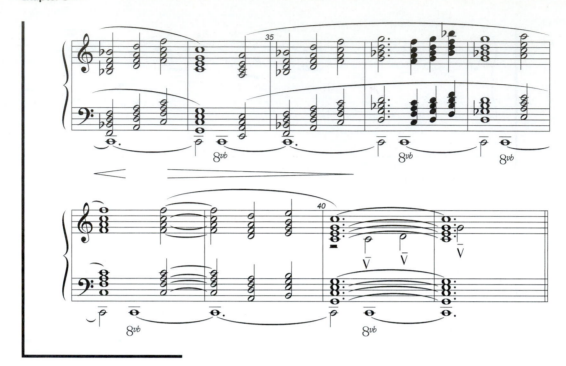

SELF-TEST 8–3

Time Limit: 5 Minutes

1. Considering the Impressionists and their music, circle T if the statement is true, or F if the statement is false. *Scoring: Subtract 6 points for a wrong answer.*

   T   F   a. Maurice Ravel is considered by many authorities to be an Impressionist.

   T   F   b. The whole-tone scale was used as early as the Baroque era.

   T   F   c. A polyrhythm involves two different meter signatures.

   T   F   d. Quartal harmony is nonfunctional.

   T   F   e. "Motivic generation" refers to building a melodic phrase from a motive.

   T   F   f. Impressionist composers rarely used binary and ternary form.

   T   F   g. The layering of two or more accompanimental voices was common in Western music from the Middle Ages.

   T   F   h. Hector Berlioz employed pandiatonicism as early as 1840.

   T   F   i. The original "Impressionists" were French painters.

   T   F   j. Mixed planing is based on a synthetic scale.

2. Choose a description from the list for each chord in the next example. Write the appropriate letter in the blank. *Scoring: Subtract 10 points for each incorrect response.*

A. Dominant ninth
B. Dominant seventh
C. Tertian triad
D. Quartal: 3 × 4
E. Added tone

F. Quartal: 4 × 4
G. Quartal: 5 × 4
H. Whole tone
I. Synthetic

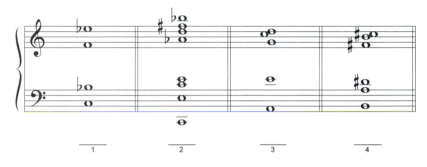

1   2   3   4

Total Possible: 100   Your Score _____

PROJECTS

Analysis

All three works available for analysis in this chapter are for piano and all three are by Claude Debussy. While other composers adopted Impressionist techniques, as we have discussed, Debussy was the model and guiding spirit of the movement. In an analysis of Impressionistic piano works, several areas will be of general interest:

a. melodic style: the range of scales and modes, motivic development; contrast.

b. key centers and cadential procedure.

c. planing and other nonfunctional harmonic techniques.

d. formal structure—both on the small scale (documenting Debussy's usual mosaic approach) and the overall shape of the movement (binary, ternary, through composed, and so on).

e. texture and textural contrast.

f. the range and employment of nuance (dynamics, expression, tempo, and the like).

g. rhythm and meter: metric consistency, the use of syncopation, hemiola, and other devices.

Text

Claude Debussy, "The Girl with the Flaxen Hair" from *Préludes I*, text pages 288–290.

Workbook/Anthology II

Claude Debussy, "The Little Shepherd" from *Children's Corner*, workbook pages 159–160.
Claude Debussy, "The Sunken Cathedral" from *Préludes I*, workbook pages 161–166.

Composition

Suite for Oboe and Piano.   The phrases on the next page are based on harmonic materials discussed in Chapter 8. Identify the most prominent techniques and be prepared to provide an analysis of both passages.

After you have analyzed the two phrases below, compose a miniature suite of three movements that together make about three minutes of music. Use the two given passages as models for the second and third movements, respectively. The first movement (prelude), for which no model is given, might be an adagio and little more than an introduction (as is common in suites of the Baroque era).

CD 2, TRACK 48-1 (2 PARTS)
Sample Suite
Second Movement

I. Prelude
(no model given)

II. Aria

CD 2, TRACK 48-2
Sample Suite
Third Movement

III. Dance

For Further Study

Movements in Art.   As we have seen from our studies of Impressionism, movements in art have often preceded similar changes in music. Prepare a presentation on one or more of the following periods in art history from which a similar musical movement takes its name. Mention two or three principal painters and show the class a few of their representative words through handouts, slides, Powerpoint, or other visual medium. Summarize essential elements of the period in art and explain some of the philosophical ideals that generated it. How were equivalent ideas carried out in musical terms? Consider playing recordings of appropriate music as you view and discuss the art work.

Renaissance Art (1400–1600)

In art, the Renaissance is often divided in to Early Renaissance (early and mid-1400s), High Renaissance (early and mid-1500s), Northern Renaissance (painters in Germany and The Netherlands 1400–1600), and Mannerism (late sixteenth century).

Baroque Art (1600–1700)

Rococo Art (1700–1775)

In music, the Rococo is a transitional period between Baroque and Classical eras.

Romanticism in Art (1775–1825)

Consider also investigating the school of Realism in the mid-nineteenth century.

CHAPTER 9

National and Ethnic Resources

In 1913, Igor Stravinsky opened his ballet *Le Sacre du Printemps* (*The Rite of Spring*, known universally as *Le Sacre*) with a simple phrase for one solo instrument. In a soprano register, the melody is stated, restated, embellished, and expanded amid constantly changing meters.

CD 2, TRACK 49

Igor Stravinsky, *Le Sacre du Printemps*

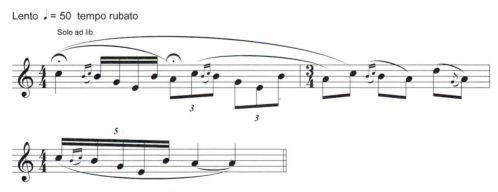

While the triplets, irregular divisions, and contradiction of metric accents in Stravinsky's melody are noteworthy, the most innovative aspect of the line is *timbre*. Earlier, we identified the phrase as lying "in a soprano register." The solo line, however, is scored for bassoon—not flute, violin, or clarinet. Today's professional bassoonists play the extremely high passage with ease, but in 1913, the unusual instrumentation—as well as many other aspects of the work—comprised a stroke of brilliance for some listeners, an abomination for others.

Many historians today speculate that Stravinsky's *Le Sacre* (and similar works) announced a period of transition in Western music. In general, however, audiences lagged behind in their musical interests. Throughout the twentieth century, important new musical styles and systems emerged in virtually every decade. Arguably, however, none of these movements has passed the test of time with the listening public.

As with other transitional periods, the traditional and the revolutionary existed side by side as the twentieth century began. Gustav Mahler (1860–1911), Jean Sibelius (1865–1927), and Gustav Holst are composers who remained faithful to traditional tertian harmony. Igor Stravinsky and Aaron Copland, on the other hand, mastered several of the new styles. Composers who adopted a single innovative system and adhered to it include Paul Hindemith and Anton Webern (1883–1945).

Technology was a major factor in late nineteenth- and early-twentieth-century Western music. The phonograph allowed listeners, for the first time, to enjoy music without attending a live performance. Moreover, favorite arias, waltzes, and popular tunes could be heard over and over again in the home. The invention of sound-recording instruments permitted scholars to document authentic versions of folk music "in the field." Often, these new melodic and rhythmic combinations accentuated the limitations of Western music notation. Finally, the invention of the radio (ca. 1895) advanced commercial possibilities in music never before imagined; by 1925, most listeners had home access to a wide variety of musical styles (as well as commercial advertisements).

NATIONALISM

The period of NATIONALISM—an increased awareness of ethnic dance, literature, music, and other aspects of culture—began in the nineteenth century. New national forms of opera emerged in Germany, France, and England; folk idioms influenced virtually all of Western music by 1875. While composers were finding inspiration in the music of their native cultures, scholars began to scrutinize music both from a historical and an anthropological standpoint. ETHNOMUSICOLOGY, an important field in music today, began at least nominally with the Nationalistic movement in the late nineteenth century.

Influences from Folk and National Rhythms

While folk melodies in Western Europe are often rhythmically predictable, those of Eastern Europe may include mixed and asymmetrical meters as well as irregular phrase structure. In the song, *Na Solnechnom Vskhode* (*At Dawn, At the Warming*), from Northeastern Russia, accents defy any one traditional metric classification.

Russian Wedding Song, "At Dawn, At the Warming"

At dawn, at the warming [of the public bath]
A bushy white birch tree stands.

Mary Howe (1882–1964) is an American composer and pianist who wrote chamber, choral, and orchestral works. She often favored exceptional accent patterns to complement the text. Unlike Debussy, however, Howe changed meters frequently—sometimes in virtually every measure, as shown in her setting of a poem in English by Elinor Wylie (1885–1928).

 CD 2, TRACK 50
Mary Howe, "Let Us Walk in the White Snow"
Mixed Meter

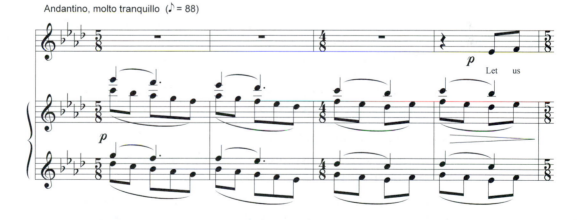

walk in the white   snow   In a   sound - less   space;

With   foot - steps qui - et and   slow,   At a   tran - quil   pace.

Led by Igor Stravinsky, a number of early-twentieth-century composers employed conventional metric and rhythmic notation, yet nullified any perception of regularity by changing the accents in virtually every measure. Most often, the beat division is constant, but the accents shift repeatedly. Study the first violin part from Stravinsky's *Le Sacre* shown in the next example. The meter changes with nearly every measure, but the sixteenth-note value remains fixed. The full score of these measures appears on the next page.

Igor Stravinsky, *Le Sacre*

CD 2, TRACK 51
Igor Stravinsky, *Le Sacre du Printemps*
Irregular Accents

Igor Stravinsky, *Le Sacre du Printemps*

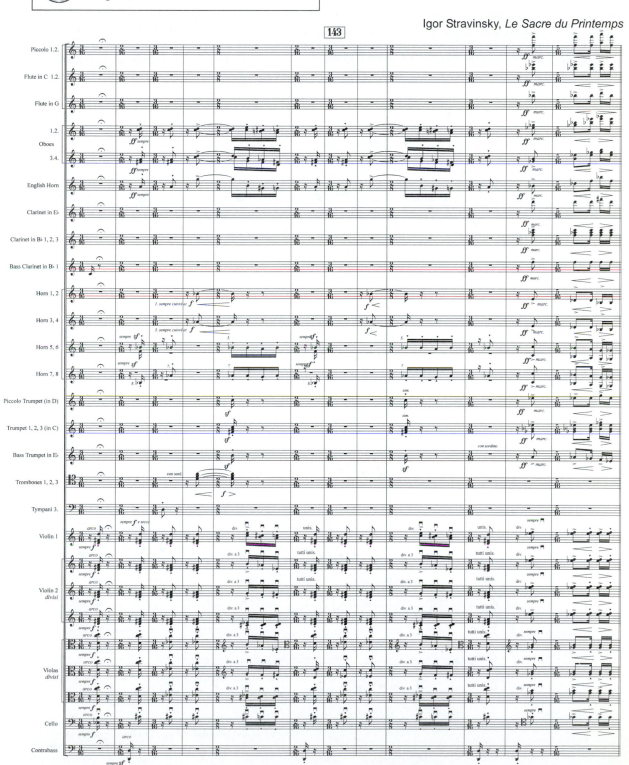

Polyrhythm and Polymeter. While not associated with one specific geographic region, several rhythmic devices became popular in the twentieth century, as composers experimented with novel effects. A POLYRHYTHM, for example, is a contradiction in one or more voices of natural accents in the notated meter. The Sonata for Oboe and Piano (1938) by the German Paul Hindemith begins in $\frac{2}{4}$, but the piano has a polyrhythm that creates $\frac{3}{8}$.

CD 2, TRACK 52-1 POLYRHYTHM AND POLYMETER (2 PARTS)
Paul Hindemith, Sonata for Oboe and Piano

Copyright 1929 by Associated Music Publishers, Inc. Used by permission.

Composers also use *different* notated meters simultaneously—an effect termed POLYMETER. In the duet below (second system), Bartók could have employed a measure of $\frac{5}{4}$ in both parts instead of the $\frac{2}{4}/\frac{3}{4}$ polymeter. The more complex notation, however, separates the two lines and underscores the asymmetry in Eastern European folk rhythms.

TRACK 52-2 POLYRHYTHM AND POLYMETER
Béla Bartók, "Song of the Harvest"

Copyright 1933 by Universal Edition. Copyright renewed.
Copyright and renewal assigned to Boosey & Hawkes, Inc.
Used by permission

The previous examples are but a few of the many new ideas in rhythm and meter that dominated the early twentieth century. As we will discuss in the next section, rhythms influenced by national styles spawned similar developments in melody and harmony.

Innovative Melody

As ethnomusicologists and composers researched and recorded authentic folk music, some of these sounds were absorbed into the musical vocabulary. Improvisation is a feature of most world musics, for example, and in the works of many composers, soaring melodies, so popular in the late nineteenth century, were replaced by a more spontaneous melodic style after 1900.

Additive Melody. In addition to the cellular melodic structure used by Mussorgsky, Debussy, and others, some composers in the following generations favored repetitive rhythms. In his early works, Igor Stravinsky devised a style often termed ADDITIVE MELODY: A cell (perhaps two or three pitches) is repeated, extended, and transformed into phrases; individual phrase length and rhythmic structure are often asymmetrical. At the age of twenty-eight, Stravinsky achieved fame with the ballet *Firebird* (1910); *Petrushka*, another work for the *Ballet Russe* in Paris, followed in 1911.

The flute solo that opens the first *tableau* of *Petrushka* is an elaboration of an ascending perfect fourth. Manipulation of this cell continues for the next forty-one measures (measures 1–5 shown).

CD 2, TRACK 53-1 TWO PASSAGES FROM *PETRUSHKA* (2 PARTS)
Igor Stravinsky, *Petrushka*
Additive Melody

TRACK 53-2
Two Passages from *Petrushka*
Polymeter

Later in the same section, flutes and oboes in $\frac{7}{8}$ form a polymeter against $\frac{3}{4}$ in the orchestra. Again, observe the manipulation of the perfect fourth heard in the opening measure.

Stravinsky, *Petrushka*

Common-practice composers usually presented a theme and then developed it; Stravinsky, however, does the opposite in *Petrushka*. In measure 42, we first hear "Song of the Volochebniki"—the Russian melody upon which the previous forty-one measures were based. Sung by beggars (*volochebniki*) wandering from one village to another at Easter time, the version given here is from a collection compiled by Nicolai Rimsky-Korsakov.

CD 2, TRACK 54-1

RUSSIAN FOLK SONG (2 PARTS)
"Song of the Volochebniki"

Stravinsky's brilliant orchestral setting suffers greatly in piano reduction, yet we can still see at one time a blending of the old, the contemporary, and the innovative. As we have discussed, the repetition, melodic angularity, and mixed meter are characteristic of Russian folk music. Planing of the melody, on the other hand, was a contemporary technique in 1911—a tried and true compositional approach conceived by Debussy and others. Finally, Stravinsky's innovative contribution is the additive treatment of melody.

TRACK 54-2
Russian Folk Song
Orchestral Reduction

New Scale Resources   Several new scales, some colored by Eastern European folk melodies, were included in the art music of early-twentieth-century composers such as Bartók and Kodály. The so-called HUNGARIAN SCALE, for example, includes two augmented seconds.

CD 2, TRACK 55-1 NEW SCALES (2 PARTS)
Hungarian Scales

Hungarian Scale on C   Hungarian Scale on B

An OCTATONIC SCALE is one with eight discrete pitches in alternating whole and half steps (and also known as the WHOLE-HALF SCALE). Enharmonic notation is acceptable in constructing whole-half scales. Like other symmetrical materials (the whole-tone scale, augmented and diminished triads, diminished seventh chords, and so on), octatonic scales have limited transpositions.

TRACK 55-2 NEW SCALES
Octatonic Scales

W H W H W H W H   W H W H W H W H
Whole-Half Scale on C   Whole-Half Scale on E

Bartók uses an octatonic scale in "From the Island of Bali," No. 109 in the keyboard collection *Mikrokosmos*. Measures 1–11 are based on a whole-half scale, beginning on the pitch A.

In addition to the octatonic scale material in "From the Island of Bali," notice that the upper voice is a transposed inversion of the lower (measures 1–4). Tonally, the lower line establishes A as a pitch center, while F is the focus of the upper line. The hemiola in measures 4 and 10 is typical of Bartók and other early-twentieth-century composers.

CD 2, TRACK 56
Béla Bartók, "From the Island of Bali"

For over three hundred years, common-practice Western music was dominated by one or another national style. Italian composers originated and developed a common musical system in the seventeenth and eighteenth centuries; after about 1800, Germans such as Beethoven, Schumann, Brahms, and Wagner breathed new life into traditional forms and techniques. The Frenchman Claude Debussy facilitated a transition into the twentieth century. From about 1875, however, many composers looked inward, to national, regional, and local resources of rhythm and melody.

WORKBOOK/ANTHOLOGY II
I. Rhythm and Melody, page 167

REVIEW AND APPLICATION 9–1

Folk Resources

Essential Terms

additive melody	nationalism	polyrhythm
ethnomusicology	octatonic scale	whole-half scale
Hungarian scale	polymeter	

1. Choose from the list and identify *the most prominent* rhythmic technique in each of the duets. Note that some of the techniques are from earlier chapters. Perform each passage.

A. Polyrhythm   D. Mixed Meter

B. Simple syncopation   E. Polymeter

C. Two-Against-Three

Béla Bartok, Scherzo

John Williams, Theme
from *Angela's Ashes*

2. Use the given focal pitches to write ascending scales as indicated. Some of the scale materials are from earlier chapters.

Ascending

a. 1. Hungarian   2. Whole-Half   3. Dorian

Ascending

b. 1. Whole-Half   2. Mixolydian   3. Pentatonic

3. Identify the predominant scale material of each melody and notate this scale on the staff.

a. Scale type: _____

Allegretto

b. Scale type: _____

Moderato

c. Scale type: _____

Andante

SELF-TEST 9–1

Time Limit: 5 Minutes

1. Some of the statements below are true, others false. Circle T if the statement is true; F, for incorrect statements. *Scoring: Subtract 8 points for each wrong answer.*

T F a. Ethnomusicology is a modern field of study that emphasizes music in a cultural perspective.

T F b. Igor Stravinsky remained faithful to functional harmony throughout his career.

T F c. Most composers abandoned time and key signatures by about 1910.

T F d. Béla Bartók was an important early-twentieth-century ethnomusicologist and composer.

T F e. Additive melody is associated particularly with Igor Stravinsky.

T F f. Simultaneous time signatures—$\frac{3}{4}$ in one voice, for example, and $\frac{9}{8}$ in another— are termed polymeter.

T F g. The folk rhythms and melodies of Eastern Europe were especially important in the music of several composers in the late nineteenth and early twentieth centuries.

T F h. *Le Sacre du Printemps* is an opera by Stravinsky.

2. Construct an octatonic scale on the given pitch. *Scoring: Subtract 18 points for an incorrect notation.*

Octatonic Scale

3. Enter a term to describe the rhythmic technique in the next example. *Scoring: Subtract 18 points for an incorrect response.*

Technique: _____

Total Possible: 100 Your Score _____

TONAL HARMONY REVITALIZED

At the turn of the twentieth century, most composers retained at least a minimal tonal orientation in their works. We will divide our study of turn-of-the-century tonal harmony into two categories: (1) Music based upon expanded tertian principles, and (2) less traditional tonal systems such as secundal harmony, simultaneity, and polytonality.

Expanded Tertian Harmony

Tertian triads and chords have appeared in Western music since the Renaissance. Consider, for example, the following table that summarizes concepts and styles discussed previously in this text.

Evolution and Development of Tertian Harmony

Period	Essential Characteristics	Representative Composers
1450–1600 *Renaissance*	Use of Church Modes. Triads emerge from converging contrapuntal lines. Descending fifth root movement common at cadences.	Dufay, Josquin, Palestrina
1600–1750 *Baroque Era*	Concept of function emerges. Stereotypical cadences. Homophonic texture popular. Major/Minor system fashionable by 1680.	Monteverdi, Corelli, Purcell, Vivaldi, Bach, Handel. D. Scarlatti
1750–1825 *Classical Era*	Functional tertian harmony clarified and refined. Longer forms unified through key. Limited use of chromatic embellishment and distant keys.	Clementi, Haydn, Stamitz, Mozart, Beethoven
1825–1900 *Romantic Era*	Expansion of tertian harmony with an emphasis on nonchord tones, ninth chords, enharmonic relationships, and nonfunctional resolutions.	Schubert, Chopin, R. Schumann, Brahms, Liszt, Franck, Wagner
1890–1925 *Impressionism*	Nonfunctional tertian harmony, planing, added-tone chords.	Debussy, Ravel, Griffes, Loeffler

After 1900, tertian harmony remained important, not only in popular music genres such as marches, waltzes, songs, ragtime, and early forms of jazz, but also in the music of some traditional European and American composers. Some modified tertian principles for use as the basis of literally dozens of inventive styles before World War II. While most of these trends were short-lived, three of them are particularly important for our present studies. First, composers like Stravinsky and Prokofiev added biting dissonances, stinging modulations, and novel root relationships to progressions that were otherwise fairly traditional. Next, a number of different composers extended the tertian system to include not only ninth chords, but elevenths and thirteenths as well. Finally, *Neo-Classicism* and a reborn interest in other historical styles proved that tonality remained viable in an evolving century.

Dissonance and Distortion.   As someone once said, "the dissonance of one era becomes the consonance of the next." We may trace the validity of this statement throughout various eras of tonal music. Passing sevenths in the Renaissance were absorbed into the harmony as seventh chords in the Baroque era. Dissonant nonchord tones in the Classical and Romantic eras became ninth and added-tone chords in the hands of the Impressionists. In addition to added dissonance, some composers in the late nineteenth and early twentieth centuries employed triads and seventh chords, but with exceptional root relationships.

Modest Mussorgsky was a member of *The Five*—a group of Russian Nationalist composers whose music was influential on later generations.[1] The

---

[1]"The Five" include Mussorgsky and Rimsky-Korsakov as well as Mily Alexeyevich Balakriev (1837–1910), César Cui (1835–1918), and Alexander Borodin (1833–1887).

second scene of Mussorgsky's opera *Boris Godunov* (1874) opens with a clash of dominant seventh chords a tritone apart and over a tritone pedal. The pitches C and F♯/G♭ are common to both chords and anchor the passage.

CD 2, TRACK 57
Modest Mussorgsky, *Boris Godunov* (Act I, Scene II)
Dissonance

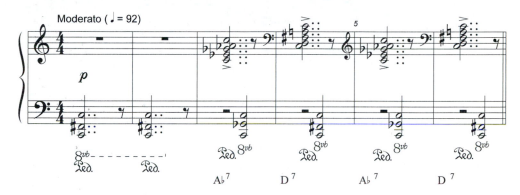

Simultaneous nonchord tones interested several composers in the twentieth century. Samuel Barber (1910–1981) is an American whose cycle *Hermit Songs* (1952), based on Medieval texts, has been popular with performers and audiences. In "The Monk and His Cat" (shown in the next example), the harmony is basically functional in F major, but the measures shown include simultaneous nonchord tones—each resolving according to prevailing functional tendencies (measures 50–51). This sparkling effect, along with the shifting metric accents, creates a playful and unpredictable mood. Notice that there are eleven eighth notes in measure 49.

CD 2, TRACK 58
Samuel Barber, "The Monk and His Cat" from *Hermit Songs*

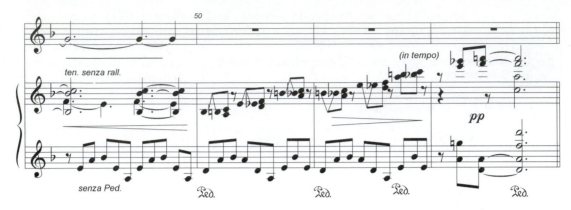

A number of twentieth-century composers added gentle dissonances to more traditional progressions. The American composer Vincent Persichetti (1915–1987) wrote for a variety of media. In his *Hymns and Responses for the Church Year*, Persichetti exemplifies an effort among several twentieth-century composers to interest congregations in contemporary sacred music. The "Opening Response" from this collection illustrates a mildly dissonant style that is based on triads and seventh chords.

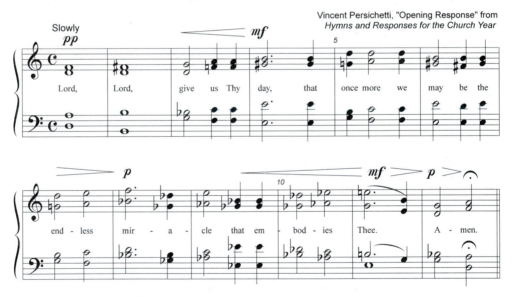

Roman-numeral analysis is not especially helpful in understanding Persichetti's "Opening Response." But while the harmony is largely nonfunctional, the tonality remains clear (D minor with an excursion to Mixolydian on A♭ in measures 8–10). Notice both the frequent third relation and the traditional plagal cadence on the syllables "A-men." Persichetti's four-part choral writing is representative of a moderately dissonant twentieth-century approach. Parallel fifths abound between soprano and alto; cross relationships and augmented seconds also occur. Still, as you sing each voice separately, notice that distant chords are connected largely through whole- or half-step movement.

"Wrong-Note" Harmony.   Although some disdain the term, WRONG-NOTE HARMONY is commonly used to describe a style adopted by Sergei Prokofiev, Dimitri Shostakovich, and other Russian (Soviet) composers in the years following World War I. The style is both tertian and tonal, but the listener is constantly teased by unexpected pitches, dissonances, or special effects. In the famous Polka from his 1930 ballet *The Golden Age*, Shostakovich establishes B♭ major through a bass ostinato. In the melody, however, there is a conflict between G♭ and G♮ (measures 7–9). Several nonchord tones add to a sense of uncertainty (hear the B♮ in measures 10–11, for example, as an embellishment of the pitch C). "Wrong-note" harmony is an apt description of a style in which the listener may ask, "was that last pitch *right?*"

Shostakovich's Polka is functional with dominant and diminished-seventh chords providing momentum and clarity through near-traditional resolutions. A brief modulation to D minor occurs in measures 13–14. With its insistence on ninths, the melody has a comic effect seen in many of Shostakovich's works.

CD 2, TRACK 59-1 (2-PARTS)
"Wrong-Note" Harmony
Dimitri Shostakovich, Polka from *The Golden Age*

In Imperial Russia, Sergei Prokofiev was sometimes compared to Mozart as a child prodigy. At the age of thirteen he entered the St. Petersburg Conservatory where he studied piano and composition. Prokofiev is remembered today mainly for a wide range of works written before and during World War II. The final movement of his Sonata No. 6 (1940), for example, provides another instance of the "wrong-note" compositional style. The movement opens in A minor, but with D♯ (which we might hear either as $\hat{4}$ in a synthetic scale or as an unresolved embellishment of the pitch E). In measures 5–6, the B♭ and G♭ seem initially out of place. A complete melodic minor scale on E♭ follows, but contrary

TRACK 59-2
"Wrong-Note Harmony"
Serge Prokofiev, Sonata No. 6, Op. 28 (IV)

motion between bass and soprano, along with a functional cadence, leads the listener smoothly back to A minor.

Extended Tertian Harmony.   In the previous discussions of seventh and ninth chords in traditional harmony, we noted that dissonant pitches may be analyzed in either of two ways: Melodic or harmonic. In the twentieth century, we must often choose from among *several* possible harmonic interpretations for a sonority. One of these is a further extension of thirds above a root to include ELEVENTH and THIRTEENTH CHORDS. In the next example, note the addition of thirds above the dominant in C major and the subdominant in C♯ minor to form increasingly dense extended chords.

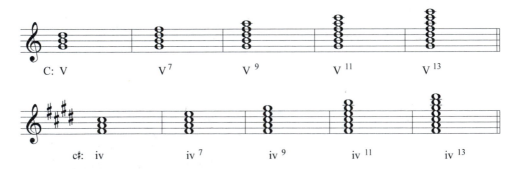

One or more pitches is often omitted in "tall" chords such as elevenths and thirteenths. We often employ a letter-name analysis in nonfunctional contexts. Likewise, the resolution of eleventh and thirteenth chords may not follow traditional guidelines for ninths and sevenths (down by step). Listen to the three versions of a relatively dissonant minor thirteenth chord on the pitch A♭.

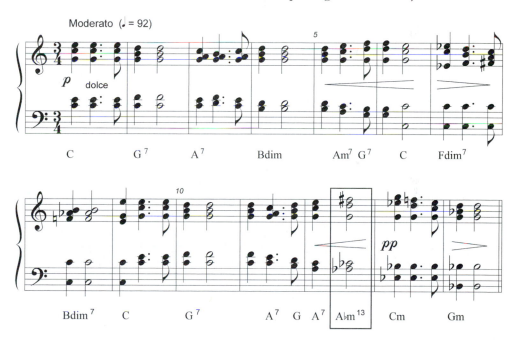

The chord in the last frame occurs in Prelude No. 1 from *Twenty-Four Preludes and Fugues* by Dimitri Shostakovich. Although we will discuss other analytical possibilities later in this chapter, we might understand the chord in measure 12 as A♭ m^{13} (boxed). Shostakovich's Prelude is in C major, has Baroque flavor, and is further enhanced by the limited range and the opening sarabande rhythm.

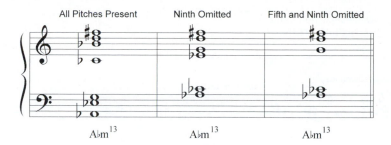

CD 2, TRACK 60-1 TALL CHORDS (2 PARTS)
Dimitri Shostakovich, Prelude No. 1, Op. 84

As composers stretched the limits of tonality and tertian structure, the most appropriate approach to analysis varies from work to work. Charles Ives, the "Yankee" maverick cited earlier, wrote in a number of unconventional styles. His *114 Songs* (1922) was published at the composer's expense and its songs date from 1884 to 1921. "Mists" (1910) is whole tone, but should we want to analyze the final chords individually, they are augmented elevenths on C and G (with intervening sonorities in this analysis recognized as embellishing chords). We might also analyze these same sonorities as superimposed augmented triads (see the discussion of polychords on pages 419–420).

TALL CHORDS TRACK 60-2
Charles Ives, "Mists"

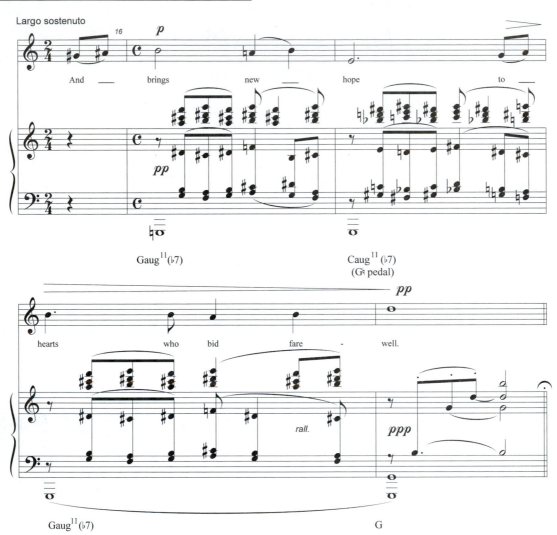

Finally, extended tertian chords quickly became (and have remained) a staple of the popular music harmonic vocabulary. The refrain of George Gershwin's *Why Do I Love You?* includes several eleventh chords in the first phrase group. We might easily find nonchord-tone or alternate harmonic explanations for Gershwin's elevenths, but in popular music, where improvisation is important, "tall-chord" designations are helpful for those composing "in tempo."

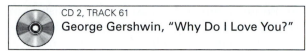

Split Chord Members. After two centuries devoted almost universally to composition in major or minor (ca. 1675–1875), Western composers in the late nineteenth and early twentieth centuries rediscovered the Church Modes, devised synthetic scales, and employed other alternate scale arrangements such as pentatonic. Another manipulation of traditional materials is SPLIT CHORD MEMBERS—tertian structures in which one member of the chord (root, third, fifth, seventh, and so on) occurs simultaneously with a *chromatically altered* version of the same pitch. Split chord members may appear chromatically (C–E♭–E♮–G, for example) or diatonically (C–D♯–E♭–G). Some theorists use an exclamation point to identify the chord member that is split. In the next example, the third is split chromatically (E♮–E♭) in the first chord (3!); the fifth is split diatonically (D♮–E♭) in the second (5!). The caret symbol is not used because the reference here is to a chord member and not a scale degree.

Ives's song "General William Booth Enters into Heaven" was published in *114 Songs* and is based on the hymn *Cleansing Fountain*.[2] We might consider several of the chords to be tertian with split chord members. The first four measures are B^9 with split seventh ($A\natural$/$A\sharp$). Notice how B^7 is outlined in the first measures of the voice part. The chord in measure 5 can be identified as C^{add6}_{add6} (5!)—C major with added sixth (A) and both a $G\natural$ and a $G\sharp$. The final chord shown is *quintal* (superimposed fifths—to be discussed in the next section).

CD 2, TRACK 62

Charles Ives, "General William Booth Enters into Heaven"

Copyright 1935 by Merion Music, Inc. Used by permission.
Text by Vachel Lindsay from *Collected Poems*.
Used by permission of Macmillan Publishing Company, Inc.

---

[2] *Cleansing Fountain* was one of Ives's favorite tunes and appears in many of his works. For another setting of the same melody and the hymn tune itself, see page 344.

Neo-Classicism

We have already noted that Bartók, Shostakovich, and some of their contemporaries were responsible for a revival of imitative counterpoint. A more unified movement, however, is one associated principally with Stravinsky and Prokofiev. NEO-CLASSICISM is a return to styles, forms, and genre of the Classical era while retaining a contemporary sound through innovative harmony and melody. A master of several twentieth-century styles, Stravinsky wrote Neo-classical works between about 1920 and 1960. His opera *The Rake's Progress* (1952) employs the same recitative and aria structure that Mozart used nearly two hundred years earlier. The Classical effect in recitatives is further enhanced through the use of harpsichord accompaniment.

A less complex Neo-Classical work is Stravinsky's Symphony in C (1940). Scored for a small orchestra, the first movement of the symphony demonstrates the inherent flexibility of Classical-Era models. After a few introductory measures (not shown), the first theme appears as an oboe solo. The movement centers on functional pillars, is cast in sonata form, and is simple in texture. While the overall effect is contemporary (with additive melody and twists and turns of harmony), the Classical flavor is conspicuous.

Igor Stravinsky, Symphony In C
First Movement

In addition to the Stravinsky works cited, we can also identify many others (Ravel's Quartet on page 357, for example) that are Classical in form, style, and stereotypical accompaniment. Prokofiev's Symphony No. 1 in D Major (1917) is subtitled "Classical."

We have surveyed only a few of the many ways that late-nineteenth- and early-twentieth-century composers exploited tertian principles to create innovative works. The development of tertian harmony continues today—not only in commercial music, but in traditional art veins. Numerous composers today have based their styles at least in part upon traditional harmony. Although his earlier works were more dissonant, George Rochberg (b. 1918) has written in a tonal style in recent years; younger tonal composers such as Lowell Liebermann (b. 1961) have also adopted the traditional tertian system as a point of inspiration and as a result, have found considerable favor with audiences.

WORKBOOK/ANTHOLOGY II
II. Tonal Harmony Revitalized, page 173

REVIEW AND APPLICATION 9–2 ━━━━━━━━━━━━━━

Tonal Harmony Revitalized

Essential Terms

eleventh chord	Neo-Classicism	thirteenth chord
expanded tertian harmony	split-chord members	wrong-note harmony

1. Use letter names and other symbols to identify the chords shown. Some of the chords are traditional and were discussed in previous chapters. Center your analysis on three chord types discussed earlier:

G^9 ninth chord on the root G (one or more pitches may be omitted)

G^7 add6   seventh chord on the root G with added sixth

G^{11} add ♯4 (3!)   eleventh chord on the root G with added sharp fourth and a split third

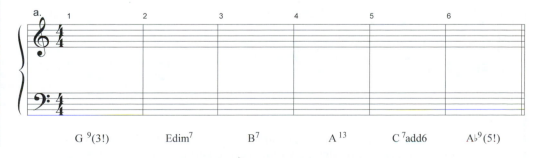

2. Construct chords as directed by the symbols. In some cases, two or more answers are possible.

a.

1	2	3	4	5	6
G^9(3!)	$Edim^7$	B^7	A^{13}	C^7add6	$A♭^9$(5!)

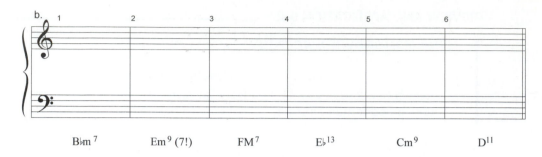

b.

| Bbm⁷ | Em⁹ (7!) | FM⁷ | Eb¹³ | Cm⁹ | D¹¹ |

3. Provide an appropriate analysis of the passage that follows. Determine key relationships, triadic structure (including extended and split chords), use of dissonance, melodic style, and so on. Be prepared to discuss the passage as directed by your instructor.

CD 2, TRACK 63
Hugo Wolf, "If My Love Were the Lark"
Review and Application 9-2, Exercise 3

Sehr mässig

a.

Singt mein Schatz   wie ein Fink,   sing'   ich Nach - ti - gal - len - sang.

ist mein Lieb - ster ein Luchs,   o   so bin   ich ei - ne Schlang'!

If my love were the lark, sweet as nightingale I'll sing;
Were he false as a lynx, with a serpent's tongue I'll sing.

SELF-TEST 9–2

Time Limit: 5 Minutes

1. Some of the statements below are true, others false. Circle T if the statement is true; F, for incorrect statements. *Scoring: Subtract 5 points for each wrong answer.*

T F a. Compositions in the "wrong-note" style are usually non-tertian.

T F b. All six pitches must be present in scoring an eleventh chord.

T F c. Charles Ives was an innovative American composer.

T F d. If a chord member is split, it is duplicated enharmonically in another voice.

T F e. Neo-Classical works often employ the Church Modes.

T F f. The analysis G (3!) designates a triad with split third.

T F g. Even in the twentieth century, composers have continued to avoid parallel fifths and octaves in choral writing.

T F h. From the early twentieth century to the present day, most popular music can be described as both tonal and tertian.

2. Where blanks appear, provide appropriate analyses for the extended tertian chords. *Scoring: Subtract 8 points for each incorrect answer.*

CD 2, TRACK 64
Nathaniel Dett, *Cinnamon Grove*
Self Test 9-2, Question 2

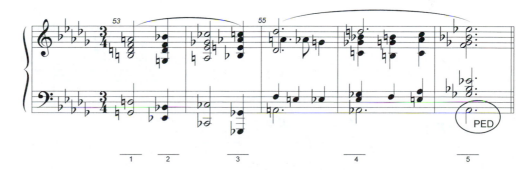

3. Construct the chords specified. Adhere to the key signature, but use accidentals as necessary. *Scoring: Subtract 10 points for an incorrect notation.*

Dm¹¹   C (5!)

Total Possible: 100   Your Score _____

NEW MUSICAL SYSTEMS

Alongside the development of tertian harmony in the late nineteenth and early twentieth centuries, several composers devised new systems for the organization of melody, rhythm, harmony, or *timbre*. These new ideas have been important sources of organization and inspiration that continue to influence today's music. Among these new systems, discussed in this section, are quartal and secundal harmony, polychords, bitonality and polytonality, simultaneity, and innovations in *timbre* such as *Klangfarbenmelodie*.

Harmonic Systems

In a quest for tonal alternatives to tertian harmony, some composers experimented with the superimposition of intervals other than thirds. As we noted in the last chapter, Debussy and other turn-of-the-century composers employed quartal harmony to contrast one section with another. In the twentieth century, a few composers adopted secundal or quartal/quintal harmony as the basis of their style.

Quartal/Quintal Harmony. QUARTAL HARMONY is based on superimposed fourths; if the harmony comprises superimposed fifths, it is QUINTAL. Because fifths and fourths invert intervallically, the same chords may be produced through a series of either interval. In studying the way intervals are stacked in a given work, however, we can usually determine whether the composer viewed the harmonic system as quartal or quintal. Remember that in either system, we might expect some chords to be exceptional (triads, groups of seconds, and so on).

The analytical symbols ("3 × 5 on D," for example) were covered in detail in Chapter 8 (see page 366–369). Remember that the first number identifies the range of pitch classes present in the chord; the second number reflects the generating interval. Specifications such as "on G" and "on B♭" document the lowest pitch when intervals are arranged vertically.

Quartal Harmony				Quintal Harmony			
3 x 4 on B	3 x 4 on A	4 x 4 on G♯	3 x 4 on F♯	3 x 5 on D	4 x 5 on B	3 x 5 on B	4 x 5 on G

Like Bartók and some of his contemporaries, Hindemith reveled in counterpoint. His series of keyboard preludes and fugues, *Ludus Tonalis* (1942), is reminiscent of Bach's imitative writing. The subject of Hindemith's Fugue in A♭ is dominated by fourths, fifths, and seconds—the intervals most typical of quartal harmony. The dotted rhythms that permeate Hindemith's music were also favored by many Baroque-era composers such as Henry Purcell. Other Neo-Baroque elements in Hin-

CD 2, TRACK 65

Paul Hindemith, Fugue in A♭ from *Ludus Tonalis*

demith's fugue include a traditional subject–answer key scheme and melodic ornamentation.

Secundal Harmony and Clusters. As unresolved dissonance continued to influence Western music in the early twentieth century, composers like Bartók, Ives, Shostakovich, and others experimented with SECUNDAL HARMONY—a system generated by superimposed seconds. If the chord is more an effect than a consistent harmonic approach, however, we use the term CLUSTER. One approach to the analysis of secundal harmony and clusters is the one employed earlier for quartal and quintal chords. If the chord comprises seconds of the same quality, this might be noted in the analysis (examples a and b); if the chord includes seconds of more than one quality (frame c), notation of the interval alone is sufficient.

a. 3 x m2 on F♯   b. 4 x M2 on F   c. 5 x 2 on F♯

An excerpt from the Polka from Shostakovich's ballet *The Golden Age* was given on page 401. The introduction to that passage (shown in the next example) includes a cluster of minor seconds stacked upon the pitch E.

 CD 2, TRACK 66-1 CLUSTERS (2 PARTS)
Dimitri Shostakovich, Polka from
The Golden Age

4 x m2 on E

Exhultation, a piano work by Henry Cowell (1897–1965), begins with a secundal harmony played with the left forearm. The notation indicates the upper and lower pitches of each chord; other pitches within the cluster are defined by the position of the arm. The simple melody in the right hand is Mixolydian on F♯. Note also a polymeter between the two parts.

 TRACK 66-2 CLUSTERS
Henry Cowell, *Exhultation*

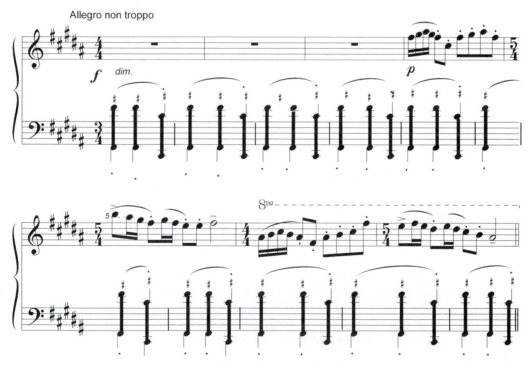

One historical measure of a composer's importance is the extent to which later generations employed his or her original techniques as a springboard for their own styles. In this light, Charles Ives emerges as one of the most important

American composers of the twentieth century. Ives experimented with clusters and secundal harmony in the late nineteenth and early twentieth centures. Cowell was greatly influenced by Ives's work and continued the older composer's experiments with dissonant and novel effects even after World War II. In the next generation, John Cage (1912–1992), one of Cowell's students, continued the line of nontraditional music in the late twentieth century to include

WORKBOOK/ANTHOLOGY II
III. New Harmonic Systems, page 177

works for *prepared piano*, electronic media, and aleatoric (chance) music.[3]

Simultaneity

Some of the most original music in the early twentieth century was written by combining (layering) two or more contrasting lines. This concept of layering in Western music can be traced to the Impressionists, but when we speak of SIMULTANEITY, we usually mean music outside any one tonal or modal system. Included in the catalogue of simultaneous effects are *tonal ambiguity, bimodality, polytonality, polychords,* and other new techniques discussed in this section.

Tonal Ambiguity. Simultaneity is one of several techniques employed by Stravinsky and other early-twentieth-century composers to create organization in dissonant music. In the four-hand piano arrangement from *Le Sacre* (shown in the next example), three lines occur simultaneously. In the first piano, the right hand declares an additive melody that combines with the second piano to establish F♯ minor (measures 19–23); later, B♭ minor is the pitch center (measures 24–26). Contrasting with this relatively stable melody and harmony, however, the left hand of the first part is a meandering chromatic line planed largely in minor triads. The effect is raw and eerie—an appropriate mood for the beginning of a sacrificial dance.

CD 2, TRACK 67
Igor Stravinsky, *Le Sacre*
Simultaneity

---

[3]A "prepared piano" is one in which objects are placed on the strings to produce novel *timbres.*

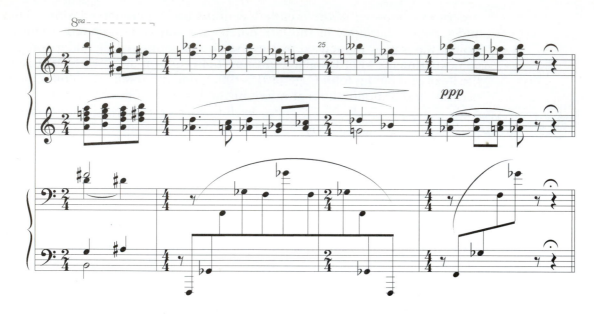

Bimodality. One of many culminating points in the evolution of tonal harmony is BIMODALITY—tonal music with a consistent use of both major and minor modes. In the next passage, from Bartók's Bagatelle VI, measures 1–5 are marked by both major and minor triads on B; the key moves to A♭ major/minor at the end of the phrase. Note the functional cadence in measures 6–7 (with A♮ and F heard as escape tones).

CD 2, TRACK 68-1 BIMODALITY
Béla Bartók, Bagatelle VI

"Blue" Notes. Bimodality is also a regular feature of early jazz. The juxtaposition of major and minor forms of a triad is often described as BLUE NOTES in jazz terminology, yet the technique is merely an adaptation of bimodality. Early jazz composers, in fact, found that many late nineteenth-century idioms fit their new style. Bimodality, an augmented triad, and a borrowed submediant ninth, for example, are all seen in the opening measures of Gershwin's famous *Rhapsody in Blue* (1924).

TRACK 68-2 BIMODALITY
George Gershwin, *Rhapsody in Blue*

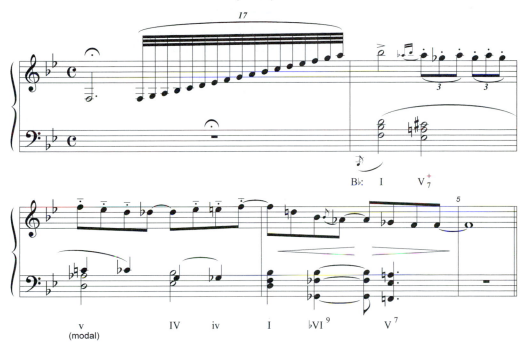

Polytonality. While a bitonal work combines two modes within a single key center, POLYTONALITY is the simultaneous use of two or more keys. Polytonality was a favorite technique of an anti establishment group of French composers known as *Les Six.*[4] Darius Milhaud (1892–1974), a member of *Les Six,* was influenced both by travel in Brazil and by the interest in jazz that preceded World War II. Milhaud is among those who extended the tonal principle to include simultaneous key centers. In the Botofogo (a Brazilian dance) from his *Saudades do Brazil,* the right hand is in F♯ minor while two different ostinatos in the lower part center on F minor.

---

[4] *Les Six* (The Six), active mainly before the end of World War I, included five men and a woman: Georges Auric (1899–1983), Louis Durey (1888–1979), Arthur Honegger (1892–1955), Darius Milhaud, François Poulenc (1899–1963), and Germaine Tailleferre (1892–1983).

Darius Milhaud, *Botofogo*

Doucement (♩ = 84)

Milhaud managed without a key signature in the Botofogo; other composers provided a key signature for each different line. In addition to the Bartók violin duet on page 390, note the use of simultaneous key signatures in his Bagatelle I, Op. 6.

Béla Bartók, Bagatelle I

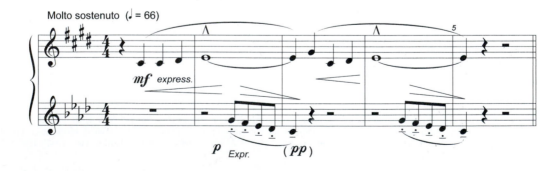

Molto sostenuto (♩ = 66)

Polychords.   In addition to bimodality and polytonality, a number of composers employed POLYCHORDS—two or more triads or chords sounded simultaneously. A polychord differs from an eleventh chord, for example, in having two roots. The first chord below is an E♭/D♭ polychord; the second is an eleventh on E♭.

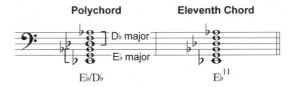

We presented the last chords graphically to illustrate the theoretical difference between them: A polychord has two roots; an eleventh chord, one. In practice of course, we must rely on factors such as resolution, planing, register placement, and continuity of individual lines to differentiate between a polychord and a superimposition of thirds.

The American William Schuman is known widely both for his compositions and his work as president of the Juilliard School of Music and the Lincoln Center in New York. He adopted a wide range of twentieth-century techniques including the use of polychords. The next example, the brief *Three Score Set*, is in three parts with a coda as shown on the time line.

Schuman, *Three-Score Set*

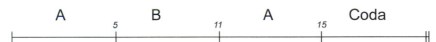

The opening and closing sections of *Three Score Set* are polychordal; the middle part is lighter in texture, with lines generated more by contrary motion than through harmonic combination. Observe Schuman's choice of chords in the first and third parts: Both triads are major (with the lower in second inversion) and are often a half or whole step apart.

CD 2, TRACK 70
William Schuman, *Three-Score Set*
Polychords

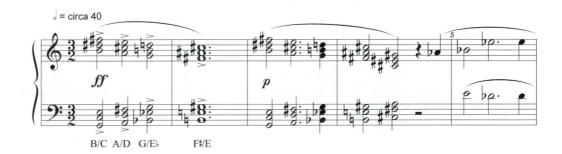

After studies at Yale University, Charles Ives began as a traditional composer, but quickly veered toward experimentalism. By the time he composed his Symphony No. 4 (between 1910 and 1916), Ives had adopted a dissonant style, in which individual lines occur simultaneously and together create a solid mass of sound. Listening to the second movement of Ives's Symphony No. 4, we may occasionally home in on one part or *timbre*, but individual lines are secondary to the construction of a complex fabric. The passage shown on the next page is one of the most dense in the second movement of Ives's Symphony No. 4, which is scored for a large orchestra with three pianos, an enormous percussion section, woodwinds, brass, and strings. In the measures shown, virtually every instrument performs a different melodic and rhythmic line—some including polychords. Some parts are at least minimally tonal; others lack a pitch focus. The overall effect is an extreme, but animated mass of dissonance that is neither homophony nor counterpoint.

Simultaneity proved to be a significant resource throughout the twentieth century as composers adapted the principle to different styles and harmonic systems. Comparing the Schuman and Ives examples, we can see that the level of dissonance and tonal ambiguity can vary with the particular lines combined. While we discussed Cowell's *Exhultation* (page 414) in terms of its clusters, the work also exhibits simultaneity in combining the secundal background and the Mixolydian melody.

New Concepts in Rhythm and Timbre

Several composers proposed novel approaches to rhythmic notation as demands on the traditional Western system began to outstrip its flexibility. Henry Cowell's book, *New Musical Resources*, appeared in 1919 and includes proposed symbols for third, fifth, seventh, ninth, and other fractional parts of a beat. While Cowell's new rhythmic system did not find favor with professionals and amateurs already highly-familiar with traditional notation, this and other experiments show us how early-twentieth-century composers wrestled with the limits of the Western musical system. The excerpt in the next example is from Cowell's *Fabric* (1922).

[Not Recorded]   Henry Cowell, *Fabric*

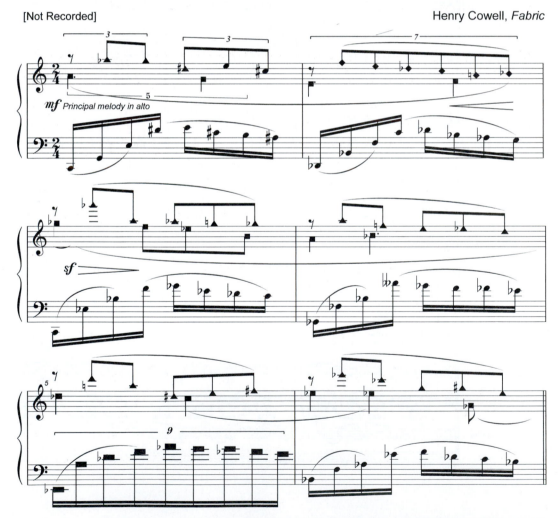

Innovations in Timbre. Harmonics, innovative articulations, and extremes in register added to the twentieth-century inventory of *timbres*. Some composers experimented with obtaining unique sounds from conventional instruments. As we noted at the beginning of the chapter, Stravinsky's *Le Sacre* begins with a bass instrument playing in a soprano register. Other composers choose to alter conventional instruments or to invent new ones. Cowell's *The Banshee* is a work for piano, but one in which the performer touches the strings in various ways: with the fingernail, with the flesh of the finger, sweeping from high to low, and so on.

Henry Cowell, *The Banshee*

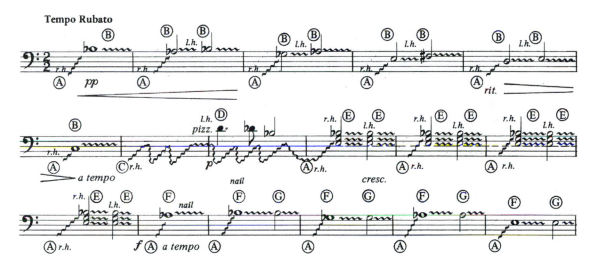

Sprechstimme. Several composers experimented with new vocal *timbres* in the early twentieth century. The German Englebert Humperdinck (1854–1921) developed a style of singing termed SPRECHSTIMME ("speech-song"). When an "x" appears on a note stem, the singer is instructed to produce the given pitch, but also add a rising or falling inflection. Arnold Schoenberg popularized sprechstimme in a number of works, including *Pierrot Lunaire* (1912). "Nacht" is one of 21 songs in *Pierrot* and is scored for bass clarinet, cello and piano. The texts are by the Belgian poet Albert Girard.

TRACK 71
Arnold Schoenberg, "Nacht" from *Pierrot Lunaire*
Sprechstimme

Ominous, black giant moths
Obliterate the glow of the sun.
The horizon lies as a sealed
magic book—silent.

Klangfarbenmelodie. Claude Debussy is credited with originating the style of orchestration based upon a kaleidoscope of shifting chamber ensembles. Arnold Schoenberg expanded this technique to include constantly changing *timbres* and dynamics. KLANGFARBENMELODIE (tone-color melody) connotes a work or section in which lines evolve as much through tone color as through changes in pitch. The third movement of Schoenberg's *Five Pieces for Orchestra* (1909) is a lengthy work scored for a large ensemble including harp and celesta. The movement unfolds in sections of carefully contrasted *timbres.*

Another composer who experimented with klangfarbenmelodie is the American Ruth Crawford (Seeger) (1901–1953). The third movement of her Quartet (1931) employs shifting dynamics, accents, and a well-crafted melodic line emerging throughout each section. The last twenty-three measures of Crawford's Quartet are shown in the next example. Note the exceptional dynamic marking that indicates a consistent intensity punctuated by sudden accents.

* The half note in measures 85-88 should be faster than the quarter notes in measure 77.

Copyright 1931 by Merion Music, Inc. Used by permission.

Our discussion of late-nineteenth- and early-twentieth-century techniques has been selective. As in any era of Western music, many composers, whose works are now forgotten, achieved popularity in their day, and contributed to a time of originality and cultural richness that continues today. A desire to escape Romanticism and functional harmony drove many to the fringes of tonality. In addition to the many techniques covered in this chapter, two concepts emerged before 1925 that are of such importance that an entire chapter will be devoted to each. *Atonality*, with its array of new sound combinations and organizational problems, will be discussed in Chapter 10. *Serial composition*, a systemized atonality, is the subject of Chapter 11.

WORKBOOK/ANTHOLOGY II
IV. New Musical Systems, page 181

REVIEW AND APPLICATION 9–3

New Musical Systems

Essential Terms

bimodality	polychord	secundal harmony
blue note	polytonality	simultaneity
cluster	quartal harmony	sprechstimme
klangfarbenmelodie	quintal harmony	

1. Construct secundal, quartal, or quintal chords as specified. Assume perfect fourths and fifths; the quality of seconds is given. Use close spatial position and add accidentals as necessary.

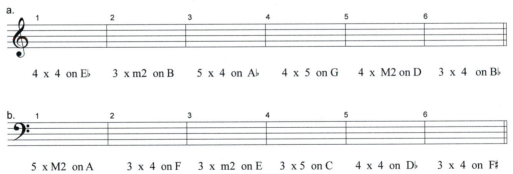

a.

1	2	3	4	5	6
4 x 4 on E♭	3 x m2 on B	5 x 4 on A♭	4 x 5 on G	4 x M2 on D	3 x 4 on B♭

b.

1	2	3	4	5	6
5 x M2 on A	3 x 4 on F	3 x m2 on E	3 x 5 on C	4 x 4 on D♭	3 x 4 on F♯

2. The following sonorities are polychords. Provide analytical symbols to identify the two triads present (AM/Em, G⁷/AM, and so on).

a.

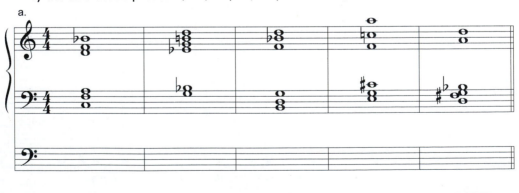

1	2	3	4	5

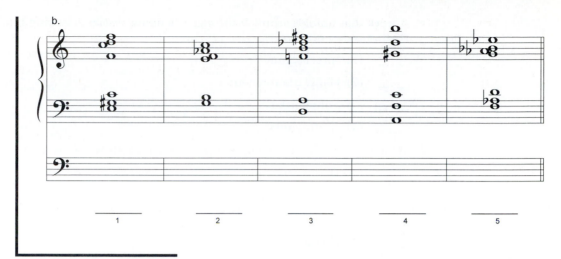

SELF-TEST 9–3

Time Limit: 8 Minutes

1. Make a check mark by the correct answer for each statement or question below. These questions cover material from the entire chapter. *Scoring: Subtract 5 points for each error.*

   a. Sprechstimme involves

      _____ (1) pitch fluctuation.

      _____ (2) rhythmic complexity.

      _____ (3) tone color.

      _____ (4) German nationalism.

   b. A cluster comprises

      _____ (1) consecutive seconds.

      _____ (2) split thirds.

      _____ (3) superimposed seconds.

      _____ (4) "tall" chords.

   c. Polytonality involves simultaneous

      _____ (1) triads.

      _____ (2) keys.

      _____ (3) modes.

      _____ (4) textures.

   d. Which of the following composers *was not* born in America?

      _____ (1) Charles Ives

      _____ (2) Mary Howe

      _____ (3) Henry Cowell

      _____ (4) Paul Hindemith

e. A work that unfolds as much through changing *timbres* as varying pitch and rhythm is described as

_____ (1) sprechstimme.

_____ (2) klangfarbenmelodie.

_____ (3) polychordal.

_____ (4) contrapuntal.

f. Which of the following composers is associated with Neo-Classicism?

_____ (1) Darius Milhaud

_____ (2) Modest Mussorgsky

_____ (3) Igor Stravinsky

_____ (4) Charles Ives

2. Provide an analytical symbol for each of the chords below. *Scoring: Subtract 9 points for an incorrect answer.*

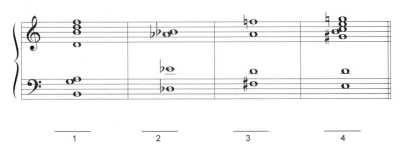

1   2   3   4

3. Provide analytical symbols for chords where blanks appear. *Scoring: Subtract 6 points for an incorrect response.*

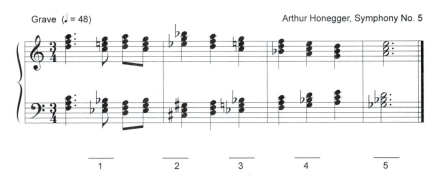

1   2   3   4   5

4. Write a term in the blank that describes the harmony in the previous Honegger passage. *Scoring: Subtract 4 points for an incorrect answer.*

*Term*_____

Total Possible: 100   Your Score _____

PROJECTS

Analysis

The analytical projects in this chapter feature a range of techniques including quartal harmony, nonfunctional tertian harmony, and tonal ambiguities. Roman numerals will be of relatively little advantage in these studies, so be prepared to tap other analytical resources.

Text

Roy Harris, "Bells" from *Little Suite*, text pages 432.
Roy Harris (1898–1979) was a native of Oklahoma who, with Samuel Barber, Walter Piston, and Aaron Copland (among others) studied both in the United States and in France and founded a distinctly American musical style in the 1930s. "Bells" affords an opportunity to analyze nontertian harmony. Comment on cadences, the scalar melody, and the contrapuntal framework between highest and lowest voices. If the workbook/anthology is available, be prepared to compare Harris's "bells" with the bell sounds in Barber's "The Bell at Night."
Antonio Carlos Jobim, "Once I Loved," text page 433.
Antonio Carols Jobim (1927–1994) was one of the foremost advocates of Brazilian song and, with João Gilberto, is prominently associated with developing bossa nova ("New Way" in Portuguese) in the 1950s. Jobim was a classically trained musician and influenced by Debussy, Stravinsky, and others. He was attracted to Brazilian popular and folk music early on, however, and is revered in North American among jazz musicians today. While "Once I Loved" dates from 1965, we have included it here because the harmonic vocabulary and techniques are those of the early twentieth century.

The chord symbols reflect the harmony precisely, but unless you are proficient in reading them, you may find that making a harmonic reduction of block chords is helpful in your analysis.

Workbook/Anthology II

Samuel Barber, "The Bell at Night" from *Hermit Songs*, Op. 29, workbook page 187.
Paul Hindemith, Fugue in F from *Ludus Tonalis,* workbook pages 188–190.

Composition

Fugue for Piano (Quartal Harmony). Compose a short fugue for piano. If the workbook/anthology is available, use Hindemith's Fugue in F as well as the material given here as a guide. Adhere to the most general conventions of fugal procedure (see Chapter 2), but matters of function, key, and voice leading may follow early-twentieth-century guidelines. The model fugue provided here has a short, three-measure subject, a brief middle section (with subject entries and an episode), and a final section that includes stretto.

Begin by composing a short subject that is quartal in structure. The answer might be at the dominant or at a different tonal level. Make your counterpoint basically nonfunctional, but include frequent cadences at different tonal levels. The next example shows a subject-answer-subject sequence. The second subject entry (not the answer) is preceded by a one measure extension (measure 7); a two-measure transition (measure 11-12) moves toward a key center on A (major/minor) for the middle section.

CD 2, TRACK 72
Sample Fugue

STATEMENT SECTION

A subject-entry group and an episode (based on new material) are shown in the next passage.

MIDDLE SECTION

The final section might begin with stretto and conclude quickly after a few overlapping statements.

FINAL SECTION (Stretto)

At about ♩ = 100, this little fugue is just over a minute in length, yet it has most of the essential elements of the traditional procedure. We have omitted dynamics to enhance the Neo-Baroque effect; your instructor may ask that you include them in your own composition.

For Further Study

The Music of Charles Ives.   The first American composer to win international acclaim was Charles Ives (1874–1954). A New Englander, Ives's father was a band leader during the Civil War. While the boy grew up with music, and showed an early talent for composition, he was often decidedly nontraditional in his approach. He once startled the congregation by playing a hymn in two different keys simultaneously. And when someone complained about a choir member's off-key singing, Ives remarked "You can't listen closely to the sounds or you will miss the music."

Write a paper or prepare a presentation that is an overview of Ives's work as a musician. You will find many sources available—including a wide range of recordings (many of them made by Leonard Bernstein and the New York Phil-harmonic). Address some or all of the following topics in your paper (depend-ing upon the scope specified by your instructor):

a. Ives's childhood and his studies at Yale University

b. Critical reaction to Ives's music in the early twentieth century

c. Ives's career in insurance

d. Ives's influence on younger American composers such as Henry Cowell.

e. Leonard Bernstein's interest in Ives and the composer's later years.

Compile a listening list of recordings in your library including songs, or-chestral works, and compositions for chamber ensembles.

[Not Recorded]

Roy Harris, "Bells" from *Little Suite*

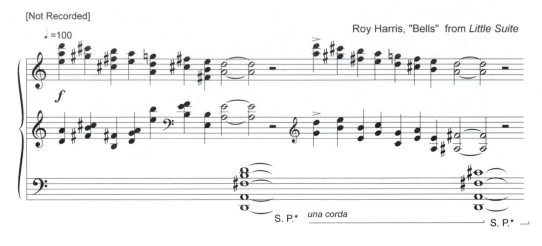

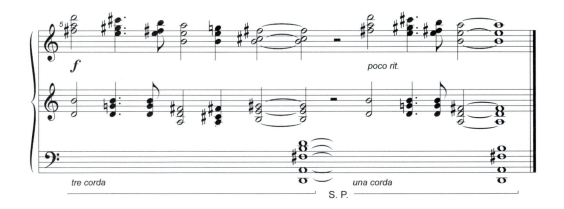

UNIT 5

The Contemporary Era

As some composers increasingly turned away from tonality in the twentieth century, several problems loomed. First, without traditional cadences to define the smallest formal elements (phrase, period, and phrase group, for example), musical line had to be structured through other principles and relationships. In addition, major sections of longer works, traditionally delineated by contrasting keys, still needed definition in atonal music. While the cell structure favored by Debussy and Stravinsky was to prove a useful tool for some atonal composers, others relied on brevity and novel approaches to organization. An essential step in the evolution of an atonal system was a means of ensuring that no one pitch could be identified as focal. Finally, for audiences, publishers, and producers who were accustomed to the music of Giacomo Puccini (1858–1924) and Giuseppe Verdi (1813–1901), for example, it was a hard sell to promote angular melody and unrelenting dissonance as equally inspirational. A few eagerly embraced "The New Music," but critics more often panned performances sarcastically as "feeding time at the zoo"; supporters were also derided as "a masochistic cult."

The debate about new music continues today. Looking back on the twentieth century, we can see that cellular structure has been an important device for atonal composers. As we will discuss in Chapter 10, a few pitches can be transposed, inverted, heard in retrograde, and in other relationships that allow the listener to perceive organization. The concept of pitch-class set developed in the years following World War II, but some of the techniques had been in use decades before. The analysis of atonal music also poses significant problems. Even if we ourselves understand a work, what common language can be employed to share our conclusions with others? *Pitch-class set*, a mathematical approach to principles of order and structure, constitutes one popular collection of analytical tools.

The *twelve-tone technique,* an approach to the problems of organization and incidental tonal emphasis, was developed almost single-handedly by the Austrian Arnold Schoenberg. Discussed in Chapter 11, serial composition was influential for half a century. While some composers continue to write serial works today, interest in the system has waned substantially since about 1985. Still, serialism is a useful method of atonal composition that has proven sufficiently flexible to support a number of allied movements.

Following in the footsteps of Charles Ives and Henry Cowell, the American John Cage thrilled some and antagonized others with *aleatoric* (chance) works like *4′–33″,* in which a performer sits in silence at the keyboard for four minutes and thirty-three seconds. Especially after 1950, composers discovered liberating new worlds of music through electronic media, *minimalism,* and an array of additional experiments. We will discuss many of these contemporary composers and their works in the final chapter of this volume.

Arnold Schoenberg was born in Vienna in 1874. Like other young musicians, he showed an affinity for composition at an early age. Schoenberg avoided a traditional conservatory education, however, and instead, studied composition and violin privately. His early works, such as the string sextet *Verklärte Nacht* (*Transfigured Night*), are basically romantic, but with more density and unresolved dissonance than those of most of his contemporaries. By 1910, Schoenberg had not only embraced atonality, but had attracted a number of students—principally Anton Webern and Alban Berg (1885–1935).

Between about 1913 and 1923, Schoenberg pondered the problems of organization in atonal music, and eventually devised the *twelve-tone technique* in which each of the twelve pitch classes is employed equally. The basis of a serial work is the *row*—the initial ordering of the twelve pitch classes. One of Schoenberg's first serial works is the six-movement *Suite for Piano,* Op. 25 (1923). We will discuss the serial technique in detail in Chapter 11; for now, consider the twelve-tone row that serves as the basis of the Menuett (given complete beginning on page 438). Notice that the row unfolds over the first seven beats between right and left hands; the first pitch of the row (E♮) is actually the fourth pitch heard.

Although Schoenberg converted to Lutheranism as a young man, he was a Jew by birth, and left his teaching post in Berlin in the early 1930s. He moved first to Paris and later immigrated to America where he accepted a position at the University of California at Los Angeles. In his later years, Schoenberg celebrated his Jewish heritage with works such as *A Survivor from Warsaw* (1950).

In addition to piano pieces, Schoenberg wrote four important string quartets and other chamber music, several large orchestral compositions including a violin concerto, song cycles, and an (unfinished) opera, *Moses and Aaron*.

Schoenberg had a significant impact on the development of Western art music in the mid-twentieth century. Some of his early atonal works, *Pierrot Lunaire* (1911), for example, are still considered masterpieces today. Long after his death in 1951, students and disciples alike continue to explore and extend the twelve-tone system. That established composers such as Aaron Copland, Igor Stravinsky, and Pierre Boulez (b. 1925) adopted the serial technique is evidence of its importance.

TRACK 73
Arnold Schoenberg, Menuett from
Suite for Piano, Op. 25

Menuett da capo

CHAPTER *10*

Atonality

Throughout the history of Western music, the effectiveness of a composition has depended on the building and maintaining of relationships in several parameters. Melodic tendencies governed the construction of melodies; formal design was carefully planned, beginning with motives and phrases, combining these to form larger formal units, and finally, shaping complete works in binary, ternary, or other forms. The establishment of these relationships has sometimes been more by instinct than design. The articulation of tonal areas through contrasting themes, for example, just "sounded right" to early eighteenth-century composers.

In atonal music, the search for alternative means of organization led early-twentieth-century composers to exploit new melodic and harmonic systems. Composers like Schoenberg instinctively chose combinations of pitches that caused the music to hold together—both in the short and long terms. These new relationships form the core of our studies in atonality. In this chapter, we will look first at sets and their transformations. Next, we will introduce *pitch-class set analysis*—an important method for the understanding and discussion of atonal music.

Atonality

ATONALITY may be defined as the absence of a tonal center. Because *serial composition* is a specifically organized atonality (Chapter 11), we often encounter the terms NON-SERIAL ATONALITY and FREE ATONALITY to specify music that is atonal, but with an organization outside the serial principles that we will discuss in the next chapter.

Even when an avoidance of tonality is the goal, however, composers may inadvertently favor one pitch class for a few beats or even a few measures. Moreover, some atonal composers (Alban Berg, 1885–1936 for example) reveled in brief cells of tonality amid an otherwise atonal work. A broader definition of atonality permits the inclusion of music that lacks a tonal center *and also* music in which tonality is established through nontraditional means.

RELATIONSHIPS IN ATONAL MUSIC

Within the many individual solutions to problems of organization in atonal music, four relationships have appeared consistently since the 1920s. These are *Transposition, Inversion, Inclusion,* and *Complementation.* One or more of these relationships forms the core of most twentieth- and twenty-first-century atonal music. Atonal relationships are often based upon a *set.*

The Set

A SET is a collection of items. The process of delineating sets within a melody or harmony is called SEGMENTATION. Any number of items may appear in a set, but the order of those items as well as any duplication among them is disregarded. Consider the following set of shapes that we will designate "Set 1."

If the order of shapes is changed, or if any of them is repeated, the collection is still identified as "Set 1."

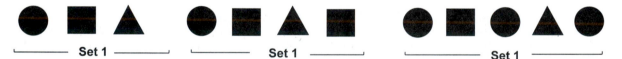

But if a set contains *new* items, or if any of the original items is omitted, the collection is *not* Set 1, but some other set (Sets 2 and 3 in the next example).

Pitch Class and Notation Class.   Transferring our discussion of sets from shapes to music, we can view the pitches C–E–G as a set of notes. We should observe, however, that the pitches B♯, F♭, and A♭♭ comprise the same set. As we have discussed, pitch class denotes a specific collection of prime- or octave-related pitches; NOTATION CLASS is a category of letter name. The pitches F, F♯, and F♭, for example, are all in the same notation class, while comprising three different pitch classes.

Despite octave doublings and enharmonic duplications, and regardless of order, each collection in the next example comprises the same set.[1]

---

[1]While composers and editors sometimes make other choices, we generally employ enharmonic equivalents freely in atonal music, avoiding double sharps and double flats.

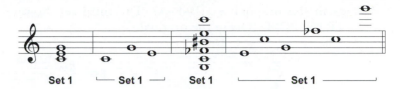

Set 1   └── Set 1 ──┘   Set 1   └────── Set 1 ──────┘

If pitches are added or omitted, a new set is formed.

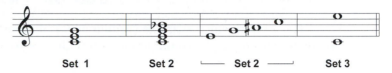

Set 1   Set 2   └── Set 2 ──┘   Set 3

Transposition

Earlier, when we transposed scales, we also engaged in set transposition. In our study of atonal relationships, SET TRANSPOSITION refers to the intervallic duplication of a group of pitches to sound higher or lower. A three-pitch set (D–F–A, for example) may be transposed by moving each pitch up or down by the same interval. For clarity, in calculating the interval of transposition, theorists consider only the eleven pitch classes *above* the original. In the next example, the first transposition is three half steps above the original; the second transposition is actually a half step lower, but we identify it as eleven half steps higher.[2]

Set A   Set A   Set A
           Transposed   Transposed
       3 Half Steps Higher 11 Half Steps Higher

Indistinct Transposition.   Certain sets may be transposed without producing new pitches. As shown in the next example, an INDISTINCT TRANSPOSITION is notated differently from the original set, but produces no new pitch classes.

Indistinct Transposition

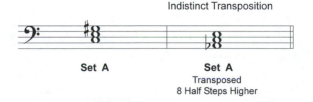

Set A   Set A
           Transposed
       8 Half Steps Higher

Ordered and Unordered Transposition.   If pitches appear in a transposition in the same order as the original, the set is an ORDERED TRANSPOSITION. Compare the first and second sets in the next example. Although transposed three half steps higher, the pitches E♯–G♯–B♯ are in the same order

---

[2]For obvious reasons, key signatures are not used in modern atonal music. For clarity, some composers attach an accidental to every pitch in a composition. Others rely on the traditional approach that cancels an accidental only within the same measure. We will follow the latter procedure in this text: Cautionary accidentals are used where confusion might arise. Finally, we will not employ double sharps or double flats in text examples.

as in the original set (D–F–A). The third set, however, is an UNORDERED TRANSPOSITION of the original.

Set A   **Set A**   **Set A**

Transposed   Transposed

3 Half Steps Higher   11 Half Steps Higher

The set in the next example (written by a sophomore theory student) is used to organize a sample piano composition throughout several sections of this chapter.

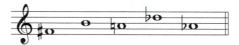

In the phrase below, our set begins in the right hand and is accompanied with an ordered transposition (two half steps higher). The phrase continues

CD 2, TRACK 74-1 SAMPLE ATONAL COMPOSITION (3 PARTS)

Transposition and Inversion

with additional statements of the set and two different unordered transpositions. Keep in mind that pitch repetition changes neither set structure nor identification (see measures 3–4, for example).

Joseph Teague, *Set Variations*

Inversion

Transposition produces eleven new versions of an original set. Inversion is another means of generating new, but related sets. SET INVERSION refers to a *mirror* image, in which intervals are duplicated in the inverted set in the opposite direction. In our next example, the original set includes the pitches C, D, and G. A mirror inversion begins with C, but duplicates the intervals in the opposite direction.

The second set in the last example is a LITERAL INVERSION—one that begins on the same pitch as the original set. If the original set is displayed harmonically, a literal inversion follows the same process. The lowest pitch of the first set becomes the highest of the inversion; other pitches duplicate those in the original set in the opposite direction.

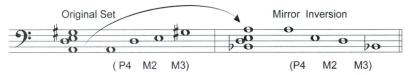

Ordered and Unordered Inversion. As with transposition, a set may be inverted in the same or a different order. The original set in the next example is followed by an ordered and also an unordered inversion.

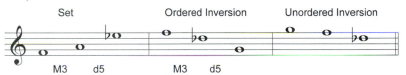

Transposed Inversion. If an inverted set is transposed, it retains its relationship with the original set as a mirror image. Transposed inversions may be ordered or unordered.

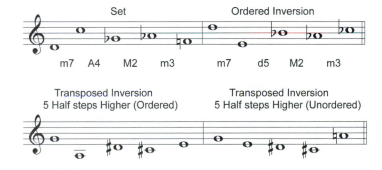

Indistinct Inversion. INDISTINCT INVERSION produces the same pitch classes as the original set *or* one of its transpositions. The set C–D–E, for example, is inverted as C–B♭–A♭.

The inversion in the last example is indistinct because the transposition of the original set eight half steps higher produces the same pitches.

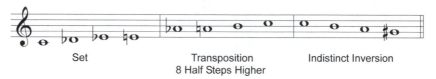

Set 1   Transposition   Indistinct Inversion
              8 Half Steps Higher

Sets that have a symmetrical intervallic structure produce indistinct inversions. The next set is comprised of whole and half steps. The transposition up eight half steps is identical with the literal inversion.

Set   Transposition   Indistinct Inversion
            8 Half Steps Higher

TRACK 74-2 SAMPLE ATONAL COMPOSITION
Transposed Inversion

The set used in the next passage continues the sample piano piece begun on page 444. Again, the basic five-pitch set is heard in the first two measures. The literal inversion as well as a transposed inversion completes the phrase.

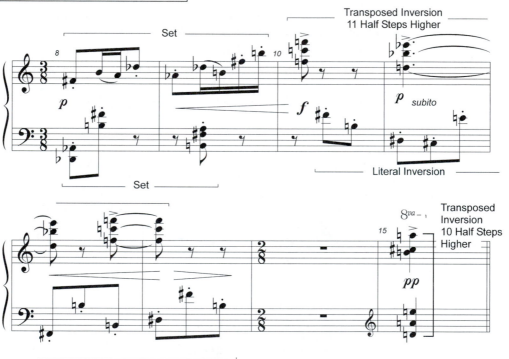

With eleven transpositions of a set and its inversion, there are twenty-four different possibilities available in either ordered or unordered versions. While a different set could be employed in virtually every measure of an atonal work, composers tend to choose forms that convey a certain group of intervals or a harmonic effect. In the next section, we will discuss two additional relationships that present even further possibilities for atonal writing: *inclusion* and *complementation*.

WORKBOOK/ANTHOLOGY II
I. Transposition and
Inversion, page 191

Inclusion

In addition to transposition and inversion, other relationships are important in atonal music. When one set *contains* another, the two sets are related by INCLUSION. In the diagram that follows, Set 1 is included in Set 2.

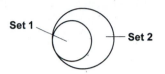

Musically, we can recognize a set comprising the pitches D and E (Set 1) as related to a C major scale (Set 2) by inclusion.

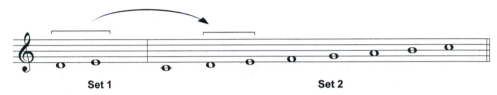

Likewise, Sets B, C, and D in the next example are related by inclusion to Set A.

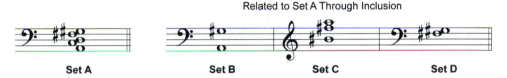

Nonliteral Inclusion. The sets in the last example represent literal inclusion: The pitch classes in the related sets are the same as pitches in the original set. If inclusion is nonliteral, however, the relationship may be by transposition, inversion, or transposed inversion. Still considering Set A in the last example, the pitches F–E are not literally included in Set A, but they are a transposition of the pitches A–G♯ which *are* related literally. Likewise, the set A♯–B is another transposition of the pitches A–G♯ which, again, are included literally in Set A.

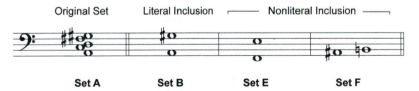

We can use inclusion to show that the pitches F♯–G♯–A♯ are related to a C major scale despite their apparent distance. If a C major scale is Set 1 and the first three pitches (C–D–E) comprise Set 2 (related by inclusion), then Set 3, F♯–G♯–A♯ (a transposition of Set 2), is also related to Set 1 through nonliteral inclusion.

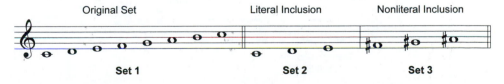

Because order is not a factor in the definition of a set, order is not a factor in determining inclusion among sets. Other arrangements of the pitches F♯–G♯–A♯ (as well as alternate spellings) are still related to the C major scale through nonliteral inclusion.

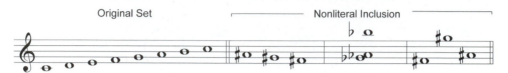

Continuing with a third section of the atonal composition begun earlier, new sets are created both by segmentation of the original and by the addition of pitches.

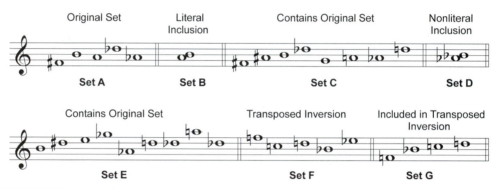

TRACK 74-3 SAMPLE ATONAL COMPOSITION
Literal and Nonliteral Inversion

The nine measures below include the original five-pitch set and several different related sets.

We can see several relationships in the voice part of "The Cage" by Charles Ives (given complete on page 450). The single stanza that Ives wrote for "The Cage" is divided into five segments that exhibit transposition as well as literal and nonliteral inclusion. The vocal line begins with a whole-tone PENTACHORD (set of five pitches).

The next segment of the voice part is a transposition of the original whole-tone set three half steps higher.

The third segment of the melody is a complete whole-tone scale. The original pentachord is included literally in the new set (Set 2), a complete whole-tone hexachord.

The music beginning on the words "A boy who had been there three hours began to wonder," includes Set 1 (the whole-tone pentachord) nonliterally.

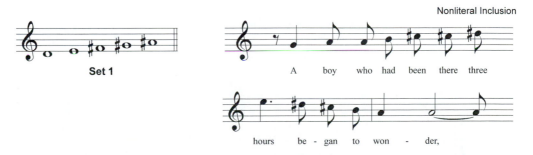

Ives's final line of text, "Is life anything like that?", is set to a literal restatement of the original whole-tone pentachord.

For many brief compositions, the original set and one or two transformations are sufficient material. In a longer work, composers may use not only transposition, inversion, and inclusion, but multiple sets as well.

CD 2, TRACK 75
Charles Ives, "The Cage"

Set Complementation

The COMPLEMENT of a set is another set: the set of all pitch classes *not* included in the original set. The complement of a C major scale, for example, is a set containing the five black notes of the keyboard. Interestingly, these com-

plementary pitches form a pentatonic scale. Like mirror inversion, complement is a mutual relationship; each set in the next example is the complement
of the other.

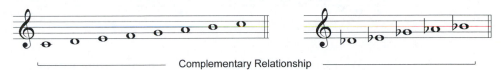

Complementary Relationship

In a harmonic context, the complement of a chord (set) is another chord
that contains all pitches omitted from the original chord. In the next example,
both sets are HEXACHORDS—structures with six discrete pitches.

Set 1   Complement Relation   Set 2

A common use of a set and its complement is a distribution between melody
and accompaniment. Using the hexachord (Set 1 in the last example) as the
melody, we have broken Set 2 (another hexachord) into two different TRI-
CHORDS for use as an accompaniment. Taken to-
gether, the melody and accompaniment contain all
twelve pitch classes.

CD 2, TRACK 76-1

SAMPLE ATONAL COMPOSITION (2 PARTS)
Complementation

Nonliteral Complement.   By definition, a set and its complement have no
pitches in common. In a literal sense, therefore, the pentatonic scale (C, D, E,
G, and A) is not the complement of a C major scale. In a nonliteral sense, however, this pentatonic scale can be the complement of a C major scale. The pitches C, D, E, G, and A constitute a transposition of G♭, A♭, B♭, D♭, and E♭—a set
that we found earlier to be the literal complement of a C major scale.

Literal Complement of Set 1 — Nonliteral (Transposed) Complement of Set 1

Set 1   Set 2   Set 3

We can now complete the brief atonal composition presented in other sections to illustrate transposition, inversion, and inclusion. The new material (measures 25–34) includes an ostinato based on the original set, while the literal complement unfolds in the bass. There are several different motives in this piano piece and any or all of them could be expanded considerably.

TRACK 76-2 SAMPLE ATONAL COMPOSITION
Nonliteral complementation

WORKBOOK/ANTHOLOGY II
II. Inclusion and Complement, page 195

REVIEW AND APPLICATION 10–1

Sets and Analysis

Essential Terms

atonality	literal inversion	set
complementation	nonliteral complement	set inversion
hexachord	nonliteral inclusion	set transposition
inclusion	ordered inversion	trichord
indistinct inversion	ordered transposition	unordered inversion
indistinct transposition	segmentation	unordered transposition

1. Analyze the given set; then comment on its intervallic characteristics.

Intervallic Characteristics:

Provide the following related sets. Remember that enharmonic spellings are acceptable and that octave placement is not a factor in set contents. Use quarter notes.

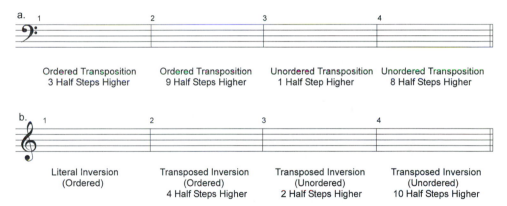

2. Provide the literal inversion for each of the following sets. Use the same rhythmic figure.

3. These questions pertain to the inclusion and complement relationships. Concerning inclusion, more than one correct response is possible. Base your composition on the following pentachord. Comment on its intervallic structure.

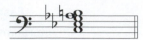

Intervallic Characteristics: _____

a. Provide three different sets that are related by literal inclusion (you may use one or more of the same pitches in different sets).

Two Pitches   Three Pitches   Four Pitches

b. Melodically, provide the literal complement of the original set. Provide two different sets that are included literally in the complement.

Literal Complement   Three Pitches   Four Pitches
                         Included in Complement

4. For each line, identify the relationships of sets in measures 2–4 with the first given. Write your analyses in the blanks. If the set is transposed, include this information in half steps above the original. Consider the following:

- identical set
- ordered and unordered transpositions
- literal and transposed inversions
- literal inclusion
- nonliteral inclusion

SELF-TEST 10–1

Time Limit: 8 Minutes

1. Choose a term from the list that corresponds to the description. Write the appropriate letter in the blank. *Scoring: Subtract 5 points for an incorrect answer.*

   A. Ordered transposition   E. Complement
   B. Literal inversion   F. Indistinct transposition
   C. Literal inclusion   G. Transposed inversion
   D. Unordered transposition   H. Indistinct inversion

   _____ a. a smaller set derived from pitch classes in the original set

   _____ b. contains all pitch classes not heard in the original set

   _____ c. a duplication of the original set higher or lower, but with different intervals between some or all pitches

   _____ d. a duplication of the original set higher or lower that produces exactly the same pitch classes as the original set

   _____ e. begins with the same pitch as the original set, but duplicates intervals in the opposite direction

   _____ f. a transposed inversion that produces exactly the same pitch classes as the original set *or* one of its transpositions

   _____ g. a duplication of the original set higher or lower

   _____ h. intervals are the same as those in the original set, but in opposite directions, *and* higher or lower

2. Provide transformations of the given set as directed. *Scoring: Subtract 8 points for each error.*

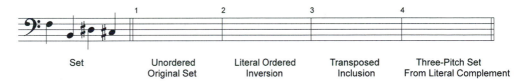

| Set | Unordered Original Set | Literal Ordered Inversion | Transposed Inclusion | Three-Pitch Set From Literal Complement |

3. The melody below comprises three different versions of the set heard in measures 1–2. Use the blanks to identify the sets used. Remember that repetitions of pitches within a set and enharmonic spellings do not affect set identity. Consider only ordered versions of the original, transpositions, and inversions. *Scoring: Subtract 8 points for each incorrect identification.*

a. _____

b. _____

c. _____

4. Provide the term for a collection of six different pitch classes. *Scoring: Subtract 4 points for an incorrect term.*

_____

Total Possible: 100   Your Score _____

ANALYZING ATONAL MUSIC

In a later section of this chapter, we will discuss an extended numerical approach to analysis that permits the convenient display of detail. For the present, we will examine several aspects of sets that are identified with letters, numbers, and staff notation. In atonal works, transposition and inversion are very common; inclusion occurs frequently, and some composers take advantage of the complement relationship. Remember that no matter how neatly we may categorize pitches into this or that set, the process of creating successful music is an artistic one. Except in teaching materials (such as the student piece on pages 444–452), we should not be surprised to find instances where the composer abandoned an anticipated structure for aesthetic reasons.

Octave Duplications and Enharmonic Equivalents.   Set analysis conveniently begins with a renotation, so that all pitches are arranged with less than an octave separating the highest and lowest, and also with the elimination of any pitch-class duplication. In addition, you may want to substitute an enharmonic version of one or more pitches in order to improve notation (this is largely a matter of personal choice). The original set, G–C–F–F♯, for example, can be studied with either F♯ or G♭ as the upper pitch.

Original Set   Reduced with   Reduced with
Original Pitch Names   Enharmonic Notation

Interval Vector

The intervals present (and *not* present) in a set are important in understanding how a musical work has been constructed. INTERVAL VECTOR is a calculation of every interval sounding in a given set. By employing interval vector, we can compare sets throughout a composition and understand their differences in terms of dissonance, strength, and elements of stability and instability. INTERVAL CLASS, the classification of an individual interval in terms of half steps, is central to calculating interval vector. There are only six different interval classes (*ic* 1–6) because a given interval is considered equivalent to its inversion and also to all enharmonic variations and compound versions of that interval.[3] A minor second, for example, falls into interval class 1 (abbreviated *ic* 1) because there is one half step between the two pitches.

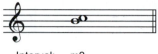

Interval: m2
Interval Class: 1

Because the major seventh is the inversion of a minor second, it also falls into interval class 1.

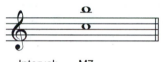

Interval: M7
Interval Class: 1

If the interval is a compound minor second (m9) or major seventh (M14), or if the pitches are notated with enharmonic equivalents, the sonority is still regarded as falling into interval class 1.

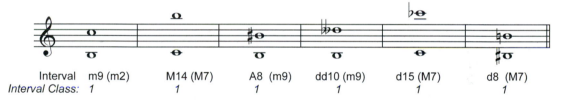

Interval	m9 (m2)	M14 (M7)	A8 (m9)	dd10 (m9)	d15 (M7)	d8 (M7)
Interval Class:	1	1	1	1	1	1

When there are two half steps between pitches (M2), the interval class is 2. Likewise, a minor seventh; a compound major second or minor seventh; or any enharmonic notation that produces pitch classes in these relationships, are also in interval class 2.

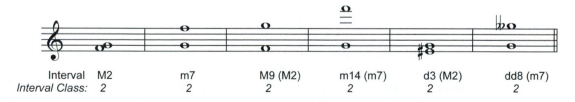

Interval	M2	m7	M9 (M2)	m14 (m7)	d3 (M2)	dd8 (m7)
Interval Class:	2	2	2	2	2	2

---

[3]While octaves and primes, including enharmonic notations, constitute a seventh interval class, they are discounted in reckoning interval vectors.

Interval classes 3, 4, 5, and 6 have three, four, five, and six half steps, respectively. As before, inversion, spacing, and enharmonic spelling have no effect on interval class.

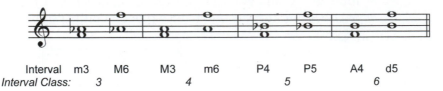

Interval	m3	M6	M3	m6	P4	P5	A4	d5
Interval Class:	3		4		5		6	

Six interval classes are sufficient, because every other arrangement of two pitch classes can be reduced to a sonority of one, two, three, four, five, or six half steps.

Interval	M10 (M3)	P5	A5 (m6)	A4	M7	dd7 (m6)
Interval Class:	4	5	4	6	1	4

Calculation and Representation of Interval Vector. We have seen how an individual interval can be classified into one of the six interval classes. Interval vector, however, is a calculation of every interval class present in a set. If there are three pitch classes in a set, for example, there will be three intervals present. Consider the set F, G, E.

In addition to the major second (*ic* 2) and major seventh (*ic* 1) above the pitch F, we also have a major sixth (*ic* 3) present between G and E. There are three interval classes present in the interval vector.

Set	M2	M7	M6
Interval Class:	2	1	3

With the interval data complete, we can classify the set (F, G, E) according to its interval vector. Use a table to keep track of the intervals present as you identify them. Write the class on an upper line with the tally in each category beneath the line. For the previous three-pitch chord, our compilation of data might look like this:

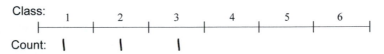

The interval vector of our chord is represented *1 1 1 0 0 0*. Notice that an accounting of each interval class is provided with zeros included as necessary. The first number is understood to represent the count in interval class 1; the second number, the count in class 2; and so on. At a glance, we can see that our chord contains no interval class above the third, that no perfect intervals are present, and that there is no tritone.

The interval vector of larger and more complicated sets is calculated in the same way. The set in the next example contains five pitch classes; there will be *ten* intervals in the interval vector. Remember that before calculating interval vector, you should first eliminate octave duplications.

Five-Pitch Set

We begin by calculating all intervals sounding above the bass, A♭.

Intervals Above A♭

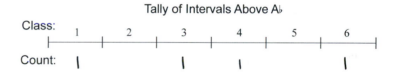

Set	M3	A4	M6	M7
Interval Class:	4	6	3	1

Enter these preliminary data into a table. Remember: Interval vector is a *running total*. We will add more data as we go.

Tally of Intervals Above A♭

Next, discount the bass pitch, A♭, since we have already computed these intervals. Assume the next lowest pitch (C in this case) as the new bass and calculate intervals as before.

Intervals Above C

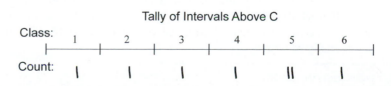

Set	M2	P4	P5
Interval Class:	2	5	5

Add these data to the table begun earlier.

Tally of Intervals Above C

Intervals are calculated above D and above F in a similar manner. No calculations beginning with the pitch G are necessary, because there are no pitches above it.

Intervals Above D and F

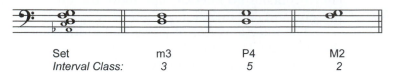

Set	m3	P4	M2
Interval Class:	3	5	2

When these data are added to the table, we have the complete interval vector.

Complete Interval Tally

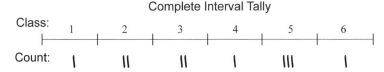

In stating the interval vector, we can enter data from the completed table, inserting zeros if necessary:

1   2   2   1   3   1

In addition to permitting a ready comparison with other sets, interval vector data provide useful information. Concerning the five-pitch set in the last example:

- The chord is mildly dissonant, containing one interval in class 1 and two in class 2.
- The predominant interval is perfect (class 5), imparting a relatively stable effect to the chord.
- The presence of one tritone (class 6) adds a degree of instability.

Many students are able to calculate relatively simple interval vectors in their heads, although you should never hesitate to use scratch paper to keep the interval tally. Observe the interval vectors of the four additional sets below.

Interval Vectors

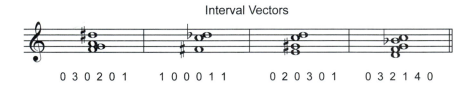

0 3 0 2 0 1   1 0 0 0 1 1   0 2 0 3 0 1   0 3 2 1 4 0

All four chords in the last example are different, but the first and third are similar in interval vector and, therefore, will have similar musical effects. The second chord is relatively dissonant in that it contains both a minor second and a tritone. Finally, the fourth chord is quartal: Perfect intervals and major seconds predominate and there is neither a minor second nor a tritone. Knowledgeable musicians might make similar observations simply by viewing a score, but the use of interval vector data enables information to be conveyed easily in words.

WORKBOOK/ANTHOLOGY II
III. Analyzing Atonal Music, page 197

PITCH-CLASS SETS

Music in the early twentieth century is sometimes too complicated for analysis with letter identifications or with phrases such as "pandiatonic" or "chord-type planing in G Dorian." With some simple concepts put forward by Allen Forte, however, the analysis of contemporary music is facilitated.[4] Forte's system, while designed for music that is atonal, is applicable as well to nonfunctional tonal works, including some by Debussy, Bartók, Stravinsky, and others. We will begin our study of pitch-class sets with a review of *pitch class.*

Pitch Class

The foundation of set analysis in music is the concept of pitch class. In this connection, it is useful to assign a number to each member pitch of the chromatic scale, starting with zero. While zero can represent any note, assigning it to the pitch C is convenient. We will follow this course in the present discussion.

Twelve Pitch Classes

Pitch Class: 0   1   2   3   4   5   6   7   8   9   10   11

All enharmonic (and octave) duplications of any one pitch are also in the same pitch class. Notice in the next example that each pitch (except A♭–G♯) has two different enharmonic equivalents within the same class. Remember, however, that atonal composers tend to avoid notation using double sharps and double flats.

Pitch Classes with Enharmonic Equivalents

Pitch Class: 0   1   2   3   4   5

Pitch Class: 6   7   8   9   10   11

Pitch-Class Set.   Traditional music notation is a graphic representation of sound. In studying twentieth- and twenty-first-century music, a major advantage of using numbers in analysis is that it facilitates our ability to compare chords, melodic cells, phrases, and so on. Spacing, octave placement, enharmonic spellings, and rhythmic complexities all contribute to possible confusion with staff notation and even note names. Numbers present a "cleaner" way of

---

[4]Allen Forte, *The Structure of Atonal Music,* Yale University Press 1973.

representing pitches, so that relationships among them (or, the *lack* of relationships) can be identified more easily. A useful concept to this end is *pitch-class set* (often abbreviated pc set). Simply put, a PITCH-CLASS SET is a collection of pitch classes. Because we deal with only twelve different pitch classes, there is a finite number of pitch-class sets (4096 of them, in fact). A chromatic scale is the universal set (containing all available elements). As a pitch-class set, a chromatic scale would be identified [0,1,2,3,4,5,6,7,8,9,10,11].

Pitch Class: 0   1   2   3   4   5   6   7   8   9   10   11

If the chromatic scale begins on G, the pitches occur in a different order. Note, however, that as pitch-class sets, the two collections are identical and identified as [0,1,2,3,4,5,6,7,8,9,10,11]. Remember that order is not a factor in identifying sets.

Pitch Class: 7   8   9   10   11   0   1   2   3   4   5   6

Other sets vary in pitch-class content according to the specific pitches present. A major triad on C, for example, is identified [0,4,7]; on B♭ as [2,5,10]; and on F♯ as [1,6,10]. Observe that pitch-class numbers are arranged from lowest to highest regardless of the order of notes in the set. The set [0,7,4], for example, is no different from [0,4,7], although if we are not concerned with normal order (page 464), ascending numerical order is customary.

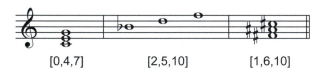

[0,4,7]   [2,5,10]   [1,6,10]

We can identify pitch-class sets for any harmonic or melodic group:

[2,4,10]   [1,7,9]

The two sets identified in the previous example appear in the piano accompaniment in the opening measures of *O'Connell's* by midwestern composer Kendall Stallings (b. 1940).

CD 2, TRACK 77
Kendall Stallings, *O'Connell's*
Pitch-Class Sets

Sets 1 and 2 are the trichords boxed in the last example. As we continue to study the accompaniment, however, a new ordering of the same pitch classes appears in measure 3. This discovery suggests that we are dealing not with two trichords (Sets 1 and 2 separately), but with a hexachord that can be identified as Set 3. The six-pitch set in the accompaniment (measures 1–6) has the identity [1,2,4,7,9,10].

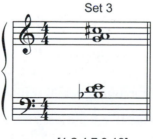

[1,2,4,7,9,10]

Turning to the melody of the Stallings piece, we might look for Sets 1, 2, or 3 by considering new pitches one by one: [7,9], [7,9,10], [1,7,9,10], [1,2,7,9,10], and [1,2,4,7,9,10]. Through the last eighth note in measure 6, the pitches unfolding in the melody are identical to Set 3 of the accompaniment.

As could be confirmed by further analysis, the final pitches of the melody in the last example (measure 7) begin a transposition of Set 3. Having found that the melody pitches to the end of measure 6 duplicate Set 3, we would anticipate that these pitches should be considered a distinct unit—another presentation of Set 3.

Pitch-class sets constitute an important tool in the analysis of atonal music. When another concept, *normal order*, is applied, however, relationships such as transposition and inversion are much easier to identify.

Normal Order

To facilitate the recognition of relationships among sets, we arrange pitch classes in a special way. When a set is in NORMAL ORDER, the pitch classes appear with the most compact spacing possible. In normal order, pitches are arranged with the smallest possible interval between lowest and highest pitches (called the BORDER PITCHES). This arrangement satisfies Allen Forte's "REQUIREMENT 1" for normal order.

Consider the set of pitch classes [1,5,11].

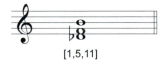

[1,5,11]

As notated in the last example, the border pitches are D♭ and B—an augmented sixth. If we rearrange the pitches as B–D♭–F, however, the border pitches are a tritone apart.

[1,5,11]

The remaining possibility for arrangement is with F as the lowest pitch.

[1,5,11]

With F in the bass, however, the border pitches are a minor sixth apart, and this configuration is less useful than the smaller B–F borders that we determined earlier. Requirement 1 is met with the arrangement B–D♭–F and this is the normal order for set [1,5,11]. The other two sets have the same pitch-class set identification, but they are less compact.

Now consider a larger pitch group, the pentachord [0,4,5,6,10]. First, we reduce pitches to a single octave.

To find the normal order of set [0,4,5,6,10], begin with the border pitches F–E (a major seventh), then rearrange the chord with the original bass pitch on top. The pitch G♭ is now the bass and this pitch borders with F (also a major seventh). Continue the rearrangement of pitches until all five possibilities have been considered. Notice that when using normal order and representing pitches with numbers, the numerical order reflects the relative compactness.

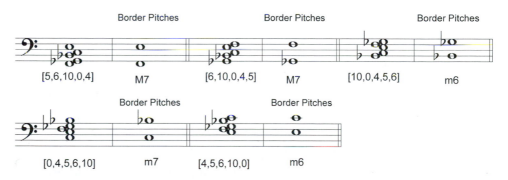

"*Requirement 2.*" The most compact border pitches are separated by a minor sixth (B♭–G♭).We have a problem, however, because the last arrangement of set [0,4,5,6,10] also has border pitches a minor sixth apart (E–C).

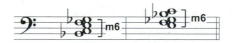

When the smallest border-pitch interval is the same in two or more orderings of the set, eliminate all other orderings and consider next the two *lowest* pitches of each set, to meet Forte's "Requirement 2." In our first arrangement of border pitches a minor sixth apart, the two lowest pitches (B♭–C) are a major second apart. In the second chord with minor sixth-borders, the two lowest pitches (E–F) are a *minor* second apart.

Both orders of set [0,4,5,6,10] satisfy Forte's Requirement 1, but only the second set meets Requirement 2 (having the least distance between the two lowest pitches). The second set, therefore, is the normal order for the original arrangement of set [0,4,5,6,10].[5]

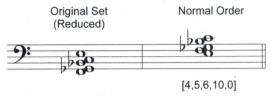

Returning to Stallings's O'Connells on page 463, we can arrange the hexachord (Set 3) with a pitch-class identification [1,2,4,7,9,10] in normal order. The diminished seventh and major-sixth border pitches in the second and fifth arrangements, however, are equivalent.

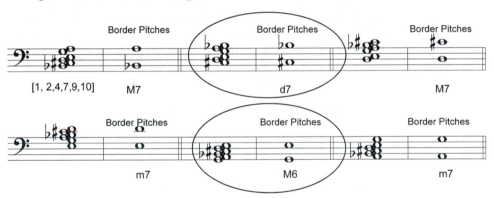

Requirement 2 allows us to identify the diminished-seventh arrangement as normal order. The two lowest pitches here are a minor second apart; in the fifth arrangement, these pitches are separated by a major second.

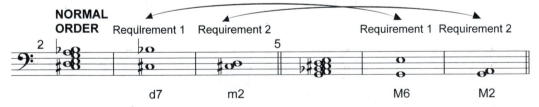

In an analysis, we would certainly want to know whether a relationship exists between Set 3 and the pitches that occur in the accompaniment in measures 7–8.

---

[5] If the two lowest pitches form the same interval, then the first and third pitches of remaining set orders are compared. If necessary, the process is continued with the first and fourth pitches, and so on, until one interval in an arrangement is found to be smaller than those corresponding to it in the other arrangements, or until all corresponding intervals of the arrangement are found to be identical (in which case all of the tied arrangements exhibit normal order).

Stallings, "O'Connell's"

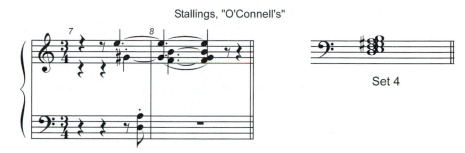

Set 4

Because this new material (Set 4) is also a hexachord [2,4,5,7,9,11], we might assume that it is related to Set 3. To verify this hunch, however, we can put Set 4 into normal order. In the next example, two arrangements of Set 4 have a major sixth (diminished seventh) between border pitches. Requirement 2 differentiates between these, however, and identifies the diminished-seventh arrangement as the normal order (there is a minor second between the lowest pitches in this configuration, as opposed to a major-second with the major-sixth version).

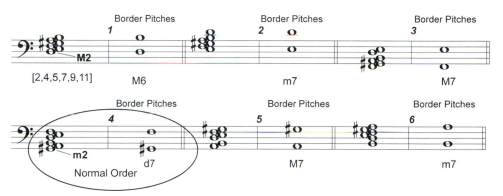

Comparing Set 3 to Set 4, we find that the latter is a literal transposition of Set 3 a perfect fifth higher (or perfect fourth lower).

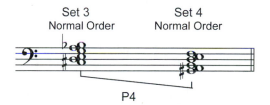

Not all relationships among sets are as straightforward as those seen in Stallings' O'Connell's. Yet, working with pitch-class sets and employing normal order when appropriate, relationships that otherwise might be missed may be discovered. Some students will find that they can figure normal order in their heads; others will need to duplicate the step-by-step comparisons as detailed in this chapter. Finally, avoid the notion that in atonal music "everything is related to everything else." In some works, this is at least partially true; in others, however, only minimal relationships among sets exist. In either event, for a work structured through set-theoretic relationships, the principles in this chapter form an introductory analytical approach.

Schoenberg, Op. 19, No. 6

We conclude this chapter with the analysis of a brief atonal work for piano. Although several important composers experimented with atonality around the turn of the twentieth century, Arnold Schoenberg is regarded by scholars as one of the most successful. His *Six Pieces for Piano*, Op. 19 was written in 1911, and comprises six brief movements. The final movement of this collection includes several important set relationships.

CD 2, TRACK 78
Arnold Schoenberg, Op. 19, No. 6

The last movement of Schoenberg's Op. 19 features two trichords:

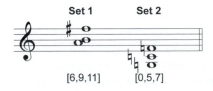

Set 1   Set 2

[6,9,11]   [0,5,7]

The interval vector of Set 1 is *0 1 1 0 1 0* ; Set 2 has the interval content *0 1 0 0 2 0*. The two sets are similar; neither contains a tritone or a minor second, and perfect intervals figure prominently into both collections. When the two sets are combined, there is no pitch duplication.

Sets 1 and 2 are repeated and a third set (Set 3, [3,4]) appears linearly. Set 3 is a minor second and is unrelated by interval content to Sets 1 and 2.

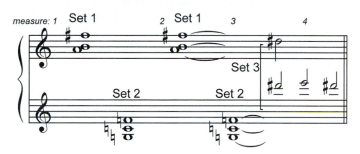

Sets 1 and 2 recur (measures 4–5); then Set 2 is transposed a perfect fourth higher (Set 4, [0,5,10]). The pitches E–D in the left hand (Set 5, [2,4]) are related to Sets 1 and 2 through nonliteral inclusion. Likewise, the pitches G♯–F♯ in measures 5–6 (Set 6, [6,8] are an unordered transposition of Set 5 and included nonliterally in Sets 1 and 2.

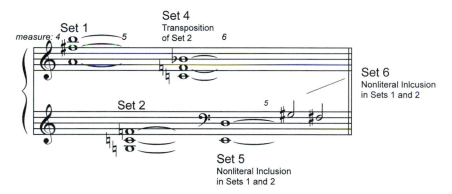

In measure 7, Set 6 is a new, four-pitch collection [1,2,3,6], although we find both Sets 5 and 6 related to it through nonliteral inclusion. Beginning in measure 8, Schoenberg employs the largest set in the work (Set 8, [0,1,2,3,4,6,7,8,11]). Note that Set 7 is included literally in Set 8. Concluding the movement, Sets 1 and 2 return in their original form, followed by Set 9 (the pitches B♭–A♭) which is a transposition of both Sets 5 and 6.

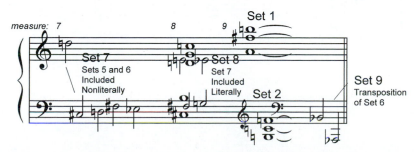

In Chapter 12 we will discuss *aleatory* or "chance" music in which one or more elements of a composition are left undetermined. This is not a requirement of atonal music, however. As can be seen in Schoenberg's Op. 19, No. 6, pitch combinations that may at first *sound* random are actually carefully planned. In tonal music, our analysis usually focuses on central and local key centers: how those centers are built and maintained, the treatment of dissonance within their contexts, and the relationship between tonality and formal design. With atonal music, such relationships are be absent. Instead, composers build cohesive works through the manipulation of motives, *timbres*, textures, and the like. The set-theoretic concepts taken up in this chapter help us to recognize important aspects of these musical structures.

WORKBOOK/ANTHOLOGY II
IV. Pitch Class and Normal Order, page 199

REVIEW AND APPLICATION 10–2

Analysis of Atonal Music

Essential Terms

border pitches	normal order	requirement 1
interval class	pitch-class set	requirement 2
interval vector	pitch class	

1. Study the following sets and determine, first, whether each given arrangement is in normal order. If the pitches do not appear in normal order, use the blank measure to rearrange them as necessary. Provide a pitch-class analysis of each set and write this identification in the blank.

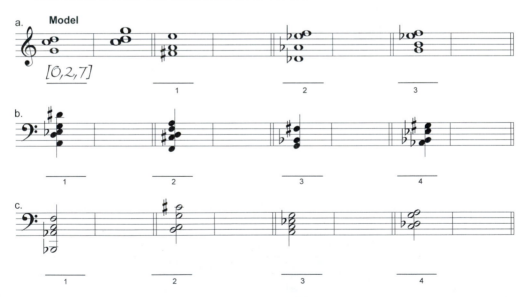

2. The next melody is atonal, employing numerous enharmonic spellings. Assign a pitch-class number (0–11) to each pitch.

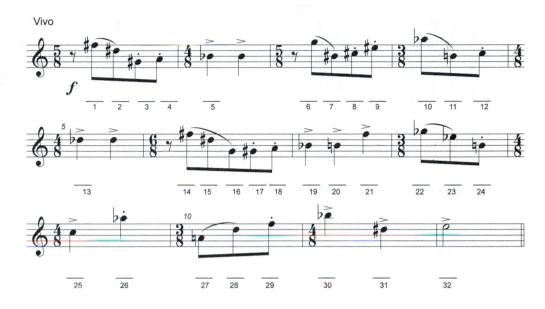

3. Earlier in this chapter, we discussed No. 6 from Schoenberg's Op. 19. The second movement, similar in length, is given below. Provide an analysis in all relevant parameters. Do not expect a wide range of set relationships; the work is relatively simple, with certain interval types predominating. Where fuller chords appear, produce pitch-class set identifications and arrange in normal order. Prepare notes for a class discussion or presentation.

CD 2, TRACK 79
Arnold Schoenberg, Op. 19, No. 2

SELF-TEST 10–2

Time Limit: 8 Minutes

1. Identify the following terms with a complete sentence or two for each. *Scoring: Subtract 7 points for each error.*

   a. Atonality

   b. Unordered transposition

   c. Nonliteral inclusion

   d. Interval vector

   e. Normal order

   f. Requirement 2

2. For each of the following three chords, provide an interval vector; then reduce the chord and rewrite it in normal order. There are two different parts for each of the three problems. *Scoring: Subtract 8 points for each incorrect part.*

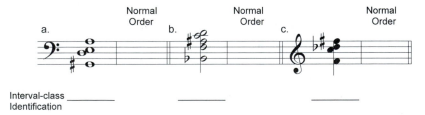

Interval-class _____   _____   _____
Identification

3. Provide the literal complement of an octatonic scale beginning on E♭ (and *not* the octatonic scale itself). *Scoring: Subtract 10 points for an incorrect answer.*

Total Possible: 100   Your Score _____

PROJECTS

Analysis

We do not always need to make chord-by-chord analyses in studying atonal music. All three pieces included in this chapter are relatively brief and reasonably straight-forward in their use of set structures. You will probably find the Stallings work in the text less challenging than the Schoenberg and Varèse compositions in the Workbook/Anthology. In the latter works, the set is not used as literally as in the Stallings. Still, you should be able to trace many atonal relationships that make the works hold together musically. In addition to an analysis of the atonal framework, be prepared to comment on the rhythm and meter, texture, and other aspects of the compositions assigned.

Text

Kendall Stallings, *O'Connell's,* text pages 476–478.
> Passages from *O'Connell's* are discussed in the text (see pages 462—464). Complete an analysis of the remainder of the work, tracing the development of sets. The work was originally for voice and piano; bassoon replaces the voice in this arrangement.

Workbook/Anthology II

Arnold Schoenberg, Six Small Piano Pieces, Nos. 2 and 3, workbook pages 201–202.
Edgard Varèse, *Density 21.* 5, workbook pages 202–203.

Composition

Trio for Trumpet, Horn, and Trombone.   Compose an atonal suite of three movements for trumpet, horn, and trombone. Use the same atonal set throughout the three movements, but employ only the trumpet in the first movement; the horn and trombone in the second; and all three instruments in the third. Make the movements brief; three minutes in all will be sufficient to establish the set and clarify relationships. Instead of the six-pitch set given in this sample assignment, compose your own set and choose permutations that you find interesting and musical (avoid the temptation to use too many different set variations).

   While professional brass performers may be expected to play more or less any passage with agility, remember that less experienced players may have difficulty with wide atonal leaps and intricate rhythms. The best readings will result from a work of modest difficulty. Your movements should be at least *twice* the length of the samples.

First Movement: Trumpet Alone

Use a moderate tempo and relatively uncomplicated rhythms. This "Fanfare" employs the original set and one transposition. Follow the sample score and trace your use of the set throughout.

I. Fanfare
(Horn and Trombone Tacit)

Second Movement: Horn and Trombone

The second movement is a legato duet for horn and trombone. The inverted set is heard in the horn with the original in the trombone.

II. Ballad
(Trumpet Tacit)

Third Movement: Trumpet, Horn, Trombone

In the *finale* to the suite, employ all three instruments. In this sample, the trumpet begins with the literal complement of the original set; the horn states the original set and the trombone has a transposed inversion.

III. March

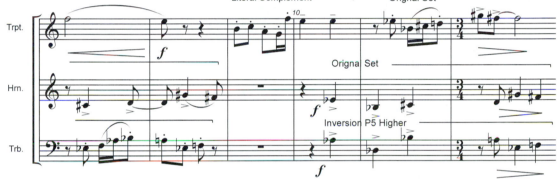

For Further Study

Music Criticism.   Atonal composers in the early twentieth century were often reviled by critics and audiences alike. Yet, we might remember that virtually all new movements in Western music have had severe critics among more conservative elements. Investigate the role of the music critic from the eighteenth century to the present day (as a paper, presentation, or personal project). First, gather information about the role of the music critic. How are the critic's views shared with an audience of readers (and listeners or viewers today)? What training does a critic usually have? For whom does the critic work? How do philosophies of criticism differ today? In the past? For a humorous look at how wrong some critics have been (in hindsight, of course), locate a copy of Nickolas Slonimsky's book *Lexicon of Musical Invective.*

Briefly trace the history of Western musical criticism. Name and comment on one important critic from the eighteenth, nineteenth, and twentieth centuries (you will find that several well-known composers were also important critics). For a look at criticism today, use the Internet or another source to find published reviews by two or three different critics (it would be interesting to locate several reviews of the same performance or composition). Be prepared to cite differences in the reviewer's respective styles.

Finally, attend a live musical performance and write a review. Model your comments after one of the reviews that you have located and studied. Your written text need not be more than two pages (about five hundred words); strive to be concise, accurate, and informative. Many reviewers include biographical or technical information about the composer or the composition. If you like the performance, write about the highlights; if the performers were relatively weaker, say so, but endeavor to find something positive to say as well (and remember to be tactful if the review is to be shared with classmates).

CD 2, TRACK 80

Kendall Stallings, "O'Connells"

CHAPTER *11*

Serial Composition

Although revered today as an innovator in music, Arnold Schoenberg was also a painter, allied philosophically in the years before World War I with the Russian Wassily Kandinsky (1866–1944) and the German Franz Marc (1880–1916). Many artists, composers, and writers during this period embraced *expressionism*, in which any real accounting of an object or theme is distorted to convey an intensely personal viewpoint. Schoenberg's musical works such as *Pierrot Lunaire* (1912) and the 1909 melodrama *Erwartung* (*Awakening*) are expressionist; dissonance and even atonality were means to such a personal expression. Atonality, however, was largely an end without means for many young composers in the early twentieth century.

Schoenberg is credited with having devised a systematic approach to atonal composition.[1] Throughout his life, the Viennese master steadfastly contended that atonal music did not *lack* anything. Rather, he preferred the term PANTONAL to describe an equal emphasis on all twelve tones of the chromatic scale. More commonly, however, we designate Schoenberg's method of composition the *serial* or *twelve-tone* technique.

SERIAL TECHNIQUE

Whether we employ the term TWELVE-TONE COMPOSITION, PANTONALITY, or SERIAL TECHNIQUE, Schoenberg's method of ensuring parity for each pitch in the twelve-tone equally tempered scale cut a swath through musical tradition in the years between the world wars. Interest in serial composition has

---

[1]Another Viennese, Joseph Hauer (1883–1959), developed a similar system of atonal composition about the same time as Schoenberg. Throughout their careers, both men claimed credit for originating the serial method.

declined in recent years, but its appeal as an alternative to traditional functional harmony attracted such major composers as Aaron Copland, Igor Stravinsky, Pierre Boulez (b. 1925), and Milton Babbitt (b. 1916).

The Tone Row

Central to Schoenberg's method of atonal composition is the *row* (*Reihe*, in German), an ordering of pitches. When we speak of a row, an array of the twelve different pitch classes is understood. As we will discuss, however, rows with more than and fewer than twelve pitches are also feasible. For the present, we will define a ROW as an ordering of all twelve pitch classes. By contrast, a set is a group of pitch classes *without* reference to order.

Construction of the Row. Serial composers impart a good deal of structure to the row, and then exploit those characteristics to create aesthetically effective musical works. The row that Alban Berg wrote for his Violin Concerto (1935), for example, is a series of superimposed major and minor triads that ends with a whole-tone fragment.

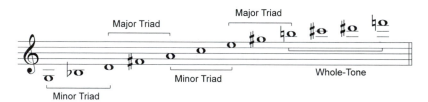

The row for Berg's *Lyric Suite* includes one occurrence of every interval type:

Throughout Western musical history, composers have used letters of the alphabet to devise motives. Robert Schumann, for example, wrote a series of variations on the name "ABEGG"; in his String Quartet No. 8 (1960), Dimitri Shostakovich devised an anagram on his own name ("DSCH").[2] Several prominent composers, including Liszt and Rimsky-Korsakov, wrote compositions on the name "BACH." In German, the letter "B" is used for B♭ while "H" connotes B♮.

B A C H

---

[2] In German, E♭ is written "es," thus, Shostakovich's motive "DSCH" is performed D E♭ C B♮.

Derived Rows.   Composers also use rows that are DERIVED—that is, comprised of related trichords, tetrachords, or hexachords.[3] Anton Webern constructed a tone row based on the pitches B♭–A–C–B♮ for his String Quartet, Op. 28. The movement begins with a transposition of the "BACH" motive beginning on G. The second tetrachord is a transposition a perfect fourth higher; the third, an inversion.

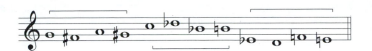

Melodic and Harmonic Application of the Row.   Tone rows appear melodically or harmonically (or both). In Alban Berg's *Lyric Suite* (1925), the first violin

CD 2, TRACK 81

Alban Berg, *Lyric Suite*

states the row in order from pitches 1 through 12. Later, the same row is divided among all four instruments. Notice that immediate reiteration of a given pitch does not affect the serial method (see measure 3 in the next example).

The Viennese composer Hanns Jelinek (1901–1969) was a student of Schoenberg who employed jazz idioms in some of his works, but turned to the serial technique later in his life. The row that Jelinek used in "Fluently" (from *Six Short Character Pieces*) is interesting in that it contains no half steps.[4]

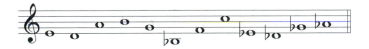

Jelinek's brief piano work appears complete in the next example. Pitches in the first two row statements, alternating between right and left hands, are identified. Trace the remaining occurrences of the row. Notice that while the pitches appear in order, octave displacements are common.

---

[3]Constructing a derived row of three- or four-pitch motives has limits. In some cases, only two or three transpositions or other manipulations of a segment are possible without pitch-class duplication.

[4]Composers vary in their use of courtesy accidentals in serial music. Some, notably Schoenberg, Webern, and Berg, add an accidental to *every* pitch regardless of its position in a measure. Other composers use courtesy accidentals liberally for clarity, but not necessarily with every pitch. We will follow this latter practice in text examples, but retain the composer's original notation where pre-existing music is cited.

Hanns Jelinek, "Fluently" from *Six Short Character Sketches*, Op. 15, No. 2

Besides a straightforward linear statement of the row (as seen in Jelinek's "Fluently"), composers often introduce the row harmonically. In this case, several pitches appear simultaneously, but order is maintained from one chord to another. The tone row that Arnold Schoenberg composed for his

Klavierstück (*Piano Piece*), Op. 33a, for example, is heard first as a series of three related tetrachords.

Row

Arnold Schoenberg, *Klavierstück*, Op. 33a

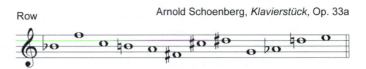

CD 2, TRACK 83-1 DISTRIBUTION OF THE ROW
(2 PARTS)
Arnold Schoenberg, *Klavierstücke*

Mässig (♩ = 120)

cantabile

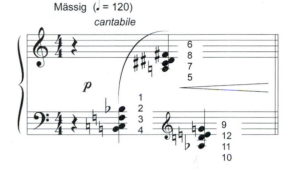

In the Schoenberg minuet given as an introduction to Part V of this volume (pages 440–442), the row

Schoenberg, Menuett Row

TRACK 83-2 DISTRIBUTION OF THE ROW
Arnold Schoenberg, Menuett

is distributed between right and left hands. In addition, notice that pitches 5–8 are heard before pitches 1–4. Serial composers sometimes employ pitches of the row out of order when musical considerations warrant. In this case, Schoenberg is working with tetrachordal segments of the row.

Moderato (♩ = ca. 88)

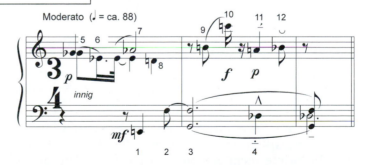

In their strictest use, twelve-tone rows are employed in order. While some composers have freely adapted the serial principle to their own tastes, the systematic use of the twelve-tone technique provided a method for atonality that spawned several additional new movements after 1945.

WORKBOOK/ANTHOLOGY II
I. The Twelve-Tone Row, page 205

TRANSFORMATIONS OF THE ROW

As we have seen, pitch-class order is central to twelve-tone composition. Within this framework, composers choose octave placements, work with row segments, employ linear or harmonic structure, and so on. While a certain amount of variety is available with the original row alone (as seen in the Jelinek piano piece), this material is not usually sufficient for a more lengthy work. Schoenberg adapted a number of traditional techniques to provide new orderings that retain their relationship to the original row. The most important permutations of the row are *transposition, retrograde, inversion,* and *retrograde inversion.*

Transposition

A diatonic or chromatic transposition of melodic material has long been an important feature of Western music. The same principle is easily adapted to serial composition. TRANSPOSITION creates eleven new versions of an original row—each retaining the same intervallic relationships. If a row is segmented into trichords, tetrachords, or hexachords, those divisions are still heard within each transposition. We will illustrate transposition and other permutations using the row that Milton Babbitt composed for Duet (given in full on page 491). The original row is also termed the PRIME FORM because it generates all other row variants.

Babbitt, *Duet*
Prime Form of Row

Stated a minor third higher, a transposition of the prime form includes all twelve pitch classes as well as the original sequence of intervals. The order of pitches, of course, is entirely different.

Row Transposed Up Three Half Steps

Identification of Transposed Row Forms.   As with cells in nonserial atonality, transpositions of a row are identified by the number of half steps between the prime form and the transposition. The prime form is identified as P_0; a transposition one half step higher (or eleven half steps lower) is designated P_1; two half steps higher (ten half steps lower) is labeled P_2, and so on. The transposition in the last example is P_3 and duplicates the prime form three half steps higher. The first pitch of a row is numbered "1" regardless of transposition or other manipulation of pitch order.

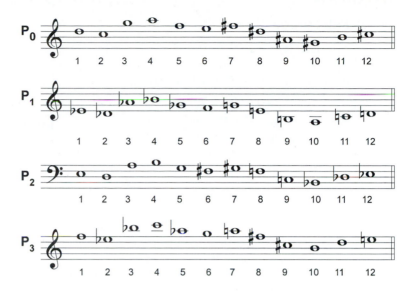

Remember that while we study row forms within an octave range, in practice, pitches may appear in any octave and with enharmonic spellings (although double sharps and flats are normally not used). Both of the lines below, for example, are designated P₇ —seven half steps higher than the prime form.

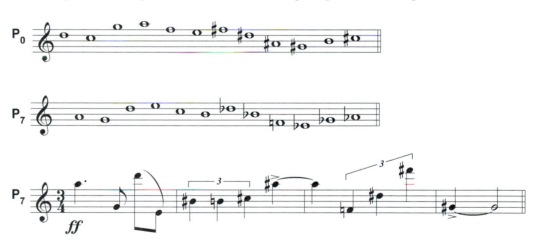

Combining Row Forms.   Composers typically employ a row in one of three ways:

1. Each voice in a polyphonic work is assigned a different row form.
2. Row forms may appear as chords in any one or in all voices.
3. One row form is divided among parts (any two or more lines).

As we have discussed, transpositions of the prime form produce eleven new versions of the row. Many composers, however, exploited still other row permutations such as *retrograde* and *inversion.*

Retrograde

The RETROGRADE form of a row is simply a statement of the prime form or one of its transpositions in reverse order. In these illustrations, we have returned to the row that Babbitt composed for his Duet.

Prime Form (**P$_0$**)

Retrograde (**R$_0$**)

The retrograde form is designated with the letter R. The retrograde of P$_0$ is R$_0$ (shown in the last example). If R$_0$ is transposed four half steps higher, it is designated R$_4$; likewise, R$_{11}$ is a retrograde statement of the row eleven half steps higher (one half step lower). Constructing any prime row form also displays its retrograde (with pitches appearing right to left).

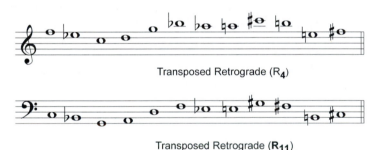

Transposed Retrograde (**R$_4$**)

Transposed Retrograde (**R$_{11}$**)

The remaining two permutations of a row are the *inversion* and the *retrograde inversion*.

Inversion

The inverted form of the row is a *mirror inversion*. Beginning with the first pitch of P$_0$, the INVERSION duplicates the intervals of the original row, but in the opposite direction.

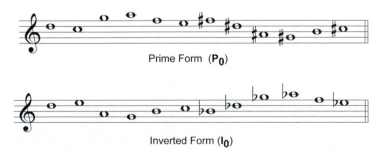

Prime Form (**P$_0$**)

Inverted Form (**I$_0$**)

Transposed inversions are identified as prime and retrograde forms are.

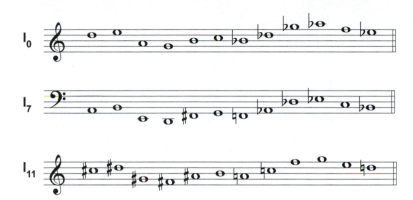

Retrograde Inversion

A reverse statement of the inversion, the RETROGRADE INVERSION, together with its eleven transpositions, completes the forty-eight standard row forms. Each of these forms is different, yet each is tied intervallically to the original. Forms RI_0, RI_7, and RI_{11} are shown in the next example.

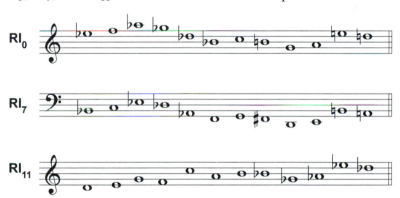

The Matrix

A graphic array called a MATRIX displays all forty-eight forms of a twelve-tone row. Composers use a matrix to find pitch combinations that create musical effects; performers, theorists, and conductors study the matrix to discover how a composer employed different row forms, and to take them into account in performance. Constructing a matrix is somewhat time consuming (and rife with the potential for error), but it is the surest way to study serial music. Construct a matrix through three steps.

1. Write the pitches of the untransposed prime form from left to right, employing letter names with any accidental symbol. Notice that this process also reveals the retrograde form (right to left). Add the indications "P_0" and "R_0" as shown.

$\mathbf{P_0} \rightarrow$ D   C   G   A   F   E   F♯   D♯   A♯   G♯   B   C♯ $\leftarrow \mathbf{R_0}$

2. Determine the inverted form and write it from top to bottom, beginning with the first pitch of P_0. The retrograde inversion will appear from bottom to top. Check carefully for any pitch duplication or omission which will indicate an error.

I_0
$\downarrow$

$P_0 \rightarrow$ D   C   G   A   F   E   F♯   D♯   A♯   G♯   B   C♯ $\leftarrow R_0$

E

A

G

B

C

B♭

D♭

G♭

A♭

F

E♭
$\uparrow$
RI_0

3. Transpose the prime form of the row to begin successively with the initial pitch of each inverted form (top to bottom on the matrix). Note that the sequence will not fall in chromatic order down the page. When these rows have been completed, however, all forty-eight forms are displayed.

Milton Babbitt, Duet
Matrix

	I_0	I_{10}	I_5	I_7	I_3	I_2	I_4	I_1	I_8	I_6	I_9	I_{11}	
P_0	**D**	C	G	A	F	E	F♯	D♯	A♯	G♯	B	C♯	R_0
P_2	E	**D**	A	B	G	F♯	G♯	F	C	B♭	D♭	E♭	R_2
P_7	A	G	**D**	E	C	B	D♭	B♭	F	E♭	F♯	G♯	R_7
P_5	G	F	C	**D**	B♭	A	B	A♭	E♭	D♭	E	G♭	R_5
P_9	B	A	E	F♯	**D**	C♯	D♯	C	G	F	A♭	B♭	R_9
P_{10}	C	B♭	F	G	E♭	**D**	E	D♭	A♭	G♭	A	B	R_{10}
P_8	B♭	A♭	E♭	F	D♭	C	**D**	B	F♯	E	G	A	R_8
P_{11}	D♭	B	G♭	A♭	E	E♭	F	**D**	A	G	B♭	C	R_{11}
P_4	G♭	E	B	D♭	A	A♭	B♭	G	**D**	C	E♭	F	R_4
P_6	A♭	G♭	D♭	E♭	B	B♭	C	A	E	**D**	F	G	R_6
P_3	F	E♭	B♭	C	A♭	G	A	F♯	D♭	B	**D**	E	R_3
P_1	E♭	D♭	A♭	B♭	G♭	F	G	E	B	A	C	**D**	R_1

RI_0 RI_{10} RI_5 RI_7 RI_3 RI_2 RI_4 RI_1 RI_8 RI_6 RI_9 RI_{11}

When a matrix is constructed correctly, the first pitch of P_0 appears diagonally from top to bottom and left to right (boldfaced letters in the above example).

Data and Analysis in Serial Music.   For the present, we will consider only serial works that are relatively strict in their employment of the method. Later in this chapter, we will discuss more liberal employments of serialism which, after World War II, were more the rule than the exception. In any event, note well that discerning row forms in serial music is no more analysis than is the collection of roman numerals in a Bach chorale harmonization. These endeavors constitute the collection of *data*; use these data to form conclusions that will aid in performance or increase your understanding of the music.

Discerning the Row.   The row is typically presented in the first voice heard either in a linear or in a harmonic setting. If you are unfamiliar with the composition, study the first twelve pitches of the melody. If there are no duplications, this is most likely the row. Conversely, if there are duplications within the initial twelve pitches, the row is probably in another voice or split between two or more voices. If there are pitch-class duplications in the first voice, consider another line alone. Again, duplications within the first twelve pitches normally preclude a statement of the row. If the lower line includes chords, remember that the row may be presented harmonically over the span of just a few beats (Schoenberg, Op. 33a, page 483). In this event, you may not be able to determine the row without close analysis of other passages that are entirely linear.

Be aware that some composers distribute the pitches of a row form among some or all of the voices available or between right and left hands in a keyboard score (as seen in the Jelinek duet on page 482 and the Webern Concerto on page 517). Occasionally, the row will appear after some introductory material in another voice.

"Chasing" Row Forms.   Make a matrix of the row once you have it identified. To trace (or "chase") row permutations, match the first two or three pitches from a line in the matrix with the first few notes of the music (being sure to check the *entire* row before making a firm identification). Label each row form as shown in the next example. Take note of these additional considerations (some are discussed later in this chapter):

1. Some composers are freer in their use of the row (as in the Schoenberg Menuett excerpted on page 483).

2. Row overlap (discussed on page 497) and other techniques make identification more challenging.

3. If the beginning of a row is not readily apparent, use the matrix to look for the *last* few pitches.

4. Extra pitches may occur.

5. Some composers create brief melodic cells and also employ nonserial passages.

6. A row form may be stated incompletely.

7. Look for exceptional intervals (possibly inverted) that occur only once in the original row.

Finally, keep track of the various permutations of the row used. Reach conclusions about the music. Speculate, for instance, on why a composer chose particular row combinations or successions. Which, if any, pitches are common within the first trichord, tetrachord, or hexachord? How is the row segmented? Which intervals or scale fragments predominate?

Babbitt: Duet.   Milton Babbitt is closely associated with the development of serialism in the 1950s and 1960s. A member of the music faculty at Princeton University, Babbitt explored various aspects of the serial technique, including combinatorality (discussed later in this chapter) as well as serialized rhythmic, dynamic, and articulation elements.

CD 2, TRACK 84
Milton Babbitt, Duet

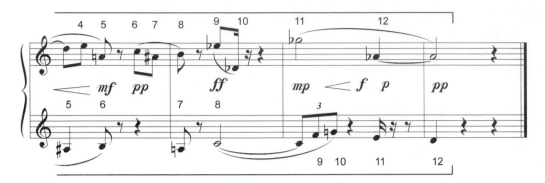

Babbitt's row is constructed so that a combination of specific forms produces all twelve pitch classes between corresponding hexachords.[5] Notice that Babbitt effects a symmetry of the two voices: Row forms begin and end at more or less the same time. The next table shows the variety of forms and how the two voices are combined.

Row Forms in Babbitt's Duet

Right Hand	Left Hand	Measures
P_0	P_6	1–6
RI_{11}	R_0	6–10
I_5	RI_5	10–14
R_6	I_{11}	14–19

Babbitt's Duet is through-composed, but numerous motives provide continuity and shape for individual lines. The opening motive in the right hand occurs in variation also in measures 5–6, 10–11, and 14–16. The motivic approach to formal design, devised by Debussy and others in the nineteenth century, remains a favorite tool of modern composers.

---

[5]This is *always* true of a prime form and its retrograde. Other possibilities are discussed beginning on page 502.

The left hand figures are more varied—including triplets—and are generally faster moving. The two lines complement one another neatly as free counterpoint. The overall effect is dissonant, of course, but notice the predominance of thirds and sixths between the two parts—especially in measures 1–10. Points of cadence are often major or minor seconds or sevenths (measures 7, 10, 11, 16), and the final interval is a tritone.

Not all serial works are as straightforward as Babbitt's Duet, but we see in the composition both a traditional employment of row forms and a close association with the principles of traditional two-voice counterpoint.

Transposition, inversion, and retrograde enable a composer to choose from among numerous row forms to combine certain pitches, trichords, tetrachords, or hexachords, and so on. Composers tend to limit their use of row forms and combine them so that certain pitch combinations predominate. On the other hand, for lengthy serial works, two or more different rows may be used.

WORKBOOK/ANTHOLOGY II
II. Transformations of the Row, page 209

In the next section, we will discuss several additional possibilities for inventive uses of the row.

REVIEW AND APPLICATION 11–1

Transposition, Inversion, and Retrograde

Essential Terms

inversion	prime form	row	transposition
matrix	retrograde	twelve-tone composition	
pantonality	retrograde inversion	serial technique	

1. Compose twelve-tone rows that have the characteristics specified. Many different answers are possible. Begin on any pitch you choose.

    a.   Perfect intervals predominate in the row

    b.   The row has a whole-tone flavor

    c.   Row on the word "BEAD" [6]

    d.   The row is constructed of minor thirds and half steps.

---

[6]Begin with an arrangement (in order) of B, E, A, and D for pitches 1–4 in the row. Next, find a transposition or inversion in which no pitches are duplicated (for pitches 5–8). Finally, choose another segment permutation for pitches 9–12 (if none is available without pitch duplication, use a similar gesture that combines the remaining pitch classes.)

2. Provide permutations of the given row as specified. After the row form is completed, scan it for duplications and omitted pitches. Next, verify the interval between pitches 1–2 and 11–12.

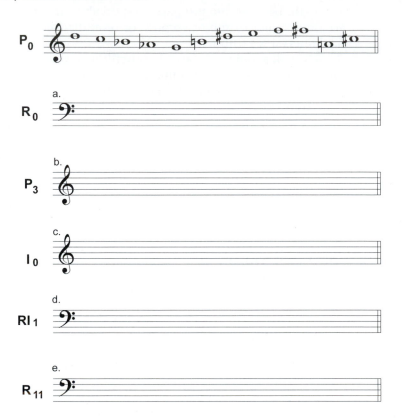

3. On a separate sheet, construct a matrix for the row that follows. Next, use this matrix to analyze the brief composition. In addition to a linear row statement in the voices separately, be on the lookout for a row form that is split between the two parts. Label row forms, and mark the beginning and ending of each.

Given Row

SELF-TEST 11–1

Time Limit: 15 Minutes

1. Some of the statements that follow are true; others are false. Write "T" or "F" in the blank as appropriate. *Scoring: Subtract 5 points for each incorrect answer.*

_____ a. "Pantonal" is a term used to refer to traditional Western harmony as opposed to music that is atonal.

_____ b. The retrograde version of a given row form is a statement of pitches backward.

_____ c. Arnold Schoenberg was a famous pupil of Anton Webern.

_____ d. By definition, serial music is atonal.

_____ e. The prime form of a row is a duplication of the same intervals in the opposite direction.

_____ f. The terms "serial" and "twelve-tone" are synonymous.

_____ g. Segmentation refers to the division of the row into hexachords, tetrachords, or trichords, and so on.

_____ h. Most rows are limited to twenty-four different permutations.

2. For the given row, provide the forms specified (you need not construct a matrix). *Scoring: Subtract 15 points for each incorrect answer.*

Given Row

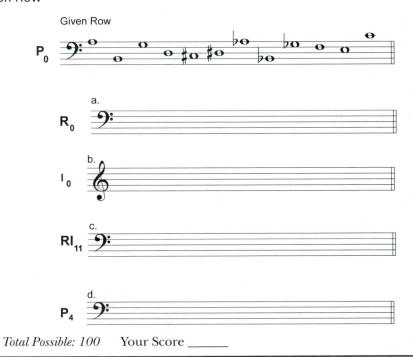

Total Possible: 100   Your Score _____

FLEXIBILITY IN THE SERIAL METHOD

Throughout Western musical history, the importance of any new organizing principle has been measured in part by its flexibility. Sonata form, for example, has served composers from the eighteenth century to the present day. On the other hand, the hyperchromaticism of the late Renaissance and late Romantic eras was a limited technique and quickly bypassed by the advent of functional harmony and atonality, respectively.

Serialism has offered an inherent flexibility and has influenced Western music for three-quarters of a century. As we have seen, serial composers are not always strict in their use of the row. Remember that while serialism provides a method for organizing atonal music, the goal remains one of aesthetically satisfactory art. We should not be surprised that from the beginning, composers added, omitted, and repeated pitches as they saw fit. Two such common exceptions to a strict use of the row include overlapping and the creation of melodic cells.

Free Use of the Row

OVERLAPPING may occur when the final pitch or two of one row form is duplicated in the initial pitches of a different form. Examining the Babbitt row, for instance, notice that the last two pitches of P_0 and the first two pitches of RI_8 are identical. Accordingly, the two rows may be combined linearly in either of two ways: The rows may follow one another (the first example below) or they may be overlapped where the pitch duplication occurs (second example).

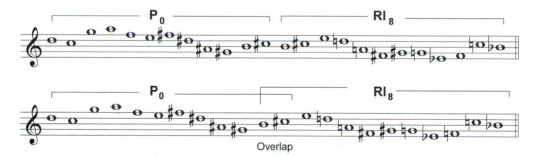

In addition to retrograde forms P_0 and R_0 (that will always have an overlapped pitch), some rows have a few variants in which two or more pitches overlap. Row forms that present the potential for overlap are easily determined from a matrix.

The Canzonet for Tuba (1972) by contemporary American composer Claude Baker (b. 1948) provides another example of row overlap as well as an example of melodic cells and an unordered set (measures 1–22 of this 54-measure work are shown in the next example).

Claude Baker, Canzonet

The canzonet begins with the prime form (ending with the pitches C and B). These same pitches occur at the beginning of RI_3 and Baker capitalizes on this overlap (measure 3). Another instance of overlap occurs in measure 4 where RI_3 and P_{10} are combined. The statement of RI_1 that follows includes an extra pitch B (measure 9). Finally, observe the melodic cells that are created in measures 11, 12, and 15. Serial composers often create such fleeting tonal references to be canceled quickly by a return to the twelve-tone sequence. Baker's statement of RI_1 begins ordinarily (measures 13), but lapses into an unordered series before a cadence on the pitch G (measure 21).

Another serialist, Alban Berg, is particularly known for his free use of the technique and for his fondness for melodic cells. The passage that follows, from *Lyric Suite* includes several different row forms—some split between two instruments—as well as melodic cells and other complexities.

Alban Berg, *Lyric Suite*

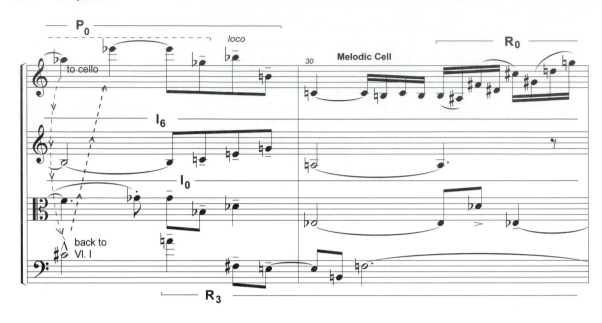

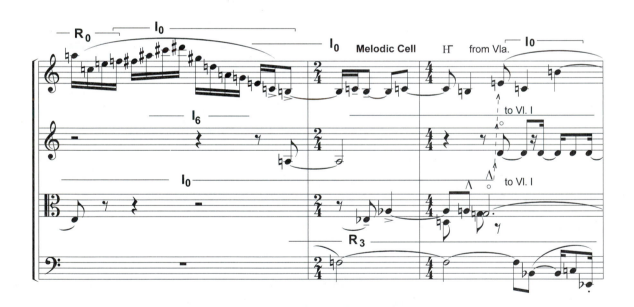

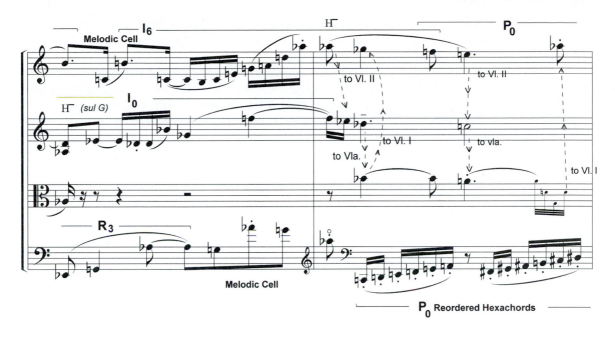

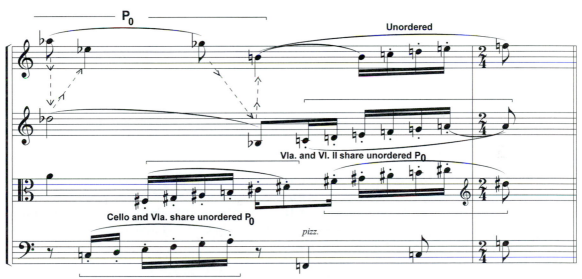

Row form R_0 begins in the second violin (measure 22 not shown), but moves to the viola in measure 23 as the second violin takes up a new form—I_6. While the pitch A appears to be omitted from I_6, it occurs at the appropriate point in the viola. Likewise, the pitch C$\sharp$ is omitted from the prime in measure 27 (first violin), but the pitch *is* heard as the cello simultaneously states R_3. Two row forms are elided in this passage: P_0/I_6 (measure 24 and again in measure 25) and R_0/I_0 (measure 29).

Several times in the excerpt shown, Berg treats two pitches as a melodic cell (labeled on the score). Also of interest is the reordered use of the first and second hexachords of P_0 as scale passages (measures 33–34). Finally, observe that while Berg's treatment of row forms is basically linear, in measure 33, RI_0 is distributed among three instruments.

The symbol $\overline{H}$ in the score stands for *Hauptstimme* or principal voice; a related symbol is $\overline{N}$ which designates the *Nebenstimme* or secondary voice. Schoenberg and his followers often used these markings on the score so that performers would be aware when they had principal and secondary roles, respectively.

Rows with More Than and Fewer Than Twelve Tones

Most serial composers employ a row of twelve tones; some, however, have extended the principle to include fewer than and more than twelve pitch classes. The Italian Luciano Berio (b. 1925), for example, used the following thirteen-tone row in *Nones* (1954):

The trichord symmetry of the row is obvious with the seventh pitch, A♭, flanked by a perfect fourth and a perfect fifth. The pitch D appears twice.

Igor Stravinsky, on the other hand, chose this five-tone row for his *In Memoriam Dylan Thomas* (1954):

Overlapping and the use of exceptional rows provided serial composers with still more novel avenues for combining forms and creating well organized music. Even before World War II, Schoenberg and others adopted several new techniques to exploit the twelve-tone principle fully. These include both combinatoriality and extended serialism.

Combinatoriality

The serial principle centers on pitch *order*. Other manifestations of twelve-tone composition, however, rely more on content. *Combinatoriality*, discussed in this section, is such a phenomenon. Before we are able to address combinatoriality, however, we need to approach the concept of hexachordal *aggregates*.

Aggregates.   If the first hexachord of the prime form (P_0) combines with the first hexachord of another row form with no pitch classes duplicated, then those two hexachords taken together are said to form an AGGREGATE. If the first hexachords comprise an aggregate, the second hexachords will form an aggregate as well. Again, aggregates are considered on the basis of hexachordal content and not order.

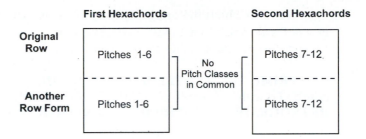

Aggregates are important to twelve-tone composers because they extend the serial principle to include simultaneity. In considering the row from Babbitt's Duet (see the matrix on page 491), look first at a row pair that *does not* produce aggregates. In a combination of P_0 and P_3 the pitches F, C, and G appear in the first hexachords of both rows.

We need only study the first hexachords of two row forms to determine whether an aggregate exists; if one or more pitches is duplicated in the first hexachords, duplications will occur in the second hexachords as well. The first hexachords of row forms P_0 and P_1 have only one pitch in common. Still, however, no aggregate is formed.

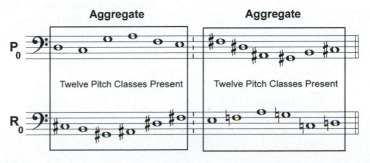

A combination of P_0 and R_0, however, produces aggregates. Comparing the first and second hexachord of P_0 with the same divisions of R_0, all twelve pitch classes are present in both hexachords.

A row in which the original prime form (P_0) can be combined with another row form to produce hexachordal aggregates is termed COMBINATORIAL.[7] Four different kinds of combinatorial relationship are possible:

PRIME	**PRIME**	**PRIME**	**PRIME**
combined with	combined with	combined with	combined with
RETROGRADE	**PRIME**	**INVERSION**	**RETROGRADE INVERSION**

The relationship between P_0 and R_0 might sometimes be termed "quarter-combinatorial" because these pairs will always produce hexachordal aggregates, even when the other pairs do not. Likewise, *any* prime form and its retrograde also produce a combinatorial relationship (P_0/R_0, P_7/R_7, and so on). Other types of combinatoriality, however, are more important and may or may not be present in a given row.

Semi-Combinatoriality.   A row is SEMI-COMBINATORIAL if, in addition to the prime/retrograde pairing that is always present, aggregates are produced between the prime and one other form:

- Prime and a transposition of the prime
- Prime and the inversion (or transposed inversion)
- Prime and the retrograde inversion (or transposed retrograde inversion)

The row from Schoenberg's *Klavierstück* (Op. 33a) is semi-combinatorial. A combination of P_0 and I_5 produces all twelve pitch classes in the first hexachords. Likewise, the second hexachords have no pitches in common and likewise form an aggregate.

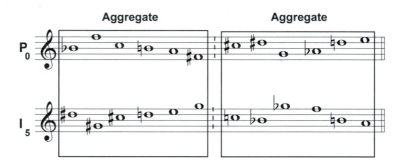

The principle of combinatoriality permits a composer to select forms that include no pitch duplications between melody and accompaniment (or between any two voices). Schoenberg was particularly fond of the P_0/I_5 semi-combinatorial relationship (seen in the next excerpt from *Klavierstück*, Op. 33a).

---

[7]While discussion in this text is limited to hexachordal combinatoriality, other kinds exist (tetrachordal, for example).

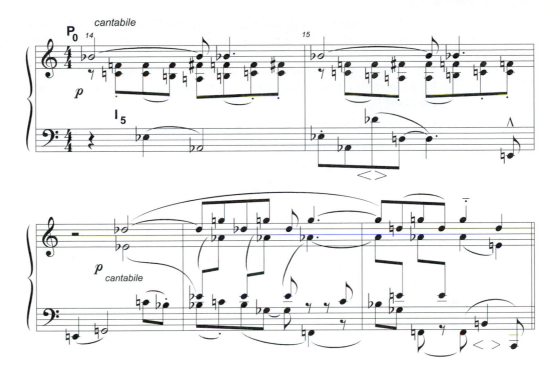

Secondary Rows.   Another feature of combinatoriality results from a linear combination of two different row forms. If a row is followed by the *retrograde* of its combinatorial partner (P_0 and RI_0 using the Schoenberg row), a new twelve-tone row is formed between the second hexachord of the first row and the first hexachord of the second. A new row produced in this way is termed a SECONDARY ROW. Like combinatoriality and other relationships, secondary rows present further possibilities for simultaneity.

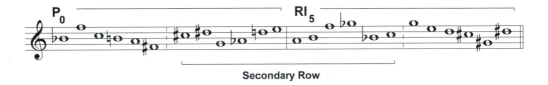

Secondary Row

All-Combinatoriality.   When a row is ALL-COMBINATORIAL, the prime form can be combined to form aggregates with every sort of row form. The prime form must combine with other row forms to meet *each* of the following conditions:

1. RI_0 or at least one transposition of the retrograde inversion forms aggregates with P_0.

2. At least one transposition of the prime itself forms aggregates with P_0.

3. I_0 or at least one transposition of the inverted form results in aggregates with P_0.

These relationships are in addition to the prime/retrograde pairing that is *always* available. These conditions must be met in an all-combinatorial row, but remember that we are talking about content and not order. The row that Milton Babbitt composed for his Duet is all-combinatorial. In addition to the P_0/R_0 combination, aggregates are produced by combining P_0 with I_{11}, P_0 with RI_5, and P_0 with P_6.

All-Combinatoriality

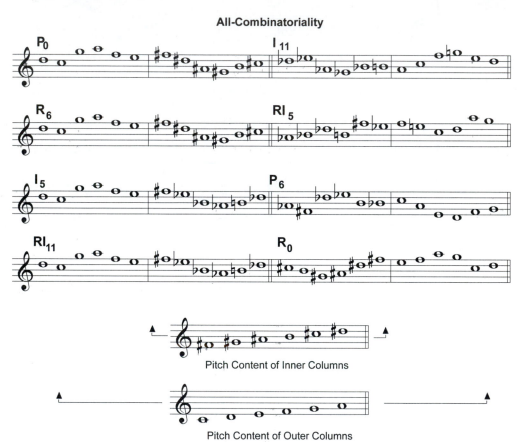

Pitch Content of Inner Columns

Pitch Content of Outer Columns

Combinatoriality allows a composer to combine row forms without pitch duplication. With pitch-class overlap and other techniques, serial composers have a wide range of means to exploit the basic twelve-pitch-class set.

WORKBOOK/ANTHOLOGY II
III Flexibility in the Serial Method, page 211

Extended Serialization

When Schoenberg devised serialism, he offered a method of composition that provided systematic control over the parameter of pitch. Almost immediately, other composers experimented with extending this control to other parameters as well. Pierre Boulez, Milton Babbitt, Olivier Messiaen, and others applied a kind of row structure to both rhythm and *timbre*. EXTENDED SERIALIZATION refers to a systematic method of controlling two or more parameters of a given composition.[8] This term is preferable to "total serialization" because, in fact, the serialization is not always "total." Composers extend the process of serialization to include pitch as well as any additional parameters.

Serialization of Rhythm. Pitch serialization is based on four row forms: prime, retrograde, inversion, and retrograde inversion. Some of these same forms are applicable to the serialization of other parameters as well. For a given set of rhythmic values (the "prime" form), the retrograde is simply a statement in reverse order. The rhythmic row in the next example has six values; rows with fewer than or more than six elements are also useful.

Inversion of Rhythmic Row. The inversion of a rhythmic row is somewhat more complex than retrograde. While pitch inversion is based on interval size and direction, rhythm has only one parameter: duration. Composers use diverse methods to determine an "inversion" of a rhythmic row. One approach is to assign a duration to each pitch of the pitch row; an inversion of the pitch row (in the usual way) also provides a rhythmic inversion. In the next example, the pitch row is from Babbitt's Duet introduced earlier (a matrix appears on page 489.

Prime

Pitch Row	D	C	G	A	F	E	F♯	D♯	A♯	G♯	B	C♯

Rhythmic Row

Inversion

Pitch Row	D	E	A	G	B	C	B♭	D♭	G♭	A♭	F	E♭

Rhythmic Row

Another system of arriving at an inversion involves mathematical manipulation of durations or rhythmic patterns. In the first of his *Three Compositions for Piano* (1947), Milton Babbitt uses a rhythmic row based on sixteenth notes containing the values 5, 1, 4, and 2, respectively.

---

[8] Some refer to the serialization of two or more parameters as INTEGRAL SERIALIZATION.

Prime

Babbitt inverts the row by subtracting each number from 6; the inverted row, therefore, is represented by the sequence 1, 5, 2, 4.

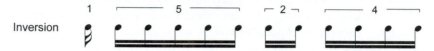

Inversion

A third method of obtaining an inversion of a rhythmic row involves segmentation. When the row is broken into segments (groups of two values in this six-element rhythmic row), those segments can be interwoven so that a new rhythmic row emerges.

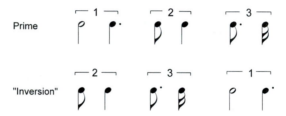

Prime

"Inversion"

While rhythmic rows can be "transposed" (doubling or halving all values, for example) with one of the methods of inversion already discussed (or another of the many possibilities), we can devise a retrograde inversion to provide at least four permutations for any given rhythmic row. The inversion in the next example was determined through interweaving segments. When composers employ rhythmic rows, more often than not, the rhythmic structure is complex—often with mixed meter or measured rhythm.

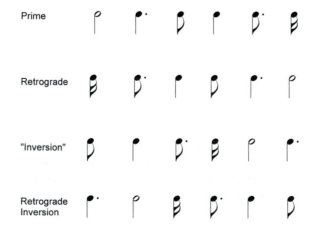

Prime

Retrograde

"Inversion"

Retrograde Inversion

Serialization of Other Parameters.   Dynamics, *timbres*, tempos, articulations, and other aspects of a musical work can be serialized as well. Inverted forms are determined by any one of the methods discussed on pages 507–508. The following dynamic and articulation rows contain six elements each. Inversions have been derived through segmentation.

Dynamic Matix

Original	*mf*	*f*	*ff*	*mp*	*p*	*pp*
Retrograde	*pp*	*p*	*mp*	*ff*	*f*	*mf*
Inversion	*mp*	*p*	*pp*	*mf*	*f*	*ff*
Retrograde Inversion	*ff*	*f*	*mf*	*pp*	*p*	*mp*

Articulation Matrix

Original	–	.	>	⊥	ʌ	ʌ
Retrograde	ʌ	ʌ	⊥	>	.	–
Inversion	⊥	ʌ	ʌ	–	.	>
Retrograde Inversion	>	.	–	ʌ	ʌ	⊥

Timbres can be serialized either according to terms that indicate a certain effect or by the combination or sequence of instrumental groupings. Two possibilities for an original row are shown in the next example. Permutations of *timbre* rows are determined by the same processes discussed for rhythm, dynamic, and articulation rows.

Timbre Matrix

Terms	*brilliant*	*dark*	*lightly*	*sharp*	*somber*	*crisp*
Instrument Groupings	clarinet	trumpet	violin	oboe	piano	flute

The composition that follows, by a second-year music student, employs the principle of extended serialization. The pitch row is the one from Babbitt's Duet; rhythm, dynamic, and articulation rows are from the matrices given on pages 508–509. The trumpet line is serialized in pitch, rhythm, articulation, and dynamics; the piano is serialized only in pitch.[9] The form of the work is a brief ABA. Only the first two measures of the second A section are given. Your instructor may ask you to complete the composition.

Kurt Dowland, Flirtation for Trumpet and Piano

[9]In the trumpet, the rhythm, articulation, and dynamic rows are identified with the letters R, A, and D, respectively. The following letter identifies the row form (P = Prime, I = inversion, and so on).

Serialism was a final event in the dissolution of common-practice music. In the early 1800s, Chopin and others began harmonic experiments that weakened the sensation of key. By the close of the century, Wagner and Debussy had rendered tonality almost secondary to color and motivic development. Remaining faithful to tonality in his early works, Igor Stravinsky helped launch an era of unrelenting dissonance in the early twentieth century. At the same time, in the cultured climate of pre–World War I Vienna, Arnold Schoenberg devised the serial principle. His pupils, Berg and Webern, contributed to the evolution of serialism while Babbitt, Boulez, Karlheinz Stockhausen (b. 1928), and many others extended the principle after 1945.

While serialism has been attractive to many composers as a means of organizing atonal works, audiences have generally been skeptical of music that, on first hearing, seemed only remotely connected to the established "classics" of Western music. Acknowledged masterpieces have been written using the twelve-tone method, but in our market-driven world, consumers of live and recorded music have remained largely preoccupied with the limited gamut of formulaic pop styles.

Twelve-tone composition was heralded in the 1930s as the foundation of a truly new Western music. In the perspective of time, however, the method peaked in the late 1960s and clearly began to wane by 1980. While many today study and use the serial method as a means of organizing atonality, use of the strict system, as practiced by the "Viennese masters" (Schoenberg, Webern, and Berg), has declined markedly among the present generation of composers.

 WORKBOOK/ANTHOLOGY II
IV. Later Developments in Serialism, page 213

REVIEW AND APPLICATION 11–2 —————————————————

Later Developments in Serialism

Essential Terms

all-combinatoriality   extended serialization   semi-combinatoriality
aggregate   row overlap

1. Construct a twelve-tone row of your own design. Next make a matrix of this row on another sheet. Be prepared to provide the following information.

  a. Indicate how you structured your row. Is the row segmented? If so, explain the divisions and their relationships. If not, which intervals predominate? Are there any additional characteristics of the row that you considered in its structure?

  b. In addition to row pairs that always have pitch overlap between the last pitch(es) of one form and the first pitch(es) of another (P_3/R_3, I_7/RI_7, and so on), which (if any) forms of your row have:

    (1) Overlap of one pitch _____ _____ _____

    (2) Overlap of two pitches _____ _____ _____

  c. Is your row semi-combinatorial? If so, which forms combine to form aggregates between corresponding hexachords?

    _____ _____

  d. Is your row all-combinatorial? If so, which three forms combine with P_0 to form aggregates?

    I _____   RI _____   P _____

2. Study the following rhythmic row. Use one of the three methods discussed on pages 507–508 to create a matrix with retrograde, inversion, and retrograde inversion. Explain how you arrived at permutations of the row.

Prime

Retrograde

Inversion

Retrograde Inversion

SELF-TEST 11–2

Time Limit: 5 Minutes

1. Choose one term from the list and match it with one of the definitions that follow. Write the appropriate letter in the blank. Be aware that the terms cover
material discussed in the entire chapter. *Scoring: Subtract 5 points for each incorrect
answer.*

A. Pantonal	F. Row overlap
B. Aggregate	G. Inversion
C. Semi-combinatorial	H. Melodic cell
D. Hexachord	I. All-combinatorial
E. Retrograde	J. Extended serialization

_____ (1)   a reverse statement of the row

_____ (2)   the serializaton of rhythm and other parameters

_____ (3)   The last pitch of one row form is available also as the first pitch of
another row form.

_____ (4)   an alternate term for atonal music, preferred by Schoenberg

_____ (5)   two or more pitches that are emphasized by being repeated as a
partial row statement or as an interruption of the row

_____ (6)   a combination of the prime and any other row form (except the literal retrograde) to form hexachordal aggregates

_____ (7)   a mirror version of the prime form, with intervals duplicated in the
opposite direction

_____ (8)   Two row forms combine so that the corresponding hexachords
contain all twelve pitch classes.

_____ (9)   a group of six different pitch classes

_____ (10) The prime form combines with a transposition, an inversion, and a
retrograde inversion to produce aggregates.

2. Some of these statements are true; others, false. Enter the letter "T" or "F" in
the blank. *Scoring: Subtract 8 points for any error you make.*

_____ a. Serial music may include melodic cells that establish a brief tonal
center.

_____ b. Rows with more than and fewer than twelve tones are not used.

_____ c. The serial method began to wane by about 1930.

_____ d. An aggregate depends on pitch-class content and not order.

_____ e. Combinatoriality is an alternate approach to serialization that was
originated by the Austrian Joseph Hauer about 1960.

_____ f. If a row is semi-combinatorial, the prime form combines only with the literal retrograde to form aggregates.

_____ g. Milton Babbit was a noted American composer who extended the serial principle.

_____ h. In German, the letter B stands for B♮.

3. Complete the statement below, by checking the correct word or words. *Scoring: subtract 2 points for any incorrect answer.*

Combinatoriality depends on
____order   ____content   ____both order and content

Total Possible: 100   Your Score _____

PROJECTS

Analysis

We must be on guard to avoid thinking that following row forms is the end (or even always the goal) in the analysis of serial music. Most often, an identification of forms is just one area of data for use in reaching conclusions about the music. As you study the structure of one or more of the pieces included in the text and workbook, "chase" the row forms, but also investigate the rhythm, texture, *timbre*, form, range, instrumentation, and other factors as appropriate. In particular, consider some of the following:

a. Is there any obvious organization to the row itself? Interval types? Segmentation?

b. Which row forms are used and what are the relationships among them?

c. Are rows employed strictly? Or are repeated or unordered cells present?

d. Is the row combinatorial? Are these relationships exploited?

Text

Arnold Schoenberg, Menuett from Suite for Piano, Op. 25, text pages 438–440.
    The movement appears as an introduction to Unit V and is discussed briefly in Chapter 11. Construct a matrix and study the serial structure of the movement.
Anton Webern, Concerto, Op. 24 (III), text pages 517–522.
    The Austrian Anton Webern was an important student of Arnold Schoenberg. Webern embraced the serial technique from about 1924 in works that are often miniatures. Webern's entire life work, in fact, is under four hours of music. The Concerto for Nine Instruments dates from 1934. The complete third movement is given in the text with rows identified through the first 20 measures. Make a matrix, complete the row identification, then analyze the work in full.
Twelve-Tone Works in Jazz Style, text pages 523–524.
    These two works illustrate one approach to the use of basic serial principles in a jazz style. "Blues for Eli" (2004) by Carl Pandolfi (b.1965) is a conventional 12-bar blues structure, employing traditional chord changes (with liberal substitutions) to support a serial melody. Composer Kim Portnoy (b.1954) does much the opposite in his "Blues for Anton" (1985). The bass line is serial while other elements create a clear tonality.

Analyze these works both as serial and tonal compositions. Which of the two harmonic approaches dominates? How do the compositions differ? Would we be correct in saying that both compositions illustrate a fusion between serial and tonal systems?

Workbook/Anthology II

Arnold Schoenberg, "Tot" from Three Songs, Op. 48, workbook pages 215–216.
Ernst Krenek, Suite for Violoncello Solo (First Movement), Op. 84, workbook pages 217–218.

Composition

Serial Work for Piano.   Review the short "Fanfare," a composition for piano solo given on page 497 of the text. The row from which this work is derived also appears that page. Using the same row and its permutations, complete a second movement that unfolds in a slow or moderate tempo and forms a complement to the "Fanfare." Where the given movement is contrapuntal, your new work might be declamatory (as in the first sample passage) or have a dance flavor (as in the second passage given here). Consider making use of repeated or unordered pitch cells in your composition. You might also quote a measure or two from "Fanfare" (in a different style). You may wish to employ a number of other row forms in the second movement. A matrix will be useful in this endeavor.

The approaches to the second movement are virtually limitless. Two samples are given here. Complete one of them or use your own ideas as directed by your instructor.

Sample 1

Sample 2

For Further Study

"The New Music."   When Schoenberg unveiled his twelve-tone method in the mid-1920s, friends, close associates, and even a few music critics hailed the development as a new era in Western music with perhaps as much expressive potential as tonality had offered in the early seventeenth century. Naturally, there were also detractors who saw serialism not as a logical outgrowth of romanticism (as Schoenberg, Webern, and Berg viewed it), but as a direct attack on Western aesthetic and moral values. From about 1925, serialism grew steadily in popularity and was accepted by increasing numbers as a new and valid alternative to tonality. While audiences never cottoned to the dissonances, many important composers (Aaron Copland, Igor Stravinsky, and others) adopted serial principles long after their careers had been established through tonal works. After World War II, serialism underwent many changes that seemed to portend an inherent flexibility.

Since about 1985, however, composers and audiences have expressed less interest in serialism. Text books continue to include the method, and students still experience the system through analysis and composition, but the MIDI generation has largely preferred to experiment with electronic media. Among another group of younger composers, there has been an unabashed return to tonal principles.

Write an essay of about three pages (750 words) in which you defend one of these statements:

- "Serialism is Dead!"
- "Serialism is *Not* Dead!"

This assignment is for an op-ed piece (for a local newspaper, perhaps) where you are entitled to give your opinions as long as they are based on factual information). Consult critical reviews, books on musical philosophy, recent surveys of twentieth-century music, and composer interviews and biographies. Your essay might have these basic divisions:

a. a brief introduction to serialism and the evolution of serialism in the twentieth century.

b. a statement of aesthetic problems (or potentialities) as they have been expressed by others in recent books and articles.

c. your own opinions (supported by facts, figures, and quotations) about the future of serialism in the twenty-first century and its overall role in Western musical history.

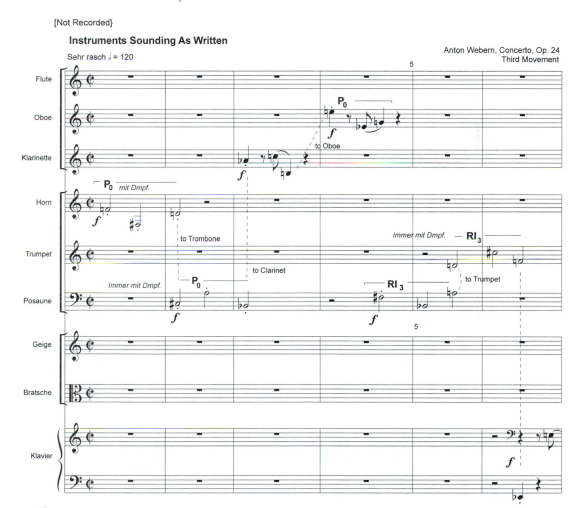

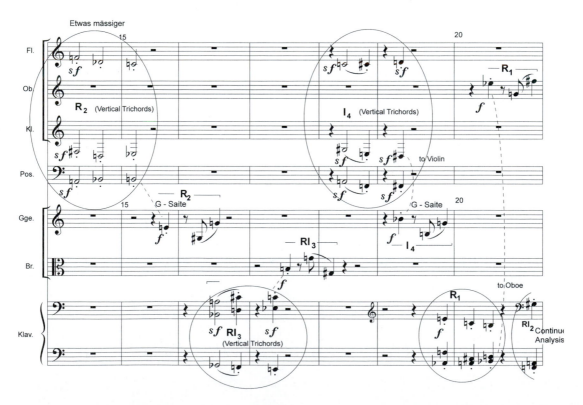

Swing Feel ♩=132

Carl Pandolfi, Blues for Eli

Kim Portnoy, "Blues for Anton"

CHAPTER *12*

Music After 1950

We often hear the terms "contemporary" and "modern" applied to the music of Stravinsky, Bartok, and Schoenberg—despite the fact that all three composers were born before 1900. No one today would describe innovations such as the phonograph record, the telephone, or an eight-track tape as "modern," yet for a substantial segment of the listening public, much music after Debussy seems unapproachable. Even more troubling, perhaps, is the reference by some to commercial music and its incredible array of style variants as our "new music." On the contrary, we can regard most commercial music as solidly common-practice in all but style. For many composers, the twentieth century brought a definitive break with past musical traditions; yet, no *new art* has emerged to fill the void.

Any comprehensive study of music after 1950 is necessarily a survey of dozens of individual methods, styles, and adaptations. Moreover, as we move ever closer to the present in our examination of Western musical theory, we lose the luxury of historical perspective to guide us in differentiating the meaningful from the competent. Bach, we should remember, was not fully appreciated until nearly a hundred years after his death; in his day, Johann Hummel (1778–1837) was considered by many to be at least the equal of Beethoven.

In the present chapter, we will consider several major trends that have been influential since 1950—especially those that continue to be at least marginally viable for new generations of composers. We may categorize these approaches as (1) those arising from new technologies and new ideas and (2) those that are at least loosely based on traditional models.

ELECTRONIC MUSIC

Just as the invention of the piano changed music in the eighteenth century, and the use of valves increased the capabilities of brass performers in the nineteenth, the twentieth century was a time of major technical developments. As music delivery systems, the phonograph and radio appeared early on. But as a new means of *creating* music, electronic innovations took place mainly after 1950.

Shortly after World War II, experiments with music that was electrically produced or altered took place in several European cities. In Paris, Pierre Schaeffer (b. 1910) and Pierre Henry (b. 1927) worked initially with disk recordings, but later discovered the many advantages of magnetic tape. Schaeffer organized and produced *The Concert of Noises* which was given on French radio in 1948.[1] Schaeffer (1910–1995) and his colleagues tape recorded acoustic sounds, then altered them electronically. In Cologne, another camp of innovative composers was led by Herbert Eimert (1897–1972) and Karlheinz Stockhausen (b. 1928). Eimert and Stockhausen veered from the French model by both *producing* and altering tones electronically.

In the early days of electronic music, the two approaches were dubbed *musique concrète* and *musique électronique,* respectively. MUSIQUE CONCRÈTE is music in which sounds are generated acoustically and then altered by electronic means. In MUSIQUE ÉLECTRONIQUE, the sounds are generated through electronic means and altered electronically as well.

Sound Manipulation in Electronic Music

Early electronic music was incredibly time consuming. From the basic sound source, the re-recording and manipulation of pieces of tape—often cut and then spliced into new arrangements—might take many hours, yet produce only a few seconds of finished music. Some of the most basic compositional techniques, however, are still important today (although the technology has advanced greatly). These include *speed change, reverse playback, overdubbing, tape echo,* and *tape looping.*

Speed Change.   Changing the SPEED of the tape alters the frequencies predictably. If we record the pitch C_4, for example, then play the tape at double speed, the resulting pitch is C_5. Varying the tape speed in small degrees produces correspondingly small changes in frequency. The resulting pitches may be quarter tones or smaller microtonal increments.

Reverse Playback.   REVERSE PLAYBACK refers to the technique of turning the tape upside down and playing it forward. In reverse playback, the normal attack and decay characteristics of the sound (known as the *envelope*) are reversed.

---

[1]Changing concepts of noise in twentieth-century music is an interesting topic for further discussion. Noise has been traditionally defined as "uncontrolled sound waves." In the hands of both electronic and acoustic composers, however, tones that *sound* uncontrolled may be, in fact, rigidly governed.

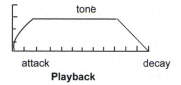

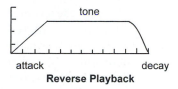

Overdubbing. Early electronic composers produced a relatively thicker texture by recording new material directly upon existing channels. This process is termed OVERDUBBING and was an important tool in the electronic composer's studio.

Tape Echo. If a composer records a sound on one channel, then records the same sound over the first, a TAPE ECHO is produced. The gap between the re-recording and the playback determines the distance between the sound and its echo.

Tape Looping. TAPE LOOPS are used to create an ostinato effect in an electronic work. The sounds a composer chooses for the ostinato are recorded on a single piece of tape and then spliced together as a loop. The loop can be played indefinitely and, with the needed equipment and staff, new loops can be created from music just played, and added to the mix.

In addition to the techniques just described, early electronic composers used devices such as reverberation units and phase shifters to alter recorded sounds. The standard electronic studio of the 1950s included a variety of multipurpose machines and a library of sounds, as well as controls for generation, filtration, and reverberation. On hand also were basic paraphernalia for editing vinyl tape, two or more tape recorders, amplifiers, loud speakers, and microphones.[2]

Performance and Notation Considerations

Electronic music has revolutionized several aspects of traditional musical performance. Chief among these are performance practice and notation.

Performance Practice. While many of the original electronic pieces were conceived for radio broadcast, electronic music today is performed in one of three basic ways: 1) as music for broadcast media, 2) as live performance altered electronically, and 3) as live performance with tape accompaniment.

Music for Recorded or Broadcast Media. Some electronic music is composed to be recorded and played through loudspeakers at a live performance, or broadcast to listeners live or prerecorded via the radio. Stockhausen's 1956 work, *Gesang der Jünglinge* (*Song of Youths*) is an early example of music conceived with these possibilities in mind. The work combines speaking, singing, and electronically generated sounds. Another important work in this vein is *Poème Èlectronique* by the French composer, Egard Varèse (1883–1965). Commissioned by the Philips Corporation for the 1958 Brussels world fair, *Poème* is a tape work intended to be broadcast over four hundred loudspeakers.

---

[2]Elliott Schwartz, *Electronic Music: A Listener's Guide* (Praeger Publishers, 1975).

Live Performance Altered Through Electronic Means.   Novel or traditional instruments are played on stage (or in studio) with those real-time sounds being altered electronically. *Atlas eclipticalis* (1962) by John Cage is an example of this technique. Mauricio Kagel (b. 1931) is an Argentine composer whose *Transición II* (for piano and percussion) includes three layers of performance: Prerecorded segments are played on one tape; live segments of the performance itself (including the prerecorded material) are recorded on another machine to form tape loops; and the two instruments also perform live along with the two tapes.

Traditional Performance Accompanied by Tape.   One or more acoustic instruments performs with a taped accompaniment. The instrument(s) may be coordinated with the tape or they may perform independently. *A Poem in Cycles and Bels* (1954) by Bruno Maderna (1920–1973) is a landmark work for tape and orchestra. *Soggiorno* by James Mobberley (see pages 532–534) is more recent, and was composed for violin and tape.

Notation.   If music is entirely electronic, any composer's "score" may more nearly resemble graphs and complex mathematical equations than pitch notation. Some composers dispense with a formal score altogether. For others, a LISTENING SCORE, intended to aid in understanding the recorded music, is sufficient. The score (page 531) for *Artikulation* (1970) by György Ligeti (b. 1923) shows frequency and dynamic levels in five-second increments.

György Ligeti, *Artikulation*

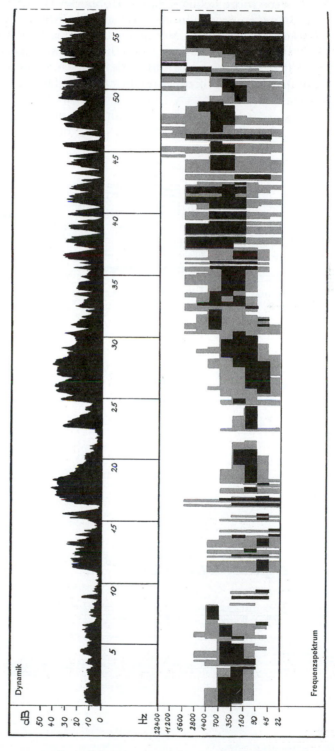

When a traditional instrument performs along with taped media, scores are often more detailed. James Mobberley (b. 1952) is a Midwestern composer who has enjoyed considerable success with his works for tape and various acoustic instruments. Mobberley began his 1989 *Soggiorno* (*Journey*) by recording samples of an acoustic violin for use in making the tape part. The first movement (47 measures) of this work is shown in the next example, and recorded on the CD that accompanies this volume. The violin part is notated in full. The tape score shows frequency, duration, and other effects, but gives no clue to the specific ways in which the tones have been manipulated electronically.

CD 2, TRACK 88
James Mobberley, *Soggiorno*

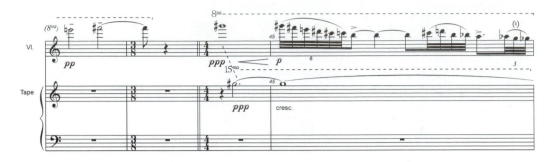

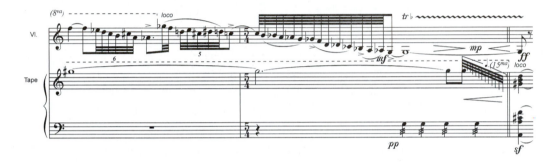

Mobberley has expressed interest in "combining sound-worlds and emotional worlds" by joining live instrumental performers with recorded playback of sounds from these same performers. At times in *Soggiorno,* it is difficult to tell what is live and what is recorded, as the relationship between performers changes over the course of the piece.

Electronic Synthesis

While electronic composers in the 1950s cut and spliced pieces of prerecorded and altered tape in a laborious and often inaccurate process, the 1960s brought a new technical innovation: *voltage-controlled synthesis.* In VOLTAGE-CONTROLLED SYNTHESIS, tones are produced and altered simply through setting and changing dials that manipulate electrical voltage. The Olsen-Belar Sound Synthesizer, built by RCA in 1955, was an early prototype. Like the first computers, the Olsen-Belar synthesizer was massive; data were input through coded paper tape. Because the synthesizer produced altered sounds by varying voltages, however, music could be produced on the spot.

"The Moog." The Olsen-Belar synthesizer was a far cry from the cut-and-splice technology that Schaeffer and his contemporaries employed, but its size, cost, and maintenance made it available only institutionally. All of this changed in the mid-1960s, however, with the first portable synthesizers. Robert Moog (b. 1934) developed a voltage-controlled machine (photo on page 535) that featured keyboard input and patch cords that allowed the composer to choose various modes of sound manipulation. Although less well known, Donald Buchla (b. 1937) developed a similar synthesizer at about the same time. Both

Moog 1C Synthesizer (1968). Courtesy of Roger Luther

Buchla's and Moog's machines attracted considerable attention, and spawned a new generation of electronic composers and performers. The album *Switched On Bach* (1968, Walter Carlos) made the general public aware of electronic sounds—perhaps for the first time.

Digital Synthesis

While the Moog and other early synthesizers were ANALOG (controlled by changes in electronic voltage), DIGITAL SYNTHESIS, in which data are input, manipulated, and exported through a microprocessor, was the cutting edge in the late 1980s. Musical Instrument Digital Interface (MIDI) technology has given art and pop composers alike an astounding range of capabilities. Users of MIDI need only a computer, a compatible electronic keyboard, guitar, or other instrument, and *sequencing* software—items that can fit together on a desktop.

SEQUENCING is the application of a software (Cubase VST is among the most popular). Composers—who may or may not read music—can play a work on keyboard or guitar, then convert their music to a variety of file types. In addition to a world of overdubbing possibilities that can transform guitar input into a symphony orchestra, available software programs create and print notated musical scores. If the composer begins with a score made through a high-end notation program like *Finale* or *Sibelius*, the music can then be heard through MIDI conversion.

Cubase VST 1900 Display.

Besides producing files that can be shared with other MIDI enthusiasts, composers can burn original CDs or convert the data to an MP3 file so that it can be sent as e-mail—virtually anywhere in the world. As microcomputers have fallen in price and increased in their accessibility to those with only limited knowledge of music or technology, MIDI software has kept pace. In a recent version of Cubase VST (1900), screen displays have the appearance of a studio control panel.

The future of digital synthesis is yet unwritten. As the power and flexibility of microcomputer software increase, the local studio with composer-performer-engineer-producer is destined to proliferate. Yet even in the world of pop, there remains ample room for the assessment of quality. True, MIDI technology affords compelling opportunities to individuals with relatively little training in music. But without the sensitivities that spring from a solid base in traditional performance, theory, and music history, untrained composer-engineers may be destined to produce only caricatures of past styles.

WORKBOOK/ANTHOLOGY II
I. Electronic Music, page 219

INDETERMINACY

INDETERMINACY is defined as the use of some random process in the course of a composition. Improvisation, as seen from Baroque-era variations to contemporary jazz, is certainly a type of indeterminacy. In contemporary music, however, the term "indeterminacy" more often refers to *structure* than to the sort of melodic spontaneity common to jazz.

Throughout the history of Western music, there have been experiments with the introduction of chance processes. The Englishman William Hayes (1708–1777), known in his time mainly for sacred music, is a case in point. Hayes's book, *The Art of Composing Music by a Method Entirely New, Suited to the Meanest Capacity,* was published in 1757 and describes how musical phrases may be combined through chance procedures. No less a figure than Wolfgang Amadeus Mozart was interested in indeterminacy as well. In his string quartet K. 294d, specifically composed musical phrases are arranged by performers through a roll of dice.

In the second half of the twentieth century, a number of composers structured entire works through chance processes.[3] John Cage is often credited with being the first composer to promote seriously the use of chance operations during the act of composing, performing, or both. Some of his works, such as *Music of Changes* (1951), are designed through a highly organized use of indeterminacy. Many such works are based on eight patterns (trigrams) of broken and unbroken lines found in the *I Ching*—a classical Chinese treatise on cosmology (also called the *Book of Changes*). Other of Cage's compositions are entirely random; his *4'-33"* (1952) stipulates only the length of a work in which a performer sits at the keyboard in silence.

As employed by twentieth-century composers, indeterminacy occurs in two principal categories: *Composer indeterminacy* and *performer indeterminacy*. Note that some compositions fall into both categories.

Composer Indeterminacy

When the composer makes chance-based decisions during the process of composition, the technique is COMPOSER INDETERMINACY. Such works may be notated traditionally with no options for the performer (who may not even be aware that the work involves chance processes). To illustrate composer indeterminacy, consider a work for unaccompanied flute, in which phrases are generated by the words in any given text. For each different text, the resulting composition will be different as well. In our sample work, we will begin with three newly composed melodic segments. The three phrases below are atonal and two of them have a whole-tone flavor. Just as easily, we could use segments that are tonal, modal, pentatonic, or based on a synthetic scale.

Next, we must formulate a plan to correlate the musical segments with words in the text. The possibilities are virtually limitless, and we will choose perhaps the most obvious: Fragments will be generated according to the number of letters in each word. Words with one letter will correlate with segment 1; those with two letters, segment 2; and so on. Since many words have more than three letters, however, we must also produce phrases for words of four, five, six, and more letters. We could compose additional phrases for longer words, but to retain unity, we will manipulate the three segments already composed. For words with four letters, we will transpose the last segment heard a major third higher; words with five letters will generate a transposition of the previous segment a major second lower; for six-letter words, we will use a retrograde statement of the previous segment. Finally, to allow additional composer control, a word of seven or more letters will be used as a "wild card" to generate a phrase or phrases as we see fit: any one of the three composed segments, a transposition or retrograde, or even new material of similar length and scope.

Our compositional process may seem a bit complicated, but remember that only the composer deals with the indeterminacy; the performer will simply read a notated score. Moreover, we may use the same process to generate a work of any length based on text using the roman alphabet.

Here is our complete matrix:

Number of Letters	Musical Segment Generated
1	Segment 1
2	Segment 2
3	Segment 3
4	Last segment M3 higher
5	Last segment M2 lower
6	Last segment in retrograde
7 and more	Composer's wild card

The text can be existing or new; carefully chosen or entirely random; in English or in another language. We might choose an arbitrary sentence from a book, for example, or use favorite words from a religious text, a speech, ceremony, patriotic statement, dictionary definition, and so on. For our sample composition we will use a hackneyed old sentence that served for many years as a typewriter test pattern:

Now is the time for all good men to come to the aid of their country.

Next, we assign a segment number to each word according to the number of letters.

	Now	is	the	time	for	all	good	men	to	come	to	the	aid	of	their	country.
Segment:	3	2	3	4	3	3	4	3	2	4	2	3	3	2	5	7

At this point, our preparation is complete. We now simply chain our precomposed segments together to produce a passable atonal work for solo flute. Different lines of text will generate new works, yet most of them will have the same whole-tone flavor and frenzied sixteenth-note motive heard in *Hummingbirds*.

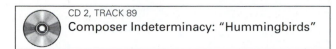

Hummingbirds
for Solo Flute

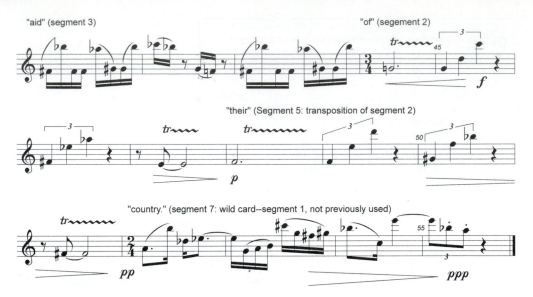

Segment 6 was not generated by this particular text (since there are no words with six letters). Still, our indeterminate process was designed to accommodate a variety of texts. Test the procedure on one or more of the three phrases below, or choose some lines yourself. In each case, the results will be quite different from *Hummingbirds*.

"One in a million; a million in one."

"Fourscore and seven years ago, our forefathers brought forth on this continent a new nation."

"Freude schöner Götterfunken Tochter aus Elysium, wir betreten feuertrunken Himmlische dein Heilig tum!"

Performer Indeterminacy

While our flautist in *Hummingbirds* does not need to know that the work is aleatoric, the performer may also take part in chance operations in several ways, including *indeterminate notation*, *mobile structures*, and *frame notation*.

Indeterminate Notation.   In works of INDETERMINATE NOTATION, the composer provides the performer with a graphic score and a set of instructions concerning the general framework of the composition. Sometimes, the performer is free to make decisions about the interpretation of symbols; in other works, the composer's directions are more specific. Single pages from three different indeterminate scores follow, by György Ligeti, Morton Feldman (1926–1987), and Cathy Berberian (1925–1983). The Ligeti and Feldman scores have relatively specific instructions; Berberian's *Stripsody* is open to a much freer interpretation.

György Ligeti, *Volumina*

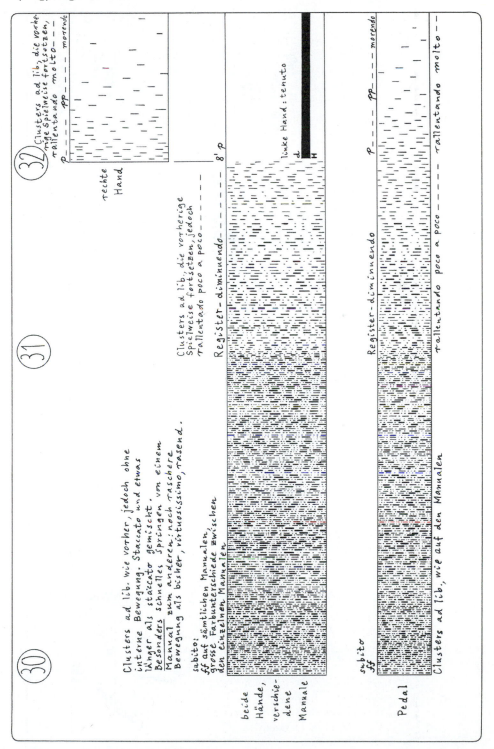

Cathy Berberian, *Stripsody*

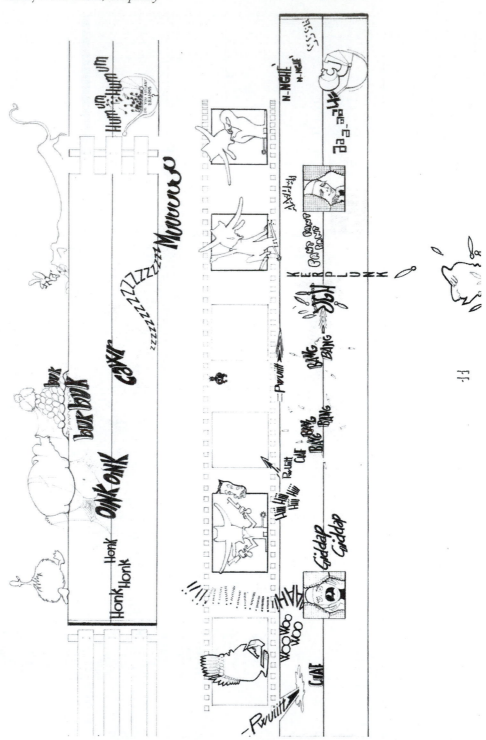

Morton Feldman, *The King of Denmark*

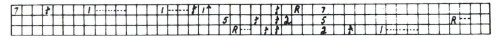

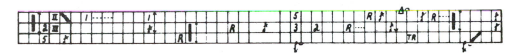

Mobile Structures.   MOBILE STRUCTURES represent a type of indeterminacy in which the composer provides the performer with a number of determined events and the performer (or conductor) must decide on their arrangement. While a given work will always be unified by the design of the component events, the possibilities for various sequences usually assure that no two performances will be exactly alike.

Earle Brown (b. 1926) is an American composer who was influenced by John Cage and the possibilities of indeterminate form. Brown's *Available Forms I* (1962) is a work for orchestra. Each performer reads from large sheets with several numbered events (see excerpt, page 544). Through hand signals, a conductor chooses the order of events and defines other specifics of performance.

Frame Notation.   FRAME NOTATION usually refers to scores that include either circles or rectangles (frames) containing pitches or rhythms in a random order. The performer is instructed to *improvise* around the pitches, rhythms, or both, as displayed in the frame. Shown on page 545, *Circles* (1961) by the Italian Luciano Berio (b. 1925), provides an example of frame notation.

Earle Brown, *Available Forms I*

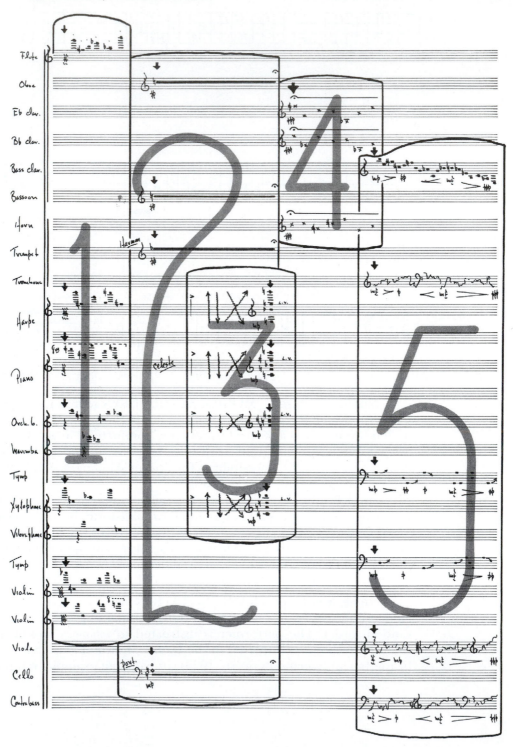

Luciano Berio, *Circles*

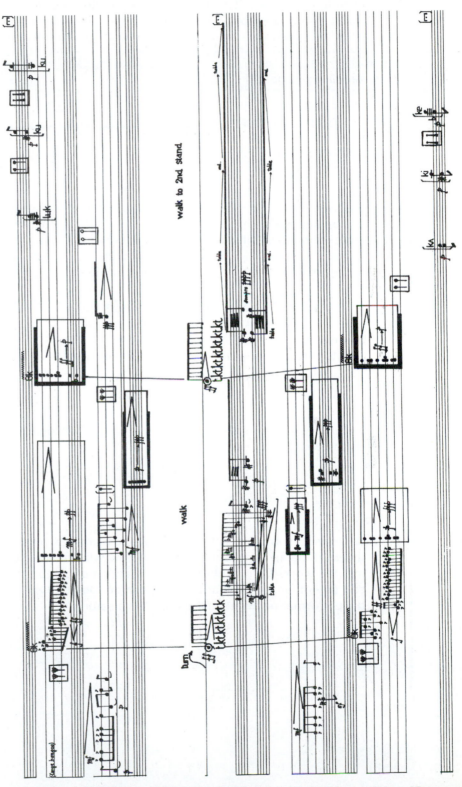

Indeterminacy has been an important technique for composers in the twentieth century. The traditional separation between composer and performer is broken down when, for example, performers have some say in how a work progresses. For composers, chance operations have sparked creativity through literary, philosophical, mathematical, and other avenues.

 REINFORCE YOUR UNDERSTANDING THROUGH WORKBOOK/ANTHOLOGY II
II. Indeterminacy, page 223

REVIEW AND APPLICATION 12–1

Indeterminacy

Essential Terms

aleatory	indeterminate notation	overdubbing
analog synthesis	MIDI	performer indeterminacy
composer indeterminacy	mobile structures	sequencing
digital synthesis	musique concrète	tape loop
frame notation	musique électronique	voltage-controlled synthesis

1. The following events may (or may not) figure into the history of electronic music. Put the events in order, and eliminate any that are fictitious or related to another twentieth-century movement in music. Finally, for each of the remaining events, write a few words of explanation and provide an approximate date.

A. The Moog Synthesizer   C. *I Ching*

B. "The Concert of Noises"   D. MIDI

2. State and comment on three ways in which electronic music is composed and performed.

(1)

(2)

(3)

3. Devise a composer-controlled aleatoric work (you need not actually compose the work here). How will you begin? How will chance elements be introduced into the work? Comment on your conception of overall length, an ending plan, and any other specifics of the composition. Do your work on other sheets. Will the performer be aware that the work is aleatoric?

4. This score by Louis J. Goldford (b. 1983) is illustrative of one or more of the three basic approaches to performer indeterminacy. Name the specific approach, and comment briefly on its application in the work shown.

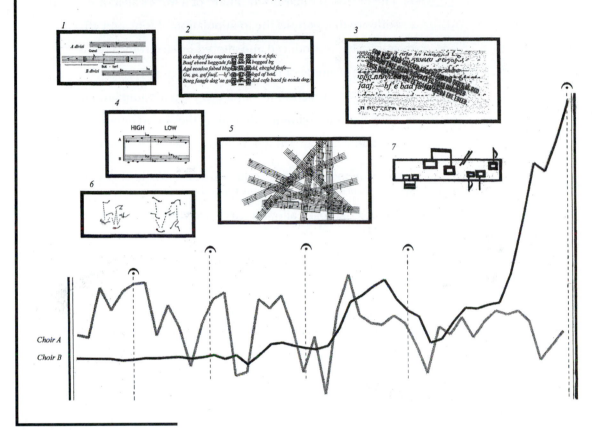

SELF-TEST 12–1

Time Limit: 5 Minutes

1. Match a term from the list with one of the descriptions given. *Scoring: Subtract 5 points for each incorrect answer.*

   A. aleatory

   B. sequencing

   C. *The Art of Composing Music by a Method Entirely New, Suited to the Meanest Capacity*

   D. composer indeterminacy

   E. indeterminate notation

   F. frame notation

   G. musique électronique

   H. reverse playback

_____ a. The performer plays within a notated segment before moving on to another.

_____ b. The performer may not be aware of a work's aleatoric structure.

_____ c. software that permits the manipulation of tone and effect

_____ d. music that is produced and altered by electronic means

_____ e. an early example of performer indeterminacy

_____ f. a process in which some or all elements are unplanned

_____ g. an electronic technique that alters the sound envelope

_____ h. a graphic display that is a mere suggestion of exact pitch

2. Some of these statements are true; others are false. Write "T" or "F" in the blank as appropriate. _Scoring: Subtract 6 points for each error._

_____ a. Reverse playback allowed early electronic composers to create echo effects.

_____ b. Performance on an acoustic instrument accompanied by tape is a common electronic genre.

_____ c. Digital synthesis concerns the manipulation of voltages.

_____ d. Mobile structures constitute a type of indeterminacy in which a performer plays within a notation block, then moves on to others in a random order.

_____ e. _The Concert of Noises_ was produced by Pierre Schaeffer and given in New York in the 1960s.

_____ f. Stockhausen's _The Song of Youths_ was conceived for recorded media.

_____ g. Robert Moog created a portable electronic synthesizer in the 1980s.

_____ h. Analog synthesis is central to MIDI technology.

_____ i. Improvisation is a type of indeterminate composition.

_____ j. Pierre Schaeffer is generally credited with being the first twentieth-century composer to employ chance operations in music composition.

Total Possible: 100   Your Score _____

COLOR AND _TIMBRE_

While many new means of musical expression evolved in the period after World War II, one group of composers has chosen to seek even more expressive potential from the piano, voice, and other conventional instruments. Moreover, they generally have accomplished this feat within the confines of traditional notation.

George Crumb (b. 1929) is an American whose works often include delicate spatial effects heard against a background of interesting *timbres.* Crumb's scores represent an extreme of traditional notation, while at the same time, maintaining the flexibility to accommodate a great deal of originality. Scored for flute, cello, and piano (all electric), *Vox Balaenae* (*Voice of the Whale*) is a 1972 work inspired by the sounds of whales. Players wear masks during the performance to "symbolize the powerful impersonal forces of nature."

Crumb employs a meticulous notation in *Vox Balaenae,* using "large" accidentals to effect more than one note. The following illustration appears in the score as an example.

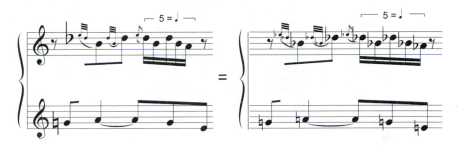

The piano part of *Vox Balaenae* directs the performer to touch strings with various objects that produce pizzicato, muted tones, harmonics, and so on. In addition to trills, grace notes, and other ornaments, the flautist is called upon to sing while playing. The cello employs SCORDATURA—that is, the strings are tuned to pitches unique to the composition (and requiring a retuning when the performance is concluded).

Standard Cello Tuning   Scordatura for *Vox Balaenae*

Study the excerpt from *Vox Balaenae* shown on the next page. Like many twentieth-century compositions, Crumb's scores are typically works of graphic, as well as musical, art.

George Crumb, *Vox Balaenae*

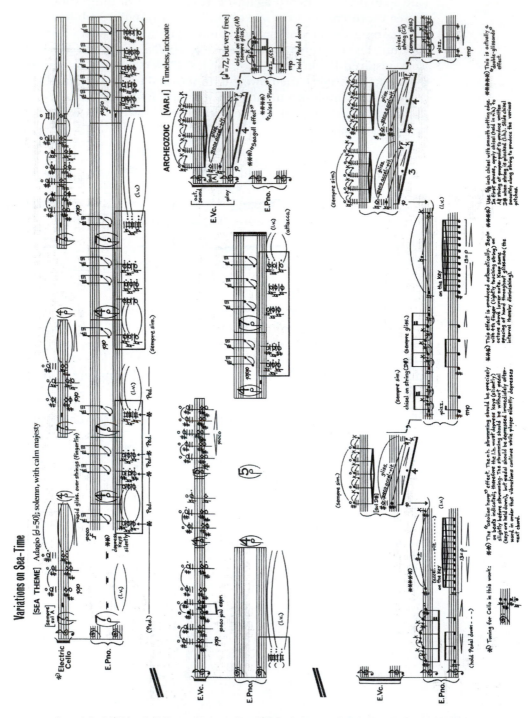

Microtonal Music

Throughout the twentieth century, some composers were attracted by the possibilities of a scale divided into *microtones*. A MICROTONE is an interval smaller than a half step, and while these divisions were present in some Hebrew and Greek melodies (upon which early Christian music was based), Western musicians quickly settled on the limitations of the diatonic scale. In the Renaissance, and throughout the common-practice period, keyboard instruments were tuned with tempered intervals that helped minimize the problems of enharmonic equivalence.[4] By the nineteenth century, most composers and audiences had become accustomed both to twelve-tone equal temperament and to its characteristic discrepancies (a wide major third, for example). For practical purposes, the advantages of far-ranging modulation and enharmonic equivalency outweighed the aural limitations.

In the late nineteenth and early twentieth centuries, composers began to re-examine microtonal possibilities. New instruments were constructed, technologies emerged, and international discussions took place among noted composers and scholars in an attempt to breach the problems of microtonal notation. Today, two separate paths in microtonal music appear to hold promise for the future: 1) alternate equal temperaments, and 2) microtonal intervals as ornaments.

Alternate Tunings and Temperaments.   Before the advent of twelve-tone equal temperament, various systems of deriving interval relationships had appeared in Western music. Pythagorean tuning, Just intonation, and Mean-tone temperament had all fallen victim to the demands of chromaticism, enharmonic equivalency, and distant modulation. In the twentieth century, however, composers revisited some of these systems, both for their purity and their expressive potential.

Just Intonation.   JUST INTONATION is a system of tuning based on the overtone series. Today we measure interval size in cents, there are 100 cents in a half step. The major thirds in just intonation are 386 cents; the fifths, 702 cents. One of several problems of just intonation is apparent in studying the size of whole steps. All whole steps in the equally tempered scale approximate the ratio of frequencies 9:8. In just intonation, however, two different sizes of whole step exist. The ratios of frequencies between C and D, for example, and between D and E, are different: 9:8 and 10:9, respectively. Other problems with just intonation make modulation all but impossible.

For some innovative contemporary composers, however, these problems present exciting challenges. The American Harry Partch (1901–1974) was one of many who favored just intervals. Basically isolated because of the complexity and the technical requirements of his music, Partch built instruments of his own that were capable of playing just and other microtonal divisions of the octave. His interests in the music of Asia (where microtonal intervals abound) spawned *Li Po Songs* (1933) and *Delusions of the Fury* (1966)—the latter a dramatic work based on a Japanese Noh play.

A student of Ben Johnston (b. 1926), Robert Chamberlin (b. 1950) has written for stringed instruments in just intonation. Like many works in the twentieth century, the full score for his 1978 Sextet (see page 552) includes explanation of the notation employed. In addition to conventional accidentals,

[4]For basic information on tuning and temperament systems, see Appendix A on page 575.

Chamberlin uses a system (devised by Johnston) of adding accidental symbols to accommodate the intervals in just intonation:

♭ lower pitch 119 cents

♭ lower pitch 141 cents

♯ raise pitch 92 cents

Robert Chamberlin, *Sextet*

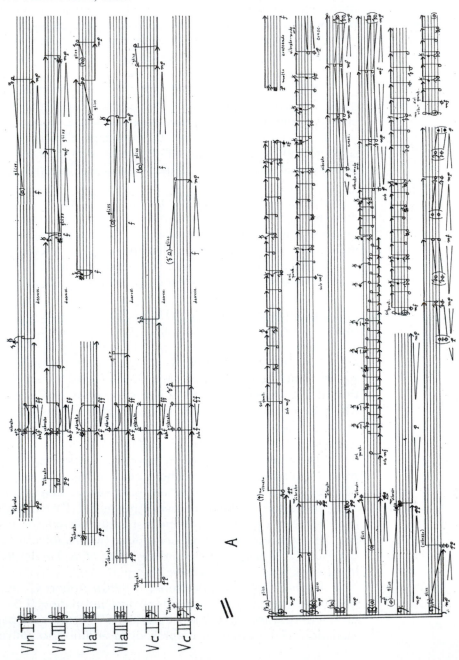

Music written for performance in just intonation has a serene and slightly haunting effect, as we immediately miss the familiar beats associated with twelve-tone equal temperament. Should we want to play a Beethoven sonata on our justly tuned instrument, however, the problems of equivalency would arise immediately.

Alternate Equal Temperaments.   Even after the general acceptance of twelve-tone equal temperament, interest in alternate tunings continued. In Beethoven's time, many lamented a loss of the intrinsic flavors that characterized each different major and minor key in other systems (the Prinz tuning, for example). While it solved numerous practical problems, twelve-tone equal temperament also "sanitized" differences among keys, and rendered any one the mere mirror image of another. Not until the twentieth century, however, did new divisions of the octave generate a degree of enthusiasm. Dividing the octave into 19, 31, and 53 equal parts is natural, since it permits performance in a wide range of tuning systems. Remember that with microtonal divisions of the octave, the composer need not *use* all of those divisions and may choose, instead, a diatonic scale approximating those in just intonation or Pythagorean tuning. The interest in the 1970s in 31-tone equal temperament, for example, was due as much to the allure of hearing Renaissance works performed accurately in mean-tone temperament as it was to interest in the range of new sounds and combinations.

An important group of microtonal composers, centered in the Netherlands, generated interest in 31-tone temperament—especially in the 1970s. Adriaan Fokker (1887–1972), performed on a 31-tone organ and, through lectures, compositions, and publications, inspired others to pursue this particular branch of microtonality. Henk Badings (1907–1987) is another Dutch scientist-composer who was captivated by microtonal possibilities. He wrote several works for the Fokker organ and another for the *Archiphone*—a portable 31-tone instrument that is based on the Fokker keyboard.

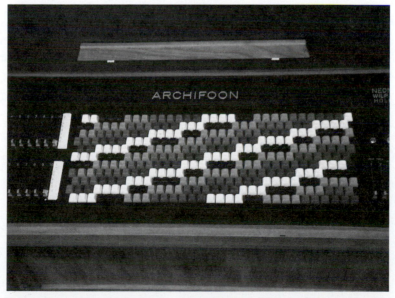

The 31-Tone Fokker Keyboard. Courtesy Huygens-Fokker Foundation.

Thirty-one tone equal temperament has intervals as small as a fifth of a tone, necessitating not only a new keyboard technique, but a range of unconventional accidentals as well. In the illustration in the next example, note that C𝄪 and D♮ are *not* enharmonically equivalent in 31-tone equal temperament.

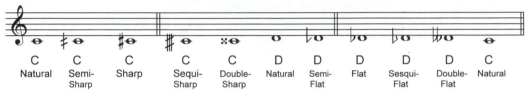

Microtonal Notation in 31-tone Scale

| C Natural | C Semi-Sharp | C Sharp | C Sequi-Sharp | C Double-Sharp | D Natural | D Semi-Flat | D Flat | D Sesqui-Flat | D Double-Flat | C Natural |

Only four archiphones were sold worldwide in the 1970s, at a price tag of about $10,000 each. Besides the price, however, the new notation, marginal technical construction, a paucity of literature, and the necessity of traveling to The Netherlands for professional instruction rendered the instrument impractical for the general public. By 1980, the initial interest had subsided and the construction of new instruments like the archiphone waned significantly.

Today, at least one of the archiphone's most serious drawbacks would be less tenable: cost. Digital synthesis, available in relatively modest tabletop units, far surpasses the technology available in the 1970s, and can be had for a fraction of the price. Such advances in technology—not to mention others that will surely follow in this century—make microtonal music one of the most promising areas for development.

Microtones as Ornamental Devices. When microtonality is not itself a system of musical structure, performers may still be asked to bend a pitch here and there within the traditional chromatic scale. Except for keyboard instruments, a quarter-tone rise or dip in pitch is usually accomplished with a minimum of physical adjustment. In his 1967 work for violin and orchestra, *Capriccio,* the Polish composer Krzysztof Penderecki (b. 1933) employs a range of microtones with rather straightforward notation that includes the "highest" and "lowest" possible pitches on the instrument:

╪ sharpen a quarter-tone

╫ sharpen a three quarter-tones

▲ highest pitch on the instrument

▼ lowest pitch on the instrument

Penderecki uses microtones for effect, but relies largely on an octave divided by half step for the majority of the work. Another kind of microtonal pitch notation in *Capriccio* is graphic. In one interesting passage, for example (page 555), the solo and first violins are instructed to fluctuate pitch over the course of several beats according to a meandering graphic line. The second violins and lower strings have the same basic notation, but are instructed to hum (mouth closed). Woodwinds take over the effect with glissandos in the passage shown.

Krzysztof Penderecki, *Capriccio for Violin and Orchestra*

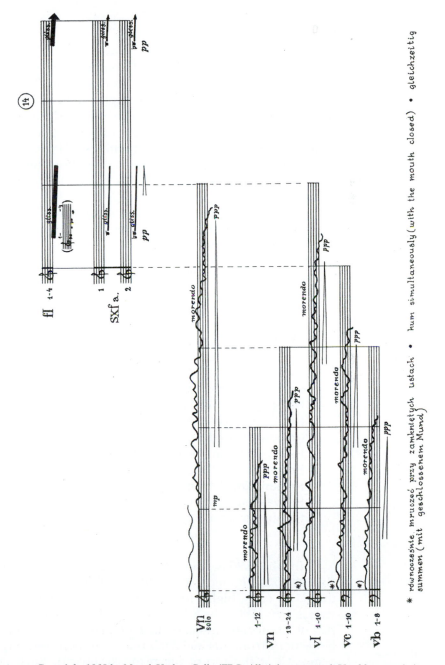

Many composers after 1950 have at least experimented with quarter-tones and other microtonal divisions. With the increased appearance of microtonal music, performers have learned to realize the composers' intentions with greater accuracy. Partly as a result, audiences have responded more favorably.

WORKBOOK/ANTHOLOGY II
III. Microtonal Music, page 225

MINIMALISM

MINIMALISM is a term borrowed from painting and sculpture to describe both a technique and a style of musical composition. The trend can be considered, in part, a reaction against the complexity of the total serialism of the 1950s (characterized by Boulez and Stockhausen). Music is reduced, and returned to the basic building blocks of simple rhythmic patterns and progressions, tonal melodic fragments, and even single notes and chords. The resulting material is then invigorated through incessant repetition, much as minimalist paintings were stripped down to deadpan basic colors and recurring fundamental shapes, such as squares and cubes.

A hypnotically powerful counterpart from a verbal art—with short phrases continually repeated and reworked—is the poem, "In Detention," by Christopher van Wyk (b. 1957). The poem comments on the blank explanations offered by government functionaries for the so-called "suicides" and accidental deaths endured by untold scores of political prisoners in South Africa.

He fell from the ninth floor
He hanged himself
He slipped on a piece of soap while washing
He hanged himself
He slipped on a piece of soap while washing
He fell from the ninth floor
He hanged himself while washing
He slipped from the ninth floor
He hung from the ninth floor
He slipped from the ninth floor while washing
He fell from a piece of soap while slipping
He hung from the ninth floor
He washed from the ninth floor while slipping
He hung from a piece of soap while washing

Used by permission of Christopher van Wyk.

In the 1960s and 1970s, American composers such as Terry Riley (b. 1935), Steve Reich (b. 1936), and Philip Glass (b. 1937) led the minimalist trend. An early, highly influential, and particularly noteworthy example of the style is *In C* (1964) by Riley (shown in full on page 557). The composition consists of 53 short fragments which are played by any number of musicians on any kinds of instruments and against a continuous pulse (provided by eighth-note, octave Cs at the top of the piano keyboard). Each performer moves ahead, faster or slower, through the fragments that add one pitch at a time. Many intriguing modal or modulatory inflections can be found as the pitches F♯ and B♭ tilt the music at times away from the centricity of C.

Terry Riley, *In C*

Riley's *In C* obviously depends on players skilled at listening to their partners so as to sense when to linger on one fragment or move on to another. This element of improvisation, which will result in a different version of the music at each performance, is not necessarily, however, an aspect of other minimalist pieces. Many are highly predetermined and coordinated with specific notation in full score like any conventional music.

Steve Reich's *Clapping Music for Two Performers* (1972) is similar to Riley's work. In *Clapping Music,* thirteen different two-voice patterns are repeated ("at least twelve times"). The lower voice begins with the same pattern as the upper, gradually moves away, then returns to the original pattern. The upper voice remains the same throughout the work. Considering the subtle variations of a single basic pattern in *Clapping Music,* we should not be surprised to find that Reich studied African drumming.

In the music of the early decades of the minimalist movement, when elements were more strictly controlled, the following listed features are often found. Not all of these features, of course, will occur in every composition. The more features present, on the other hand, the greater the likelihood that a given work will earn the label "minimalist."

- persistent repetition (often in the form of ostinatos)
- tonal (or modal) pitch centers
- modular construction (the use of short patterns and fragments)
- phrase and phrase shifting: patterns sounded against themselves at slightly faster or slower tempos (like runners or race car drivers lapping one another)
- steady-state, nonnarrative quality (lack of dramatic goals or climax points)
- long movements
- colorful, shimmering scoring (brightness and clarity highlighted)
- rhythmic pulsation; stable tempos
- gradual change (with tiny variations)
- coolness (emotional detachment; dispassionate expressive content)
- subtly evolving listener perceptions as the center of the experience (instead of a display of the composer's feelings)
- process-driven composition (feed the piece with musical material and then let it run its course)

During the 1980s and to the present, composers such as John Adams (b. 1947), Arvo Pärt (b. 1935), and others, developed the minimalist style further by adding or substituting other traits. Some of these, summarized in the following list, are Neo-Romantic.

- listener accessibility (immediate appeal)
- roving tonal centers (a high degree of modulation)
- fluid tempos
- more complex formal schemes (departure and return)
- lush nineteenth-century orchestration
- more emotionally resonant ambience
- hyper-lyrical quality (long-phrased melodies)
- motivic development
- chromaticism
- polyphony
- virtuosity
- more dramatic curve (*e.g.*, stillness followed by outbursts; build-up of tension; heroic endings; and so on)

Nowadays, in an era of blended styles, minimalist techniques have permeated many other types of music, to the point at which it is no longer possible to sort out precisely whether a composition deserves the label "minimalist." Strict pigeonholes, in other words, do not always do justice to the richness of music. Minimalism, nevertheless, has proven its merit over time—in evolving from a purer to a more eclectic form—as something more than a mere fad.

WORKBOOK/ANTHOLOGY II
IV. Minimalism, page 227

THE NEW TONALITY

While new ideas and technologies proliferated in the second half of the twentieth century, it has also been a time when some composers found inspiration in past styles and methods. In earlier chapters, we discussed how a renewal of counterpoint and ornamentation effected a Neo-Baroque style in the works of Paul Hindemith and others. Likewise, a return to simple textures, small ensembles, and venerable forms in Stravinsky's *Symphony in C* (for example), reminds us of the late eighteenth century. Particularly after 1950, a resurgence of late nineteenth- and early twentieth-century principles surfaced in the works of several important composers. Because these styles may fall only loosely within the category "Romantic," however, we will employ the term NEO-TONAL in the present discussion, rather than "Neo-Romantic."

In a contemporary work, the new tonality might be manifested in relatively larger ensembles, periodic melodies, functional or quasi-functional harmony, strong and vacillating emotions, and so on. Unlike the composers of austere twentieth-century works that seem almost intentionally aloof, many of the new tonal composers have enjoyed considerable favor with the listening public.

Among dozens of successful populist composers today is New Yorker Lowell Liebermann (b. 1961). A student of David Diamond and Vincent Persichetti at the Juilliard School of Music, Liebermann has numerous major publications in a variety of genres: two piano concertos, a symphony, a flute concerto, and a two-act opera (*The Picture of Dorian Gray*, 1996). Liebermann's Concerto for Piccolo and Orchestra (1996) embodies many of the characteristics that we associate with the new tonalists, and we will give a brief summary of the work here. The orchestra includes harp, piano, and a range of percussion. The $\frac{5}{4}$ meter of the first movement echoes a time, in the late nineteenth century, when composers first began to view asymmetrical meters as equivalent to duple, triple, and quadruple. Harmonically, we find an eclectic blend of nineteenth- and twentieth-century materials including modes, ostinatos, free dissonance, polychords, and even serialism. The melodies are singable and vary from the tranquil opening theme to the angular energy of the *finale*.

The concerto opens with a shimmering effect (largely missing in the piano reduction) that sets a Lydian ostinato in the harp against a widely spaced tonic pedal in the strings. The piccolo entry in measure 3 breaches this atmosphere only slightly; the simplicity of the lower-register Lydian melody, together with unassuming embellishments, effects a lyric musing reminiscent of Debussy and Ravel.

Lowell Liebermann, Concerto for Piccolo and Orchestra (I)
Theme

Andante comodo (♩ = c. 80)

Liebermann, Concerto
Second Theme

A second theme (in the dominant key) begins in measure 39. Throughout the movement, Liebermann exploits various intervals in this theme, as well as its half-note pulse.

Poco più mosso (♩ = c. 72)

The second movement opens with upper strings in a kaleidoscope of non-functional triads (reminiscent of Chopin's chordal mutation). At the same time, however, a complete twelve-tone row unfolds *pizzicato* in the cellos and basses. Beginning in D minor, both the piccolo melody and the tone row are subject to later variations. The mixture of nineteenth- and twentieth-century techniques, common in neotonalist music, is evident in the next passage (measures 1–25).

CD 2, TRACK 91-1 NEW TONALITY, CONTINUED (2 PARTS)
Lowell Liebermann, Concerto for Piccolo and Orchestra (II)
Second Movement

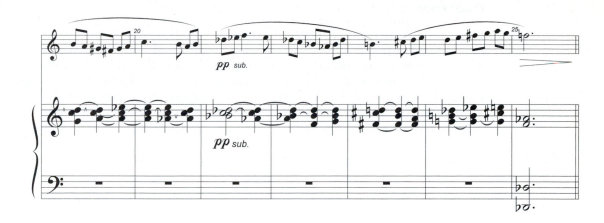

Following a conventional nineteenth-century practice, Liebermann concludes the concerto with a lively presto. The sharp flute lines and liberal treatment of dissonance offer the same wry wit that audiences before 1950 found in Prokofiev and Shostakovich.

Quotation

As we have discussed previously, musical quotation has long been a way for composers to pay homage to colleagues—past and present. Following in this tradition, a number of contemporary composers have drawn inspiration from earlier colleagues. In the *finale* of his piccolo concerto, Liebermann delights knowledgeable audiences by blending the opening two chords of the third movement (D major with added minor second page 563) with a similar effect in the first few measures of Beethoven's Symphony No. 3 in E♭ Major. After the famous E♭ triad outline, however, Liebermann returns quickly to free chromaticism.

CD 2, TRACK 92-1 QUOTATION (2 PARTS)
Lowell Liebermann, Concerto for Piccolo and Orchestra Quotation 1 (Beethoven, Symphony No. 3)

Earlier in the third movement, there are unmistakable references to Mozart's Symphony No. 40; in several passages, John Philip Sousa's *Stars and Stripes Forever* surfaces—*without* the familiar piccolo (shown in the next example).

TRACK 92-2
Liebermann, Concerto
Quotation 2 (Sousa, "Stars and Stripes Forever")

Liebermann's explanation of the quotations could just as easily have been cited by most other tonalists: 1) Homage to a composer who has been a major career influence, and 2) purely personal aims and preferences.[5]

The reasons for these quotations are threefold: Because of motivic reasons; because the Mozart and Beethoven are pieces from which the piccolo is excluded; while the Sousa is the stereotypical piccolo piece, the bane of every piccolo player's existence; and lastly, the Mozart is an implicit homage to Shostakovich, who has been one of my biggest influences, and who cited the same piece in his Second Violin Concerto.

While far from a unified movement, the new tonalists have often pleased audiences with languid adagios, sparkling *finales*, familiar textures, and the occasional Beethoven, Schubert, or Rossini passage wafting through unexpectedly. On the other hand, some critics have been less favorably disposed, openly

---

[5] Notes by Richard Freed that accompany the BMG recording.

regarding new tonal works as "superfluous" and "pedestrian." But while we can acknowledge that the new tonality is probably not the new *music*, we must also remember that the tonal system originated over four hundred years ago—in the sixteenth century, began to be challenged in the 1800s, and was declared officially moribund in the twentieth century. Today, however, the familiar sounds and combinations of tonal music continue to enrich our lives.

THE FUTURE

In attacking Machaut and other innovative composers of the *Ars Nova,* Jacob of Liège (ca. 1270–1330) proclaimed the "old art" more perfect, rational, and simple than the new. "Music was originally discreet …," he wrote in *Speculum musicae,* "Have not the moderns rendered it lascivious beyond measure?"

For Jacob, the work of thirteenth-century composers like Leonin and Perotin was music; the striking new ideas of younger composers was apparently impossible for him to accept. Yet, even without Jacob's permission, music changed. In later centuries, the concept of meter (to which Jacob objected) became an integral part of Western musical art.

Familiar as we are today with the elegance of a Mozart sonata or the lush sonorities of a Brahms symphony, it is easy to forget that at the beginning of the seventeenth century, the composers who conceived the "new music" (*nuove musiche*) were attacked just as bitterly as were Machaut and his contemporaries three hundred years earlier. In his treatise *Delle imperfezioni della moderna musica* (1600), Giovanni Artusi (also cited on page 1 of this volume) complains about the new concepts of dissonance employed by Monteverdi and others:[6]

> … tell me first why you wish to employ these dissonances as they employ them …. why you do not use them in the ordinary way, conformable to reason, in accordance with what … Palestrina … and so many, many others in the Academy have written? … even if you wish dissonance to become consonant, it remains necessary that it be contrary to consonance; by nature it is always dissonant and can hence become consonant only when consonance becomes dissonant; this brings us to impossibilities.

Today, of course, what Artusi considered "impossible" (dissonance as a form of consonance) is a regular feature of music in some styles. Listening to a work by John Cage or Karlheinz Stockhausen, we can speak of density, of tension and release, but not really of consonance and dissonance. Can we even imagine how Artusi would have reacted to a work in which the performer sits in silence at the keyboard for four and a half minutes?

Neither should we assume the perpetuity of valued paraphernalia like the symphony orchestra, piano, and guitar. The insert on page 565 shows composer Tod Machover (b. 1952) with the *FXOS Dexterous Hand Master,* a HYPERINSTRUMENT (one intended to enhance "real-time" musical performance). Worn as a glove by conductor or performer, the complex electronic device

---

[6]See Oliver Strunk, *Source Readings in Music History* (W. W. Norton, 1950), for other fascinating excerpts from our musical past. The Jacob of Liège and Artusi quotations are both from this source.

measures minute hand movements. These data are then read by a computer that has ultimate control over the performance.

We may find it difficult to accept a device such as the Dexterous Hand Master as a viable participant in performance. But we also might imagine how virginalist William Byrd (1543–1623) would have reacted to a nine-foot concert grand piano—let alone a Moog synthesizer. Could Fokker and Badings have imagined in 1970 that technology far superior to that in their $10,000 archiphone could be had for a few hundred dollars just a generation later?

Tod Machover and the FXOS Dexterous Hand Master. © 2004 Peter Menzel/menzelphoto.com.

As we have discussed in this chapter, we live today in an eclectic musical world where many different styles coexist. Moreover, the boundaries between some styles—classical, ethnic, folk, world, jazz, rock, crossover, and pop, among others—have become remarkably fluid since the 1950s. We are witnessing the emergence of new musical combinations and classifications continuously.

The modern era currently supports this multiplicity in a way that has never existed in the past. Before, one basic set of analytical concepts and stylistic descriptions satisfied a wide range of pieces and composers within a given historical period. Today, in the twenty-first century, we sometimes have to invent new conceptual frameworks and vocabularies for each new composition. While such a flexibility puts extraordinary demands on our educational system (as we strive to keep pace with new trends), we can choose to celebrate and relish the diversity and wealth of listening experiences that our present age provides. Perhaps the future will weave together stylistic strands in such a way that more established categories and groupings will emerge with clarity and stability. Or, perhaps the current stylistic mix and state of flux will continue. Only time will tell.

WORKBOOK/ANTHOLOGY II
V. Quotation and the New Tonality, page 229

REVIEW AND APPLICATION 12–2 ──────────────────────

Microtonal and Other Modern Trends

Essential Terms

just intonation   microtone   minimalism   neotonality

1. Two score excerpts follow for study. First, classify each excerpt into one of the following categories (with the understanding that the work as a whole may exhibit variety). Note also that the categories include techniques covered in the first half of the chapter. Next, write a paragraph or create an outline (as directed) that summarizes your analysis of the excerpt.

A. Electronic

B. Microtonal

C. Composer Indeterminacy

D. Minimalism

E. Performer Indeterminacy

F. Traditional Notation (new techniques and *timbres*)

G. New Approaches to Tonality

a.

b.   Morton Feldman, "Straits of Magellan"

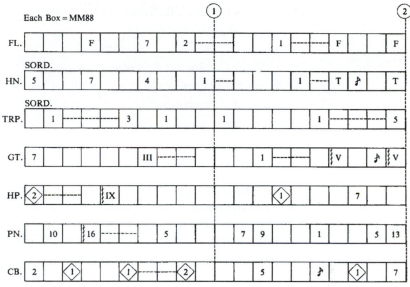

SELF-TEST 12–2

Time Limit: 5 Minutes

1. Place a check mark in the blank by the best answer to each question. *Scoring: Subtract 8 points for each error.*

a. Scordatura refers to

_____ (1) microtonal intervals.

_____ (2) *timbre* in string instruments.

_____ (3) tuning in string instruments.

_____ (4) performer indeterminacy.

b. Steve Reich and Terry Riley are associated with

_____ (1) microtonality.

_____ (2) minimalism.

_____ (3) rhythmic complexities.

_____ (4) electronic composition.

c. Two different sizes of whole step occur in

_____ (1) unequal temperament.

_____ (2) twelve-tone equal temperament.

_____ (3) minimalism.

_____ (4) just intonation.

d. Composers who seek new color and *timbres* in traditional Western idioms include
_____ (1) Henk Badings.
_____ (2) George Crumb.
_____ (3) Karlheinz Stockhausen.
_____ (4) Morton Feldmnan.

e. Among techniques adopted recently by neotonalists is
_____ (1) serialism.
_____ (2) microtonality.
_____ (3) quotation.
_____ (4) alternate keyboard arrangements.

2. Match the technique with one of the movements listed. Write the appropriate letter in the blank. You may use some answers more than once. *Scoring: Subtract 6 points for each error.*

A. Minimalism   E. New Colors and *Timbres*
B. New Tonality   F. Microtonality
C. Electronic Music G. Not applicabile to any of the listed movements
D. Indeterminacy

_____ a. may include tape and an acoustic instrument.

_____ b. may include complicated and precise rhythmic and melodic notation.

_____ c. diatonic planing a common technique

_____ d. makes possible accurate performance of works originally written in mean-tone temperament.

_____ e. may be controlled by the composer or the performer.

_____ f. works may be in sonata and other traditional forms.

_____ g. may feature mobile structures.

_____ h. includes digital synthesis.

_____ i. may be in just intonation or another alternate tuning.

_____ j. may be combinatorial.

Total Possible: 100   Your Score _____

PROJECTS

Analysis

Because many of the materials and techniques are unfamiliar, our studies in twentieth- and twenty-first century music center on listening, composition, and score study. Therefore, except for the Riley and Reich minimalist pieces (pages 557 and 558), no complete works for analysis appear in either the text or the workbook.

Text

Terry Riley, In C, text page 557.
Steve Reich, *Clapping Music*, text page 558.

Workbook/Anthology II

See the Listening list on workbook pages 231–232.

Composition

Composer Indeterminacy. Compose an indeterminate work for five perform-ers. Begin by drawing large symbols on each of five pieces of $8\frac{1}{2} \times 5\frac{1}{2}$ paper or card stock. The symbols or objects can be chosen more or less at random, or they can make up a theme. In any event, the symbols should be instantly recog-nizable. Consider one of the following, for example:

Monetary Symbols

Shapes

Miscellaneous Symbols

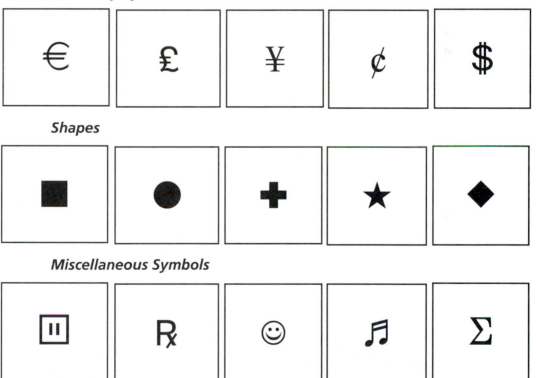

Make a set of parts for the performers that tells them how to respond to your selection of one or another of the symbols. Each performer might respond in the same way, of they might perform differently according to your instructions. Using the last set of symbols, for example, a performer's part might look like this:

Improve a simple clapping pattern beginning with beat units, then moving to divided beat patterns as the time continues.

Rx Whithout opening your mouth, hum a familiar song phrase, then improvise on that melody for a few seconds.

☺ Make clicking sounds with your tongue. Space the sounds several seconds apart and try to retain exactly the same distance throughout the passage.

♫ Sing (on "la") two different pitches in a slow alternation. Begin with pitches about a major third and gradually decrease the distance until you are singing a microtone.

Σ Stamp your foot at irregular intervals and in varying dynamic degrees.

Have the performers gather around a table facing the audience. As composer, you can stand facing the performers to control the flow of the composition. Keep the face of the cards hidden from the performers until you want them to respond. You will think of many additional possibilities for using the cards and your instructions, but here are a few suggestions.

1. If you hold up a card, all five performers respond in the same way (of course, their interpretations will be quite different).

2. If you place a card in front of you on the table, players may respond when and if they choose.

3. If you place a card in front of one performer, that individual responds (of course you can place different cards in front of different players at the same time).

4. Consider slipping a blank card into the "deck" and let the performers respond as they choose.

You will have to decide how to end the composition (or whether to allow the performers to determine that, perhaps).

For Further Study

Women Composers: The Twentieth and Twenty-First Centuries. After about 1970, the music establishment slowly became more sensitive to the music of women and minority composers. Trade books about women and minority composers began to appear and these composers and performers were more often included in anthologies, scholarly articles, and references in major dictionaries and encyclopedias.

Prepare a report on important American women composers during the twentieth century. Choose two composers from the period 1900–1950 and another two women who lived after 1950. As directed by your instructor, provide the following information for each composer you choose:

a. a brief biography including training and major influences

b. range of compositions; favorite style or styles

c. teaching positions (if any)

    d. experiences as a professional woman composer (possibly more germane for women in the period 1900–1950)

    e. an annotated listening list of two or more representative works.

There are many composers to choose from. You will find copious material on these:

Bauer, Marion (1897–1955)	Howe, Mary (1882–1964)
Beach, Amy (1867–1944)	Mahler-Werfel, Alma (1879–1964)
Boulanger, Nadia (1887–1979)	McLeod, Jennifer (b. 1941)
Clarke, Rebecca (1886–1979)	Musgrave, Thea (b. 1928)
Fine, Vivian (b. 1913)	Oliveros, Pauline (b. 1932)
Glanville-Hicks, Peggy (1912–1990)	Tower, Joan (b. 1938)
Hays, Doris (b. 1941)	Weir, Judith (b. 1954)
Hölszky, Adriana (b. 1953)	Zwilich, Ellen Taaffe (b. 1939)

APPENDIX A

Tuning and Temperament

On the modern keyboard, the pitches A♯ and B♭ are played with the same key, despite the fact that their frequencies *should* be slightly different. In effect, we tune the modern keyboard *out of tune* so that enharmonic pitches may be played with the same key. This modern "equalization" is not the only (or perhaps even the best) solution for determining the various frequencies for pitches in a scale.

The Cent. We have discussed how certain interval qualities (the perfect fifth, for example) are expressed as ratios like 3:2. An additional measurement, the *cent* is helpful in studying the size of intervals. A CENT is 1/100 of a semi-tone. By definition, there are 1200 cents to the octave; each half step is comprised of 100 cents.

When two pitches have the ratio 3:2 (a perfect fifth), natural the interval in modern tuning is comprised of 702 cents. Likewise, the major third (with frequencies in the ratio 5:4) has 386 cents between pitches.

Pitches in Ratio 3:2	Pitches in Ratio 5:4
702 cents	386 cents

Just Intervals. Measurements like 700 and 400 cents reflect intervals that have been altered from the natural relationships as represented in the overtone series. Intervals that result from simple ratios are termed JUST or PURE INTERVALS. Intervals that are larger or smaller than the pure versions are TEMPERED.

Examples of Just Intervals

702 Cents   386 Cents

Examples of Tempered Intervals

700 Cents   400 Cents

Pythagorean Tuning

String, wind, and vocal performers can fine-tune pitches by a few cents whenever necessary, but this is not possible on keyboard instruments. The frequency of each pitch in a scale is determined by projecting a certain interval type (such as a perfect fifth) over several octaves. A system based on just perfect fifths is known as PYTHAGOREAN TUNING (after Pythagoras, the Greek mathematician who lived during the sixth century, B.C.E.). This system was employed for tuning organs and other keyboard instruments throughout the Middle Ages. In Pythagorean tuning, the pitches of the diatonic scale are derived from tuning one just fifth below, and four just fifths above a given pitch. To tune a diatonic scale beginning with the pitch C, we would begin with a just fifth *below* C, then proceed to tune identical intervals through the last pitch, B.

Pythagorean Scale

The modern perfect fifth is 700 cents, but the just fifth, upon which the Pythagorean scale was based, is *702* cents. The difference was not problematic until the fourteenth century, when chromatic experimentation necessitated the use of enharmonic equivalents (F♯ = G♭, for example). Early theorists studied and discussed intervals by comparing string lengths and mathematical relationships. Today, we can accomplish the same thing more simply by reckoning cents. In addition, we can recreate the problem with Pythagorean tuning when we remember that an octave has 1200 cents. If we project seven octaves, the highest pitch is 8400 cents above the first.

8400 Cents

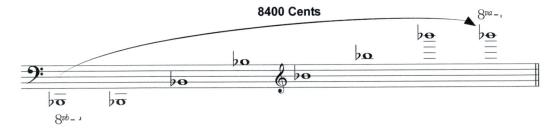

Two cents make an imperceptible difference for most listeners, but the problems that such a difference can make in a system of tuning are considerable. To play chromatic music, enharmonic equivalents must be available. Projecting twelve just (702-cent) fifths above B♭♭$_0$ (for example), we arrive at A♯. For the system to be effective, A♯ and B♭ must be heard as identical, yet our A♯ is actually 24 cents too high (8424-8400 = 24).

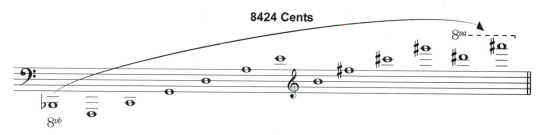

The 24-cent discrepancy between *any* pair of enharmonic equivalents is about one–quarter of a half step—still a small interval, but one that would be noticeable to many listeners. Using Pythagorean Tuning to derive pitches of a chromatic scale, we must inevitably make a choice between B♭ and A♯ (unless the keyboard were constructed with "split keys" as was common in the Middle Ages). On a modern keyboard, if we choose to tune to B♭, then any A♯ will be out of tune by 24 cents. Again, the same will be true of *every* pair of enharmonic equivalents (F♯–G♭, C♯–D♭, and so on).

While early music was not chromatic, another problem with Pythagorean Tuning troubled Medieval musicians. As we have discussed, the just major third is 386 cents in modern measurements. The Pythagorean third, however, is 408 cents—22 cents wider. Thus, while the fifth is just in Pythagorean Tuning, other intervals are problematic.

Mean-Tone Temperament

When we speak of Pythagorean or any other TUNING, the method of deriving the pitches of a scale is based on just intervals (such as the 702-cent fifth or the 386-cent major third). A TEMPERAMENT is a similar system, but one derived from values that have been altered from just intervals. One solution for the problems of Pythagorean tuning, called MEAN-TONE TEMPERAMENT, was proposed by theorists in the Renaissance. If the fifth were tempered to 696.5 cents (rather than the 702-cent just fifth), they proposed, then the resulting major third would be 386 cents as it is in just intonation. We can prove this by a projection of four 696.5-cent fifths. The fifth tone (D in our present example) is 2786 cents higher than the first pitch. Subtracting 2400 cents for the two-octave difference, the result is 386.

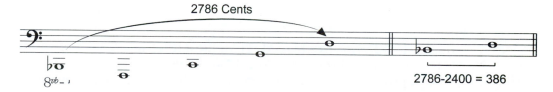

Mean-tone temperament solved the problem of a wide major third that is associated with Pythagorean tuning, but the system was not without its own inherent problems. First, enharmonic "equivalents" that are *not* really equivalent are even more significant in mean-tone temperament than in Pythagorean tuning. Twelve 696.5-cent fifths, projected to reach an enharmonic version of the first pitch, result in 8358 cents above the beginning point. If we begin with B♭₀ as we have with other examples in this section, the pitch A♯ is a substantial 42 cents too low.

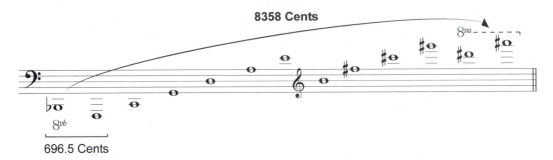

This discrepancy (about half of a half step) is discernable even by many untrained listeners. Again, we have the problem of choosing between enharmonics for a keyboard tuning. If we tune to A♯, then an interval like E–B♭ would be replaced by E–A♯, which is 42 cents too narrow. As long as composers remained in keys with only two or three flats or sharps, the just thirds and only slightly narrow fifths made mean-tone temperament preferable to Pythagorean tuning. For Western music to develop fully, however, a new solution was needed.

Twelve-Tone Equal Temperament

As early as the sixteenth century, theorists began to gravitate toward a new approach to tuning keyboard instruments. If the fifth were tempered by 2 cents to 700, theorists reasoned, then enharmonics would be truly identical. Discrepancies such as the 408-cent Pythagorean third and the 42-cent difference between enharmonic pairs virtually disappear.

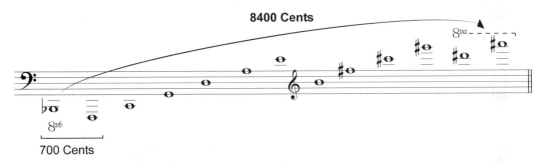

TWELVE-TONE EQUAL TEMPERAMENT has been the standard for keyboard instruments since before 1750. While many other tuning systems have been proposed, none has found favor with performers and instrument manufacturers. Compared to just intervals, the equally-tempered major third is 400 cents—14 cents too wide. Still, the differences, perceptible to many, are sufficiently slight that they are outweighed by the advantages of true enharmonic equivalents and the freedom to modulate to virtually any key.

APPENDIX B
Instrument Ranges and Transpositions

INSTRUMENT RANGES

The following table provides instrument transpositions and ranges in the order in which they are typically included on an orchestral score. In some cases (the oboe and flute, for example), less expensive instruments lack one or more lower notes that are available on higher-priced models. On the table, these lower notes (which may or may not be available on a given instrument) are shown with solid note heads.

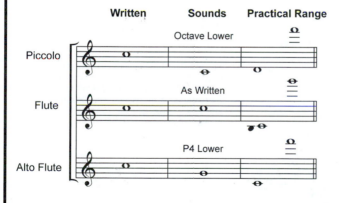

	Written	Sounds	Practical Range	Comments (Average Performers)
Piccolo		Octave Lower		Upper register brillant to shrill. Extremes of register difficult. Capable of impressive passage work.
Flute		As Written		Lower register warm, but difficult to project. Middle range clear and bright; upper register shrill for average performers. Capable of great technical facility.
Alto Flute		P4 Lower		Extends flute range down a perfect fourth. Instrument not often available ourside professional groups.

	Written	Sounds	Practical Range	Comments (Average Performers)

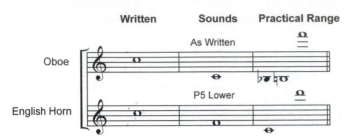

Oboe — As Written

Low register difficult to articulate. In the hands of a beginner, tone may be reedy and harsh. Ability to blend varies with experience.

English Horn — P5 Lower

Comments about oboe also apply. Lower register warm; upper register may be thin and weak. Instruments available with professional groups.

	Written	Sounds	Practical Range	Comments (Average Performers)

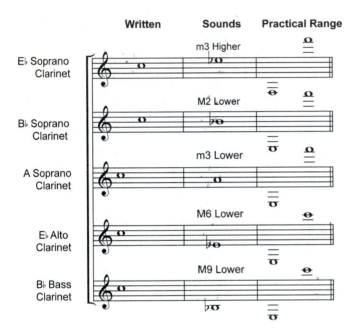

E♭ Soprano Clarinet — m3 Higher

Not always available in non-professional ensembles. Upper register bright to shrill. Capable of great technical facility.

B♭ Soprano Clarinet — M2 Lower

Standard orchestral and wind ensemble instrument. Lower register warm; middle and upper registers clear and bright. Written pitches G_4-$B\flat_4$ ("throat tones") may be reedy and muffled.

A Soprano Clarinet — m3 Lower

Used in orchestra only and in conjunction with B♭ clarinet (instrument specified by composer). Performer may change instruments from one key to another.

E♭ Alto Clarinet — M6 Lower

Band instrument commonly used in place of violas in transcriptions. Rare in orchestra.

B♭ Bass Clarinet — M9 Lower

Common instrument in both orchestra and wind ensemble.

	Written	Sounds	Practical Range	Comments (Average Performers)

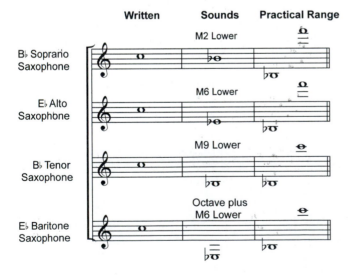

B♭ Soprano Saxophone — M2 Lower

All saxophones common in wind and dance ensembles. Alto and tenor saxophones appear occasionally in orchestras. Like other conical instruments, lower register may be difficult to articulate. Saxophones are used in wind ensembles in place of violas and cellos.

E♭ Alto Saxophone — M6 Lower

B♭ Tenor Saxophone — M9 Lower

E♭ Baritone Saxophone — Octave plus M6 Lower

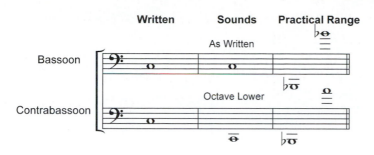

	Written	Sounds	Practical Range	Comments (Average Performers)
Bassoon		As Written		Lower register warn and reedy, although attacks may be difficult. Capable of considerable technical facility. Upper register often notated in tenor clef.
Contrabassoon		Octave Lower		Available only in large orchestras.

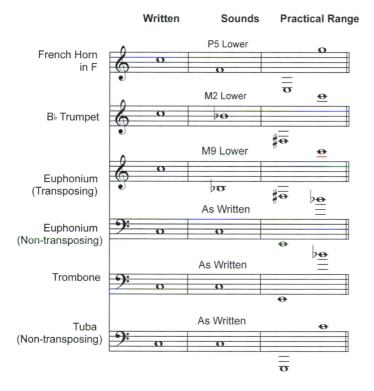

	Written	Sounds	Practical Range	Comments (Average Performers)
French Horn in F		P5 Lower		Usually written in four different parts; Horns 1 and 3 higher, 2 and 4 lower.
B♭ Trumpet		M2 Lower		Bright, clear tone in middle and upper registers. Lower notes often unstable with young performers. Other instrument keys common (C, D, E♭, but performer expected to transpose)
Euphonium (Transposing)		M9 Lower		Used in Wind ensembles to sujpport tenor range. Parts usually supplied for both B♭ (transposing, treble clef) and non-transposing (bass clef).
Euphonium (Non-transposing)		As Written		
Trombone		As Written		Capable of glissando, technical facility, and with a wide range.
Tuba (Non-transposing)		As Written		Tubas exist in a variety of sizes and keys. Advanced performers are expected to transpose as necessary.

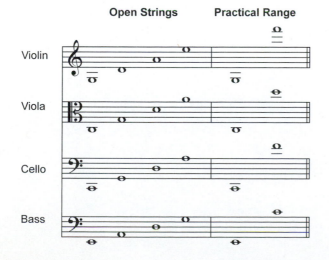

	Open Strings	Practical Range	Comments (Average Performers)
Violin			**All Strings:** Intonation difiicult for beginners. Advanced players capable of considerable facility. Performers expect bowing indications to be provided (see Workbook/Anthology, Appendix A). Strings may be bowed (arco) or plucked (pizzicato).
Viola			
Cello			
Bass			Bass: Sounds octave lower than written.

Credits

p. 14 SYMPHONY NO. 3 by WILLIAM SCHUMAN © 1942 by G. SCHIRMER. All rights reserved. Used by permission. **p. 331** "GIANT STEPS" by JOHN COLTRANE © 1974 Renewed 1992 by JOWCOL MUSIC. Used by permission. **p. 339** PRELUDE by CARLOS CHÁVEZ © 1940 G. SCHIRMER, INC. International copyright secured. All rights reserved. Used by permission. **p. 346** VISION FUGITIVE, Op. 22, NO. 6 by SERGE PROKOFIEV © 1922 by Hawkes & Son (London), Ltd. Copyright renewed. Reprinted by permission of Boosey & Hawkes, Inc. **p. 385** LE SACRE DU PRINTEMPS by IGOR STRAVINSKY © 1912, 1921 by Hawkes & Son (London), Ltd. Copyright renewed. Reprinted by permission of Boosey & Hawkes, Inc. **p. 390** SONATA FOR OBOE AND PIANO by PAUL HINDEMITH © 1929 by ASSOCIATED MUSIC PUBLISHERS, INC. Used by permission. **p. 390** SONG OF THE HARVEST by BÉLA BARTÓK © 1933 by UNIVERSAL EDITION. Copyright renewed. Copyright and renewal assigned to Boosey & Hawkes, Inc. Used by permission. **p. 391** PETRUSHKA by IGOR STRAVINSKY © 1912 by HAWKES & SON (London) Ltd. Copyright renewed. Revised version © 1948 by Hawkes & Son (London) Ltd. Copyright renewed. Reprinted by permission of BOOSEY & HAWKES, INC. **p. 394** "FROM THE ISLAND OF BALI" from MIKROKOSMOS by BÉLA BARTÓK © 1940 by HAWKES & SON (London) Ltd. Definitive corrected edition © Copyright 1987 by HAWKES & SON (London) Ltd. Reprinted by permission of BOOSEY & HAWKES, INC. **p. 395** ANGELA'S ASHES by JOHN WILLIAMS © 1999 by ENSIGN MUSIC CORPORATION and UNIVERSAL SONGS of POLYGRAM INTERNATIONAL, INC. International copyright secured. All rights reserved. Used by permission. **p. 399** THE MONK AND HIS CAT from *HERMIT SONGS* by SAMUEL BARBER © 1952 by G. SCHIRMER. Reprinted by permission. **p. 400** "OPENING RESPONSE" from HYMNS AND RESPONSES FOR THE CHURCH YEAR by VINCENT PERSICHETTI © by Elkan-Vogel CO., All rights reserved, Used by permission. Text by Conrad Aiken from the poem "Stones Too Can Pray" from *Brownstone Eclogues.* Used by permission. **p. 401** POLKA from *THE GOLDEN AGE* by DIMITRI SHOSTAKOVICH © Permission pending. **p. 402** SONATA NA. 6, Op. 28 by SERGE PROKOFIEV © by G. SCHIRMER, INC. **p. 403** PRELUDE NO. 1, OP. 84 by DIMITRI SHOSTAKOVICH © by G. SCHIRMER, INC. **p. 404** MISTS by CHARLES IVES © 1933 by MERION MUSIC, INC. Used by permission of the publisher. **p. 405** "WHY DO I LOVE YOU" by GEORGE GERSHWIN, B. G. DESYLVA, and IRA GERSHWIN © 1925 (Renewed) WB MUSIC CORP. and NEW WORLD MUSIC COMPANY, LTD. ALL RIGHTS OBO NEW WORLD MUSIC COMPANY, LTD. Administered by WB MUSIC CORP. All rights reserved. Used by permission. Warner Bros. Publications U.S. Inc., Miami Florida 33014. **p. 406** "GENERAL WILLIAM BOOTH ENTERS INTO HEAVEN" by CHARLES IVES © 1935 by MERION

Terms Index

Fugue, 3, 64, 72*ff,* 413
  analysis,
    time-line, 88, 90, 94
  answer, 76
    definition, 76
    episode and, 89–90
    real, 76–79
    tonal, 76, 78–82
  complementary material, 65,
    86–87
  counter-statement, 88
  countersubject, 86–87
  double, 88
  exposition, 88*fn*
  final section, 92–96
    recognizing, 92
    pedal, 92
    stretto, 94–96
    subject statement, 92
  form and, 72
  free counterpoint, 77–78,
    91
  improvisation, 73
  middle section, 89–92
    development, 89–90
    episode, 89–90
    sequence, 89
    subject entry, 89
  pedal, 92
  statement section, 88–89
    elision, 88
    link, 88, 88*fn*
    transition, 88
  stretto, 94–96
    definition, 94
    subject/answer pairs and,
      94
  subject, 73–76
    augmentation, 90–91
    cadences, 73
    characteristics of, 75–76
    diminution, 90–91
    end of, 78
    false entry, 91–92
    final statement, 92
    inversion (mirror), 91
    length, 73
    development of, 73
    melody,
      character,75
      compared,73
      range,75
    meter, 75
    motive compared, 73

  overlapped, see Stretto
  prominent fourth/fifth,
    80–81
  rhythm, 75
  ricercar-type, 75
  tonal answer, 80–82
  tonality, 75–76, 78–82
  sonata form and, 193
  subject-answer pairs, 76–78,
    415
  technique and, 72
  tension, 73
  tonality, 75–76, 78, 80, 90, 92
  voices, 75–77
Functional logic, 324–325

G
Gamelan, 336
German augmented sixth
    chord, 131–143, 152, 188
  analytical symbol, 131
  construction, 133
  dominant seventh and, 165
  enharmonic, 133–134
  modulation, 165–167, 298
  resolution, 132–133
Gigue, 7
Goldberg Variations, (J. S. Bach),
    10, 16, 61–64
Grand form, 176
Gregorian chant, 351, 366
Ground bass, 8–10, 25, 145
  variation in, 15

H
Half cadence, 126, 148, 301
Harmonic rhythm, 308
Harmony, 285
  ambiguous (obscured), 121,
    135, 148, 162–165, 249,
    315–317, 319
  augmented triads, 315–316
  bimodality, 416–417
  definition, 315
  diminished triads, 317
  dominant, 299
    augmented,
    minor (modal), 299–300
    weakened, 299
  function, 122, 167, 299–300,
    318, 335, 363, 377, 401
  Impressionist, 363–369
  minor (modal) dominant, 299
  nonfunctional, 291, 315*ff,*
    317, 321, 363–366

nonchord tones, 293
pandiatonicism, 357
  parallel, 317, 319
  parenthetical, 318–321
    chordal mutation, 322–325
  pillars in, 321, 363
  polychord, 419–422
  quartal harmony, 366–369,
    406, 412–413
    analysis, 368–369, 412–413
    cadence and, 367
    dissonance, 367
    function and, 367
    root, 368
  quintal, 368–369, 406,
    412–413
  revitalization, 397*ff*
  secundal, 413–415
  tertian, 306, 398, 409
    extended, 398–406,
  tonic, 58
  wrong-note, 401–402
Harpsichord, 42–43, 57, 67*fn,*
    106, 143, 145, 407
Hauptstimme, 502
Hemiola, 191, 371–372, 394
Hemiola cadence, 16
Hexachord, 451, 484, 492
Homophony, 57, 72–73, 285,
    372*fn,* 373
Hyperinstrument, 564–565
Hypermeasure, 16

I
Idee fixé, 295, 369
Imitation, 73
Imitative counterpoint, 64*ff*
  point of imitation, 64–69
  revival, 407
Impressionism, 286, 335*ff,*
    341, 343
  cadences, 351–353
    authentic, 351
    plagal, 351–352
    predominant approach, 351
  form, 369–371
    mosaic, 369
    motivic generation,
      369–370
  harmony, 349*ff,* 357
    added-tone chords,
      364–366
    function, 353, 377
    pandiatonicism, 357–358
    quartal harmony, 366–369

Composers Index

NOTES

NOTES

NOTES

NOTES

NOTES

NOTES

NOTES

NOTES